]

Towards an Ecumenical Metaphysics, Volume 2.

"To act wisely in the present, one must understand the past. This sweeping, erudite history of the development of ecumenical consciousness offers profound insights to all who care about unity in the Spirit today and desire to bridge the sad divisions that have arisen in the church. The book is a masterful, engaging complement to the author's first volume on ecumenical metaphysics."

— **THOMAS ALBERT (TAL) HOWARD**, Valparaiso University

"This monumental work — inspired not only by Nikolai Berdyaev's *Essay In Eschatological Metaphysics* but also by Sergij Bulgakov's 'sophiology,' Eric Voegelin's appeal to an 'ecumenic age,' Gadamer's hermeneutics, John Milbank's 'Radical Orthodoxy,' French personalist philosophy, and Pope Francis's gospel of the Creation — aims at nothing less than an exit from the many ruptures — between science and wisdom, phenomenology and metaphysics, religion and secularism, philosophy and theology — that have shaped modernity and postmodernity. This broadening of ecumenical inspiration will no doubt seem too 'ecumenical' or too 'irenic' to some; but its ambition is essential if we are to measure up to today's challenges. The book will of course be of interest to readers who are themselves believers, but it also opens up new transdisciplinary and dialogical dimensions within the ecumenical idea (including secular humanisms). Its originality lies in showing how, through many convergences between contemporary thinkers and activists, a new model of thought and action is being sought at a global level. Hence this book's method of bringing the history of Church and socio-political actors into relation with the history of ideas, rather than dealing with them separately. Working in concert with many colleagues in many institutions, both intellectual (such as the Collège des Bernardins in Paris) and religious (such as the World Council of Churches), here is a book determined to understand how to act upon our hopes and thoughts for the world to come."

— **EMMANUEL GABELLIERI**, Université Catholique de Lyon

"In this critique of agnostic and rationalist historiographers who have nothing to say about divine-humanity, Antoine Arjakovsky appeals to an 'ecumenical metaphysics which seeks . . . to think the divine and the human together without confusion and without separation.' His insistence on divine-humanity is essential today, especially within a Protestantism harboring an ultra-liberal current — an increasingly powerful 'new Arianism.' In becoming *incarnate*, the eternal Son of God took upon himself all the realities of our world. Thus the author is right to insist on divine-humanity. To reject the realities of the world would be to reject the incarnation. There are thus no 'non-theological' factors. There is in principle no tension between Faith and Constitution, Mission and Evangelization, and practical Christianity (or 'Life and Work'), even if it is not easy to keep the different domains balanced with each other. The impressive synthesis of the history of the ecumenical movement provided here opens up new paths for the future."

— **MARTIN HOEGGER**, Haute École de Théologie de Suisse Romande

"Direct and engagingly informative, this second volume of a trilogy further pursues the perspective of ecumenical consciousness. Having traced different historical meanings of the term *oikouménē*, it proceeds to cast the history of the Christian tradition in its engagement with the world anthropologically and cosmologically, thereby showing how ecumenical metaphysics is both a resource for understanding our present-day interdenominational situation and for integrating different narratives within Western consciousness and with the spiritualities of the different faith traditions of the world, including that of political theology. Its integrative sweep opens new vistas for understanding and transcending barrios and divisions in our various theological traditions. Its novelty and intellectual freshness spring from a perspective linking different periods of human consciousness through intellectual traditions and personalities as they move from Western to global consciousness. Well worth reading for those who wish to gain an overview of religious pluralism through the lens of ecumenical consciousness."

— **ABRAHIM H. KHAN**, Trinity College in the Univ. of Toronto

Towards an Ecumenical Metaphysics

TOWARDS AN
Ecumenical Metaphysics

VOLUME 2

A History of Christian Ecumenical Consciousness

• • •

ANTOINE ARJAKOVSKY

Angelico Press

First published in the USA
by Angelico Press 2022
Copyright © Antoine Arjakovsky 2022

For information, address:
Angelico Press, Ltd.
169 Monitor St.
Brooklyn, NY 11222
www.angelicopress.com

Paper 978-1-62138-853-1
Cloth 978-1-62138-854-8

Book and cover design
by Michael Schrauzer

CONTENTS

For the ancient mystics, man must disappear into divinity. This is the mysticism of India, of Plotinus, the ascetic Syrian mysticism, and, in part, that of Meister Eckhart. For Plotinus, man must turn away from the world of the many and turn towards the world of the One. It is a monism contrary to the Gospel. Christianity has a divine-human character.

(Nikolai Berdyaev, *On Mysticism* [unfinished], 1948)

PART ONE
General Introduction

HAVING SET OUT IN THE FIRST VOLUME OF this work the principles and methods of ecumenical metaphysics, we must now tell the story of how, historically, ecumenical consciousness came into being. In the face of the crisis in contemporary historiography, which has been "in pieces," according to François Dosse, since the collapse of structuralism,[1] the history of ecumenical consciousness is, in my view, the appropriate response to the pressing demand for a new history, a history both of the world and of individual areas, a history both anthropological and cosmological. I shall begin by explaining why this new "history of the present day" starts out from a metaphysics centered on ecumenical consciousness. I shall show at the same time how this new narrative, both distanced and participatory, seeks to re-articulate the history of men, of the cosmos, and of God, in a manner which is both coherent and accurate, both creative and faithful.

This history of ecumenical consciousness is still practically unknown to the churches. It has been observable, indeed, that in their own seminaries the latter have held on, most of the time, to a strictly denominational pedagogy, even when it comes to ecumenical training. The instruction given there reduces the history of human consciousness, often enough, to the denominational history of the Church.[2] Thus, for example, the Pontifical Council for the Promotion of Christian Unity, in a vade-mecum of 2020 intended for Catholic bishops, refers to the decree of Vatican II, *Unitatis Redintegratio*, to affirm that the essence of ecumenical formation is that "the Catholic faith must be explained

---

1 Francois Dosse, *L'histoire en miettes, Des Annales à la 'nouvelle histoire'* (Paris: La Découverte, 2005).
2 Of course, I am not reducing the Church to a few departments within its institutional apparatus. In France, for example, the newspaper *La Croix* defines itself as both Catholic and ecumenical. See, for example, the opinion column by the paper's publisher, Antoine Bellier, of April 8, 2021: "Pour lutter contre le séparatisme, redevenons catholiques!," la-croix.com.

I

more profoundly and precisely, in such a way and in such terms as our separated brethren can also really understand."[3] (11)

In the same way, in most secular universities, religious faith has been expelled from the field of knowledge, and so ecumenical metaphysics is treated as a marginal phenomenon. Consequently, the history of human consciousness at the present time is becoming more and more problematic. I have set out elsewhere the story of the eighteenth-century historicist turn in the way history is narrated.[4] It was the misfortune of medieval historiography that it crushed human freedom beneath the action of an Omnipotent God, of a *Pantocrator* in the history of men. Jean-Jacques Rousseau's "Letter to Voltaire on Providence," written on August 18, 1756, after the publication of the latter's poems "Sur la loi naturelle" [On natural law] and "Sur le désastre de Lisbonne," as well as the publication of *Candide, ou l'Optimisme* in Geneva in 1759, represent important landmarks in the critique of providentialist Christian theology and of "theologo-cosmolo-nigological" metaphysics.[5]

The story has also been told of the consequences for French historiography of the rupture with the modern narrative provoked by Michel Foucault's postmodern philosophy. In *The Order of Things*, Foucault showed that between 1775 and 1825, with Kant, Cuvier, and Darwin, European scholars discovered that nature, work, and language each had a historicity of their own. The sapiential knowledge of truth, open to the action of the divine Spirit within history, as it could still be seen in the work of Bossuet, was transformed into a chronological knowledge of the rhythms proper to the development of things and men. French republican historiography, from Jules Michelet to Ernest Lavisse, devoted a century to drawing out all the consequences of this historicist turn, while still retaining a providentialist aspect to French history. But after the Second World War, after the simultaneous discovery of the terrifying "dialectic of reason" (Adorno/Horkheimer) and of a disturbing dialectical materialism, and especially with the realization of the danger represented by an excessively

---

3   Pontifical Council for Promoting Christian Unity, "The Bishop and Christian Unity: An Ecumenical Vademecum," preface by Cardinal Kurt Koch and Mgr Brian Farrell, www.christianunity.va, 9.

4   "Le rôle de l'historien est-il de ressusciter le passé?" August 27, 2017, www.theconversation.com.

5   "[L]a métaphysico-théologo-cosmolo-nigologie" is the subject of which Pangloss is satirically said to be a teacher in Voltaire's *Candide* (1759). See Voltaire, *Romans et Contes*, ed. Frédéric Deloffre and Jacques van den Heuvel (Paris: Gallimard [Éditions de la Pléiade], 1979), 146. — *Translator*.

nationalist vision of the past of the republican State, the landscape of French historiography exploded. In order to narrate the history of France, historians sought to find a universal element, either from the perspective of the homeland (Jean Sévillia) or from that of social justice (Michelle Zancarini-Fournel) or, again, from those of myth (Patrick Boucheron) or memory (Pierre Nora).[6]

This explosion of historiography can be found all over the world today. Historians everywhere try to get beyond disciplinary, national, chronological, or ideological compartments, in order to arrive at a history founded on a new ontology that would be more relational or more rhizomatic, more holistic or more Anthropocene.[7] The new narrative of the *longue durée* of world history consequently finds itself divided between those promoting a new ethical narrative associating human history with the law of evolution on planet Earth (Dipesh Chrakrabarty, b. 1948) and the apostles of a joined-up history who want to tell the story of the victims of Western rationality (Sanjay Subrahmanyam, b. 1961), but also between the representatives of a historicity founded in the interlocking viewpoints of different communities of memory (Paul Ricœur, 1913 – 2005) and the defenders of a historicity newly respectful of the god Chronos and centered on the experience of the incommensurable (François Hartog, b. 1946).[8]

Everything goes on as though contemporary historiography had not managed to rid itself of its distrust towards European thought, which is regarded as ontologically violent and colonial (Edward Said, 1935 – 2003), and towards metaphysics, which is identified exclusively with modern

---

6   According to Boucheron, the true historian must be capable, by means of a chronological narrative of events, of bringing to mind what could have happened in the past, which still constitutes a hidden reserve of wounds or potentially creative developments within a community of communities. This is why he declares himself to be in favor of an "open, diverse, inhabited and engaging" history. Boucheron, who teaches at the Collège de France, does not deny the power of myth in history, nor the desire of individual peoples for a national romance. But his narrative tries to keep myth in its proper place. This approach has been criticized by Pierre Nora, who has seen in it a way of rehabilitating a dangerous national mythology. "Peut-on se passer de la Providence pour comprendre l'histoire de France?," September 7, 2017, www.theconversation.com.

7   Pierre-Yves Saunier, *Transnational History* (London: Palgrave Macmillan, 2013); Alessandro Stanziani, *Les entrelacements du monde. Histoire globale, pensée globale: XVIe-XXIe siècles* (Paris: CNRS Editions, 2018).

8   Dipesh Chakrabarty, *The Climate of History in a Planetary Age* (Chicago: University of Chicago Press, 2021); Sanjay Subrahmanyam, Henning Trüper, and Dipesh Chakrabarty, *Historical Teleologies in the Modern World* (London: Bloomsbury, 2015); Paul Ricœur, *La mémoire, l'histoire, l'oubli* (Paris: Seuil, 2003); François Hartog, *Chronos, l'Occident aux prises avec le temps* (Paris: Gallimard, 2020).

onto-theology.[9] Still marked by Hegelian idealism, contemporary historiography has not, in summary, managed to reconcile anthropology and history, sophiology and theology. It treats human consciousness as necessarily unhappy. Divided between an empirical and mortal self, and a self that experiences the infinite and incommensurable, it never manages to become a unity, and cannot produce coherent knowledge. Moreover, despite the work of deconstruction carried out by the anthropologist Philppe Descola, a prevailing scientism continues to separate cosmic and sapiential consciousness from human consciousness.[10] Or, conversely, this cosmic and sapiential consciousness is mixed up with human consciousness to such an extent that the borders between human beings and non-human beings seem to disappear.[11] Personalist thinkers, however, have shown the limits of Hegelian thought's monism and of Kantian thought's dualism.[12] And some contemporary scientists do not shrink from hypothesizing a "consciousness of the sun," without, however, confusing this with the self-consciousness of human beings, who possess language and a finite experience of the infinite.[13]

It is, nevertheless, true that the systemic crisis revealed by the COVID-19 pandemic has reinforced the realization in historical circles that we share a common destiny. In his book *The Climate of History in a Planetary Age*, published in 2021, the Indian-American scholar Dipesh Chakrabarty acknowledges that most of his academic colleagues have until now, under

---

9   Thus Bruno Latour, for example, who is much influenced by Bultmannian demythologization, identifies the "religious" with faithful memory, and does not imagine this as being in tension with correct truth, knowledge of justice, or participatory glorification. See Latour, *Rejoicing, or the Torments of Religious Speech*, trans. Julie Rose (Cambridge: Polity Press, 2013). Cf. also Henning Schmidgen, *Bruno Latour in Pieces* (New York: Fordham University Press, 2015).

10   Philippe Descola, *Beyond Nature and Culture*, trans. Janet Lloyd (Chicago: University of Chicago Press, 2014).

11   Bruno Latour, *We Have Never Been Modern*, trans. Catherine Porter (Cambridge, MA: Harvard University Press, 2002).

12   Nikolai Berdyaev, *The Beginning and the End*, trans. R. M. French (San Rafael, CA: Semantron Books, 2009).

13   Rupert Sheldrake, "Is the Sun conscious?," *Journal of Consciousness Studies*, 28 (3–4), 2021: 8–28. "Field theories of consciousness propose that some electromagnetic fields actually are conscious, and that these fields are by their very nature integrative. When applied to the sun, such field theories suggest a possible physical basis for the solar mind, both within the body of the sun itself and also throughout the solar system. If the sun is conscious, it may be concerned with the regulation of its own body and the entire solar system through its electromagnetic activity, including solar flares and coronal mass ejections. It may also communicate with other star systems within the galaxy."

the influence of subaltern studies,[14] been suspicious of any unitary or universalistic spirit, a spirit that is by definition suspected of ulterior motives of a dominating, colonial, racial, or chauvinist kind. But the systemic and environmental crisis of planet Earth changes the deal. It must, for Chakrabarty, give rise to a neo-holistic consciousness at once humanist and focused on the fate of the planet.

The lines of demarcation are shifting, not only in respect of the "Gaia hypothesis," to use James Lovelock's expression, but also so far as the recognition of the value of spiritual rationality within scientific discourse is concerned. The sociologist of science Bruno Latour does not abstain from considering knowledge and faith together, in the name of the most constructive epistemology and its principle of symmetry. Similarly, Michel Serres (1930 – 2019), a member of the Académie Française, was one of the first to rehabilitate the resurrection of Christ as a possible means of freeing oneself from unhappy consciousness:

> When they arrived at the entrance to the empty tomb, the women did not know what to do with their sweet spices, that Easter morning, the moment when this great and colossal Mediterranean (and, perhaps, global) Antiquity draws to a close: the unique moment when coming out into the light of day, or entering into glory after death, take place without any preparation, without any act of observance or any incense, without any veils or draperies, without any apparatus, any labor, any technique, or any knowledge. Forget the dead body, direct your activities towards other objects than the corpse, free yourselves from death. Then time and history topple. If you delve into the earth, like historians, like archaeologists, like those who revere the dead past, you will, from now on, find nothing but empty tombs. Personal and collective life, existence and human history themselves, once led in one direction only: towards death. From now on, we are counting time in the other direction. The end no longer lies before me, before us, but behind me, behind us: let the dead bury their dead. This is a first significance, a historical and very human one, of the Resurrection.[15]

The exteriority that faith provides within the rational judgement is the source of a more realistic and more open way of imagining historical

---

14   The phrase "subaltern studies" is in English in the original text. — *Translator.*
15   Michel Serres, "Devenir," Lent talk at Notre Dame, March 12, 2006, www.paris. catholique.fr.

change. It announces a new era, which Serres calls "the Christian era," which has, up until now, hardly begun. It also inaugurates a new epistemology grounded in the meeting of different religious traditions. In the *Cahier de l'Herne* devoted to Michel Serres, the French philosopher Anne Baudart presented this heir of Leibniz as a weaver, and thus as a prophet heralding the ecumenical age:

> The Resurrection makes it possible to exit from a History governed by the evils of revenge, of mounting violence, brutality, domination, and hatred. It lays low the law of Death. It inaugurates a new, absolutely new, era which has, no doubt, not yet really begun, and which it is necessary to bring about. It helps us to understand how fundamental religion is, in that it links us closely to the Earth, to the life force, which is made up of both human and divine elements. Penelope becomes the paradigm of religion (*religare* and *relegere*): "She remained at her work of tapestry-making day and night. In the same way religion goes back over, spins, knots together, gathers, collects, ties, ties again, winds up, reads, and sings the elements of time" (*Le Contrat naturel* [The Natural Contract], 80). Short and long durations structure the religious fabric. Today, however, displays, by contrast, neglect (*neglegere*), disconnection, a falling back on the local and an isolation from the world and from what is temporally or spatially global. We need to "stitch time back together again," the time of paganism and Christianity, the time of words and things, the time of the universe and of men, the time of sciences and of beliefs, the time of law and of morality, the time of arts and of manners. One sole law must inspire the work of the great weaving: the love of our two fathers, "natural and human, the soil and our neighbor; [the love of] humanity, our human mother and our natural mother, the Earth" (*Le Contrat naturel*, 83). The neighbor and the stranger, the nearby and the distant, the singular and the universal, reconciled at last by the royal weaver — a pagan, a Christian, a pantheist, a Cathar, sometimes, even, a "mystical unbeliever." The philosophy of Michel Serres works continually towards this cross-grafting made into a new ethics. [16]

Ecumenical consciousness must, however, be distinguished from syncretistic consciousness. Let us recall that ecumenical consciousness is neither

---

16   Anne Baudart, "Le philosophe-tisserand: paganisme et christianisme," *Cahier de l'Herne Michel Serres*, ed. François L'Yvonnet et Christiane Frémont (Paris: L'Herne, 2010), 260.

a universalistic consciousness that suppresses differences, nor is it a consciousness of autonomy that legitimizes divisions. Ecumenical consciousness is the intuition on the part of living beings of their shared belonging to a single body, at different degrees of density. These degrees vary from the psychic consciousness of the smallest amoeba possessing a tangential and a radial energy, [17] to the spiritual consciousness of the human being, who possesses the ability to know himself through other people, according to differing representations of this alterity, from totemism to shamanism, from Judaism to Christianity, from Hinduism to Buddhism. This ecumenical consciousness is also characterized by a form of knowledge that does not separate in any radical way the leap of the hypothesis from careful attention to proof. Finally, the personalist and sapiential consciousness of the universal is a form of life-wisdom, that of the "included middle," in perpetual tension between potentialization and actualization. [18]

Such a level of consciousness produces a new, balanced narrative of the history of interactions between the earth-system, men, and their gods. This history goes beyond any framing within the Christian community alone, and beyond the limits of the chronology of Christianity. Nevertheless, for reasons that will be indicated — starting with the limitations of the author's own expertise — attention will be focused here on the level of consciousness which Christians have, historically, crafted from this history. Because of the principle of non-duality that marks symbolic consciousness, this new history of the concept of the *oïkoumènè* is at the same time the story of their own ecumenical consciousness.

This history is all the more necessary because collective consciousness is today swept along by a denominational mythology that does not stand up to historical scrutiny. Despite the advances of ecumenical historiography, many media outlets, newspapers, and journals, even the best-informed continue to base their communications on *doxa* dating from the denominational epoch. It is continually repeated, for example, that the break between Eastern and Western Christians goes back to the fateful year 1054, [19] whereas there were breaks before, as well as reconciliations after, this date. [20] It goes without saying, however, that such a history of ecu-

---

17   Pierre Teilhard de Chardin, *Le phénomène humain* [The Phenomenon of Man] (Paris: Seuil, 1955).
18   See the first volume of the trilogy for more details on all this.
19   Loup Besmond de Senneville, "Les relations entre Moscou et Constantinople," *La Croix*, January 15, 2021, 14–15, www.la-croix.com.
20   Antoine Arjakovsky, *What Is Orthodoxy?*, trans. Jerry Ryan and Penelope Cavill (New York: Angelico Press, 2018).

menical consciousness, centered on Christian consciousness, is a call for a new historiographical movement on a global scale.

HOW IS THE STORY OF ECUMENICAL CONSCIOUSNESS TOLD?

In the Christian context to which we are limiting ourselves here — a context which, on its own, already concerns a quarter of the people on the planet — it is important to avoid the trap of an exclusively ecclesio-centric narrative, a narrative grounded in a single tradition of memory. For example, the three-volume history of the ecumenical movement published by the World Council of Churches, while it has the merit of existing, does not commence its narrative until 1517, that is, from the beginning of Luther's reformation onwards. [21] In contrast to a mainly Protestant apologetic position, Hans Küng's work is marked by a unilaterally critical discourse with regard to the denominational period of the Church, which also prevents an impartial view of events from being taken. [22] Similarly, the identification which most Orthodox Christian historians make of the universal Church with the church that calls itself "Orthodox" is no more satisfying, as one can well imagine, for most historians of Christianity. [23] This is all the more so because according to this same Orthodox Church,

---

21 A History of the Ecumenical Movement, Volume 1 (1517–1948), ed. Ruth Rouse and Stephen Charles Neill (Geneva: World Council of Churches, 1954). The period covering the ecumenical movement before Luther is covered in twenty-six pages of a first volume comprising of more than eight hundred.

22 Nevertheless, in Christianity: Its Essence and History (1995), Hans Küng developed a new conception of the history of Christianity, founded on the development of Christian consciousness through six main periods. The history of Christian consciousness in the twenty-first century is governed, according to Küng, by a "post-modern and ecumenical" paradigm. He understands the idea of a paradigm in the same way as Thomas Kuhn, that is, as "a complete constellation of beliefs, values, techniques, and so on, shared by the members of a given community." More precisely, for Küng, "a theological and ecclesial paradigm consists of a constellation of typical ways in which members of the Church think and act, both individually and collectively, and is marked by typical theological and institutional structures and by typical ways of relating to society as a whole, to the state, to the economy, to the arts, etc." "Editor's note," in Hans Kung, Can we save the Catholic Church? (London: William Collins, 2013), 339–45, 343.

23 Some historians think that nothing much happened in twelve hundred years between the Seventh Ecumenical Council of 787 and the Pan-Orthodox Council in 2016. (See "Preparation of the Holy and Great Council: A Comprehensive Timeline" at https://www.orthodoxcouncil.org.) Now, even if the Ecumenical Council of Florence was disavowed in 1484 by a Council of inferior rank convoked under Ottoman domination, this decision (which was itself contested) cannot by itself wipe out its historical reality from ecclesial memory. Cf. Antoine Arjakovsky, En attendant de concile de l'Église Orthodoxe [Waiting for the Orthodox Church Council] (Paris: Cerf, 2011).

the ecumenical councils cannot keep to themselves all the action of the Spirit at work in ecclesial consciousness.[24]

By contrast, new publishing projects presenting themselves as scholarly [*scientifique*], in the modern sense of the term, and offering a more ecumenical history of Christianity, have come into being in France and in Great Britain in the 1990s and 2000s. But this approach is not without difficulties of its own. In the preface to the first of nine volumes of the *Cambridge History of Christianity*, the authors make no secret of their project of contradicting the "myth" according to which the Christian church would originally have been a united one:

> Once upon a time, historians of the early church wrote a simple story of a pristine faith received from Jesus Christ and communicated to his disciples. With an agreed gospel summed up in the Apostles' Creed, they dispersed to spread the word in all directions. In time, however, this unified message was frustrated by distortions called heresies, which produced their own offspring, multiplying and diversifying, by contrast with the one truth entrusted to the apostles. Despite heresy and persecution, however, Christianity triumphed with the conversion of Constantine. Doubtless, that is an over-simplification of an over-simplification, yet it is towards the goal of emancipation from such a schematized view of earliest Christianity (a perspective inherited from the ancient sources themselves) that much modern critical scholarship has been directed. The recognition of diversity within Christianity from the very beginning has transformed study of its origins. Simple models of development, or single theory explanations, whether they be applied to organizational, liturgical, doctrinal or other aspects of early church history, are recognizably inadequate. We have endeavored to capture the complexity of early Christianity and its socio-cultural setting, while also indicating some of the elements that make it possible to trace a certain coherence, a recognizable identity, maintained over time and defended resolutely despite cultural pressure that could have produced something other.[25]

---

24   Sergij Bulgakov, "Obladaet-li pravoslavie vneshnim avtoretom dogmaticheskoj nepogreshimosti?" ["Does Orthodoxy possess an external authority of dogmatic infallibility?"] *Put'* 2 (January, 1926), 47–58.

25   "Preface" to *Cambridge History of Christianity*, vol. 1, *Origins to Constantine*, ed. Margaret M. Mitchell and Frances M. Young (Cambridge: Cambridge University Press, 2008), xiii.

As shown in an earlier work of mine,[26] this will to demythologization means that the ecumenical movement is only treated from an institutional standpoint. This is why the ecumenical movement is tackled only in the ninth volume of the set, in the section devoted to the twentieth century.[27] Such a situation cannot satisfy those historians who take seriously the event of Pentecost as the foundation of a new type of ecclesial community.

The same difficulty is found in the fourteen-volume *Histoire du Christianisme* [History of Christianity] overseen in France by Jean-Marie Mayeur, Charles and Luce Pietri, André Vauchez, and Marc Venard. As Émile Poulat remarked in the final volume, *Anamnesis*, the risk taken by such collective projects, bringing together more than one hundred and thirty historians, is that of by-passing the mystical dimension of the Church.

> The risk for historians of Christianity is that they find themselves disqualified in the name of a faithful understanding of the Church which they lack or which they suspend out of methodological caution and loyalty to their profession.[28]

The historians participating in the *Oxford History of Christianity* have, for their part, openly acknowledged their modern concern to separate their beliefs from their knowledge:

> The writers of the various chapters of this book belong to the confraternity of professional historians of the "scientific" kind; whatever as individuals they believe about human destiny, whatever spiritual contacts they expect or do not expect in their own lives, they write, within their lights, impartially, with detachment from their convictions.[29]

These histories of Christianity reject the classic conception of a divine Providence at work in history. Their objective is not to grasp the divine-human nature of the Church, but to understand it in its entirety through its spread across the planet. That is why, with a great deal of erudition, the history of Christianity is narrated exhaustively across the whole surface of the globe and in all ages. The difficulty with this sort

---

26 Arjakovsky, *What Is Orthodoxy?*.

27 David M. Thompson, "Ecumenism," in *The Cambridge History of Christianity*, vol. 9: *World Christianities, c.1914–c.2000*, ed. Hugh McLeod (Cambridge: Cambridge University Press, 2006), 50–70.

28 Émile Poulat, "Anamnèse," in François Laplanche, ed. *Anamnèsis*, vol. 14 of *Histoire du christianisme* (Paris: Desclée, 2001), 268.

29 John McManners, ed. *The Oxford History of Christianity* (Oxford: Oxford University Press, 1993), 17.

of modern and technical approach, which refuses any sort of questioning about the meaning [*sens*] of history, is that it produces a history which is literally incredible [*insensée*].

> Our book has no conclusions, for we did not write to a common formula, and a history of Christianity raises problems which outrun by far the scope of the professional techniques available to us.[30]

I shall also try here to avoid a strictly philosophical approach, an approach which certainly has meaning and is capable of embracing all the movements of consciousness on the planet, but is too general to be relevant to history.

Interesting efforts at such a philosophical approach appeared after the Second World War at the moment when thinkers perceived the limits of Hegelian and Marxist historiosophies. Thus the German-Swiss philosopher Karl Jaspers' account of what he calls humanity "noetic consciousness" highlights its "axial period" between the ninth century before Christ and the second century of our era.[31] For Jaspers, this was a way of avoiding allowing historical narrative to sink into a post-modern vision, that of Spengler or Toynbee, of a world shattered into declining civilizations. But Jaspers only extended beyond Christianity the Hegelian mythology of the "absolute epoch." Further examples will be given below of attempts at scientific conceptualization (Gebser, Neumann, Eliade, Teilhard de Chardin) of the meta-individual phenomenon of consciousness. Although these approaches are unsatisfactory, they are interesting for their pioneering character. They are all the more useful because today we are witnessing the emergence of the phenomenon of a "global consciousness." This mediatized consciousness, which is producing more and more rapidly, on a global scale, especially through the internet and social networks, but also through non-governmental organizations and international institutions, a mirror which presents itself as that of human consciousness.

It is necessary to explain here my choice to describe the development of ecumenical consciousness within Christianity in a way which is more historical than theological or philosophical.

The paradigm of the "ecumenic age," first conceived by the Austrian-born American philosopher Eric Voegelin (1901–1985), presents human

---

30   Ibid., 17.
31   Karl Jaspers, *The Origin and Goal of History*, trans. Michael Bullock (New Haven: Yale University Press, 1953).

consciousness as the most appropriate place in which to find a meaning in the history of the world. Voegelin emphasized, in particular, the role played by Christian faith in putting a stop to the consciousness of finitude, which was dominant in the age of the Roman Empire, and in orientating the latter towards divine-humanity. This eschatological conception of history greatly exceeded the merely Judaeo-Christian context, and now poses questions for all peoples on the planet.

WHAT IS AT STAKE FOR A HISTORY OF UNIVERSAL CONSCIOUSNESS

The level of ecumenical consciousness is largely unknown to public opinion. Conversely, the media are conscious that the era of globalization cannot abstain from further reflection on civilization's final goal and universal nature. It is enough to mention the widely publicized reports of the Intergovernmental Panel on Climate Change on global warming to understand the contemporary relevance of this question. This is leading everyone to redefine their identity, their priorities, and the way in which they define the universal, and is pushing us to find new syntheses between different branches of knowledge, different nations, and individuals. Let us take an example to illustrate this point.

In November 2020, the French president, Emmanuel Macron, suggested to his European and African colleagues, to representatives of the World Bank, and also to the non-governmental organizations, that they should adopt a "Paris consensus " at the next Paris Peace Forum.[32] The French president wishes to reverse the ultra-liberal and uni-polar logic of the "Washington consensus" tacitly adopted in 1989 by economic institutions and international bankers.[33] This Washington consensus itself represented an evolution in the ethical, rather than merely in the economic, thinking of the planet's leaders. It marked a rupture with the two-power model made up of the politics of planning, on the one hand, and the politics of the providential State on the other, which dominated the world in the years 1950 – 1970.

This new "Paris consensus," which wishes to be seen as both multi-polar and participatory, has as its objective to bring order back to a world which has become a-polar. It proposes a consolidation of the new paradigm of "sustainable growth" set out in 2015 by the United Nations, with its

---

32   "Le Forum de Paris forge un consensus sur le monde post-Covid," November 11, 2020, www.la-croix.com.

33   John Williamson, "A Short History of the Washington Consensus," https://www.piie.com/publications/papers/williamson0904-2.pdf.

seventeen Sustainable Development Goals for 2030. It aims to begin a campaign against the growth of inequality in the world by adopting new, fairer, and more consistent trade rules. It suggests adopting new finance rules at COP [Conference of the Parties] 26 in order to make possible the implementation of the COP 21 climate accords.

In this way the Paris consensus means to bring together the conditions for universal access to a COVID vaccine and to combat pandemics by mobilizing non-governmental organizations and other foundations. It suggests that the World Health Organization, as a trusted mediator, should become a regulatory instrument between states and the laboratories. It wants mechanisms to be put in place such as the Access to COVID-19 Tools Accelerator making it possible for everyone to get access to treatments, or the COVAX initiative for vaccine purchasing and sharing. Lastly, it calls for the fundamental rights declared in the United Nations Charter to be defended by new coalitions against all forms of terrorism and for a batch of legal and penal responses to be coordinated against online hate and disinformation on social networks.

This new development in the consciousness of the planet's leaders was immediately criticized. [34] The economist Romaric Godin does not believe that the new consensus suggested by the French president is sincere:

> Once the moment of urgency has passed, there will once more have to be sacrifices to the "normal" functioning of the economy: competition will have to be reintroduced and the public finances will need to be cleaned up. The "Keynesian flash" of urgency will be followed by a return to the stick of austerity. *Capital rules*, more than ever before. [35]

As we shall see in volume three, more and more thinkers are calling for a fairer and more ecological society. They are proposing a new paradigm, a new relation to the *oïkouménè* [household, economy] founded on a "politics of vision" which consists in making public everything that impinges on such a society: working conditions and exploitation of child labor in Indian factories, the dying-out of bees in the United States as a result of glyphosate use, abattoirs in Europe, ultra-polluted hidden cities in Russia, the impact of climate change in Latin America, the seventh continent of

---

34   Romaric Godin, "Le 'consensus de Paris,' nouveau concept creux du Macronisme," November 17, 2020, https://blogs.mediapart.fr/romaric-godin/blog/.
35   Romaric Godin, "Gare à l'effet d'optique: un 'flash keynésien' n'est pas un changement de paradigme," March 11, 2020, https://blogs.mediapart.fr/romaric-godin/blog/.

plastic in our oceans.[36] For David Schlosberg, Professor of Environmental Politics at the University of Sydney, visibility is a key component in bringing about a change in consciousness in the Anthropocene:

> The effort to recognize this new geologic era of human influence is one of *making visible* what we have previously refused to recognize. The Anthropocene *enables* sight, and, so, reflection. Such a vision requires heightened critical reflexivity about our ecological selves, a life with constant awareness of the environmental systems in which human life is immersed. It opens us to a *receptivity* to our impacts on the planet and, so, a potential reconstruction of the relationship between human and non-human.[37]

However relevant they might be, these quests for a "new consensus" or for a "credible successor to neo-liberalism" are directly linked to the topic of the present work. Against the neo-liberal vision of John Rawls which marginalizes the notion of the good in favor of a particular conception of justice, it is today a question of thinking the just and the good in a balanced and universal way while respecting social and environmental differences. Whether one supports or opposes these propositions, this development of ethical consciousness impels every person to take a position.

Now, ecumenical metaphysics seeks precisely to think and to configure the true, the just, the good, and the beautiful in a harmonious whole that is at once personalist, sapiential, and ternary. It offers a deepened and distanced reflection on the way (both one and diverse) in which human consciousness inhabits the world. But in order to "make visible" this ecumenical consciousness, which pulses within and beyond the walls of the visible borders of the Church, its story must be told.

THE PARADIGM OF THE ECUMENIC AGE

The philosopher Eric Voegelin, whose polyglot erudition and depth of philosophical and historical culture are out of the ordinary, told in 1974 the story of what he called the "ecumenic age" of the consciousness of humanity.[38] This idea was, for Voegelin, polysemic, and could be parsed

---

36   Olivier Monod, "Y a-t-il vraiment 5 continents de plastique dans les océans?" *Libération*, September 7, 2018, www.liberation.fr.
37   David Schlosberg, "Environmental Management in the Anthropocene," in Teena Gabrielson, Cheryl Hall, John M. Meyer and David Schlosberg (eds.), *Oxford Handbook of Environmental Political Theory* (Oxford, Oxford University Press, 2016).
38   Eric Voegelin, *Collected Works*, vol. 17, *Order and History*; vol. IV, *The Ecumenic Age*, (Columbia and London: University of Missouri Press, 2000).

in multiple ways in the cosmologies of different civilizations. He devoted a whole chapter of the fourth volume of his book *Order and History*, for example, to *tianxia*, "everything under heaven," the basis of the Chinese political theology that preceded the Han empire, which ruled over China from 206 BC onwards.[39]

For Voegelin, the "ecumenic age" did not refer only to a period of human history extending roughly from the rise of the Persian Empire to the fall of the Roman. For the very fact of dividing history into epochs was already, according to him, the result of an ecumenical consciousness, because the awareness of a historical dynamic is indissociable from a confrontation between a universal truth and one's own identity. Certainly, this historical period called "ecumenical," through which run dreams of universal empire, from Alexander the Great to Marcus Aurelius, has indeed fashioned a deep stratum of humanity's consciousness. But a first development occurred in the second century BC. The expression *oikouménē gē*, which originally signified nothing more than the "inhabited world" in the geographical sense, was given a new meaning by the historian Polybius (208 – 126 BC), that of "the peoples who are drawn into the process of imperial expansion." As Voegelin writes, with Polybius, "instead of the philosopher who articulates the order of the soul, there appears the historian who articulates the dynamics of political events, of the *praxeis*; instead of the Platonic dialogue or the Aristotelian treatise, there is the Polybian *pragmateia*."[40] The *oikuménē*, as Polybius understood it, was an object, an organization, rather than a subject. It was not organized for action as was the case in the Egypt of the Pharaohs, with the people of Israel, or in the Greek city-state.

According to Voegelin, a new event of the first importance occurred with Christianity:

> The term *ecumene*, which originally means no more than the inhabited world in the sense of cultural geography, has received through Polybius the technical meaning of the peoples who are drawn into the process of imperial expansion. On this Polybian

---

39 "The foundation of the empire can be defined, therefore, in Chinese terms, as the victory of the *kuo* over the *t'ien-hsia*: The empire was an inflated *kuo* without spiritual legitimacy. With the Han dynasty, as a consequence, there began the struggle among the movements and schools for providing the spiritual substance of which the power colossus was so embarrassingly devoid. But the new synthesis of spirit and power that was found and variously changed, until it became stabilized in the neo-Confucian orthodoxy, could never restore the order of the early kingdom before it had dissociated into *t'ien-hsia* and *kuo*." Voegelin, *Order and History*, 4, 370.

40 Voegelin, *Order and History*, 4, 179.

stratum of meaning could later be superimposed the meaning of the mankind under Roman jurisdiction (Luke 2:1; Acts 17:6; 24:5), and ultimately of the messianic world to come (Heb. 2:5).[41]

The apostle Paul understood and proclaimed to the Hebrews that the static vision of the *oikumnēnē*, under the domination of the Roman emperor, must give way to the eschatological vision of "the *oikouménē* to come."

> The basis of Paul's missionary action is furnished by the passage of Matthew 24:14, which reads: "And this gospel of the kingdom shall be preached over the whole ecumene, as a testimony to all the nations [*ethnesin*]; and then the end [*telos*] shall come." The ecumene in the pragmatic sense is established; but beyond the Polybian telos of the process through the Roman conquest, there becomes now visible a further telos through the spreading of the gospel. The ecumene is not rejected at all, but its establishment is reduced to the rank of a prelude to the drama of salvation. The differentiation of the new meanings becomes manifest in the temptation scene of Luke 4:5, where Satan offers Jesus power over "the kingdoms of the ecumene."[42]

Christ's response to the devil was to allude to Deuteronomy 6:13–14 ("Thou shalt worship the Lord thy God, and him only shalt thou serve" Matt. 4:10). By making this reply, spoken at the beginning of his mission in the Judaean desert, Christ crushed the demon's attempt to usurp power, and, with it, the modern illusion of princely power. By witnessing to his faithful memory in Scripture, he reminded us of the white-hot limit separating earthly kingdoms from the Kingdom of God, while laying the basis for a new liturgical theology of politics. This new vision of a theology of politics, and particularly the angelology that accompanies it, today inspires some post-modern thinkers, such as Giorgio Agamben.[43] It is in the Radical Orthodoxy movement, however, that it finds, as we shall see, its fullest ecumenical development.[44]

Voegelin was one of Hegel's main adversaries in the twentieth century. He called Hegel "the greatest egophanic thinker of our time."[45]

---

41   Ibid., 138.

42   Ibid., 189.

43   Giorgio Agamben, *Homo Sacer: Sovereign Power and Bare Life*, trans. Daniel Heller-Roazen (Stanford, CA: Stanford University Press, 1998).

44   Catherine Pickstock, *After Writing: On the Liturgical Consummation of Philosophy* (Oxford: Blackwell, 1997).

45   "Human and divine nature (*Natur*) are the same. In this declaration, while using the language of the dogma, Hegel flatly rejects the Definition of Chalcedon with its

It is well known that for Hegel the Christian religion, the apex of all religion, was called to leave its denominational framework behind. But Christianity was still a discourse of representational thinking [*vorstellendes Denken*], still dependent on the sensory. It was therefore fated, for Hegel, to be absorbed back into philosophical thought in the modern age.[46] Voegelin's main argument, by contrast, was that modernity was rooted in the violent political attempt to make paradise come down to earth, and to make access to the means of happiness here below into the ultimate goal of all politics. Now, the advent of Christianity was, for Voegelin, the advent of humanity's realization of its divine-human vocation, here and now.

> Ecumenicity will mean the tendency of a community that represents the divine source of order to express the universality of its claim by making itself coextensive with the ecumene; universality will mean the experience of the world-transcendent God as the source of order that is universally binding for all men. To the spiritual communities of this type we will apply the term ecumenic religions, paralleling the term ecumenic empires.[47]

With access to this new, eschatological, sense[48] of the *oikouménē*, the theology of politics is turned upside-down. With the good news in the Gospel of the imminent arrival of the Kingdom of God on earth, a new force for the transfiguration of the world entered into history. This force, although experienced in the first place by the Judaeo-Christian community, goes well beyond the limits of its initial context.[49] Henceforth man

---

concern about making divine and human nature, which are supposed to be different, intelligible as copresent in the one person of Christ." *Order and History*, 4, 329.

46 G. W. F. Hegel, *Lectures on the Philosophy of Religion*, trans. P. C. Hodgson (3 vols, Oxford: Clarendon Press, 2007), vol. 3.

47 Voegelin, *Order and History*, 4, 192.

48 Ibid., 376: "The historical dimension of humanity, thus, is no more a given than the reality of man's personal existence in the Metaxy. Universal mankind is not a society existing in the world, but a symbol that indicates man's consciousness of participating, in his earthly existence, in the mystery of a reality that moves toward its transfiguration. Universal mankind is an eschatological index."

49 Ibid., 337: "Structure and transfiguration do not begin when they become conscious through the theophanic events of the Ecumenic Age; they are experienced as the problems of reality both before and after their differentiation. Transfiguring incarnation, in particular, does not begin with Christ, as Paul assumed, but becomes conscious through Christ and Paul's vision as the eschatological telos of the transfiguring process that goes on in history before and after Christ and constitutes its meaning."

is permanently caught between two poles, the divine and the human, which Voegelin defines by means of the Platonic term *metaxu*, the between. We find here the tense logic of ecumenical metaphysics, which leads, in Voegelin as in Nicolescu, Desmond, or Gabellieri, to a new definition of time and space.[50] As Voegelin lamented, by contrast, the reduction of the real and of spiritual life to their phenomenal and secular character, developed in idealist philosophy in the nineteenth century, was at the origin of reactionary totalitarian movements marked by their closedness to the Other and to Otherness, and by a forgetting of the spiritual foundations of political life. Voegelin also inveighed against the loss of the cosmic meaning of the notion of *oikoumenē* in modern thought.[51] Shaped by the work of Rudolf Otto, and especially by Otto's book *Mysticism East and West* (1932), Voegelin came to the conclusion, as he writes in his *Autobiographical Reflections*, that "[w]hen consciousness becomes luminous for itself as the site of divine-human cooperation in the historical process of differentiation, the end of all things has by no means come, as some of the contemporaries of this great event believed."[52]

But Voegelin, probably because he was largely unfamiliar with the ecumenical movement of the twentieth century, did not manage to bring his project to completion. For him, the spiritual experience of universality

---

50 Ibid., 408: "There is a process of the Whole of which the In-Between reality with its process of history is no more than a part, though the very important part in which the process of the Whole becomes luminous for the eschatological movement beyond its own structure. Within this process of the Whole, then, some things, as for instance the earth, outlast other things, as for instance the individual human beings who inhabit the earth; and what we call 'time' without further qualifications is the mode of lastingness peculiar to the astrophysical universe that permits its dimension of time to be measured by its movements in space. But even this ultimate mode of lastingness, to which as a measure we refer the lasting of all other things, is not a 'time' in which things happen but the time dimension of a thing within the Whole that also comprises the divine reality whose mode of lastingness we express by such symbols as 'eternity.' Things do not happen in the astrophysical universe; the universe, together with all things founded in it, happens in God."

51 Ibid., 263: "Oikoumene and okeanos belong together as integral parts of a symbolism that, as a whole, expresses a compact experience of man's existence in the cosmos. Man is not a disembodied psyche. His experiencing consciousness is founded in a body; this body is part of the life process through the generations; the human life process is part of the life that also comprises the animal and vegetable realms; this larger life process is founded in the earth on which it takes place; and the earth is part of the whole of reality that the Greeks have called the cosmos. The oikoumene, in the literal sense, is man's habitat in the cosmos."

52 Eric Voegelin, *Autobiographical Reflections: Revised Edition with Glossary* (Columbia, MO: University of Missouri Press, 2011), 137.

was insufficiently differentiated from the desire for ecumenical expansion within what he called the ecumenical religions. His vision of religions, a vision which was in the end very political, remained that of the period before the creation of the World Council of Churches and Vatican II. This probably prevented the American philosopher, the child of a Viennese Catholic mother and a German Lutheran father, from conceiving an authentic metaphysics of ecumenism.

That is why the time has probably come to tell the story of how the Christian *ekklesia* becomes aware, in a way that is so decisive for the global consciousness of humanity, of its ecumenical *telos*, beyond all distinctions of sex, race, and social class. This new consciousness, indeed, has been at work within the Church for two millennia, and, through the Church, has been at work in all humanity. We will show how this consciousness took hold, in a discontinuous way, of the dynamic brought by the new ecumenical metaphysics. In the light of this, we shall find in particular that the external unity of human beings is not the first objective of ecumenical consciousness. The theanthropo-cosmic horizon of ecumenical metaphysics, which appeared in Galilee in the first century of our era, is that of the eschatological, personal, sapiential, and ternary meeting-point of justice, law, truth, and beauty. Two short phrases addressed by Jesus Christ to his disciples allow us to summarize this eschatological turn brought about by Christianity: "The kingdom of God cometh not with observation . . . for, behold, the kingdom of God is within you" (Luke 17:20 – 21).

THE THIRD GRAND NARRATIVE OF THE EMERGENCE OF ECUMENICAL CONSCIOUSNESS

Let us from now on begin from the present moment of human global consciousness. The current age of Western consciousness, which has become global by means of a series of successive hybridizations, is today undergoing a mutation without precedent since the age of the Renaissance. As early as 1991, the Canadian Catholic philosopher Charles Taylor had brought to light the malaises of Modernity: the loss of meaning, the eclipse of goals, and the loss of freedom within a society that was more and more individualistic and was fascinated by mechanistic materialism. Following Bergson, Taylor reminded us that Modernity was wrong to have conceived time in an analogous way to space, with moments that follow upon each other like the inch marks on a ruler, whereas, as Emmanuel Mounier puts it, "the present has a thickness which is precisely that of freedom in the world." Taylor also condemned the myth of the "liberty without hindrance" of the egocentric self, disconnected from the world, a self which was supposed to have broken the chains of modern man and was lauded by post-modern thinkers. In order to make room for a conception of eternity capable of reconnecting all moments in the one movement of this world, in order to arrive at an ethics of self-fulfillment, it was necessary, for Taylor, to find new paths towards truth, "subtler languages," which, in *Sources of the Self*, he called epiphanies of being.[53]

The Radical Orthodoxy movement, started in in 1990s[54] by the Anglican theologian John Milbank, envisaged the history of Western consciousness in a different way.[55] The Cambridge Christian thinker liked then to present himself as a "post-modern Christian traditionalist."[56] He called for a radical return to orthodoxy in faith in order to withdraw from modernity. In the fifth part of this volume we shall analyze in more detail this important movement in spiritual consciousness and contemporary ecumenism. Here let us simply note that, for Charles Taylor, Modernity cannot be rejected in so radical a way. For the Canadian thinker, the post-modern era is full of promise. It is, first of all, characterized by the realization that "we live on several different levels." At one level, our self stops wanting to control everything and to claim that it is disengaged and capable of doubting everything. It discovers all the resources of authenticity. It is then enough to be present to oneself and to live the present moment, as the German thinker Eckhart Tolle, who lives in Canada, argues.[57]

But Charles Taylor has a rather narrow vision of "orthodox Christianity," because in *A Secular Age* he summarily links it to the decadent scholasticism of the sixteenth century, which made a radical distinction between the natural world, on the one hand, and the supernatural world on the other.[58] In my view, Taylor did not sufficiently allow for the extent to

---

53 "Part V: Subtler Languages," in Charles Taylor, *Sources of the Self: The Making of the Modern Identity* (Cambridge: Cambridge University Press, 2012), 391–493.

54 The birth of the movement can be dated from the appearance of John Milbank's *Theology and Social Theory* in 1990.

55 *Radical Orthodoxy: a New Theology*, eds. John Milbank, Catherine Pickstock, and Graham Ward (London: Routledge, 1999).

56 John Milbank, *Theology and Social Theory: Beyond Secular Reason*, 2nd edition (Oxford: Blackwell, 2013).

57 Eckhart Tolle, *Le pouvoir du moment présent: Guide d'éveil spirituel* [*The Power of Now: Guide to Spiritual Awakening*] (Outremont: Éditions Ariane, 2000).

58 Charles Taylor, *A Secular Age* (Cambridge, MA: Harvard University Press, 2007). The same horror towards orthodoxy in faith is found in the work of Pierre Magnard.

which faith-reason has developed over the course of the centuries, as Milbank showed in 1990 in *Theology and Social Theory*.

As a matter of fact, the difficulty of these two meta-narratives consisted in orthodoxy's being understood only as "what is consistent with correct and sound doctrine" (Taylor), or as the memory faithful to "the exemplarity of the patristic matrix" (Milbank).[59] But in reality these approaches correspond to a static vision of orthodoxy and, what is more, grasp only two of the four forms of orthodoxy in faith, as I showed in 2013.[60]

John Milbank recognized this point in the foreword he wrote to my book when it was published in English in 2018.[61] Furthermore, it is true that Charles Taylor was correct in pointing to the limits of the denominational period of the Church — that is, its desire to free itself from all creativity and all responsibility of its own by relying on sources of certain authority such as the Pope or the Scriptures (and, we for our part have added, the Councils and the Fathers of the Church, for Eastern Christianity). This is why Taylor was right to propose in the end, in *A Secular Age*, a unified vision of the spiritual, intellectual, and civilizational history of Europe, which associated the narrative defended by Milbank — the narrative of a wrong interpretation of Christian revelation from the fourteenth century onwards (the "ID" narrative, for Intellectual Deviation) — with that of a permanently self-reforming Christian thought and spirituality (Reform Master Narrative).[62]

This summary recounting of these two explanations of the dynamic of Modernity, explanations resulting from post-modernity and from the limits of the denominational representation of orthodoxy in faith, seemed to me indispensable to the understanding of the contemporary development of Western consciousness. The French sociologist Jean-Paul Willaime has described post-modernity as an epoch characterized not only by the loss of the referent, as in the modern epoch, but also by uncertainty, by

---

Magnard identifies orthodoxy as "the reign of a single thought," and "the alibi of the abstract universal," which can only "enter into a logic of the exclusive." Pierre Magnard, *Pourquoi la religion?* (Paris: Armand Colin, 2006), 72.

59 "In what sense orthodox and in what sense radical? Orthodox in the most straightforward sense of commitment to credal Christianity and the exemplarity of its patristic matrix. But orthodox also in the more specific sense of re-affirming a richer and more coherent Christianity that was gradually lost sight of after the late Middle Ages." *Radical Orthodoxy: A New Theology*, 2.

60 Arjakovsky, *What Is Orthodoxy?*.

61 John Milbank, "Foreword" to Arjakovsky, *What is Orthodoxy?*.

62 The final sentence of Taylor's book *A Secular Age* is: "Thus we need both ID and RMN to explain religion today." (776)

fear, by a new endemic cycle of violence. Something was broken within humanity's consciousness between the two world wars of the twentieth century and with the invention of the atomic bomb in 1939. The dominant contemporary consciousness finds itself to have broken both with the medieval belief in the coercive omnipotence of God and with the modern faith in the ineluctability of human progress.

Contemporary consciousness is marked by the whole current which, from Nietzsche to Foucault, rejected faith in a creator God, as well as Cartesian rationality. Having become incapable of accepting the possibility of divine revelation in history, and horrified by the very thought of a "blind watchmaker" at the controls of evolution,[63] it has ended up by imagining evolution as it pleases.[64] This post-modern consciousness is sometimes extremely clear-sighted about the collapse of some of the pillars of modernity, such as the notion of progress, as well as about the need to find new paths towards transcendence, and about all the phenomena of "emergence" or self-transcendence.[65] But as Olivier Roy laments,[66] it does not possess the weapons that would allow it effectively to resist the various fundamentalist movements, which are themselves increasingly dissatisfied by the powers of secularization.[67]

Of course, more and more people are arriving at new syntheses — the people whom Paul H. Ray and Sherry Ruth Anderson call the "cultural creatives." These are people who privilege personal and spiritual development in their lives, who privilege communion with nature and with others, and who seek the authenticity and personal integrity extolled by Taylor and Tolle.[68]

---

63 Richard Dawkins, The Blind Watchmaker (London: Penguin, 1986).
64 Jean-Pierre Dupuy, La marque du sacré (Paris: Carnets Nord, 2008).
65 Marc Weinstein, Pas de société sans auto-transcendance (Aix: Éditions du Croquant, 2020). Self-transcendence [l'auto-transcendance] is the fact that in human societies before industrial capitalism, the horizontal power of the people spontaneously ascended into verticality. Some native Americans erected a totem; the Greeks revered the "good and beautiful" city. The thesis, or the hypothesis, of this short enquiry is that self-transcendence is a constitutive invariant of all human societies. (For "emergence," see, for example, Philip Clayton and Paul Davies, eds., The Re-Emergence of Emergence: The Emergentist Hypothesis from Science to Religion [Oxford: Oxford University Press, 2006], where emergence is described as the idea that "at each level of complexity, new and often surprising qualities emerge that cannot, at least in any straightforward manner, be attributed to known properties of the constituents." — Translator.)
66 Olivier Roy, La Sainte Ignorance (Paris: Seuil, 2013).
67 "Face à la montée des fondamentalismes: pour une nouvelle anthropologie du droit," March 13, 2017, https://theconversation.com.
68 Paul H. Ray and Sherry Ruth Anderson, The Cultural Creatives: How Fifty Million People are Changing the World (New York: Three Rivers Press, 2001).

Yet it is as if this sector of the population, which has integrated the human soul's capacities to bring together identity and alterity through the intermediary of a transcendent middle, has been weakened, in the age of "believing without belonging,"[69] by its reluctance to belong to communities and therefore to institutions.

It seems necessary above all to add a third approach that would allow us to grasp the depth of the crisis in contemporary consciousness, but also the renewal heralded by the emergence of new intellectual and psychological spiritual profiles. This narrative supplements that of the intellectual deviation (ID) in relation to a Catholic understanding of truth (John Milbank, but also, in France, Marie-Joseph Le Guillou) and that of the reforming matrix (RM; Charles Taylor, or Jean-Paul Willaime in France) of Western consciousness. This third grand narrative is that of the emergence of ecumenical consciousness (ECE) in contemporary consciousness. It is no more anti-modern than post-modern; it is trans-modern. It is neither theocentric, as in the Middle Ages, nor anthropocentric, as in the modern era, nor technocentric, as in the postmodern era. If I may, I shall describe this third grand narrative as the theo-anthropo-cosmic, in that its description of the evolution of ecumenical consciousness holds together within human consciousness the manifestations of cosmic consciousness and the hierophanies of divine consciousness. The person, as an emergent part of cosmic consciousness, as an interface between God and his creation, thus finds itself at the heart of this process, as a third referent. In this way, by combining personalism, sophiology, and ternary thought, this third narrative institutes human consciousness as the epistemological key to the understanding of the world and the constitution of the real.

This narrative is, therefore, at once historical and metaphysical. First philosophy, indeed, according to Louis Lavelle, can justly be called the *science of consciousness* in contrast to all those sciences which are concerned with objects. This science is, by definition, universal. "Consciousness, however, far from being the self's closing-in upon itself, is that opening upon itself without which the self would be nothing."[70] Such a science is also dialogical insofar as it passes from subjectivity to objectivity by means of intersubjectivity. The history of ecumenical consciousness is therefore that of the intersecting gazes of men and women who participate in God and in the world in the adventure of divine humanity.

---

69   "[B]elieving without belonging" is in English in the original text. — *Translator.*
70   Louis Lavelle, *L'existence et la valeur* (Paris: Collège de France, 1991), 26.

THE FIRST ATTEMPTS AT A NARRATIVE OF ECUMENICAL CONSCIOUSNESS

Apart from Eric Voegelin, a number of scholars tried in the twentieth century to tell the story of the emergence of ecumenical consciousness within Western consciousness. We shall mention only the four following thinkers, because of their belonging to different disciplines: the philosopher Jean Gebser, the psychologist Erich Neumann, the historian Mircea Eliade, and the theologian Pierre Teilhard de Chardin. A few words should be said about the interest, but also about the limitations, of these scholars' thought, before setting out the approach to be taken here.

JEAN GEBSER

The German philosopher and linguistician Jean Gebser (1905–1973) gave in 1965 a talk called "The image of man and of consciousness," in which he put forward a sketch of a chronology of the stages of the development of human consciousness.

> The structure which actually makes it possible for us to live and to react is at least threefold, if not fourfold, in kind. We have what could be called an archaic consciousness, an original consciousness, of which most people are not really any longer conscious; we have a magical consciousness that is grounded in vitality; we have a mythical consciousness that is more physically based; we have a mental, rational consciousness, whose home is more in thinking; and there is perhaps also a fifth consciousness: a new level of consciousness, which I have described as integral, is being formed.[71]

Hostile to Nazism, Jean Gebser found refuge in Switzerland from 1939 onwards. He had written his great work during the thirties of the twentieth century and published it in 1949 under the title *Ursprung und Gegenwart* [The Ever-Present Origin]. In this work he foresaw the end of the rational age of global human consciousness and the dawn of an "a-rational thought" whose premises he found in Paul Klee and Sri Aurobindo.[72] In the light of the discoveries of Einstein and Heisenberg, he remarked upon the collapse of the four pillars of modern thought, namely Euclidian geometry, Aristotelian logic, Democritus's atomism, and Aristarchus's heliocentrism.

---

71   Jean Gebser, "Menschensbild und Lebensgestaltung (1965)," *Gesamtausgabe* (Schaffhausen: Novalis, 1975–1981), 6: 360–75, 360.

72   The Jean Gebser Society, "A brief biography," https://gebser.org/.

Gebser was one of the first to herald the mutation of human consciousness towards a new integral stage, that is, a stage capable of integrating
the lessons of the previous stages, while opening the way to a new stage,
the de-centering of the ego and the becoming-open to self. Gebser's problem, however, is that he assimilated the world of faith to that of mythical
consciousness, that is, to the world of the irrational and the collective.
Consequently, it was difficult for him to understand faith as the synthesis
of a symbolic and living rationality, at once conceptual and non-dual.

ERICH NEUMANN

The same difficulty is found in the story of the thinking of Erich Neumann (1905 – 1965), a German-Jewish psychologist who became an Israeli
citizen. This analytical psychoanalyst was close to C. G. Jung, and developed
his research on the origins of consciousness in close association with Jung's
depth psychology. For both men, indeed, the appearance of collective
archetypes began from childhood onwards. These archetypes, Neumann
writes in *The Origins and History of Consciousness*, are the pictorial forms of
the instincts, because the unconscious is revealed to the conscious spirit
by means of images that, as in dreams and fantasies, begin the process of
conscious reaction and assimilation.

> It is the task of this book to show that a series of archetypes is a
> main constituent of mythology, that they stand in an organic rela-
> tion to one another, and that their stadial succession determines
> the growth of consciousness. In the course of its onto-genetic
> development, the individual ego consciousness has to pass
> through the same archetypal stages which determined the evo-
> lution of consciousness in the life of humanity. The individual has
> in his own life to follow the road that humanity has trod before
> him, leaving traces of its journey in the archetypal sequence of
> the mythological images we are now about to examine. [73]

This approach has affinities with Rudolf Steiner's anthroposophy. But
as Martin Buber remarked about the work of Jung, for depth psychology
God is only a state of the soul and not a person. In Jung, "metaphysical
expressions are expressions of the soul; they are therefore of a psychological nature." [74] This is why, as Buber lamented, psychology becomes

---

73   Erich Neumann, *The Origins and History of Consciousness* (London: Routledge,
1954), 400.
74   Dominique Bourel, *Martin Buber, Sentinelle de l'humanité* (Paris: Albin Michel,
2015), 587.

the only authorized metaphysics. Now for Buber, psychology runs the risk of idolizing the instincts, instead of sanctifying them in faith. Moreover, Neumann limits the development of the human being's religious consciousness to the stages of childhood and adolescence. This is why, for Neumann, "the aim of all education, and not in our culture alone, is to expel the child from the paradise of his native genius and, through differentiation and the renunciation of wholeness, to constrain the Old Adam into the paths of collective usefulness."[75] Here we are distant enough from the religious understanding of education as an apprenticeship, by means of successive initiations, in mastering the cosmic powers which are found in the human being.

MIRCEA ELIADE

The historian of religion Mircea Eliade (1907 – 1986) was formed by the influence of the German Lutheran theologian Rudolf Otto. In The Philosophy of Religion Based on Kant and Fries (1909), Otto defended the German philosopher Jakob Friedrich Fries's theory of knowledge against Kant's. For Fries, indeed, the idea of Godhood was present in the human subconscious, in the relational category of reciprocal action. Nevertheless, as the notion of the creature did not for neo-Kantian thought correspond to a rational category, Otto made the choice to abandon all concepts in favor of the "ideogram of the pure content" of an inexplicable "numinous" feeling.

This is how Otto came, in his 1917 work Das Heilige [The Holy], to define the concept of the "sacred" as a numinous being, a notion relative to a "non-rational experience which does without the senses and the feelings, and whose first and immediate object is found outside oneself." According to Otto, the experience of the numinous takes place in four stages, from awareness of oneself as a creature to emotion, and from the discovery of mystery to a form of rapture from which follow love, compassion, devotion, and benevolence. For Otto, as for another representative of neo-Kantian philosophy, the German Protestant theologian Ernst Troeltsch (1865 – 1923), the fundamental and essential element of all religion is therefore mysticism, that is to say, a faith in the active presence of a supernatural power, and in the possibility of an inner relationship with that power. In place of the Durkheimian idea that religion should be understood as the product of social interactions, Otto postulated an inner revelation and a hermeneutics of the signs of the sacred. The same was true of the Swedish thinker

---

75   Neumann, Origins and History of Consciousness, 400.

Nathan Söderblom (1866 – 1931), a former pupil of Durkheim's, who in 1914 became the primate of the Swedish Lutheran church. The Lutheran Archbishop distanced himself from religious sociology. He believed that even in Buddhism, despite the impermanence of everything, one finds a transcendent reality: Nirvana, the state sacred to Buddhists. In a similar way, in his 1926 book *Mysticism East and West*, Otto explained that, despite his rational concern to compare the work of the Christian mystic Meister Eckhart (1260 – 1327) and that of the Hindu mystic Adi Shankara (788 – 820), his approach was mystical rather than metaphysical. He justified his approach in the following way:

> It is characteristic of the mystic vision that it sees the manifoldness and multiplicity with which it is surrounded in the One. This and this alone is its distinguishing feature. It is no concern of the mystic to discover how the dispersive vision (i.e., the scientific vision) does its work, and so still more to strengthen and to exercise it. The seeker after salvation . . . finds the given empirical situation and seeks how this is to be overcome and not how it is to be explained.[76]

Mircea Eliade was also influenced by the work of René Guénon (1886 – 1951) and by a whole current of metaphysical and esoteric thought which is called "perennialist" or "traditionalist."[77] Guénon's work certainly represented a salutary reaction in relation, on the one hand, to the progressive loss of the sense for symbolism in the West from the sixteenth century onwards, and, on the other hand, to the rejection of intellectual intuition from Kant onwards. But as Jean Borella has shown,[78] this thinking collapsed into a form of gnosis that divided the world into the pure forms above, the archetypes, and the world below, characterized by the rule of quantity and decay.[79]

---

76 Rudolf Otto, *Mysticism East and West: A Comparative Analysis of The Nature of Mysticism* (Wheaton, IL: Theosophical Publishing House, 1987), 248.

77 Xavier Accart, *Guénon ou le renversement des clartés. Influence d'un métaphysicien sur la vie littéraire et intellectuelle française (1920 – 1970)* (Paris: Édidit, 2006).

78 Jean Borella, *René Guénon et le guénonisme* (Paris, L'Harmattan: 2020). See Borella, *Christ the Original Mystery: Esoterism and the Mystical Way (With Special Reference to the Works of René Guénon)*, trans. John Champoux (Brooklyn: Angelico Press, 2018).

79 "It might appear that there is, in a sense, multiplicity at the two extreme points, in the same way that there is correlatively, as has just been pointed out, unity on the one side and 'units' on the other; but the notion of inverse analogy applies strictly here too, so that while the principial multiplicity is contained in metaphysical unity, arithmetical, or quantitative 'units' are on the other hand contained in the other and inferior multiplicity. Incidentally, does not the mere

These approaches, symbolic rather than conceptual, nevertheless had a direct influence on Mircea Eliade. The Romanian thinker placed *homo religiosus* — that is, man as capable of entering into contact with transcendence by virtue of the original organization of Mind itself — at the heart of his research. Bestowing particular attention, in *The Sacred and the Profane*,[80] on myths, symbols, and rituals, Eliade showed that each revelation is an act which displays a reality of an order which differs from the natural order. The act of revelation, from cave art to the Tour de France, was, for Eliade, a hierophany, a religious phenomenon perceived by *homo religiosus*, even in the secular world. He believed that phenomena of violence or of the commercialization of the instinctive responses of individuals were only offshoots of the fundamental misrecognition of the human condition in self-sterilized modern societies.

In connection with this vision of the world, he worked out a comparative view of religions by finding proximities between varying cultures and historical moments. His monumental history in three volumes of religious beliefs and ideas, which claimed to cover the entire subject, was the great work in which he was engaged up until the end of his life.[81] Yet history as such was not in reality for Eliade a discipline genuinely relevant to the study of the manifestations of the sacred. In fact, as he writes in the preface to his trilogy, the sacred is an expression of individuation that does not depend on the phenomenon of temporalization:

> In short, the "sacred" is an element in the structure of consciousness and not a stage in the history of consciousness. On the most archaic levels of culture, living, considered as being human, is in itself a religious act, for food-getting, sexual life, and work have a sacramental value. In other words, to be — or, rather, to become — a man signifies being "religious."[82]

---

possibility of speaking of 'units' in the plural show clearly enough how far removed the thing so spoken of is from true unity? The multiplicity of the lower order is by definition purely quantitative, it could be said to be quantity itself, deprived of all quality; on the other hand, the multiplicity of the higher order, or that which can be called so analogically, is really a qualitative multiplicity, that is to say the integrality of the qualities or attributes that constitute the essence of beings and of things." René Guénon, *The Reign of Quantity and the Signs of the Times* (Hillsdale, NY: Sophia Perennis, 2001), 9.

80   Eliade, *The Sacred and the Profane*, trans. Willard R. Trask (San Diego, CA: Harvest, 1968).

81   Eliade, *A History of Religious Ideas*, trans. Willard R. Trask (3 vols, Chicago: University of Chicago Press, 1978 – 1982).

82   Eliade, *History of Religious Ideas*, 1: xiii.

Eliade's phenomenological method, critical towards the positivism dominant in his era, presented itself as integral and aimed to understand the essence and structure of myth. His research rehabilitated the symbolic thought which, for him, distinguished *homo sapiens*, in that it holds together, in every sign, a signified, a signifier and a referent, and, in every hierophany, a mediator able to make manifest the sacral dimension of the divine.

Eliade's theories were developed by numerous experts across the world. They were the origin of new disciplines with names such as integral metaphysics, the science of the religious, and religious anthropology. These disciplines themselves possess many branches which greatly differ one from another, sometimes critical of Eliade's work, and which go from Gilbert Durand[83] to Julien Ries,[84] and from Fritjhof Schuon[85] to Michel

---

83   Gilbert Durand, *Les structures anthropologiques de l'imaginaire* (Paris: Dunod, 1992).

84   Julien Ries, *Symbole, mythe et rite* (Paris: Cerf, 2012).

85   Frithjof Schuon, *Résumé de métaphysique intégrale* (Paris: Le Courrier du Livre, 1985). In this book, Schuon puts forward his ecumenical synthesis by means of an esoteric conception which is non-Christian, because it integrates the personal transcendent God into an impersonal Divinity. "The supremely Real is absolute, and, being such, it is infinite. Whatever does not admit of any addition or subtraction, nor of any repetition or division, is absolute; therefore, the absolute is at once uniquely itself and completely itself. And that which is not limited by any border is infinite; it is, first of all, Potentiality or Possibility in itself, and ipso facto the Possibility of things, thus Virtuality. Without Omnipossibility, there would be neither Creator nor creation, neither maya nor samsara." (3) This gnosis can thenceforth find a simple enough solution to the riddle of religious diversity: "The key to the riddle is that there is only one personal God — who is, so to speak the 'human' or 'humanized' Face of supra-personal Divinity — but that there is also, beyond and by virtue of this first hypostatic degree, what we might call the 'denominational Face' of God: this is the Face of God turned towards a particular religion, the Look which he casts upon that religion, without which that religion could not even exist. In other words, the 'human Face' or the 'personal Face' of God assumes various modes which correspond to so many religious, denominational, or spiritual perspectives, such that one can say that each religion has its own God, without denying that God is one and that this unity can at any moment pierce the veil of diversity; the fact that the God of Islam is revealed — or can be revealed — differently from the God of Christianity cannot prevent its being the case that in substance Christians and Muslims worship the same God. The divine Being contains all spiritual possibilities, and, consequently, all religious and mystical archetypes; and, having projected these into existence, he looks at each religion with a Look particular and appropriate to it; it is in a sense analogous to this that the angels have been said each to speak the language which suits them. This 'Look' or 'Face' is a sort of new 'divine subjectivity,' subordinated to that of God in himself and transmitting God's subjectivity in a particular way to man; it is in this way that colorless light, without ceasing to be light, throws out the colors of the rainbow; and it is in this way that water,

Meslin.[86] It is, nevertheless, certain that these various disciplines, which all take as their subject the study of symbolic thought and its various hierophanies, each in their way make a contribution to the history of ecumenical consciousness.

Yet they cannot be fully satisfactory from the point of view of ecumenical metaphysics, as I shall go on to explain. I shall confine myself here to the critique of Eliade's work mounted by Michel Meslin (1926 – 2010), a professor of religious anthropology and a former President of the Sorbonne.[87] Meslin's three main books were published in 1973 (*Pour une science des religions* [Towards a Science of Religions]), in 1988 (*L'expérience humaine du divine* [The Human Experience of the Divine]), and in 2010 (*L'homme et le religieux. Essai d'anthropologie* [Man and the Religious Dimension: an Anthropological Essay]). These works will be examined so as to shed light on the deep critique which the French academic developed of the Romanian thinker, who, in the 1960s, became a professor at the University of Chicago. But the limitations of Meslin's work will also be shown.

Meslin recognized the interest of a critical approach to the purely empirical human sciences. He also recognized to the full the interest of mysticism in trying to think in a coherent way about the variety of experiences of the numinous. Thus in his final book he draws on the mysticism of Sankara and of St John of the Cross, but also on Islamic mysticism, to describe the overcoming of the phenomenon of individuation:

> Thus *tajrid*, the abandonment of all concepts and the overcoming of any empirical form, is necessary to arrive at a state of union; it leads to *tafrid*, which is a state of radical forsakenness that follows from the overcoming of the self. For Islamic mysticism, total submission to God can therefore only be brought about by a complete relinquishment of self, which in the end allows *tawhid* to be attained, the proclamation of divine Unicity within one's most inward being.[88]

---

transformed into ice, gives rise to crystallizations and thus to different and even opposed forms of manifestation." (23)

86   Michel Meslin, *L'expérience humaine du divin. Fondements d'une anthropologie religieuse* (Paris: Les Éditions du Cerf, 1988).

87   Daniel Vidal, "Michel Meslin, L'homme et le religieux. Essai d'anthropologie," *Archives de sciences sociales des religions* [online], 156 [October–December 2011, document 156–80, uploaded February 16, 2012]; J. Richard, "Anthropologie religieuse et théologie. À propos d'un récent ouvrage de Michel Meslin," *Laval théologique et philosophique*, 46 (3), (1990), 383–402.

88   Michel Meslin, *Pour une science des religions* (Paris: Éditions du Seuil, 1987), 388.

But Meslin directly disputed Mircea Eliade's theories. Eliade, in making nature the site of the sacred, treated the latter as a transhistorical paradigm. For Eliade the real was the sacred. Daniel Vidal has finely remarked that

> The cosmic is thus immediately assimilated to the ontological. But then there is no quest which is of any use to the human being, because the principle of transcendence is immanent within things, such that the latter appear in the light of transcendence and in the depths of the existence of transcendence. This is just what the author [Meslin] finds a problem: "it is men, and only men, who are the measure of the sacredness of beings and things, because they are the ones who sacralize them."[89]

To summarize the matter, then, Meslin wished to separate anthropology from its idealist foundations. He did not think it possible that the religious element might appear "in the process of self-revelation." For Meslin, spiritual experience was the product of a personal encounter with a transcendent God as with one's neighbor. "The foundation of every religion," Meslin explains, "is an existential experience in which the human being constructs himself in relation to a God, and in which he is at once the creator and the creature responsible for his own new being."

As a result of this commitment, however, Meslin rejected any approach of a metaphysical or theological kind. This is why his conception of religious anthropology has nothing to say about God himself. It could only speak of the human being in his or her religious dimension, in his or her openness to the divine, with the assistance of all the tools of phenomenology, beginning with hermeneutics. In the end, the work of the former rector of the Sorbonne is continuous with that of Ernst Troeltsch, but also with that of Paul Ricœur and Paul Tillich, that is to say, with an existentialist philosophy of Protestant obedience. The latter does not aim to change the world. It begins from cultural and religious facts so as to notice in them, through the ages, testimony to and expressions of human self-understanding. It retains its value, nevertheless, from the perspective of ecumenical metaphysics, because as Meslin writes, "anthropology (in general) postulates a unity, and, in a certain sense, an identity among men, and seeks to reveal, beyond the diversity of cultures, the very structures of the human mind as they manifest themselves in the actions and works of collectives as well as in those of individuals."[90]

---

89 Daniel Vidal, "Michel Meslin, L'homme et le religieux," 3.
90 Meslin, *L'expérience humaine du divin*, 8.

Yet there is still no bridge between Meslin's work and Eliade's. As Jean Richard quite correctly reminds us in his review of Meslin's book, the Protestant theologian Paul Tillich, in his last talk on "The Significance of the History of Religions for the Systematic Theologian" (1965), asserted the urgent importance of correlating and combining systematic theology and the historical sciences of religion. In a certain way, religious anthropology allows one to see the divine in the human without confusion. In this sense it is a useful response to Eliade's comparative mythology, which tried to show, for its part, the unity without separation of the divine and the human. Ecumenical metaphysics seeks, on its part, to think the divine and the human together without confusion and without separation.

PIERRE TEILHARD DE CHARDIN

The Christian theologian and palaeontologist Pierre Tielhard de Chardin (1881 – 1955) developed a history of evolution as a history of cosmo-anthropic consciousness. His history has the interest of presenting itself as personalist.[91] For Chardin, a French Jesuit, the science of consciousness must avoid the spiritualist trap just as keenly as it avoids the materialist one. This is why Teilhard devises a phenomenology (which he also calls a "generalized physics") that studies the interior face of things as well as the exterior face of the world. The originality of Teilhard's thought was to grasp vision as the interface between the two worlds, interior and exterior, of cosmic consciousness. "Unity," he writes, "only grows when it is supported by a growth in consciousness, that is, in vision." Now it is man, the apex of cosmo-genesis and anthropo-genesis, who is the universe's center of perspective and center of construction.

> It is a virtue, as well as a matter of necessity, then, that it is to man that all Science must come back in the end. If truly to see is to be more, let us look at Man, and we shall live more.[92]

The thought of the French palaeontologist, influenced by that of the Russian chemist and mineralogist Vladimir Vernadsky, the father of the idea of the biosphere, possesses some of the characteristics of sophiology, even if he does not use that word himself.[93] Teilhard writes, in the

---

91   Pierre Teilhard de Chardin, Le phénomène humain (Paris: Seuil, 1955). In this work the Jesuit thinker presents the history of human consciousness from its origins to its omega-point.

92   Teilhard, Le phénomène humain, 27.

93   Cf. especially Vernadsky, Filosofskie mysli naturalista [Philosophical Thoughts of a Natural Scientist] (Moscow: Nauka, 1987). There are nevertheless differences between

epilogue to *The Phenomenon of Man*, that the culmination of the Noosphere in the Omega Point can be compared to the vision of St Paul, for whom, at the end of time, "there will no longer be anything but God as 'all in all' [*en pasi panta theos*]."[94] For Teilhard, in contrast to Vernadsky, the history of evolution is therefore that of the tension within created Wisdom, from the tiniest amoeba to the omega point of anthropo-cosmic consciousness capable of joining in play with its Creator, as in the Book of Proverbs.[95]

Teilhard's personalist approach is combined with a conception of created Wisdom which he situates within the process of the emergence of Spirit (noögenesis):

> To make room for thought in the world, I have needed to "interiorize" matter: to imagine an energetics of the mind; to conceive a noögenesis rising upstream against the flow of entropy; to provide evolution with a direction, a line of advance and critical points; and finally to make all things double back upon *someone*.... The only universe capable of containing the human person is an irreversibly "personalising" universe.[96]

In the end, Teilhard's vision of the world is ternary in the sense that it is opposed to the binary vision of spiritualism (body/soul) and the monist approach of materialism (matter), even the most dialectical. He recovers

Teilhard's point of view and that of Vernadsky, as I showed at a colloquium dedicated to Vernadsky at the Centre for Russian Culture in Paris in 2015. Vernadsky was ready to recognize that all inanimate matter possesses the capacity to become living, as is shown by the presence of calcium in plants. But he was not ready to take the next step after that, which was taken by Florensky and Bulgakov, which is to regard divine Wisdom as being at work in natural evolution. https://www.msha.fr/msha/archives.
94 Ibid., 327.
95 For Vernadsky, the evolution of human consciousness from its remotest origins tends towards an emancipation of life by the domestication of the sun's energy and an emancipation in respect of the need for biological nutrition. "If this emancipation were brought to fulfillment, man would free himself from living matter. From being a heterotrophic social being, he would become an autotrophic one. Such a phenomenon would have enormous repercussions for the biosphere. It would mean the splitting of the forces of the living, and the creation of a third independent branch of living matter. There would appear on the earth's crust, for the first time in the geological history of the planet, an autotrophic animal. It is difficult for us today — perhaps even impossible — to imagine the geological consequences of such an event; but it is clear that it would be the culmination of a long palaeontological evolution, and would represent not an action of free human will, but the manifestation of a natural process." Vernadsky, "L'autotrophie de l'humanité," *Revue générale des sciences pures et appliquées* (Paris, 1925), 18, http://www.larecherchedubonheur.com/article-24979015.html.
96 Teilhard de Chardin, *The Phenomenon of Man*, trans. Bernard Wall (London: Fontana, 1965), 318.

the vision of Man as formed of a body, a soul, and a spirit that was shared by Europeans at least until the ninth century. He also integrates, between identity and alterity, the power of the third element capable of uniting the "I" and the "Thou," without, however, annihilating them. As Dany-Robert Dufour writes, the Trinity is inscribed into man's condition as a speaking being. It is the capacity of the "I" to tell the "Thou" stories that it has got from the "He." "In other words, every human being, because he speaks, whatever are his beliefs, whether he is a pagan, a Buddhist, an atheist, a Jew, or a Christian, puts into practice a Trinitarian schema, anterior to any particular religious actualization."[97] In this sense it can be said that, anticipating the transhumanist temptation to increase human power by means of the technique of a binary digital language, Teilhard from 1921 onwards put forward a ternary vision of the world founded in man's recognition of his own createdness:

> To act like Titans? — impossible.... The further we advance along the highways of matter towards the perfecting of our organism, the more imperative will it become for the unity our being has won to be expressed, and to be completed, in the fibres of our consciousness by the predominance of spirit over flesh, by the harmonisation and sublimation of our passions. And the closer we come, through the diligent convergence of our efforts, to the common centre to which the elements of the world gravitate, the more will it become our duty, as conscious atoms of the universe, to submit ourselves "constructively" to the more and more far-reaching ties, to the dominating, universal influence of this more fully known centre — and the more incumbent will be the duty of worship.[98]

Teilhard de Chardin's work is not exempt, however, from limitations which have been amply discussed, both in the Catholic church and in scientific circles.[99] The French scholar's thought, after having been clarified and corrected by a number of experts such as Gérard Donnadieu in France, has nevertheless been widely rehabilitated in the Catholic church.[100] It remains true, nevertheless, that it must, today, be supplemented, as the British biologist Celia Deane Drummond recommends, with the sapiential

---

97   Dany-Robert Dufour, Les mystères de la trinité (Paris: Gallimard, 1990), 17.
98   Pierre Teilhard de Chardin, Science and Christ, trans. René Hague (London: Collins, 1968), 33.
99   Pierre Boutang, "Un chevalier de l'impossible," Le Monde, April 11–12, 1965, https://www.teilhard.fr/.
100   "Archives Dossiers de Noösphère," https://www.teilhard.fr/.

and eschatological thought of the Orthodox theologian Sergij Bulgakov. Teilhard himself used the term "pantheism" to describe his thought, and acknowledged that he had not sufficiently integrated the idea of evil into his conception of evolution, despite the innumerable extinctions of species and cruelties of all kinds that have peppered the history of the "phenomenon of man."

It is better to understand the history of the world, with Bulgakov, as a meeting between two wisdoms, that is to say, between two freedoms, created and uncreated, which is indissociable from the possibility of "falling" in created freedom, but also from the divine work of incarnation and redemption. Cosmic evolution is like a cross that links the order of nature with the ethical order of the divine-human relation. Celia Deane Drummond teaches today at the University of Notre Dame in the USA. In the year 2000, she devoted one of her major works, *Creation Through Wisdom: Theology and the New Biology*, to Father Sergij Bulgakov.[101] She rejects the reduction of Wisdom to pure rationality, as happened in the replacement of Sophia by Logos in medieval theology.[102] In her sapiential and ternary approach, true science is not separate from virtue. For Deane Drummond, positivistic evolutionism, which is incapable of distinguishing among the different qualities of temporality, and is hypnotized by the vitalist viewpoint centered on the behavior of the "selfish gene," as in the work of Richard Dawkins, cannot explain certain anomalies of evolution, nor certain complexities of human behavior, such as, for example, celibacy. Deane Drummond allies herself with the views of the British biologist Rupert Sheldrake, for whom the inheritance of acquired characteristics is epigenetic, rather than merely genetic, and takes place by means of chemical changes that do not affect the underlying genetic code. The sequencing of the human genome, indeed, has shown that the variety of forms among animal species does not correspond to a variety of genes. A simple flower, the *Paris japonica*, contains more genes than the human body.[103] It has also been discovered that the behavior of genes is neither individualistic nor selfish. On the contrary, Sheldrake writes, "they work co-operatively in the development and functioning of organisms. . . . Through morphic resonance, animals and plants are connected with their predecessors. Each individual both draws upon and contributes

---

101   Celia Deane Drummond, *Creation Through Wisdom: Theology and the New Biology* (Edinburgh: T & T Clark, 2000).

102   Ibid., 136.

103   https://en.wikipedia.org/wiki/Genome_size.

to the collective memory of the species."[104] The form and the behavior of an animal are, in Sheldrake's view, transmitted by morphic resonance, a little like a television set which receives transmissions by means of waves originating far away. These limitations of Teilhard's work have clouded its reception. From his definition of consciousness, only the "emerged" part has been retained, that is, "the specific effect of complexity."

CONCLUSION

Taking account of what has just been said about the interest of the main theses of the pioneers of the science of consciousness, it becomes possible once more to imagine a new narrative of the global development of human consciousness, a narrative that goes beyond the aporias of postmodernity by bringing together a spiritual, ethical, and rational view of the real. At a moment when humanity is realizing that "everything is connected," to follow the expression used many times by Pope Francis in his encyclical *Laudato Si'*, and at a moment, too, when more and more works are appearing on the topic of metaconceptual phenomena of all kinds (premonition, telepathy, out-of-body experiences, etc.),[105] it is necessary to find an approach to the history of human consciousness that is at once rational, spiritual, and holistic.

For my part, I define the noösphere as the space-time of the human spirit which links the cosmic universe to divine Wisdom. Through human consciousness's power to name, and animated by the various expressions of religion and belief which exist on the planet, the noösphere (which can be designated by the theological term "created Wisdom") interacts with the divine Mind [*Esprit divin*] acting within the geosphere (inanimate matter) and within the biosphere (biological life). Consciousness is thus situated at the heart of evolution, and if faith plays a significant role in evolution as the capacity for vision and creation, on an internal as well as an external level, and if in the end the expression of faith is thought of as the sap of the life of the Church, then it makes sense to put forward a history of ecclesial consciousness, as the beginnings of a more global history of ecumenical consciousness on the planet.

Such a history, moreover, makes it possible to understand the differences of emphasis among the various spiritual and belief traditions, and thus to grasp the ways in which these might be reconciled with each

104   Rupert Sheldrake, *The Science Delusion: Freeing the Spirit of Enquiry* (London: Coronet, 2012), 185.
105   Miriam Gablier and Sébastien Lilli, *Les mystères de la conscience* (Paris: Hachette pratique, 2019).

other. By bringing to light the universal polarities of faith-reason, this reconciliatory history of consciousness allows a number of phenomena converging in the real to be brought to attention through and beyond denominational, religious, and civilizational traditions.

HISTORY OF THE CHRISTIAN FAITH AND OF ECUMENICAL CONSCIOUSNESS

In many ways the history of nations, or of federations of nations, represents an advanced form of the story of the ecumenical consciousness of different peoples, even if the religious dimension of this consciousness sometimes finds it difficult to get a hearing within this story. In my research, I have tried to provide a transnational, transdisciplinary, and transreligious history of European consciousness. [106] There are also a few rare histories of ecumenical consciousness in individual religious traditions which are written in this spirit, that of a mosaic history of overlapping perspectives. We can, for example, refer here to the excellent *Histoire des relations entre juifs et musulmans des origines à nos jours* [History of the Relations between Jews and Muslims from the Origins until Today] overseen by Abdelwahab Meddeb and Benjamin Stora and published by Albin Michel in 2013. As has been said, the focus here will be on the history of ecumenical consciousness in the Christian world.

ORTHODOXY IN FAITH AS A FORM OF RATIONALITY

The Christian faith was a leaven that shaped the development of Western civilization. It is neither "rationalist," since St Paul presents it as foolishness in the eyes of the Greeks of his time, nor "fideist," since the same apostle presents it as a scandal for the Jews. It took many centuries before Christians were able to define the specificity of their faith, between rationalism and irrationalism. For the first Fathers of the Church, faith, when it is "orthodox," is a compass which holds together the faithful memory of Revelation with the right glory of Jesus Christ as true God and true Man, and which allows correct behavior and right judgements to be adopted by means of a logic of referring to God through the Scriptures, through Tradition, and through the Magisterium.

In my book *What Is Orthodoxy?* I showed that the two metanarratives of Western consciousness, that of structural deviation and that of

---

106   Antoine Arjakovsky, ed., *Histoire de la conscience européenne*, with a preface by Hermann van Rompuy (Paris: Salvator, 2016).

recurring reform, bear witness to the difficulty of grasping the notion of faith-truth in all its complexity, as at once revelation and development. Let us begin by bringing to mind the experience of faith for the first Christians. Faith was not for them a "feeling," as postmoderns hold it to be, nor a dull-witted and disconnected certainty of the real, as modernity has had a tendency to define it as being. For St Paul, "faith is the substance of things hoped for, the evidence of things not seen" (Heb. 11:1). Faith is therefore not a private conviction or a cheap form of rationality; it is, instead, a fulfillment of reason, an *epignosis*, an over-knowledge. Yet it is necessary that this faith should be "orthodox," as the whole tradition of the Church says. Hence the importance both of defining the notion of orthodoxy and of the method selected in order to arrive at such a definition. The Oriental method for making the truth spring forth is that of the purifying struggle with the energies of the world, an interior ascesis that alone permits access to what is authentically real. In the West, on the other hand, a method has been developed which consists in withdrawing from the world, so as to be in a position to grasp its logic and to remake it. These two different kinds of approach cannot be reconciled by means of a postmodern syncretism. It is best to adopt a method that is at once evolutional and involutional, symbolic and conceptual, antinomical and eschatological. Modern thought, in binary fashion, distinguishes subject from object, noumenon from phenomena, identity from alterity. The method of ecumenical science, conversely, is personalist (and thus convivialist), sophiological (and thus centered on a sapiential understanding of being), and ternary (capable of thinking identity and alterity together).

The historical formation of Christian orthodoxy possesses a structural dimension, linked to the kerygma of the Gospels and to the event of Pentecost, and an evolving dimension, linked to the leaps and jumps in the history of the Church and of the world.

After having closely studied the historiography of the idea of orthodoxy in the grand narratives of the history of the Church and of the world, from the four Gospels to contemporary histories of ecclesial consciousness, I showed that the Christian faith is structured like a compass, with four poles and the lines of tension between them, according to the levels of representation which Christian communities have in the history of what the Church is. The orthodoxy of faith, in the East as in the West, for the Catholic, Protestant, and Orthodox worlds, is a compass which Christians have consulted in their advance towards the Trinitarian God revealed by Jesus Christ. Orthodoxy was lived as an existential style of life allowing daily access to Jesus Christ, and thus to Him who declared himself to be "the way, and the truth and the life" (John 14:6). But this faith-reason was practiced differently in different contexts and space-times, sometimes simultaneously, sometimes not, at first as the *right glory* of Christ as true God and true Man; then, after the legalization of the Church in 313, as the capacity to define the *correct truth* making it possible to unite the good and the true; and subsequently, from the sixteenth century onwards, as the *faithful memory* of the promise of Union; and finally, as is increasingly the case today, as the *knowledge of justice* of the Kingdom of God on earth, the vision for which orthodoxy cannot be distinct from orthopraxy.

As the sources in the Gospels and the tradition of the Church show, this compass with four poles was chiefly entrusted by Christ to four apostles: Simon Peter, who was given primacy over the gathering of the apostles; James, called the son of thunder, who died as a martyr (Acts 12:2); John, the other son of thunder, the visionary of the end of time; and, finally, Paul, the apostle to the Gentiles, whose forename, Saul, was also changed by Christ, the sign of a calling specific to him. These four levels of consciousness can be likened to the path of divine-humanity followed by Christ himself: prophetic consciousness (at the beginning of his public life); sacerdotal consciousness (before his crucifixion); kingly consciousness (after his ascension); and missionary consciousness (before and after his resurrection). The history of Christianity shows that in different ages and places, one of the four paradigms has dominated the other three, leading to a perpetual motion of imagination/anticipation of the Kingdom, of resistance/reform, regulation/deviation, expansion/retraction.

I also showed how classical, modern, and post-modern consciousness developed in tandem with the semantic evolution of the notion of truth as correspondence, stability, coherence, and efficacity. I arrived at the conclusion that for several decades, Western consciousness has been undergoing both a shattering of its epistemology and the end of the denominational period characterized by defining faith as faithful memory. This definition of faith was, indeed, radically questioned, first in the nineteenth century by a number of Christian thinkers such as Newman, Solovyov, and John R. Mott, but also, still more, by the masters of suspicion, Marx, Nietzsche, and Freud. As we shall see in the account of ecclesial consciousness below, the contemporary era is that of the crisis in the paradigm of faithful memory, of the emergence of an inter-denominational and then transdenominational consciousness, of the domination of the secular paradigm of the knowledge of justice, but also of the gradual realization, both religious and secular, of the need to keep together justice and the moral law, openness to the Spirit and the acknowledgement of different religious and belief traditions.

The consequences of this ecumenical narrative of Christian consciousness are important. If we want to get out of the modern and post-modern cycle of division and violence, we need to recover a holistic vision of faith-reason that is capable of holding together the four poles of the field of consciousness. This approach makes it possible to work out a spiritual conception of the governance of the State founded in the principles of imagination and shared sovereignty, and of participation and regulation. It also puts in place the indispensable supports to the proper functioning of ecclesial life: the principles of personal primacy and synodality; of recognition of the divine image in each human being; and of the Church's calling to look for the Kingdom of God on earth.

Faith is never a magic wand. It demands an effort of man's whole being, including his rationality, and of the community that faith brings together, for the transcendent Spirit to become a reality active here and now. Faith is what the French thinker Jacques Ellul calls the tension towards "truth-reality." It can move mountains only if it addresses itself to creative all-powerfulness, while accepting at the same time the role of an ear listening to the Word.[107]

Orthodoxy in faith, then, is not merely a conformity to the norm, which is what secular consciousness mostly reduces it to. It is true that the rigidity of certain circles might lead us to think it that. In reality, when faith is understood as a compass, it draws as much on the resources of tradition as it opens itself to new impulses of the Spirit. The orthodoxy of faith does not belong to Christians alone, because no one, strictly speaking, can possess the truth. It is a particular form of wisdom in which all religious and belief traditions participate. It rests on the experience of revelation and on that of experimentation; on the process of subjectivation as well as on that of objectivation.

ECUMENICAL ECCLESIOLOGY AS A SYNTHESIS IN MOTION OF THE FOUR "NOTES" OF THE CHURCH

The Christian churches, and, by extension, most religions, have since the sixteenth century, and especially since the Treaty of Westphalia in 1648, been called upon by modern states to delimit the institutional borders of grace. This call has subsequently shown itself to be, for the

---

107   Jacques Ellul, La foi au prix du doute (Paris: La Table Ronde, 2015), 255.

churches as well as for modern states, a dramatic trap. Modernity invented denominational identity — that is, a binary representation of the history of the Church in which the invisible mystical Church is associated with a Church defined by a confession of faith. In "branch theory,"[108] each denomination — Catholic, Anglican, and Orthodox — possesses only part of the expression of the truth, because of schisms. But each miraculously conserves the undivided faith and the apostolic succession of primitive Christianity.[109] This vision of the Church can be considered as a form of relativism of the expression of faith.

The fundamentalist reaction to this sort of thought identifies the borders of grace with the borders of the ecclesial institution, without paying attention to the historical limitations of the institution, for example in its level of political dependence. As a "Noah's ark," each denomination claims to be the sole site of salvation.[110] In the modern era, Cyprian of

---

108   https://en.wikipedia.org/wiki/Branch_theory: ". . . the theory that, though the Church may have fallen into schism within itself and its several provinces or groups of provinces be out of communion with each other, each may yet be a branch of the one Church of Christ, provided that it continues to hold the faith of the original undivided Church and to maintain the Apostolic Succession of its bishops. Such, it is contended by many Anglican theologians, is the condition of the Church at the present time, there being now three main branches."

109   https://en.wikipedia.org/wiki/Branch_theory: William Palmer (1803–1885), an Oxford theologian, was the principal originator of the branch theory. His two-volume *Treatise on the Church of Christ* (1838) formulated the notion. The theory was then popularized during the Oxford Movement, particularly through the work of the Tractarians. Although the Anglican Roman Catholic International Commission, an organization sponsored by the Anglican Consultative Council and the Pontifical Council for Promoting Christian Unity, seeks to make ecumenical progress between the Roman Catholic Church and the Anglican Communion, it has made no statement on the topic, and no support for the branch theory has been expressed anywhere outside Anglicanism itself. The branch theory "has received mixed reception even within the Anglican Communion." In 1983 the Holy Synod of Bishops of the Russian Orthodox Church Outside Russia stated: "Those who attack the Church of Christ by teaching that Christ's Church is divided into so-called 'branches' which differ in doctrine and way of life, or that the Church does not exist visibly, but will be formed in the future when all 'branches' or sects or denominations, and even religions will be united into one body; and who do not distinguish the priesthood and mysteries of the Church from those of the heretics, but say that the baptism and eucharist of heretics is effectual for salvation; therefore, to those who knowingly have communion with these aforementioned heretics or who advocate, disseminate, or defend their new heresy of Ecumenism under the pretext of brotherly love or the supposed unification of separated Christians, Anathema!"

110   Thus the Ecumenical Patriarchate of Constantinople does not hesitate to assert that it understands itself to be the sole Church of Christ on earth. In a 2019 text, "For the life of the world, towards a social ethos of the Orthodox church," it writes:

Carthage's phrase, *salus extra ecclesiam non est* [there is no salvation out-side the Church] has again been adopted, and it has been reduced to a strictly human representation of the Church: outside the "Catholic," or "Orthodox," or "Evangelical" Church . . . no salvation![111] Father Bernard Sesboüé prefers, today, to speak of "salvation by means of the Church" so

---

"§50. The Orthodox Church understands herself to be the one, holy, catholic, and apostolic Church, of which the Nicene-Constantinopolitan symbol of faith speaks. It is the Church of the Councils, continuous in charism and commission from the time of the Apostolic Council in Jerusalem (Acts 15:5–29) up to the present day. It lacks nothing essential to the full catholicity and full unity of the body of Christ, and possesses the fullness of all sacramental, magisterial, and pastoral grace. As Father Georgij Florovsky wrote: 'The Orthodox are bound to claim that the only "specific" or "distinctive" feature about their own position in "divided Christendom" is the fact that the Orthodox Church is essentially identical with the Church of all ages, and indeed with the "Early Church." In other words, it is not a Church, but the Church. It is a formidable, but a fair and a just claim. There is here more than just an unbroken historic continuity, which is indeed quite obvious. There is above all an ultimate spiritual and ontological identity, the same faith, the same spirit, the same ethos. And this constitutes the distinctive mark of Orthodoxy. "This is the Apostolic faith, this is the faith of the Fathers, this is the Orthodox faith, this faith has established the universe."'" https://www.goarch.org/social-ethos#_ftn54.

111   An example of the exclusivist approach: "This expression comes from the writings of St Cyprian of Carthage, a bishop of the third century, and is found in his Letter 72, *Ad Jubajanum de haereticis baptizandis*, and in Latin reads as follows: *Salus extra ecclesiam non est*. The axiom is often used as a summary of the doctrine confirmed by the Roman Catholic church, that the Church is absolutely necessary to salvation (the 'one true faith'). The theology of this doctrine is founded in the beliefs that: 1) Jesus Christ personally established a Church; and 2) the Church serves as the means by which the graces won by Christ are communicated to believers. This assertion implies that all non-Catholic religions are false, that only the Catholic church contains the entirety of the deposit of truth given by Christ to the Apostles, and that the entirety of this deposit — rather than most of it or part of it — is necessary for salvation." https://foicatholique.me/catholicisme-doctrine-catholique/763-2/hors-de-leglise-catholique-point-de-salut-2/. Bernard Sesboüé, meanwhile, compares this approach with that of the Second Vatican Council, and more particularly with *Gaudium et Spes*, 22: "All this holds true not only for Christians, but for all men of good will in whose hearts grace works in an unseen way. For, since Christ died for all men, and since the ultimate vocation of man is in fact one, and divine, we ought to believe that the Holy Spirit in a manner known only to God offers to every man the possibility of being associated with this paschal mystery." Sesboüé refers to Father de Lubac to propose a correct interpretation of this formula of Cyprian's, taken up by the Council of Florence: "As Christ cannot be separated from the Church, we must therefore infer that the necessity of the link to Christ for salvation is to be translated as the necessity for a particular kind of link with the Church. In order to respect the element of truth in the formula, we can follow Fr de Lubac's example and change it to read no longer 'No salvation outside the Church,' but 'Salvation by means of the Church.'" Cf. Henri de Lubac, *Catholicisme*, 5th ed. (Paris: Cerf, 1952).

as to avoid exclusivist interpretations of this patristic adage. The Jesuit theologian has shown that the denominational interpretation of this expression, a consequence of the Council of Florence's having been forgotten in the sixteenth century, has given rise to a neo-fundamentalist current among Christians:

> What does the term Church mean, exactly? "In the patristic texts," writes Yves Congar, "*ecclesia* meant both what we today call the Christian community — that is to say, the body of the faithful — and the institution of salvation founded by Christ: *Sponsa Christi, Mater fidelium* [Bride of Christ, Mother of the Faithful]" (Yves Congar, *Sainte Église. Études et approches ecclésiologiques*). It is a matter of the greater Church, that which St Augustine called the Catholic Church, in its etymological sense rather than in its Roman denominational sense. The Fathers of the Church developed a very broad conception of "the Church since Abel" (*Ecclesia ab Abel*), thus tracing God's plan of salvation back as far as the origins of humanity. From this point of view, the Church embraces all of history. But the late Middle Ages developed a discourse of its own on the subject of the Church, a discourse that was more focused on its visible institutions. "In the modern era," continues Congar, the word 'Church' is, in association with a whole new development in ecclesiology, taken more and more in the sense of the institution of salvation: to the point that some texts distinguish between and even oppose 'the Church and men, or the Church and the faithful.'"(Congar, ibid.) This ecclesiology of the institution became a "hierarchology." In this movement, linked to the Roman centralization of the second millennium, the Church becomes more and more identified with the Roman Church. Now, whether one is inside this Church or outside it depends upon whether one is in communion with the Pope or not. The adage therefore takes on a more and more institutional meaning. The term "Church" noticeably shrinks.[112]

Now, the denominational representation of the Church that comes from Anglicanism, separating faith from its institutional expression, is also motivated by a vision of the world characterized by a breaking of the links between reason and faith, words and things, authority and power. The nation was substituted for the Church in the understanding of catholicity. The Church of England fed the British state with its proselytizing

---

112   https://www.cairn.info/revue-etudes-2004-7-page-65.htm.

vision of the evangelization of the globe, which was the beginning of the building of the British Empire. This led to a loss of the initial Christian vision of the oikoumếnē, of a universality not only of the inhabited world but also of divine love. In the end, this denominational, nationalist, and colonial vision of the Church shattered on two world wars and a cold war, which have themselves today given way to a striking series of global crises (economic, ecological, political, etc.).

Only a recovery of the metaphysical foundations of the Church makes it possible to exit from the vicious circle between a denominationalist vision and a fundamentalist vision of the Church. From a metaphysical point of view, ecclesial consciousness can be understood as the common faith of Christians, which forms itself into shared institutions in search of the truth of the Spirit. It should not, therefore, be idealized, as is sometimes the case in some apologetic treatises devoted to the *sensus fidelium*. It is expressed in history, instead, in the form of tentative steps. It is nevertheless true that it represents, as Olivier Clément put it, an "antenna of Spirit." The book of the Acts of the Apostles shows on several occasions that for primitive Christian consciousness, the Spirit acts in history through the life of men who are turned towards God (Acts 2) and through the gathered ecclesial community (Acts 15:28). The history of Christian ecclesial consciousness shows us a comprehensive evolution, from late Antiquity to the medieval age, from an eschatological consciousness held out towards the Kingdom of God on earth, to a more political consciousness that recognizes the lines of transmission of celestial power towards the earth through political power, to its present state of a plural denominational consciousness distinct, in most cases, from public power.[113] An ecumenical history of this ecclesial consciousness makes it possible to grasp its past, present, and future dynamic.

The term "ecumenical" is concrete, marked by a history. In antiquity, it signified the "inhabited earth." Then, after the crisis of Christian eschatological consciousness in the fourth century, in the Byzantine era, it designated the "universal power" of the Emperor, and, as a consequence, of the Patriarch of Byzantium. In the modern era, the term has been applied to the "movement for reconciliation among Christians." This movement

---

113   This is not an exhaustive history of ecumenical consciousness. Reference can be made to the works already cited, as well as to the *Dictionary of the Ecumenical Movement*, ed. N. Lossky et al. (Geneva: World Council of Churches, 2002), or to the excellent book by the German Catholic theologian Peter Neuner, *Ökumenische Theologie: Die Suche nach der Einheit der christlichen Kirchen* (Darmstadt: Wissenschaftliche Buchgesellschaft, 2005). Each of these books contains a full bibliography.

was associated not only with the new encounters that had been established from the nineteenth century onwards between Catholics, Protestants, and Orthodox, but also concerned new syntheses at work between faith and reason, between the life of the Church and the life of the world, and between the faith of Christians and the organization of the Church. By extension, it was also applied to new dialogues between Christians and representatives of other religions.

In the course of its turbulent history, the term "ecumenical" was thus laden with the meaning which the term "catholicity" had to begin with, to designate a kind of universality peculiar to the Church.

This term "catholicity" had itself, as Avery Dulles showed, several levels of signification. For some Fathers of the Church, the Catholicity of the Church signified that the latter lived "according to the whole" (*kath' hōlon*) of the Trinity. But in the sixteenth century, the Reformation disputed the Roman Catholic Church's exclusive possession of this quality. Indeed, while the Church of Rome insisted on fidelity to the Bishop of Rome as a constitutive element of catholicity, the reformers Luther and Calvin rejected any automatic link between catholicity and the Roman Church. They adverted to the indestructible link existing between catholicity and faithfulness to Scripture.

Thus in the modern age, the notion of ecumenism, in addition to its earlier senses of civilizational universality, eschatological universality, and political universality, has come to acquire the fourth sense of "ecclesial universality in the course of being brought about."

This does not, of course, remove from the Roman Catholic Church its faith according to which the sole Church of Christ exists in that Church. But it corresponds to the movement of humility that gripped the fathers attending the Second Vatican Council, in not reducing the universal Church to the Roman Church.

To define it very concisely, the ecumenical movement is the discipline that unites science [*science*] and consciousness [*conscience*].[114] Ecumenical consciousness has, today, broadened to the point at which the term has also taken on a sense of divine-human universality, integrating all religious

---

114   In the course I teach on ecumenical science at the Collège des Bernardins, the first definition given of ecumenical science is the following: "Ecumenical science is the discipline that disputes the modern representation of the radical break between subject and object, between doxa and epistēmē, between culture and nature, and between liberalism and socialism. It aims to think science and consciousness, faith and reason, unity and diversity, freedom and responsibility, love and work, beauty and truth, goodness and justice, together." http://www.collegedesbernardins.fr.

traditions, but also, with the extension of the notion of the "shared house" to that of the "ecumene," to the whole of the created world.[115] This semantic evolution is convergent with the Christian faith, which proclaims that the full universality of the Church will be fulfilled when God is "all in all" (1 Cor. 15:28).

In the course of this account we shall examine some recent ecumenical agreements that testify to contemporary Christian consciousness's development towards new levels of global consciousness that are more and more transdenominational (trends towards spiritualism, integrationalism, fanaticism, and commitment to action), while denominational loyalties, which are still powerful, are more and more put in question by the dominant secular paradigm. It will be explained that these new trends in Christian consciousness on a global scale will only be able to break through to a new plateau of consciousness, that of ecumenical radicality, if certain conditions are met. Since the 1990s, indeed, there has been talk of a "crisis of the ecumenical movement." This is linked, in part, to the contradiction between the desire to remain faithful to one's denominational tradition and the wish to share the spiritual experiences of other Churches.[116]

In order to resolve this major difficulty, the ecumenical movement today seeks to help the different denominational traditions to rediscover themselves and to recognize each other as fully Christian.

This implies rediscovery as a shared metaphysics, capable of going beyond lines of tension while also respecting the levels of consciousness of each community and while becoming open to all spiritual and belief horizons.

The ecumenical movement and the Catholic Church itself have been seeking at least since Vatican II to define a new place for the Roman Church in the Christian world. This, of course, depends upon the Churches' first acknowledging the specific pastoral role over His whole Church which Christ conferred upon Peter. It also, for the Catholic Church, means putting the principle of affective synodality more effectively to work, in

---

115   *Oxford English Dictionary*, 2nd ed., "oecumene, ecumene (n.)," "The inhabited or civilized world, spec. that known to the ancient Greeks. Also (in extended use): the inhabited or developed world (or part of it) as known to or embraced by a later civilization." — *Translator*.

116   An example of such "ecumenical fatigue" can be found in the testimony of Father Stéphane Bigham, who was brought up in a Presbyterian community, moved to the Anglican church, and then to the Orthodox church. See his profile at www.academia.edu.

conformity with the promises of the Second Vatican Council.[117] This also implies that the Catholic Church should act, on both a local and a global level, according to the double principle of subsidiarity and unity in diversity, in the image of the life of the Trinity.[118] These points will be on the agenda for the synod of 2022, whose theme will be the following: "For a synodal Church: communion, participation, and mission."[119] The International Theological Commission of the Catholic Church published in 2018 an important text on "Synodality in the Life and Mission of the Church," in which, in point 117, it sets itself the following objectives:

> The quality of synodality or conciliarity reflects the mystery of the trinitarian life of God, and the structures of the Church express this quality so as to actualise the community's life as a communion [World Council of Churches' Commission on Faith and Order]. Consensus on this vision of the Church allows us to focus our attention, serenely and objectively, on the important theological knots that still need to be untied. In the first place, there is the question concerning the relationship between participation in synodal life by all the baptised, in whom the Spirit of Christ arouses and nourishes the *sensus fidei* and the consequent competence and responsibility in the discernment of mission, and the authority proper to Pastors, which derives from a specific charism that is conferred sacramentally; in the second place, there is the interpretation of communion between the local Churches and the universal Church expressed through communion between their Pastors and the Bishop of Rome, with the determination of how much pertains to the legitimate plurality of forms expressing faith in various cultures and what belongs to its perennial identity and its Catholic unity.
>
> In this context, the implementation of synodal life and a deeper appreciation of its theological significance are a challenge and an enormous opportunity in continuing on our ecumenical journey. In creative fidelity to the *depositum fidei* and consistent with the criterion of the *hierarchia veritatum*, the horizon

---

117   Peter De Mey, "Synodality as a Key Component of the Pontificate of Pope Francis: The Difficult Way from Theory to Practice," in M. D. Chapman and V. Latinovic, eds., *Changing the Church: Pathways for Ecumenical and Interreligious Dialogue* (London: Palgrave Macmillan, 2021).

118   Groupe des Dombes, *Le ministère de communion dans l'Église universelle* (Paris: Le Centurion, 1986), no. 157.

119   "Le Pape convoque un synode sur l'Église et la synodalité en 2022," *Vatican News*, March 7, 2020, www.vaticannews.va.

of synodality actually shows us how promising that exchange of gifts is, by which we can enrich each other as we journey towards unity: the reconciled harmony of the inexhaustible riches of the mystery of Christ, reflected in the beauty of the face of the Church.[120]

This development is not in conflict with the famous "Toronto statement" (1950) of the World Council of Churches, nor with its document "The Church: towards a common vision" (2012).[121] On the contrary, in accordance with the spiritual, Christological, and Trinitarian deepening of the Churches, the personal unity of the Church must be balanced with its conciliar life. We could, upon condition of the Eastern churches' also taking part,[122] speak of "an ecumenical Church" or of a "Church of churches," to use the Catholic theologian Jean-Marie Tillard's expression (Tillard is the former president of the Faith and Order Commission at the World Council of Churches). In this fully universal Church, unity, sanctity, catholicity, and apostolicity are no longer only *gifts* of God. These four notes are also *tasks* to be accomplished, vocations to be made real.

This implies in the first place, as the Dominican Catholic theologian Benoît-Dominique de la Soujeole has written, the need to acknowledge that local churches are *in* and *of* the universal Church, both as regards their foundation and as regards how they are regulated. "The local churches united by coming from the same origin and being subject to the same regulation are the universal Church — an effect which comes to pass *by means* of and *starting out from* these local churches."[123] All the churches ought therefore to acknowledge that their catholicity remains to a certain extent imperfect. This is why, as the Swiss Catholic theologian François-Xavier Amherdt adds, the four "notes" of the Church — unity, sanctity, catholicity, apostolicity — are symbols of the mystical and symphonic reality of the Church rather than criteria of juridical valuation and institutional affirmation.

---

120   International Theological Commission, "Synodality in the Life and Mission of the Church," www.vatican.va.

121   "The Council rejects any idea of transforming itself into a unified ecclesiastical structure, independent of the churches which come together in it, or into an organization subject to the authority of a central administration." "Toronto Statement," www.oikoumene.org.

122   The Eastern churches are once again gradually learning, after the Pan-Orthodox Council at Kolymbari in 2016, to live out synodal decision-making effectively at the local and pan-Orthodox level. But the task is complicated by the post-2019 schism between the sees of Constantinople and Moscow.

123   Benoît-Dominique de la Soujeole, *Introduction au mystère de l'Église* (Paris: Parole et Silence, 2006), 579–90.

It is important to take together the four characteristics which the
Niceno-Constanitopolitan creed attributes to the Church. They
are to be seen from the point of view so strongly emphasized
by the most recent Council, that the Church is a mystery: that
is, these four characteristics are to be seen both as having been
already achieved in the mystery of the death and resurrection of
Christ, and as *still to be made real* and to be further disseminated
through the Church in the course of its pilgrimage. "The notes
of the Church designate, then, the breaches which the work of
the Spirit unceasingly opens up in humanity so that that the
communion of saints can already begin to be registered in it."
They constitute a dominant seventh chord, C, E, G, B flat, beautiful and sonorous in itself, but drawn all the time towards resolution in a perfect, divine, and eschatological triad with three
Trinitarian sounds. [124]

To sum up, catholicity, understood as denominational universality, is
no longer by itself a sufficient criterion by means of which to judge the
degree of orthodoxy or orthopraxy in a Church. Catholicity is, according
to John St-Helier Gibaut, an Anglican theologian and a former secretary
of the Faith and Order Commission, "a gift of the Holy Spirit inherent in
the very nature and mission of the Church, a fulfillment of the promise of
its risen Lord, who promises us that he will be present among us until the
end of time, despite ourselves." [125] Given this, for Stanley Hauerwas, an
American Methodist theologian, and Bruce Kaye, an Australian Anglican
theologian, catholicity must be understood as "the quality of life of the
church that makes possible the cultivation of the virtues of humility and
love." [126] From this point of view, catholicity can be redefined, to borrow
the expression of Met. Jérémie Calligiorgis, the Orthodox Metropolitan
of Switzerland, as "a mode of expression of ecumenical consciousness." [127]

Ecumenical science, then, uses the notion of ecumenicity to throw
light on that of catholicity, because ecumenicity is the capacity to hold
together unity and sanctity, catholicity and apostolicity. As what we have
here is a synthesis in perpetual motion, with its advances and its setbacks,

---

124 François-Xavier Amherdt, "Comment l'Eglise romaine comprend elle la catholicité?" *Vers une catholicité œcuménique? Actes du colloque "Ensemble et divers—vers une
catholicité œcuménique?" à l'Institut œcuménique de Bossey, les 6 et 7 septembre 2010*, ed.
Amherdt (Fribourg: Academic Press, 2013), 31.
125 John Gibaut, "La catholicité et l'unité de l'Église," *Vers une catholicité œcuménique*, 228.
126 Stanley Hauerwas, *Approaching the End: Eschatological Reflections on Church, Politics,
and Life* (Grand Rapids, MI: Eerdmans, 2013), 117.
127 Met. Jérémie, "Vers une catholicité œcuménique," *Vers une catholicité œcuménique*, 117.

a metaphysics conscious of ecumenicity must put forward an account of ecumenical consciousness in action that is itself synthetic, rather than necessarily exhaustive. This metanarrative is neither apologetical nor critical, but tells the story of denominational identities from the perspective of their ecumenical consciousness. Such a consciousness is inscribed into the wider development, both historical and metahistorical, of human consciousness in interaction with divine consciousness.

THE ECCLESIOLOGICAL RELEVANCE OF THE SUBJECT

In proposing a new account of ecumenical consciousness in the course of the last two millennia, we are quite aware that we are touching on a question of acute contemporary relevance, since it has since 2018 been on the agenda of the Joint International Commission for Theological Dialogue between the Catholic Church and the Eastern Orthodox Church.[128] The World Council of Churches has also been concerned for many years with the question of the nature and mission of the Church. We know, too, that in both cases, this question of an accurate history of ecclesial consciousness is so explosive that no consensus among the churches has yet been arrived at about it.

The theologians invited to write a new history of Christian ecclesiology are taking a good deal of time to do so; the first text published in 2007 on the ecclesiological and canonical consequences of the nature of the sacraments was already on the agenda in 1990 at Odessa. The Catholic and Orthodox theologians gathered in Italy, at Ravenna in 2007 – 2008,[129] and at Chieti in 2016,[130] took the view that the historic ruptures between their Churches were the result of a theological divergence about the meaning which ought to be attached to primacy and synodality in the Church. At Ravenna, the signatories of the final document made explicit the institutional and theological character of their shared research:

> On the basis of these common affirmations of our faith, we
> must now draw the ecclesiological and canonical consequences
> that flow from the sacramental nature of the Church. Since the

---

128   Fr Andrea Palmieri, "Catholiques/orthodoxes: 'le dialogue se poursuit,'" *Zenit*, January 21, 2020, https://fr.zenit.org.

129   "Ecclesiological and Canonical Consequences of the Sacramental Nature of the Church: Ecclesial Communion, Conciliarity and Authority," October 13, 2007, www.christianunity.va.

130   "Synodality and Primacy during the First Millennium: Towards a Common Understanding in Service to the Unity of the Church," September 21, 2016, www.christianunity.va.

Eucharist, in the light of the Trinitarian mystery, constitutes the criterion of ecclesial life as a whole, how do institutional structures visibly reflect the mystery of this koinônia? Since the one and holy Church is realised both in each local Church celebrating the Eucharist and at the same time in the koinônia of all the Churches, how does the life of the Churches manifest this sacramental structure? Unity and multiplicity, the relationship between the one Church and the many local Churches, that constitutive relationship of the Church, also poses the question of the relationship between the authority inherent in every ecclesial institution and the conciliarity which flows from the mystery of the Church as communion.[131]

The Ravenna document on "Communion, conciliarity, and authority" explains that conciliarity has its foundation in the mystery of the Trinity. Primacy (which is in the image of divine Fatherhood and which has prerogatives) and conciliarity (which realizes the life of the Trinity and the Eucharist) are, therefore, interdependent. This Eucharistic approach leads to an ecclesiology of communion. The one and holy Church is realized in each local church that celebrates the Eucharist, and, simultaneously, in the communion of all churches, which is underpinned by the institution of primacy or the *protos*. Neither the Church of Rome nor that of Constantinople should, therefore, be thought of either as super-churches, superior to local churches, nor as churches equivalent to the other churches, because of the particular authority which was granted them by Christ and by history. But in reality, the Roman bishops' conferences do not enjoy the same regional autonomy as the autocephalous Orthodox Churches. Conversely, the autocephalous Orthodox Churches are not always able to see in Constantinople a helpful source of authority.

At Chieti in 2016, a new document of the Joint Commission's was adopted: "Synodality and Primacy during the First Millennium." In it, the Church is defined as "an *'eikon'* of the Holy Trinity,"[132] in Maximus the Confessor's phrase. The text also quotes John 17:11, which records a prayer of Christ's addressed to his Father: "that they may be one, as we are." The existential model of the Church is that of *koinonia*, of *communio*, of unity in diversity. We find in this document an equal insistence on complementarity between the *protos* (the function of primacy that

---

131   Joint International Commission for the Theological Dialogue between the Orthodox Church and the Roman Catholique [sic] Church, "Communique," www.ecupatria.org.
132   Ibid., point 1.

belongs definitively to Jesus Christ and is expressed in service) and the *synodos* (which places Rome at the head of the ecumenical communion). This text also explains that this model of communion was broken in the second millennium, and that this needs to be explained:

> In the second millennium, communion was broken between East and West. Many efforts have been made to restore communion between Catholics and Orthodox, but they have not succeeded. The Joint International Commission for Theological Dialogue between the Roman Catholic Church and the Orthodox Church, in its ongoing work to overcome theological divergences, has been considering the relationship between synodality and primacy in the life of the Church. Different understandings of these realities played a significant role in the division between Orthodox and Catholics.[133]

The current discussions of the Joint International Commission for Theological Dialogue between the Roman Catholic Church and the Orthodox Church concern the relationship between synodality and primacy as it was lived by the Churches in the second millennium.[134] Current research suggests that we should locate ecclesial consciousness in the tension which exists between primacy and synodality, because the Church, in the image of divine life, is a personal reality and a communion. Nevertheless, this same ecclesial consciousness is also pulled at by the poles of freedom and justice, that is to say, by the concern with forming a local Church, and by the desire to participate in the Kingdom of God on earth. This is why the life of the Church cannot be entirely distinguished from the life of the world. Now, contemporary theologians have a tendency only to study the history of the "consciousness of the Church" in the second millennium within the framework of a *canonical inquiry*. They thus prevent themselves from understanding the deep causes of the *alienation* that has gradually eaten away at the unity of the Church, not only before, but, even more, after the Council of Florence in 1439. Moreover, the main limit of current discussions on the history of Christianity in the second millennium resides in the impasse arrived at on all sides over the event of the Council of Florence itself. No general conclusion has been drawn from the fact of the agreement to the union of the Churches which was

---

133   Ibid., point 5.
134   Joint International Commission for Theological Dialogue between the Roman Catholic Church and the Orthodox Church, "Coordinating Committee Meeting: Bose (Italy), 11–15 November 2019," http://www.christianunity.va/.

secured at the Council on July 5, 1439, and which was given expression in the bull *Laetentur cœli*, "Let the heavens rejoice."

The main reason for this collective amnesia is that most of the representatives of the Catholic and Orthodox Churches today place the regional synod of Istanbul of 1484 on the same level as the ecumenical Council of Florence of 1439. However, in canonical terms, they cannot be compared with each other. Whereas the synod, held under Ottoman domination, can claim at best only a regional authority, the ecumenical Council, whose decisions were adopted by the Pope, the ecumenical Patriarch, the Emperor, and almost all the delegates from East and West alike — something which had never happened in the whole history of the ecumenical Councils — possesses an altogether higher canonical legitimacy.

The truth is that this last Council bringing together Christians from East and West causes terrible problems for the denominational logic of contemporary ecclesial institutions. So they continue to act as though there had not in the Renaissance been any true reconciliation, even a provisional one, between the Churches of the East and the West. Now, this reconciliation, from the point of view of canon law, was never formally suspended, because a Council can only be abrogated by a Council of equal importance. After the fall of Constantinople in 1453, the Byzantine Patriarchs lost all their independence, and from then on, and until the twentieth century, they received their power from the Sultan.[135] In 1484 some Eastern hierarchs chose to deny their commitment to the truth of the Christian faith and the unity of the Church, sadly dragging many of their faithful, who did not have enough historical equipment to distinguish what was true from what was false, along with them into the polemic.

As the colloquiums at the Collège des Bernardins and at the University of Fribourg in 2018 showed, this victory for zealotry, in the East as in the West, led the Churches towards a form of amnesia, of traumatic memory.[136] In a recent presentation at the Pan-Orthodox Council of Kolymbari in 2016, bringing together ten of the fourteen Orthodox Churches, amateur historians even explained that there had been no Council at the same level as that of Kolymbari for twelve hundred years, that is to say, since the Council of 879![137] But beyond the fact that assertions of this sort are factually incorrect, a realistic look at the past must admit that the

---

135   Lina Muhr Nehmé, *1453, Mahomet II impose le schisme orthodoxe* (Paris: François-Xavier De Guibert, 2001).

136   Antoine Arjakovsky and Barbara Hallensleben, eds., *Le concile de Florence, une relecture œcuménique* (Fribourg: Aschendorff, 2021).

137   "Preparation of the Holy and Great Council," www.orthodoxcouncil.org.

Orthodox Churches which rejected the Council of Florence in the sixteenth century, whether in Moscow or Istanbul, were not free. They were then dominated by Muslim regimes, from 1441 in Moscow and from 1484 in Istanbul, which were hostile to any rapprochement among Christians.

It is therefore essential today, thanks to the historical distance we can now take, to understand that, as we shall see in the following pages, the Council of Florence was in its time a real success, because, out of the hundreds of delegates present, only one did not sign the agreement, something that was especially remarkable in comparison to the first ecumenical Councils. As many historians from Joseph Gill to Olivier Clément have shown, the Council proposed in 1439 a due balance between the acknowledgement of the universal primacy of the Pope and the recognition of the privileges of the Eastern Patriarchs, that is to say of the local churches. In the West, it made possible a rehabilitation of the authority of the Pope in the Western Church, at least until the Reformation. In the East, it re-established the Churches of the East as separate and integral Churches possessing their own law, as they are today.

Beyond this, this council found a solution to all the dogmatic differences between the Churches, despite the fact that the conceptual tools at the disposal of the theologians of the period were at least incomplete. Later, these agreements on the question of the procession of the Holy Spirit, on the use of unleavened bread to celebrate the Eucharist, and on the eschatological reality of purgatory, were even approved by the Churches of the East, which represents an exceptional fact, if one remembers that these Churches had been separated from the Chalcedonian Churches for nearly a thousand years. No trace of any dogmatic differences is found until the seventeenth century in the Slavic lands, thanks to the Council of Ferrara-Florence.

The Council of Florence was thus at the origin of the political success of the Union of Lublin, on July 1, 1569, between the Kingdom of Poland and the Grand Duchy of Lithuania. This Union of Lublin was not only a victory over the wars of religion that were then tearing Europe apart, but was also a way of overcoming the isolated and separatist law of the nation-states that was then being set up, and that triumphed in the Treaty of Westphalia. The Union of Lublin was a kind of miniature anticipation of the European Union, before the return of imperial logics and the dramatic carving-up of Poland in the eighteenth and nineteenth centuries. It is indeed true that a single Council could not sort out forever all the problems existing between the Churches. It is also certain that the logics of power of the modern empires and nation-states, logics that became dominant after 1648, long rejected the model of a synthesis between primacy and synodality put forward at Florence. And yet even today, the Council of Florence possesses an unrivalled legitimacy.

As a consequence, the recovery of the deep bonds that unite Christians cannot rest on a vision of the Church's history that is merely institutional, canonical, and binary: primacy/synodality or even unity/schism. We have in any case seen that the approach through canon law argued for a reevaluation of the Council of Florence. It is also known that a denominational logic can no longer be adequate in the age of the Church's ecumenical consciousness. A metaphysical, personalist, sapiential, and ternary definition of the Church makes it possible, conversely, to exit from this modern reading of the history of the Church and of the world. According to this vision, the Father brings the Church into existence as both personal and collegial, by the joint mission of the Son who founds it, and the Spirit who constitutes it. Thenceforth, the history of ecclesial consciousness cannot be a binary history of the legal and political expansion of this or that church. A ternary history of ecclesial consciousness brings out the action of the Spirit, or the absence of such action, in the history of divine humanity.

The binary history of the Church considers that in the second millennium the primacy of the bishop was verticalized, at Rome alone, by privileging the glory belonging to the clergy at the expense of the priesthood of lay people. It judges, similarly, that in the same period, in Constantinople and Moscow alone, synodality (and thus the ability of clergy and lay people to move forward together with Christ by becoming incarnate in history) became unstable, to the benefit of the political power.[138] But the historical reality is more complex than this, as the St Irenaeus Group has recognized. This group of twenty-six Catholic and Orthodox theologians, founded in Paderborn in 2004, also chose "Primacy and Synodality" as its central research topic. In 2017, the group began to devote itself to defining a historical and systematic hermeneutics of primacy and synodality.[139] It came to understand in the course of its work that the excessive verticalization of ecclesial power in the second millennium was not brought about by the Roman Church alone.

---

138   Antoine Arjakovsky, "Primauté et juste gouvernance dans l'Eglise," *Istina* 58 (2013), 345–60.
139   "Groupe de travail orthodoxe-catholique Saint-Irénée (Hervé Legrand, op)," *L'Église Catholique à Paris*, www.paris.catholique.fr.

In the Ottoman Empire, the structure of the Rum-Millet [the name for the Eastern Orthodox community in the Ottoman Empire — *Translator*] brought about a centralization of the Orthodox Church. The Ottoman era, consequently, witnessed an enhancement of the importance of the Ecumenical Patriarchate at the expense of the other Orthodox patriarchates, which according to law were subordinated to the ecumenical patriarchs. This would have far-reaching consequences for the church in the 19th century, when the national movements within the Ottoman Empire became stronger, especially in the Balkans. Those Orthodox, who were not Greek, no longer saw in the patriarch someone who represented them, especially not in their political efforts to achieve national emancipation. For this reason, the Patriarch of Constantinople, instead of representing all Orthodox within the Empire, increasingly represented the Greek subjects only. [140]

Thus it is necessary to revisit the history of Christianity from a wider and more metaphysical perspective than that of institutional and canonical mechanisms alone.

---

140   Saint Irenaeus Joint Orthodox-Catholic Working Group, "Communique — Trebinje, 2019," www.christianunity.va.

PART TWO

A Short History of
Christian Consciousness
from its Origins to the Modern Era

THE ESCHATOLOGICAL CONSCIOUSNESS
OF THE CHURCH (1–313)

A PERSONALIST, SAPIENTIAL, AND TERNARY CONSCIOUSNESS

Christian consciousness has from its origins sought to understand the notion of universality on the model of the covenant of God with men, symbolized in Genesis by the episode of Noah's ark (Gen. 9:13). In Deuteronomy the word Qahal designates the gathering-together of the people of God, on the day of the promulgation of the Law, by the intermediary Moses on Sinai, which is the day of the renewal of this covenant (Exodus 24:3 – 8). The Jewish community, taking note of the failure of the monolithic project of the Tower of Babel, conceived of this covenant between God and men on the basis of the book of the covenant composed by Moses, then on the basis of the Ark of the Covenant, and then, finally, with the Temple at Jerusalem, as the Creator's dwelling-place with his creatures on earth.

For its part, the Christian community posited the Body of Christ as the symbolic place *par excellence* for such a meeting between God and humanity. This is why the Nativity of Christ was introduced into the liturgical calendar, and today represents one of the most important feasts for Christian consciousness. The Church is wherever Christ is; and Christ is present each time the Eucharist is celebrated, that is, in the act of the exchange of praises. As the Russian Orthodox theologian Father Nikolai Afanasiev writes, "the eucharistic assembly in the early period was the solemn gathering of the entire local church."[1] In John's gospel, Christ

---

1   Nicholas Afanasiev, The Church of the Holy Spirit, trans. Vitaly Permiakov (Notre Dame, IN: University of Notre Dame Press, 2007), 55.

says to the Jews, of the Temple in Jerusalem, "Destroy this temple, and in three days I will raise it up" (John 2:19). Christ adds that such a personal understanding of the universal is possible only if one consults the Holy Spirit. He explains to the Samaritan that "the hour cometh, and now is, when the true worshippers shall worship the Father in spirit and truth: for the Father seeketh such to worship him. God is a Spirit: and they that worship him must worship him in spirit and in truth" (John 4:23–24).

This is why the *ekklesia* described by Luke in his book of the Acts of the Apostles is founded on the event of Pentecost, that is, on the transmission by the resurrected Christ of the Spirit received from the Father in the first Christian community, in all languages, among both Jews and converts (Acts 2:11). Now, Pentecost took place on Shavuot, the feast of the gift of the Torah, which also has a cosmic meaning, because it marked the beginning of the harvest season. For Nikolai Afanasiev, as for the Catholic theologian Jean-Marie Tillard, the *Ekklesia*, in Luke, is thus not merely a Greek word indicating the assembly of the citizenry. It takes on the significance of the gathering-together of the people of God. It fulfills in a universal way, beyond the Jewish people alone, the Qahal knit together at Sinai by the celebration of the Law:

> The Pentecostal community — the mother cell of the Church — thus appeared as the manifestation, the *epiphaneia*, of the beginning of the time of Salvation. It is such in a radically unbreakable meeting of three elements: the Spirit; the apostolic witnessing which refers to Jesus Christ; and the communion in which human multitude and variety are embraced by unity, and in which unity is expressed in multitude and variety. These three elements belong to the very essence of the Church.[2]

The New Testament reports many cases of divisions between the different spiritual types of Christian, but also instances of reconciliation among them, as was the case for example at Antioch when non-Jews were welcomed into the Church, and of deciding whether the latter had to be circumcised or not (Acts 15). It is quite certain that the emergence of certain connecting factors internal to the life of the Church, which very soon began to be referred to as ministries, facilitated such internal cohesion. It is averred in particular that the primitive Church put in place almost everywhere, from the second century onwards, a ternary structure for these ministries, with an episcopal college, a college of presbyters, and a

---

2   Jean-Marie R. Tillard, *Eglise d'Eglises. L'ecclésiologie de communion* (Paris: Cerf, 1987), 22.

college of deacons. This organization ordered the flourishing of charisms and of different spiritual types that had appeared in the course of the first century, and which St Paul had echoed in his epistles.

> Now there are diversities of gifts, but the same Spirit. And there are differences of administrations, but the same Lord. And there are diversities of operations, but it is the same God which wor-keth all in all. But the manifestation of the Spirit is given to every man to profit withal. For to one is given by the Spirit the word of wisdom; to another the word of knowledge by the same spirit; to another faith by the same Spirit; to another the gifts of healing by the same Spirit; to another the working of miracles; to another prophecy; to another discerning of spirits; to another divers kinds of tongues; to another the interpretation of tongues; but all these worketh that one and the selfsame Spirit, dividing to every man severally as he will. (1 Cor. 12:4 – 11)

In the face of the importance which the vertical organization of minis-tries has acquired over the course of the ages, the First World Conference on Faith and Order in Lausanne in 1927 nevertheless reminded us that, in the primitive Church, the episcopal structure and the collegial-presbyterian structure were in communion with each other.

THE ESCHATOLOGICAL COMMUNITY: KOINOINIA, LEITOURGIA, MARTYRIA, DIAKONIA

Eschatological consciousness, the consciousness of a radical openness to Spirit, was not, therefore, synonymous with an absence of conflicts, yet nor was its fundamental unity broken. It signifies simply that the final purpose of bringing about the Kingdom was what structured all communities within which different spiritual types, but also different charismatic leaders, could come into contact with each other. It identified the Kingdom of God with the *koinonia*, the communion of the commu-nity with Christ, and between the community's members, in the Spirit. In this way, it managed to overcome most disputes thanks to a judicious blend, both at the local level and at that of the whole Church, of the exercise of top-down primacy and bottom-up conciliarity. Paul knew how to show firmness towards "unruly and vain talkers and deceivers." He recommends to Titus quite simply that their "mouths must be stopped" (Tit. 1:10 – 11). He prefers to remind the Corinthians, conversely, of the very great responsibility of Christians who are called to judge the world. He thus encouraged them not to delegate their own conflicts to worldly justice. "Do ye not know that the saints shall judge the world? How much more things that pertain to this life?" (1 Cor. 6:2). The important thing is always to be aware that the Christian identity, which is "hid with Christ in God" (Col. 3:3), is distinct from the identity of the Empire.

This new knowledge expressed by "the faith of the gospel" is founded on the hope of attaining to a new level of awareness of oneself, such that man will be able to know himself as he is known (1 Cor. 13:12). Paul sets out to the Corinthians the level of consciousness that can be described as "baptismal" by using the analogy of the body:

> For by one Spirit are we all baptized into one body, whether we be Jews or Gentiles, whether we be bond or free; and have all been made to drink into one Spirit. For the body is not one member, but many.... And the eye cannot say unto the hand, I have no need of thee: nor again the head to the feet, I have no need of you. Nay, much more those members of the body, which seem to be more feeble, are necessary: And those members of the body, which we think to be less honourable, upon these we bestow more abundant honour; and our uncomely parts have more abundant comeliness. For our comely parts have no need: but God hath tempered the body together, having given more abundant honour to that part which lacked: That there should be no schism in the body; but that the members should have the same care for one another. And whether one member suffer, all the members suffer with it; or one member be honoured, all the members rejoice with it. Now ye are the body of Christ, and members in particular. (1 Cor. 12:13–14, 21–27)

Starting out from this level of baptismal consciousness, the apostle Paul conceives of an organization of ministry in the Church founded on the necessary cooperation between the different charisms of the baptized, whether they be apostles, prophets, teachers, miracle-workers, healers, assistants, directors, polyglots, or interpreters.

As Voegelin remarked, Christians had a sense of the end of history which expressed the two aspects of the Kingdom of God, that which transcends history and that which is internal to it. The Kingdom of God, as the Russian Orthodox philosopher Nikolai Berdyaev explained, is "above" history in its complete extent, while also being "in relation" with it. The Kingdom crosses history in a qualitative way each time humanity fulfills the shared work of the Beatitudes proclaimed by Christ. The new level of eschatological consciousness therefore signified both the fact that the Kingdom of

God exceeded this world, of which it signified *the end* [*la fin*] (in the sense of *finitude*), but also the lively awareness of the *telos*, of a *final purpose*, of possible participation, at each moment and in all places, in the fulfillment of the meaning of history. From this second perspective, the past and the future come together in the present. The eternal "now" includes both of them, without their being, however, absorbed into the present. Here is what the Protestant theologian Paul Tillich writes about this:

> The fulfillment of history lies in the permanently present end of history, which is the transcendent side of the Kingdom of God: the Eternal Life . . . . [T]he ever present end of history elevates the positive content of history into eternity at the same time that it excludes the negative from participation in it . . . . What happens in time and space, in the smallest particle of matter as well as in the greatest personality, is significant for the eternal life. And since eternal life is participation in the divine life, every finite happening is significant for God.[3]

This eschatological consciousness makes it possible to grasp the political consciousness of the first Christian communities. The latter separated the Kingdom of God from the Kingdom of Caesar, but not as if they were two equivalent spheres belonging to the same space-time. It was a matter of facing political persecution, but also of defending one's rights, while bearing witness to the possibility of a different way of ordering life in society. When the apostles James and John argued over who would be sitting at the right hand of the Lord at the moment of his entry into the Kingdom, Christ replied to them:

> Ye know that they which are accounted to rule over the Gentiles exercise lordship over them; and their great ones exercise authority upon them. But so it shall not be among you: but whosoever will be great among you, shall be your minister: And whosoever of you will be the chiefest, shall be servant of all. For even the Son of man came not to be ministered unto, but to minister, and to give his life a ransom for many. (Mk 10:42–45)

Eschatological consciousness, then, is not apolitical. If the Kingdom of God is not *of* this world, it is certainly brought about *in* this world. Baptism, the Eucharist, and chrismation come to fulfill the Law. Thus the act of baptism inaugurates a new form of citizenship that integrates women,

---

3   Paul Tillich, *Systematic Theology: Combined Volume* (James Nisbet: Digwell Place, 1968), 422–24.

children, slaves, and the members of different ethnic groups. Social and political divisions are overcome in the act of communion with Christ. This act produced a significant number of martyrs, to the point of making the Roman Empire give way, in 313, with the publication of the Edict of Milan by the Emperor Constantine putting an end to persecutions. Put simply, this consciousness turned towards the Kingdom of God on earth prefigures a theology of political sovereignty that starts out from the last words of the already resurrected Christ to his apostles: "All power [*exousia*] is given unto me in heaven and earth" (Matt. 28:18). For Christ, this powerful affirmation meant that the apostles had to allow their contemporaries to attain to a baptismal consciousness. This is why his last will was as follows: "Go ye therefore, and teach all nations, baptizing them in the name of the Father, and of the Son, and of the Holy Ghost: Teaching them to observe all things whatsoever I have commanded you: and, lo, I am with you always, even unto the end of the world" (Matt. 29:19 – 20).

Eschatological consciousness therefore brought into being a model of social and missionary engagement founded on the possible complementarity between different members of the ecclesial community. [4] The example of the interaction between Paul and Apollos is interesting because it gave the apostle occasion to reflect on the ecumenical stakes of mission. In his letters to the Corinthians, he tries in the first place to explain to his congregation that they must not identify him with Christ, neither him nor Apollos (the latter had at first recognized only John's baptism, and had been initiated by Paul, but also by Priscilla). Paul and Apollos, by virtue of the gifts of the Spirit which they receive through the Wisdom of God, must be understood as messengers, connectors, or pioneers. The missionary has, therefore, a sapiential awareness of himself, since Paul makes reference to divine Wisdom as distinct from the wisdom of men. He writes: "we speak the wisdom of God in a mystery, even the hidden wisdom, which God ordained before the world unto our glory" (1 Cor. 2:7). The Christian missionary is conscious of being bound by divine Wisdom to the Christ who is the way, the truth, and the life. This is why Paul explains that divine Wisdom is accessible only to Christians who live in the Spirit. Moreover, Paul understands that that mission is necessarily the fruit of a shared action, and particularly of an action shared among those who plant and those who water (Acts 18:27 – 28; 1 Cor. 3:6). The important thing is to understand that in both cases "God gave the increase." This is

---

4 "Qu'est-ce donc qu'Apollos? Qu'est-ce que Paul? (1 Cor. 3:5)," https://www.bible-notes.org/.

why Christian mission — and this is the third lesson of the interaction between Paul and Apollos — must rely on the virtue of those carrying it out. When the latter are conscious of the grace which God is bestowing on them, their virtue brings about a change in consciousnesses. In particular, the virtue of humility and the sense of freely given effort stop them giving way to the demons of the spirit of competition, of jealousy, and of thirst for recognition and honor.

Ecclesiology and canon law developed very early in the life of the Churches, particularly in the third century, in works of ecclesiology such as the De ecclesiae unitate of Cyprian of Carthage (251), or, in the fourth century in Syria, with the collection of eighty-five ecclesiastical canons, called the Apostolic Canons. The famous thirty-fourth Apostolic Canon identified the life of the Church with the life of the Holy Trinity:

> The bishops of every nation must acknowledge him who is first among them and account him as their head, and do nothing of consequence without his consent; but each may do those things only which concern his own parish, and the country places which belong to it. But neither let him (who is the first) do anything without the consent of all; for so there will be unanimity, and God will be glorified through the Lord in the Holy Spirit. [5]

The eschatological consciousness of the first Christians certainly rested on the necessary analogy between the life of the Church and that of the Kingdom. Christians prayed each day for the will of the Father to be fulfilled "on earth as it is in heaven."

TENSIONS AND RUPTURES

This type of theological and juridical regulation was set to work to smooth out many disputed topics. The most famous polemics concern how to fix the date of Easter. There were two practices running in parallel: to celebrate Easter following Jewish custom, on the 14th of the month of Nisan, whatever the day of the week (as the churches of Asia Minor did), or to celebrate it on the following Sunday (as Rome did). In the second century, Pope Anicetus and Polycarp, the Bishop of Smyrna, did not manage to come to an agreement, but exchanged signs of peace, which led de facto to an acknowledgement of the possibility of two different calendars. Consensus was also arrived at concerning other thorny topics. On that of the validity of baptism when performed by heretics,

---

5   "The Apostolic Canons," https://www.newadvent.org/fathers/.

Cyprian of Carthage put forward theological arguments to the effect that whoever does not have the Holy Spirit cannot transmit the Spirit through baptism. At Rome, the practice was to recognize such baptisms, and the Bishop, Stephen, replied to his interlocutors that it was necessary to follow this tradition, and not to innovate. On the topic of the admission of the *lapsi*, Cyprian suggested, in his treatise *On the Lapsed* of 251, a mixture of firmness towards those who had complied with the order to make sacrifice to the Emperor, and a period of penitence for those who had only obeyed Decius's decree under torture. It was also found possible to settle the canon of Scripture for the New Testament. A first list, enumerating twenty-two of the twenty-seven books, was set out in Rome towards the year 200. In 382 a synod held under Pope Damasus settled the canon of twenty-seven books. The same list is found in the East in the thirty-ninth letter of Athanasius on the Paschal festival, dated 387.[6]

This capacity to sustain the tensions of religious consciousness was probably the result of monastic spirituality. Jean-Guilhem Xerri,[7] a contemporary Catholic theologian, has summed up in a few accessible phrases the wisdom of the Desert Fathers and Mothers, as well as their science of moderation, for men and women of the twenty-first century. These ascetics were subject to passions like anger, pride, avarice, or envy. But they forced themselves always to promote the idea of moderation by balancing the four poles of religious consciousness:

> They do this by balancing the four fundamentals, which are sobriety, care for others, meditation, and scrutiny of the heart. Indeed, if there is only sobriety, one can become an athlete of ascesis, but life becomes a hell. If I am entirely absorbed in care for the other, highly committed, I will exhaust myself and others. With meditation alone, I shall be playing the "Zen super-monk," and will be totally and utterly narcissistic. And if one pays attention only to what is going through one's head, one will soon become asocial. These approaches need, therefore, to be linked to each other, in order to balance each other and in order to have an effect. My deep nature has a need of that for its own inner psychic equilibrium, necessary to unfurl that breath which, for Christians, is the dwelling of the Holy Spirit.[8]

---

6   Hubertus R. Drobner, *The Fathers of the Church: A Comprehensive Introduction* (Grand Rapids, MI: Baker Academic, 2016).

7   Jean-Guilhem Xerri, *Prenez soin de votre âme* (Paris: Cerf, 2018).

8   Stéphane Bataillon, "2021, comment retrouver l'essentiel?" *La Croix*, January 1, 2021, www.la-croix.com.

Not all schisms could be avoided — for example, the Novatian schism in the third century, or the Donatist in the fourth. Nevertheless the witness borne by the martyrs, the apostolic tradition, the reference to Scripture, and liturgical practice together allowed the Church to maintain its unity and its coherence all around the Mediterranean reasonably well, and to grow very quickly within the Empire between the first and the fourth centuries. The custom developed of adjudicating conflicts by combining the authority of a *protos* who possessed the institutional power of the keys, either directly or by delegation, with the constitutional authority of a Council capable of referring the source of conflict back to "the whole Church," of initiating dialogue, of invoking the divine Spirit [*l'Esprit divin*] and of settling matters. Moreover, agreements and disagreements were embedded in Eucharistic practice. The workings of grace within the community were understood as the site of the realization of the Passion and Resurrection of Jesus Christ and the moment of receiving the gift of the Holy Spirit [*l'Esprit Saint*]. It constituted, therefore, the privileged space-time of participation in the Kingdom of God on earth, understood as a life in Christ in the Holy Spirit. This Kingdom, however, was not yet perfectly visible and homogenous, lasting and extended. It was woven together out of different types of consciousness, and therefore out of privileged moments and degrees of belonging that distinguished among those provisionally excommunicated, catechumens, the baptized, and the saints.

The first lasting and deep rupture in the history of Christianity consisted in the refusal by part of the Jewish community to acknowledge Jesus of Nazareth as the Messiah. On the other hand, the first ecclesial community lived as an anticipation of the theanthropic covenant.[9] Similarly, the lack of consensus at the beginning of the fourth century in understanding the life of the Trinity, as well as that of Christ's divine humanity, precipitated divisions among Christians. The legalization of the Church in 313 at Milan by the Emperor Constantine, and the summoning of the first ecumenical and imperial Council of Nicaea in 325, did not manage completely to settle the problems with which Christian eschatological consciousness was faced. In many ways, the confusion of the Kingdom of God with the kingdom of Caesar brought about by the Emperor's involvement in the Church's affairs only complicated matters. It sent whole regions that refused the authority of the Byzantine Emperor

---

9 Venance Grumel, "Le problème de la date pascale aux IIIe et IVe siècles. L'origine du conflit: le nouveau cadre du comput juif," *Revue des études byzantines*, 18 (1960), 163–78.

into schism. It fixed as opposition doctrinal trends that were in their origin only partial and provisional opinions. The consciousness of the Church became more political and less eschatological.

THE POLITICAL CONSCIOUSNESS OF THE CHURCH (313–1453)

A NEW THEOLOGY OF POLITICS

The first Christian communities then used two different terms to describe the universal dimension of their gathering-together: the term "ecumenical," and the term "catholic."

For Herodotus, the word *oïkumēnē* signified the whole of the inhabited world, and, by extension, the whole of humanity. After the conquests of Alexander the Great, in the fourth century before Christ, the concept became more restricted, and designated the Hellenized world in contrast to the barbarous regions where one could not make oneself understood by the inhabitants. The term thenceforth took on a political connotation. The *oïkouménē* thenceforth referred to the Roman Empire, then to the Byzantine Empire.

Whereas, in the Septuagint, the term *oïkouménē* designated all cultivated land, in the Gospels the term is used when the Roman Empire is being discussed, for example, when Augustus orders that there should be a census of the whole inhabited world (*oïkouménē*) (Luke 2:1).

The term used by the author of the Letter to the Hebrews takes on a new sense when it indicates that God has entrusted the *oïkouménē* to come to Christ rather than to the angels: "For unto the angels hath he not put in subjection the world [*oïkouménē*] to come, whereof we speak" (Heb. 2:5). Here the *oïkouménē* to come signifies the Kingdom of God, proclaimed by the "signs and wonders, and . . . divers miracles" (Heb. 2:4) brought about on earth by Jesus Christ, in opposition to the present *oïkouménē*, which is perishable.

The term therefore possesses a double meaning: geographical universality, and the plenitude of the Kingdom in spirit and in truth.

For the Fathers of the Church the term *oïkouménē* is associated with that of catholicity. As Avery Dulles reminds us in *The Catholicity of the Church*, the term *kath' hōlon* means "according to the whole." In the book of Acts, Luke refers to catholicity as a category at once geographical and spiritual. "Then had the churches rest throughout all Judaea and Galilee and Samaria, and were edified; and walking in fear of the Lord, and in the comfort of the Holy Ghost, were multiplied" (Acts 9:31). In the second century, in the time of Ignatius of Antioch, the *katholikos* was found in each local church. The Bishop of Antioch writes in his Epistle to the Christians of Smyrna: "Wherever the Bishop appears, there is the community, just as wherever Christ is, there is the catholic Church" (*Epistle to the Smyrnaeans*, 8:2). Thus the term *katholikē* for the Church must be understood fractally. It is different from the notion of a particular church that is part of a whole. For St Augustine, the orthodoxy of ecclesial faith is found at the level of the universal Church. But the Church is still understood as ecumenical insofar as it is the anticipation of the Kingdom. As the contemporary Catholic theologian Peter Neuner writes, "in the work of Origen and Basil, the Church appears as the new *oïkouménē*, as the cosmos sanctified by the Gospel."[10]

Let us highlight here the fact that the ecumenical opening-up on the part of the Fathers of the Church — because it was rooted in the Gospel, and particularly in Christ's dialogue with the Syro-Phoenician woman and with the Roman centurion — was very broad in scope. St Justin the Philosopher (c.100 – c.162) speaks of "seeds" cast by the Logos into different religious traditions. By the Incarnation of God, the manifestation of the Logos becomes complete (St Justin, *First Apology*, 46:1 – 4; *Second Apology*, 8:1; 10:1 – 3; 13:4 – 6). For Irenaeus, the Son, as the visible manifestation of the Father, was revealed to men "from the beginning," yet the Incarnation nevertheless brings something essentially new (*Against the Heretics*, 4.6: 5 – 7; 4.7:2; 4.20:6 – 7). According to Clement of Alexandria, "philosophy" was given to the Greeks by God as a "covenant," an intimation of philosophy according to Christ (*Stromata*, 1:5; 6:8; 7:2).

The break with the primitive Judaeo-Christian conception of the *ekklesia* as an eschatological gathering-up is completed at the moment when the Church is legalized by the Empire. The Church of the circumcised was not given a voice at the Council of Nicaea, as Cardinal Schönborn laments. The Jewish messianic theologian Mark Kinzer is today developing the concept of a "bilateral ecclesiology" that insists on the presence of both Jews and non-Jews in the single Body of Christ. This concept presents the Messianic Jews as the part of Israel that welcomes Jesus as the Messiah, the Son of God and the Savior of the world, just as the apostles and the community of Jews who believed in Jesus at Jerusalem welcomed him, initially, from within the people and the tradition of Israel.[11]

---

10   Peter Neuner, *Théologie œcuménique* (Paris: Cerf, 2005 [1997]), 17.
11   Mark Kinzer, *Searching Her Own Mystery. Nostra Aetate, the Jewish People, and*

In the fourth century, however, the atmosphere was completely different. The definition of catholicity in the thought of Cyril of Jerusalem, who was the Bishop of Jerusalem between 350 and 386, was opposed to the Jewish conception of the synagogue. The Bishop of Jerusalem founded his eighteenth baptismal catechetical lecture, devoted to the exposition of the Credo, on an explicit rejection of the synagogue in favor of the catholic Church. In the fourth century, the term acquired new meanings. Catholicity is the expression of the orthodoxy of the faith, which, following the four poles on which we have remarked, offers a synthesis between correct ritual, teaching, care, and the virtues:

> The Church is called Catholic because it is spread throughout the world, from end to end of the earth; also because it teaches universally and completely all the doctrines which man should know concerning things visible and invisible, heavenly and earthly; and because it subjects to right worship all mankind, rulers and ruled, lettered and unlettered; further because it treats and heals universally every sort of sin committed by soul and body, and it possesses in itself every conceivable virtue, whether in deeds, words, or in spiritual gifts of every kind.[12]

The Councils described as "ecumenical" during this period of ecclesial consciousness are the sign of a political conception of the Church's catholicity. Each of the seven ecumenical Councils held between 325 and 787 and remembered today by the Orthodox Church corresponds to seven interventions made by the Emperor in the life of the Church in order to settle internal or external conflicts.

A new theology of politics, unimaginable a century earlier, was defined by Eusebius, the Bishop of Caesarea.[13] He formulated it in two speeches given at Constantinople before the Emperor Constantine in 335 and 336. For the German theologian Gerhard Podskalsky, in Eusebius's work "the immanent Emperor took the place of the transcendent Christ." This semi-Arian vision was recognized as orthodox, and was imposed on the consciousness of the Christians of the Empire:

---

the Identity of the Church, Foreword by Christoph Cardinal Schönborn (Eugene, OR: Cascade Books, 2015).

12 Cyril of Jerusalem, "Catechesis XVIII," section 23, in Works, trans. Leo P. McCauley, S. J., and Anthony A. Stephenson, 2 vols (Washington, DC: Catholic University of America Press, 1969), 2:132.

13 Eusebius of Caesarea, La théologie politique de l'Empire chrétien. Louanges de Constantin (Triakontaétérikos), ed. Pierre Maraval (Paris: Cerf, 2001).

It is from Christ's hand that our Emperor, dearly beloved of God, received sovereign power to govern his State as God governs the world. The only Son of God has reigned since before time itself, and will reign after time ends, with his Father. Our Emperor, who is loved by the Word, has reigned for several years by an overflowing of and a participation in divine authority. The Savior draws the world, which he governs as his Kingdom, to the service of his Father, and the Emperor submits his subjects to obedience to the Word. The common Savior of all mankind, by his divine power, chases away like a good shepherd the rebel powers that fly about in the air and that set traps for his flock. The Prince whom Christ protects undoes by his assistance the enemies of truth, forces them to obey him, and condemns them to the punishment they deserve. The Word, who is reason itself, existing before the world, casts into our spirits the seeds of science and truth which make them capable of serving His Father. Our Emperor, who burns with a sincere zeal for the glory of God, calls all nations once again to know Him, and proclaims the truth aloud to them, as the Interpreter of the Word. [14]

A century later, in the Western Church, Augustine of Hippo (354 – 430) could only note, after the sack of Rome, the failings of the semi-Arian theology of sovereignty. After 413, he began writing the *City of God Against the Pagans*. It was, for him, necessary radically to distinguish the heavenly city from the earthly one.

The two cities then were created by two kinds of love: the earthly city by a love of self carried even to the point of contempt for God, the heavenly city by a love of God carried even to the point of contempt for self. Consequently, the earthly city glories in itself while the other glories in the Lord. For the former seeks glory from men, but the latter finds its greatest glory in God, the witness of our conscience. The earthly city lifts up its head in its own glory; the heavenly city says to its God: "My glory and the lifter of my head." In the one, the lust for dominion has dominion over its princes as well as over the nations that it subdues; in the other, both those put in charge and those placed under them serve one another in love, the former by their counsel, the latter by their obedience. The earthly city loves its own

---

14 "Harangue à la louange de l'Empereur Constantin, Prononcée en la trentième année de son règne par Eusèbe Evêque de Césarée," in *Histoire de la vie de l'Empereur Constantin écrite par Eusèbe* (Paris: D. Foucault, 1686).

strength as revealed in its men of power; the heavenly city says
to its God: "I will love thee, O Lord, my strength."[15]

But Augustine, as he admits in Book Eleven, believed that God had
created the fallen angels in order to serve the interests of the just. The
ecclesial authority could therefore use coercion in order to curb sin. In
the same way, he acknowledged that recourse to coercion of a temporary
kind on the part of the political authorities was legitimate, while await-
ing the second coming of Christ. The Church, in Augustine's work, is
the manifestation of the City of God on earth. As William T. Cavanaugh
writes, Augustine's vision always relies on an eschatological conception
that never views the state as anything other than a fallen reality.[16] The
difference between the two Cities is a temporal, not a spatial, difference.
Nevertheless, if the Church has the right to command the two swords, it
may, given the sinful nature of humanity, delegate part of its authority to
the temporal power if the latter aligns its law with that of divine justice.
The new barbarian kingdoms, sometimes Arian, sometimes Christian,
demanded no less. Augustine's model of a "provisional Kingdom" made
possible the advent of Christianity.

In 529, the Justinian Codex put forward a first synthesis between the
law of the Empire and the law of the Church. This was completed in the
Digest, which established a jurisprudence and which was then brought
to Pisa, and then expounded at the University of Bologna in the twelfth
century. The Codex, as well as the Digest, had a powerful influence on
European civilization by introducing humanist norms within Roman
legislation. Thus, freed slaves, for example, immediately became citizens
of the Empire. These works also prompted a political transmutation of
ecclesial consciousness. The latter, indeed, was obliged to take responsibility for a number of terrestrial realities, such as marriage law, which had
previously been a matter for internal canon law alone.

The political dimension of this conception of ecumenicity had the
disadvantage of limiting ecclesial consciousness according to how far it
belonged to the Empire. Moreover, the phenomenon of cultural estrangement between the Christian East and the Christian West led to a narrowing
of the meaning of conciliarity within the *oikouménē*, to the extent that
trends hostile to the Empire led to a rejection of the orthodox faith. With

---

15   Augustine, *The City of God Against the Pagans*, trans. Philip Levine, 7 vols (Cambridge, MA: Harvard University Press, 1966), 4: 405–7 (XIV: 28).
16   William T. Cavanaugh, "Church," in *The Wiley-Blackwell Companion to Political Theology*, ed. Cavanaugh and Peter Scott (Hoboken, NJ: John Wiley and Sons, 2019), 398.

the collapse of the Byzantine Empire in 1453 the imperial Church came under the control of the sultans. This political conception of ecumenicity also, as we shall see, had the consequence of producing a canon law on an imperial scale, overriding the legislation of regional councils, as well as producing a general private, administrative, fiscal, and penal law.

A SHORT HISTORY OF THE ECUMENICAL COUNCILS

The First Ecumenical Council of Nicaea took place in June 325. It was presided over by the Emperor Constantine in person. This new political dimension of ecclesial consciousness was continued with in Byzantium until the Fall of Constantinople in 1453. It prompted the American Mennonite theologian John Yoder (1927 – 1997) to say that "there was nothing ecumenical about the ecumenical Councils." For the Orthodox theologian Alexander Schmemann, this theocratic era of the Church of the Christians of the East continued until the fall of Tsarism in 1917. It began, according to him, with the intervention of the Emperor, who was not yet baptized, in the Donatist schism in North Africa. The Council of Arles in 317 had condemned the bishops of Numidia and their leader Donatus, who had disputed the election of Caecilian to the episcopacy, because his ordination had been carried out by a bishop who was a *traditor*.[17] Unprecedentedly, the Council's decree acquired the force of law by the will of the Emperor. The persecution that followed transformed the schismatics into martyrs. According to Schmemann, because of this fatal intervention of the Emperor, "[t]he Donatist schism, even more than the invasion of the Vandals, was the beginning of the end for the great and glorious African Church."[18]

The priority at Nicaea was to condemn Arianism, which, in refusing to recognize Christ's divinity, threatened not only the orthodoxy of the faith but also the civil peace of the Empire. The Fathers of the Council, and especially Athanasius of Alexandria, who was still a deacon, replied to Arius (250 – 336), a priest living in Alexandria, that Christ was perfectly God and perfectly man. It is because of this double nature that he unites humanity with God. Jesus Christ is "of one substance" (*homoousios*) with the Father. In this simple Greek term, which is not found in Scripture,

---

17 "The name given in Africa in early times to Christians who surrendered the Scriptures when their possession was forbidden in the persecution of Diocletian." F. L. Cross and E. A. Livingstone, *The Oxford Dictionary of the Christian Church*, third edition revised (Oxford: Oxford University Press, 2005). — *Translator.*
18 Alexander Schmemann, *Historical Road of Eastern Orthodoxy* (Crestwood, NY: St Vladimir's Seminary Press, 1977), 68.

there is an overturning of ancient philosophy. If God became man, it is so that man might become God. God is not a pure act, as in Aristotle. He is capable of coming out of Himself. God ec-statically exceeds [s'ex-tasie] his own transcendence, as Father, Son, and Holy Spirit, so as to allow His creation to participate in His divine life. This is why, according to St Irenaeus of Lyon, "the glory of God is man fully alive."

But as Father Sergij Bulgakov wrote in 1932, the non-Biblical terms *hypostasis* and *ousia* were still synonymous at this time. This was the source of confusion, and then of schisms. "One can say," wrote the Russian theologian, "that christological theology functioned *without* a terminology, as if in semi-darkness."[19] At the Council of Constantinople in 381, the apostolic faith was made more precise in its account of the Trinity so as to respond to new heresies such as that of the Pneumatomachi, who refused to grant full divinity to the Spirit. The Council also recognized the pre-eminence of the episcopal sees of Rome and Constantinople.

In 431, at the third Council of Ephesus, the Emperor Theodosius II secured not only a recognition of the title of *Theotokos* for the Virgin Mary (who gave birth to Him who is God) but also the condemnation of Nestorius, the Patriarch of Constantinople (c. 381–451). The latter acknowledged only that Mary should bear the title *Christotokos*. This had the result of producing a break with the Syrian church — that is, with Christians living in Mesopotamia.

The Council of Ephesus also took an important decision concerning the Church's organization. Its eighth canon guaranteed the freedom of local churches. At the time, the princes of Antioch had managed to conquer the island of Cyprus, and the Patriarchate of Antioch wanted to take advantage of this to extend its authority over that church and to take control of the ordination of its Metropolitan and its bishops. The bishops of Cyprus had protested, and the dispute was brought before the Third Ecumenical Council, which decided in favor of the Church of Cyprus, in a canon which affirmed that the bishops of the Church of Cyprus should continue to elect and to ordain their own successors themselves, together with their Metropolitans (or archbishops), "so that the Church of Cyprus should not lose the freedom which it gained by Christ's precious blood, and so that it should be the same in all other Churches." This canon of the Third Ecumenical Council confirmed the freedom and independence which the Church of Cyprus had always had since the time of St Paul, St

---

19 Sergius Bulgakov, *The Lamb of God*, trans. Boris Jakim (Grand Rapids, MI: Eerdmans, 2008), 4.

Barnabus, and Lazarus. The canon at the same time guaranteed the freedom of all the other local churches.

Twenty years later, in 451, the Council of Chalcedon affirmed that the two natures of Jesus Christ were "without confusion, without change, without division, without separation; the distinction of natures being in no way annulled by the union." The definition aimed to reconcile the Antiochene school, which distinguished from each other the two natures in Christ, human and divine (at the risk of falling into the heresy of "Nestorianism," which was thought to deny the humanity of Jesus Christ) with the Alexandrian school, which unified the concepts of nature, person, and hypostasis (at the risk of falling into the heresy of Monophysitism, the failure to recognize the two natures of Christ). According to Sergij Bulgakov, this formula was a theological and political compromise, in which the doctrine of St Cyril of Alexandria was "somewhat unnaturally united" to the Tome of Leo, the Pope of Rome, which was marked by the influence of the Antiochene school.[20] Furthermore, the Council condemned the monk Eutychus of Constantinople, who held that Christ's divine nature had absorbed his human nature. These political and theological factors explain the fact that the Council's findings were rejected by the Churches of Egypt and Syria, which then formed the Coptic Orthodox Church and the Syrian Orthodox Church, as well as by the Armenian Church.

In the year 544, the Emperor Justinian published an edict of three chapters, the first condemning Theodore, the Bishop of Mopsuestia in Cilicia (c. 352–428), and the two remaining chapters condemning the writings of Bishop Theodoret of Cyr (c. 393–460), which had been judged Nestorian, as well as the letter addressed by Bishop Ibas of Edessa (435–457) to Mari, Bishop of Hardashir, in Persia. All were accused of making Nestorian propaganda among the Eastern Syrians. The edict had no other result than simultaneously to displease Rome, Chalcedonian circles, and those who were called Monophysites. In the face of the failure of these attempts at persuasion, Justinian convoked a Fifth Council at Constantinople in 553. He secured from the Council a further condemnation of Nestorianism, as well as of the "three chapters" of Theodore, Theodoret, and Ibas, which had been judged heretical. But the Council's decisions provoked great hostility in the provinces Justinian had just reconquered, where the Christians called Monophysites, more at variance than ever, were entrenched in their positions. Today, scholars hold that if the conceptual structures of each Church had been respected it would

---

20   Ibid., 57.

have been possible to recognize as orthodox the writings of these thinkers on the topic of their faith in the divine humanity of Christ. Bulgakov judges the thought of Theodore of Mopsuestia as follows:

> The focus of Theodore's system is, without question, the affirmation of moral freedom, autonomy, and self-determination in the Lord's humanity. Owing to this focus, Theodore does not allow the humanity to be absorbed by the divine nature and transformed into an instrument (as in Apollinarius) or into an attribute (as in St Cyril). This element of his doctrine, which characterizes the entire school of Antioch, leads Theodore to diophysitism [two natures in Christ], enables him to anticipate the future dithelitism, [two wills in Christ] and becomes an integral part of the Christology of the Church.[21]

Similarly, the image used by Ibas, of a temple of the flesh as the dwelling-place of the Logos, was quite familiar from Athanasius of Alexandria. The formula of union between the two schools of Antioch and Alexandria, composed by John of Antioch in 433, used the following way of speaking: "God the Word is unified in the temple which He received from the Virgin." Ibas spoke of two natures in Jesus Christ but of one virtue, and one sole person. This condemnation, which was made in haste and was thus highly political, also complicated relations with Pope Vigilius, who had, before the Council, supported the Three Chapters. It was in this context of imperial voluntarism, and of an absence of dialogue or mutual understanding, that the birth of Islam came to pass. After Mohammed died in 632, his successors conquered Palestine in 638 and Egypt in 642.

In 680 – 681 the Sixth Ecumenical Council, gathering for the third time in the imperial capital under the presidency of Constantine IV, condemned Monothelism, the doctrine according to which Christ has only one will. This rehabilitated Maximus the Confessor (580 – 662) and Pope Martin (c. 600 – c. 656), who had both been arrested in 653 and then condemned. Maximus had died in exile in Lazica (today, Georgia), while Pope Martin died in the Tauridian Chersonese (today, the Crimea). The Council anathematized those who had been corrupted by the Monothelite heresy, that is, the Patriarchs of Constantinople, Alexandria, and Antioch, but also Pope Honorius. Rome made no protest. "It was thought at Rome that a mistake made by a single Bishop of Rome did not affect the inerrancy of

---

21   Ibid., 39.

the Roman Church as such."[22] Moreover, the Popes recognized without qualification the right of the Emperor to convoke councils. For its part, the conciliar assembly asked the Emperor to name a new Patriarch as a replacement for Patriarch Macarius of Antioch, who had been deposed as a heretic. The Emperor had therefore become the guardian of the orthodoxy of the faith. Constantine IV was even acclaimed by the bishops as the "new David." He took advantage of this moment of high prestige to depose his two brothers Heraclius and Tiberius, who had until then been emperors, and to exhibit them, their noses slit, before the ecumenical assembly.

The rise of Islam helped to call into question the cult of images that had been traditional in the Church from the earliest times. In 729, Emperor Leo III condemned the cult of images as idolatry. This decision led to a new breaking-off of communion between the provinces of Rome and of Constantinople. The local Lateran council, thirty years later, defended those who venerated images, with the support of the Patriarchs of Alexandria, Antioch, and Jerusalem. At Nicaea, in 787, at the Seventh Ecumenical Council, the Empress Irene secured protection for the venerators of images, as well as a condemnation of the iconoclasts. The Acts of the Council once more announce a political intervention in the life of the Church: "The holy and great Ecumenical Council assembled by the grace of God and by the devout order of the Emperor. . . ." But the controversy was so intense that the ecumenical Council was no longer considered as a site of consensus enjoying indisputable authority. Only iconodule bishops were now allowed into the Council, whereas in the previous ecumenical Councils, the opposing party — for example, the Monothelites in 680 — had still been invited to join the debate. At the Second Council of Nicaea in 787, it was asserted from the outset that the iconoclasts were outside the Catholic Church. After the Council, Patriarch Tarasios of Constantinople (730 – 806) nevertheless addressed Pope Hadrian as follows: "thanks to the Council, the separated members have become one. The Catholic Church has recovered its unity."[23] This assertion was contradicted by the facts. Even in Byzantium, the Council's decision provoked further unrest, so much so that the iconodules had to be rehabilitated a second time in 843. For its part, the Carolingian Empire did not accept the rulings of the Second Council of Nicaea. Later, successive ruptures between Rome and Constantinople made it impossible to keep alive in the West the memory

---

22   Wilhelm de Vries, *Orient et Occident, Les structures ecclésiales vues dans l'histoire des sept premiers conciles œcuméniques* (Paris: Cerf, 1974), 210.
23   Ibid., 226.

of either the Second Council of Nicaea or the Eighth Ecumenical Council, the council of reconciliation of 879 – 880. At the latter Council, nevertheless, the Churches of East and West acknowledged the possibility that the Churches might have differing liturgical customs without their impeding the profession of the same apostolic faith.

The rivalry between Rome and Constantinople was also linked to questions of title. Patriarch John IV of Constantinople (582 – 595) had decided to be styled "Ecumenical Patriarch," *oikoumenos patriarches*. This expression had been adopted in the new laws passed by the Emperor Justinian in the 530s. Constantinople, moreover, had been for two centuries the capital of the Roman Empire. Pope Gregory the Great (540 – 604) had, for his part, refused the title of *papa universalis*. Pope Martin I called himself "a servant of the servants of God, and, by His grace, Bishop of the holy catholic and apostolic Church of the city of Rome, in one accord with our holy Council of most reverend priests . . . ."[24] The Popes did not yet style themselves "Bishop of the Catholic Church," but only "Bishop of the city of Rome." In Byzantium, the Popes were held, at this period of the Pentarchy, to be "Patriarchs of the West."[25]

Nevertheless, the Popes were not, for all this, ready to grant an "ecumenical" authority to the Byzantine Patriarchs. This led to a famous dispute with Pope Gregory the Great, who in a series of letters in 595 called upon the Patriarch John the Faster to renounce a title which, in its Latin translation, *universalis episcopus*, questioned the primacy of the Bishop of Rome over the whole Church. The See of Rome at that time defended the notion of the catholicity of the Roman Church on the grounds that, since Ignatius of Antioch, who had died a martyr's death at Rome at the beginning of the second century, the Church of Rome had been called upon to "preside in charity." Emperor Phocas (602 – 610) maintained good relations with the papacy, and recognized the primacy of Rome in religious matters. He prohibited the title of "Ecumenical Patriarch" in an edict of 607.

A new breakdown in relations nevertheless occurred between Rome and Constantinople under Pope Theodore (642 – 649) and Patriarch Paul II of Constantinople (641 – 653). The former suspected the latter of adhering to the heresy according to which Christ was moved by one will alone. But the Byzantine Emperor Constantine II, who supported the Monothelites, had Pope Martin arrested in Rome in 653 and had him accused of high treason and put on trial in Constantinople. The Sees of Constantinople

24 Ibid., 211.
25 Ibid., 219.

and Rome were reconciled at the Ecumenical Council of 680 – 681. But the dispute flared up again in the ninth century when Pope Nicholas refused in 867 to recognize the nomination of Photius to the position of Patriarch of Constantinople by Emperor Michael III. Patriarch Photius decided in his turn to condemn Pope Nicholas for having introduced the *filioque* into the Credo said at Rome. For Photius, the Holy Spirit as a person could only proceed from the Father (and not also from the Son). The Emperor tried to re-establish unity between the two Sees of Rome and Constantinople on the occasion of a council in 869, so as to combat Arab conquests in Sicily and southern Italy. But this led only to the condemnation of Photius and the abolition of the primitive Christian belief in the existence, in each human being, of a body, a soul, and a spirit. The traditional trichotomy was replaced by a dualist conception in which man is made of a body and a soul. Ten years later, Rome and Constantinople were reconciled. The Ecumenical Council of 879 abrogated the Council of 869, suppressed the *filioque*, ratified the Seventh Ecumenical Council, and found a formula to allow Christian mission to the Balkans. But it did not settle the underlying problem of the rivalry between an apostolic and an imperial conception of the life of the Church, nor that of the soul as an entity uniting body and spirit. The Council of 869 is, today, held by Rome to have been its Eighth Ecumenical Council. Francis Dvornik has shown that it is after these two dates, 869 and 879, that the two space-times of Rome and Byzantium began to diverge within the *oïkoumérè* or Christendom. [26]

This short history of the "ecumenical" Councils brings out three points which are important for the history of Christian ecumenical consciousness. First, we have seen the way in which the logic of consciousness founded in dialogue arrived at a first transmutation of the conceptual and religious categories of Rome, Athens, and Jerusalem. Ecclesial consciousness produced a new metaphysics by virtue of its dialogue with the religious philosophy of its time, as has been amply demonstrated by the contemporary American philosopher David Bentley Hart:

> In affirming the consubstantiality and equality of the persons
> of the Trinity, Christian thought had also affirmed that it is the
> transcendent God alone who makes creation to be, not through
> a necessary diminishment of his own presence, and not by way
> of an economic reduction of his power in lesser principles, but
> as the infinite God. He is at once *superior summo meo* and *interior*

---

26   Francis Dvornik, *Le schisme de Photius, Histoire et légende* (Paris: Cerf, 1950).

intimo meo: not merely the supreme being set atop the summit
of beings, but the one who is transcendently present in all beings,
the ever more inward act within each finite act. This does not,
of course, mean that there can be no metaphysical structure of
reality, through whose agencies God acts; but it does mean that,
whatever that structure might be, God is not located within it,
but creates it, and does not require its mechanisms to act upon
lower things. As the immediate source of the being of the whole,
he is nearer to every moment within the whole than it is to itself,
and is at the same time infinitely beyond the reach of the whole,
even in its most exalted principles. And it is precisely in learning
that God is not situated within any kind of ontic continuum with
creation, as some "other thing" mediated to the creature by his
simultaneous absolute absence from and dialectical involvement
in the totality of beings, that we discover him to be the ontological cause of creation. True divine transcendence, it turns out,
transcends even the traditional metaphysical divisions between
the transcendent and the immanent.[27]

Second, despite all the tensions between Rome and Constantinople,
and despite the destabilization introduced by the intervention of the
political power, it was possible in the first millennium for the different
local Christian churches to co-exist, thanks to the Christians' deep faith
in the analogy existing between the life of the Church and the life of
the Holy Trinity. The Church gave evidence of a great ecclesiological
flexibility consisting in subsidiarity and mutual recognition, thanks to
its faithfulness to the words Christ addressed to Peter, telling him to lead
His flock, and his words to John, telling him to regard the Virgin Mary
as his own mother. The bishops of the East and the West were conscious
of belonging to the one Church. In the letters of communion sent each
time a bishop was elected, they possessed a system well suited to mutual
recognition. As the Catholic and Orthodox theologians assembled at Chieti
for the Joint Commission for Theological Dialogue write, the pastoral
primacy of the Bishop of Rome, acknowledged by the four Patriarchs of
the Eastern Churches, did not mean that the Pope of Rome was able to
interfere in the internal affairs of those Churches.

> The canons of Sardica (343) determined that a bishop who had
> been condemned could appeal to the Bishop of Rome, and that

---

27 David Bentley Hart, *The Hidden and the Manifest: Essays in Theology and Metaphysics*
(Grand Rapids, MI: Eerdmans, 2017), 111.

the latter, if he deemed it appropriate, might order a retrial, to be conducted by the bishops in the province neighboring the bishop's own. Appeals regarding disciplinary matters were also made to the See of Constantinople, and to other Sees. Such appeals to major sees were always treated in a synodical way. Appeals to the Bishop of Rome from the East expressed the communion of the Church, but the Bishop of Rome did not exercise canonical authority over the Churches of the East. [28]

Lastly, the first millennium witnessed a rise in the power of a new theology of politics, shaped in the East by Eusebius of Caesarea, a "Caesaro-Papism" that gave rise to many divisions. The Dominican Yves Congar showed that the affirmation of the papacy as the head of the universal Church was the basis of the schism that separated the Church of Constantinople from the Church of Rome in 1054. [29] The controversy over the Roman Church's use of unleavened bread was, in reality, only a pretext for Patriarch Michael Cerularius and Pope Leo IX to mark their fundamental divergence over how the universality of the Church was to be defined, and how the Church was to be governed. This is why the other local churches, from Antioch to Kiev, still for a long time remained in communion with Rome. But this evolution of the consciousness of the Church led symmetrically, in the eleventh century, to the coming in the West of what many Russian thinkers have called "Papo-Caesarism," especially after the Gregorian reforms.

FROM CAESARO-PAPISM TO PAPO-CAESARISM

In the eleventh century, Popes Leo IX (1048 – 1054), Nicholas II (1058 – 1061), Gregory VII (1073 – 1085), and Urban II (1088 – 1099) put in place a structure centralized around the Papacy. This reform aimed, in the first place, to bring an end to the practice of the Pope's being nominated by the Emperor, as was the case under the Ottonian dynasty. The reform also freed the Papacy from imperial interference in the domain of faith. Pope Benedict VIII was, for example, obliged in 1014 by the Emperor, Henry II, to reintroduce the *filioque* clause into the Credo, despite the decisions taken by the Council of 879. In 1059, Pope Nicholas II created the College of Cardinals, which elected the new Pope. The pontifical curia,

---

28 Joint International Commission for Theological Dialogue between the Roman Catholic Church and the Orthodox Church, "Synodality and Primacy during the First Millennium: Towards a Common Understanding in Service to the Unity of the Church," section 19, https://www.ecupatria.org/.

29 Yves Congar, *L'Église de saint Augustin à l'époque moderne* (Paris: Le Cerf, 1997).

which had the task of checking everything that was decided upon in the Church, developed at the same time. In March 1075, in the Dictatus Papae, Gregory VII affirmed that "The Roman Church was founded solely by God. Only the Pope can rightly be called 'universal.' He alone can depose or reinstate bishops." The Pope wished to free himself from lay powers of appointment to Church offices. This verticalization of ecclesial power had political consequences. "All princes," Gregory wrote, "shall kiss the feet of the Pope alone. It may be permitted him to depose Emperors.... He himself may be judged by no one." Pope Gregory VII went so far as to depose, and then to excommunicate, Henry IV, the Holy Roman Emperor, who opposed the reform. Despite his act of penitence at Canossa in 1076, it was only in 1122, at the Concordat of Worms, that the Emperor relinquished the power to make appointments using religious symbols such as the cross and the ring, and accepted the free election of bishops by the canonical chapters of cathedrals. This was the end of the Caesaro-Papism of the Holy Roman Emperor. The Popes, drawn by their dream of a theocracy, even attempted to make the Emperors subordinate to themselves. But the struggle between the "two swords" continued throughout the Middle Ages, to the point at which Pope Gregory IX denounced the Emperor Frederick II as the Antichrist. At the Council of Lyon in 1245, Pope Innocent IV presented himself as the custodian of both swords.

Patriarch John X Camateros (1198 – 1206) tried in vain to remind Pope Innocent III of the ecclesiology of the Sister Churches as it had been lived in the first millennium, with its ruptures and its reconciliations:

> Where do you find it written in the holy Gospels that Christ said that the Roman Church is the head, and a universal mother, and the most Catholic of all the Churches of the four points of the compass; by what Ecumenical Council was what you say of your Church decided?... It is thus not for these reasons that Rome is the mother of the other Churches, but, since there are five great Churches adorned with the dignity of having a Patriarch, the Church of Rome is the first among equal sisters... The Church of the Romans, therefore, stands first in rank, it is the first of the other Churches which, like sisters [adelphōn] equal in honor [timē] are born of the same heavenly Father from whom, according to Scripture, all fatherhood in heaven and on earth flows down.[30]

---

30   Martin Jugie, Theologia dogmatica Christianorum Orientalium ab Ecclesia Catholica dissidentium (Paris, 1931), 386–87, 456; quoted in Yves Congar, Diversités et Communion (Paris: Cerf, 1982), 128–29.

This warning, coming from the successor of the apostle Andrew, was ignored. The reform of the Papacy culminated on November 18, 1302, with Pope Boniface VIII's bull *Unam sanctam*. This concerned the unity of the Church, and affirmed the political theology of the two swords:

> We are informed by the texts of the gospels that in this Church and in its power are two swords . . . . Both, therefore, are in the power of the Church, that is to say, the spiritual and the material sword, but the former is to be administered *for* the Church but the latter *by* the Church . . . . However, one sword ought to be subordinated to the other and temporal authority, subjected to spiritual power. [31]

Boniface VIII thus declared the spiritual power superior to the temporal power, and, accordingly, the Pope superior to kings, these latter answering to the head of the Church. The French King Philip the Fair (1268 – 1314), the head of the most populous state in Christendom, opposed this decision. He assembled a council of the bishops of France, as well as assemblies of nobles and burghers in Paris, to condemn the Pope. Philip then had himself called the Most Christian King. In order to oppose the Bishop of Rome's theocratic project, he had the city of Anagni, where the Pope had taken refuge, occupied in 1303. From this date onwards, everyone understood that the King of France held a monopoly on the legitimacy to say what was right. The state became the producer of the justifications on which he based his own decisions.

This affirmation of Roman power also led to a break with the Churches of the East, especially after the Fourth Crusade, which was launched by Pope Innocent III. This Crusade led to the sack and pillage of Constantinople by the crusaders in 1204, as well as to the setting up of parallel Latin hierarchies in lands overseen by the ecumenical Patriarchate. The Crusade therefore further deepened the division between the Christians of the East and the West in the thirteenth and fourteenth centuries, until the Council of Florence. The two unity Councils of Lyon in 1245 and 1274 were motivated only by political considerations: in the first case, the dismissal of Emperor Frederick II at the behest of Pope Innocent IV, in 1245, and in the second, the desire of the Byzantine Emperor, Michael VIII Palaiologus, to avoid further Latin crusades in his lands, especially because he already had the Seljuk Turks to fight.

---

31   Pope Boniface VIII, "Unam Sanctam: One God, One Faith, One Spiritual Authority," *Papal Encyclicals Online*, www.papalencyclicals.net/.

In the fourteenth and fifteenth centuries, movements resisting the power of the Bishop of Rome appeared all over Europe, and even within the Catholic Church itself. At Oxford, in 1378, John Wyclif, a doctor of theology, disputed the new Roman conception of the ecclesial order. He believed that only a man in a state of grace could legitimately exercise authority. It was not the (exterior) office of a power-holder, but his (interior) holiness in which was founded the legitimacy of his exercise of that power. He concluded that the bishops and the Pope could not found their right to exercise a power of temporal or spiritual jurisdiction on their status as successors of the apostles or of St Peter, especially as the English sovereign was anointed in the Holy Spirit by the Archbishop of Canterbury in the coronation rite in Westminster Abbey. The following century, in 1534, Parliament passed into law the Act of Supremacy, which made the King the supreme head of the Church of England. Queen Elizabeth I (1558 – 1603) transformed this Act by declaring herself "the only supreme governor of this realm . . . as well in all spiritual or ecclesiastical things or causes, as temporal." She was careful to maintain a balance between the priority given by the Puritans to justice and the Catholic sense of tradition and apostolic succession. After the Gregorian reform, the Pope believed that he had the right to depose sovereigns. The Queen was therefore excommunicated by Pope Pius V in 1570. The following year, under the still decisive influence of the thought of the earlier Archbishop of Canterbury, Thomas Cranmer (1489 – 1556), Parliament adopted the Thirty-Nine Articles, the Church of England's confession of faith. The English sovereigns had no choice but to separate from Rome, and they harshly persecuted the community of Christians remaining loyal to Rome.

In Continental Europe, the Reformation was also a reaction to the new theology promulgated by the Popes. In Prague, the theologian Jan Hus, a rector of the University of Prague, asserted in 1413 that "the Pope and the curia can be mistaken both about the truth and in their morals." But the Council of Constance (1414 – 1418), convoked by the Emperor Sigismund I and the Anti-Pope John XXIII, condemned the reformers Hus and Wyclif as heretics. The Emperor ordered that they should be burnt alive. The end of the great Western schism, which was brought about thanks to the election of a new Pope, Martin V, and his return to Rome, did not, however, manage to resolve the crisis, in which proponents of a vertical organization of the Church found themselves in opposition to advocates for a conciliarist conception of governance. The Council of Basel, from its beginning in 1431, asserted that its authority was higher than the Pope's.

This contestation of papal power had the result in France of strengthening the local church's desire for independence from the Papacy. In 1438 the Pragmatic Sanction was adopted by the French clergy, assembled at Bourges, in which King Charles VII asserted that he was the guardian of the rights of the French Church. In 1516, with the Concordat of Bologna, King Francis I was recognized by the Pope as the master of the French church.[32]

In Wittenberg in 1517 Martin Luther condemned the sale of indulgences. The Augustinian monk was not trying to create a new church, but to reform the Catholic Church:

> What is this new piety of God and the Pope that for a consideration of money they permit a man who is impious and their enemy to buy out of purgatory the pious soul of a friend of God and do not rather, because of the need of that pious and beloved soul, free it for pure love's sake?[33]

The Catholic priest Ulrich Zwingli, meanwhile, asserted publicly at Zurich in 1520 that only the Gospel of Christ, and not the Pope, was the source of faith. He added, in contrast to Luther, that it was for the secular power to spread the good news. The French theologian John Calvin, in his *Institutes of the Christian Religion* (1536) held that it was faith, and not formal participation in the Roman Church, that established ecclesial order. For him, the authentic Church, made up of those who are predestined to be saved, was invisible. But the visible Church, gathered together by baptism, the Lord's Supper, and the Law, had to be structured by strong ecclesiastical discipline. Such a conception made possible the emergence of a legitimate diversity within the Churches of the Reformed tradition that began to form in Europe, and, from 1620, in North America, with the Pilgrim Fathers. The Calvinist influence was especially strong in George Fox (1624 – 1691), the founder of the Religious Society of Friends (the Quakers).

---

32   In 1682, the French clergy adopted the Four Gallican Articles, which established the freedoms of the Gallican Church with the support of Louis XIV. The reigning pontiff has only a spiritual authority; princes are therefore not subject to the authority of the Church in temporal matters; the Pope can neither judge kings nor depose them; the subjects of the King cannot be released from their oath of obedience; the exercise of pontifical power is governed by the canons of the Church, but alongside these canons, the immemorial principles and customs of the Gallican Church continue in force; the Ecumenical Council, an assembly of all the bishops of Christendom, takes decisions that outrank those of the Pope, whose authority is therefore limited by that of these Councils; in matters of dogma, the Pope is infallible only with the consent of the universal Church.

33   Martin Luther, "The Ninety-Five Theses," in Timothy F. Lull, ed., *Martin Luther's Theological Writings* (Minneapolis: Fortress Press, 1989), 28 (thesis 84).

According to Pierre Legendre, the Gregorian reform gave rise not only to denominational separations and national identities, but also to the foundation of the modern state.

> Without the Gregorian reform of the eleventh century announcing the "imitation of the [Roman] Empire" by the Church — it is said of the Pope, for example, that "he alone may use the Imperial Insignia . . . his title is unique in the world" — and without the revival of Roman law (which had been more or less moribund in the West since the sixth century) by the pontifical vicariate, acting on the theological justification of a mandate given by Christ, the great juridical innovations, and the idea of the State itself, would have been inconceivable. Such institutional issues, later exacerbated by the bloody conflict on the millenarian topic of the Reformation of the Church in the sixteenth century, were handed on *to a Modernity in search of divine legitimation.*[34]

The German Catholic theologian Hans Küng adds that the political conception of ecumenicity has led, especially following the Crusades, to a whole series of ruptures between the Christians of the East and the West:

> Whereas the ecumenical paradigm of the early church was fundamentally sacramental, collegial and conciliar, the new medieval Roman Catholic paradigm is primarily legalistic, monarchical and absolutist: We no longer have the scheme of the early church and the Orthodox church today: God–Christ–apostles–bishops–church. — What we have is the new constitution of the medieval church: God–Christ–Peter–pope–bishops–church. Only since the high Middle Ages has the Catholic Church had the appearance that it presents to us today: The pope claims the primacy of honour over the whole church, over all patriarchs, bishops, priests and every believer: this is still rejected by the Eastern churches. — The authority of the clergy is in principle superior to that of the laity: this led to the great dispute between the pope and the emperor and then between the pope and the modern state, a dispute which the papacy has lost all along the line. — The prohibition of marriage is now a law which applies to all the clergy: this goes against the millennia-old tradition of priestly marriage even in the Western church and causes countless unnecessary problems, at present above all a catastrophic lack of priests.[35]

---

34   Pierre Legendre, *Le Point fixe, nouvelles conférences* (Paris: Mille et une nuits, 2010), 43.
35   Hans Küng, *Tracing the Way* (New York: Continuum, 2002), 220.

These harsh words of Hans Küng must be weighed against those of another Catholic theologian, the French Jesuit Bernard Sesboüé. According to the latter, the medieval Church was able to evince unity within diversity. He recognizes, nevertheless, that the good news of the Gospel was so radical that each local church was led to choose and to privilege a single aspect of the Kingdom over the others. Sesboüé takes the example of the formation of the religious orders in the Catholic Church. These orders display the different spiritual types that came into being — in tension with each other, it is true, but also maintaining the cohesion and liveliness of the Church on a continental, and, in the modern era, on a global scale.

> The peace of the Benedictines, wholly given over to contemplation and to the absolute priority which is to be given to God over everything else, is a necessary sign of the Gospel. It does not, however, exhaust the Gospel. It leaves the field to the multiplicity of active charisms, such as that of the Dominicans, who seek the truth so as to convey the fruit of their contemplation to the people of God through preaching. The dynamic of the mission of the Company of Jesus in the service of the Church aims to imitate Jesus's peregrinations proclaiming the Kingdom, in full obedience to the mission received from the Father. . . . Each person, then, must aim towards the whole, even if they are doing so along different axes.[36]

From this brief review of the main stages of Christian political consciousness, we can grasp the origins of the triple tension between Christians and Jews in the Hellenistic period, between Eastern and Western Christians in the medieval period, and, finally, between Protestant, Orthodox, and Catholic Christians in the modern period. As well as the ambiguities attached to the political character of the term "ecumenical" and the anti-Jewish dimension of "Catholic" ecclesial consciousness, Christians progressively ceased to share the same representations of what the Church is. For some, especially those who describe themselves as Orthodox in the modern period, the Church was to be understood, as we might put it today, fractally. As is well known, a fractal figure is a mathematical object, such as a curve or a surface, which displays a similar structure at all scales. This conception of the Church was capable of being realized in its Eucharistic life, through its communion with the Father through Christ in the Spirit, the same

---

36   Bernard Sesboüé, *La théologie au XXe siècle et l'avenir de la foi, Entretiens avec Marc Leboucher* (Paris: DDB, 2007), 221.

universality in different locations. For others, especially those who will call themselves Catholics, the Church is inseparable from the form in which it is incarnated in Rome, the form of Peter's successor. The pastor designated by Christ assumed, in communion with the other apostles, the unifying function of presiding over the Eucharistic community, both at the time of the first, Galilean, community, and, later, at Rome. Lastly, for those who follow the Reform begun by Luther and Calvin, the Church cannot be associated with a pyramid-like conception of authority, because Christ alone is the Head of it. It rests above all on the Word of God handed down in Scripture.

Father Congar was certainly right to speak of a growing estrangement from the ninth to the fifteenth century between Eastern and Western Christians. He enumerated some of the reasons for this cultural distancing: as well as the verticalization of the power of the Pope, the loss of bilingualism in the West, the difficulty of learning Latin in the East, the retreat of papal jurisdiction from Illyricum in the East (and, conversely, the loss of Byzantine territories in Italy), the Carolingians' poor understanding of the meaning of the veneration of icons that was defended by the Byzantines, there was also Patriarch Photius's inattention to the fact — decisive for the Latins — that Christ is indeed He who sends the Holy Spirit upon his apostles (John 20:22), as well as, lastly, the setting up of Latin hierarchical structures after the taking of Jerusalem by the Crusaders in 1099 and the conquest of Constantinople in 1204.

Nevertheless, at the beginning of the fifteenth century, the different representations of the Church that had appeared in the course of the previous centuries were still superimposed upon each other in a non-contradictory manner. The political consciousness of the Church had not erased the symbolic consciousness of Christians. The terms "catholicity" and "ecumenicity" were still considered as synonyms. Thus the three Creeds of the ancient Church were called the *tria symbola catholica sive oecumenica* by the Reformers.[37]

THE TURNING-POINT OF THE COUNCIL OF FLORENCE

A synthesis even emerged at the Council of Florence on July 6, 1439, and, for several years, made it possible to reconcile Eastern and Western Christians, as well as papists and conciliarists.[38] This Council is of such importance for the history of ecumenical consciousness, now and in the past, that it is well to pay close attention to it.

---

37 Neuner, *Théologie Œcuménique*, 20.
38 Arjakovsky and Hallensleben, eds., *Le concile de Florence*.

The Council opened on April 9, 1438, at Ferrara. The two Churches of East and West acknowledged each other from the outset as Churches on an equal level, as is illustrated by the episode of the kiss exchanged by the Pope and the Patriarch. In January 1439, the Fathers decamped to Florence because of an outbreak of the plague.[39] Emperor John VIII and Patriarch Joseph II of Constantinople were present with a 700-strong Byzantine delegation, among them 200 well-known figures such as the future Patriarch of Constantinople George Scholarios, the humanist Bessarion, Bishop of Nicaea, and Isidore (c. 1385–1463), the Metropolitan of Kiev.[40] The Roman side numbered 360 clerics, among whom were more than 160 cardinals, archbishops, bishops, and abbots accompanying the Pope. On the Greek side, there were, according to one witness, in addition to the Emperor and the Patriarch, "twenty archbishops and eight abbots and three Staurophoroi who are called the cardinals of the Constantinopolitan church, very many calogeri ['good old men,' i.e., 'monks'], priests and monks and nobles of the laity, as well as orators of the most serene princes and emperors of Trebizond and of the King of the Georgians and ambassadors of the Walachi. There were present also two Armenian archbishops, procurators of the Patriarch or Archbishop of the whole of Armenia."[41] The Council took place against the background of Turkish pressure on Constantinople and in the context of the Pope's wish to reject the decisions of the Council of Basel.

At the end of the Council an agreement was signed in the cathedral of Santa Maria del Fiore: the bull *Laetentur cœli*, of July 6, 1439, which covered the *filioque* (a compromise was found, affirming that the Holy Spirit proceeds from the Father through the Son, *per Filium*), unleavened bread (the Greeks could keep leavened bread), and purgatory (the juridical approach based on Anselm's soteriology of justification was adjudged compatible with the eschatological approach that treated salvation as a personal spiritual growth continuing in the life to come). The Greeks also accepted the legitimacy of indulgences (which could reduce the punishments to be undergone in purgatory) and the claims of the Papacy: Rome

---

39   Joseph Gill, *The Council of Florence* (Cambridge: Cambridge University Press, 1959); *Christian Unity: The Council of Ferrara-Florence (1438/39–1989)* (Leuven: Leuven University Press, 1991).

40   Joseph Gill, *Personalities of the Council of Florence* (New York: Barnes and Noble, 1964). Mark Evgenikos, the Metropolitan of Ephesus, did not speak Latin, and took up a defensive position.

41   *Fragmenta protocolli, diaria privata, sermones*, ed. G. Hoffmann (Rome, 1951), 30; quoted and trans. in Gill, *The Council of Florence*, 109–10.

was agreed to possess primacy over the whole world, *quemadmodum etiam in gestis œcumenicorum conciliorum.* This formula, which was understood by the Romans to mean "as it results from the acts of the Councils," was understood by the Byzantines to mean "in such a way and in such conditions as the Councils shall determine." The Patriarchs, for their part, secured the maintenance of all their rights and privileges from the Pope and the Council. According to Gabriel Hachem, two points were especially important to the Greeks: the Pope could not convoke an Ecumenical Council without the agreement of the Emperor and the Patriarchs; and the Pope could not summon a Patriarch to be tried before a papal tribunal.

The Council of Florence succeeded, in this way, in finding a formula of "differentiated consensus," as we would put it today, on an ecclesiological level, despite the methodological divergences between Western scholasticism and Eastern apophatic theology. The agreement signed by the Pope and by seventy Western bishops, as well as by almost all the Byzantine delegates (except Mark Evgenikos [1392 – 1444], the Bishop of Ephesus, and the representative of Georgia, who had fled so as not to have to sign the agreement) was announced in Constantinople in 1452. It was adopted by the Armenian Apostolic Church, whose headquarters were in Sis, in Cilicia, by the decree *Exultate Deo* of November 22, 1439. In 1441 the Council continued at Rome, without the participation of the Chalcedonian Eastern churches. It led to an agreement on February 4, 1442, with the Jacobite Church of Alexandria and Jerusalem, in the decree *Cantate Domino*; on September 30, 1444, with the Jacobite Syrian Church, in the decree *Multa et admiribilia*; and, finally, with the Chaldeans and Maronites, in the decree *Benedictus*, of August 7, 1445.

This Council could have been viewed as a victory for the unitary consciousness of the Church, but the union was not lasting, for several reasons. From 1439 onwards, the papal bull *Non mediocri* gave the cardinals precedence over the Patriarchs, the cardinalate being considered as an institution "of divine origin." Moreover, the rising power of the see of Moscow, which rejected the Council in 1441, and which separated from Constantinople in 1448, made the Orthodox world more fragile. Above all, the Fall of Constantinople to the Ottomans in 1453 put an end to the hope of implementing the decisions of the Union of Florence. In 1483 – 1484, at Constantinople — and thus under Turkish domination — a local synod of the Eastern church was held in Pammakaristos Church. [42] It was convoked

---

42   "Tomos Konstantinopol'skogo sobora 1484g." [*Tomos* of the Council of Constantinople, 1484], https: //vk.com.

by Patriarch Symeon I. [43] It was held in the presence of representatives of the Patriarchs of Alexandria and Jerusalem, [44] churches which were then under Ottoman sway. [45] This synod was the first to condemn the Council of Florence, arguing that it had not been canonically summoned or constituted, and that its decrees were therefore null and void. In its *tomos*, after having referred to the condemnation of the Ecumenical Patriarch John XI Bekkos in 1285 by the Synod of Blachernae, and having affirmed that the Holy Spirit "proceeds from the Father alone," the Synod of Constantinople in 1484 erased the Council of Florence at a stroke:

> Moreover, with this conciliar decree, we reject the council held at Florence, and we declare all the chapters contained in its decisions to be null and void. This council is now regarded by us, and will henceforth be regarded, as not having taken place, for on the question of the procession of the Holy Spirit and on everything else it is not in accord with the decrees of the eight Holy Ecumenical Councils, and directly contradicts them. We also reject the offering of the Sacrifice in unleavened bread, and everything which has been affirmed at Florence and contained in that council's definition of faith, as explained above. [46]

The Synod, nevertheless, while adopting a ritual for welcoming converted Catholics into Orthodoxy by chrismation, did not demand re-baptism (as was the case in the Greek world from 1755 onwards). But the decrees of the Synod were not universally implemented. Twentieth-century Orthodox theologians, moreover, were divided over whether this decision of this council had an obligatory character (as Elie Melia held) or a relative one (as Ioannis Karmiris believed), given the contrary decision of the council of 1755 not to recognize the baptism of Latin Christians.

In reality, if the history of the memory of this council is studied more closely, it can be seen that the Orthodox Churches long upheld the Council of Florence. [47] Only Mark Evgenikos refused to sign at Florence, out

---

43   The Patriarch signed the *tomos* as "Archbishop of Constantinople, the new Rome, and Ecumenical Patriarch."

44   "Tomos sunidokos tēs en Constantinoupolei Synodikos" [*Tomos* of the Council of Constantinople], January 27, 2016, http://sathanasoulias.blogspot.com/.

45   Edward Gibbon, *The History of the Decline and Fall of the Roman Empire* (London: Penguin, 1995), 3: 142–43.

46   "Tomos Konstantinopol'skogo sobora," https://vk.com.

47   The main sources for the Council of Florence are the Latin Acts (this is a summary made in the course of the proceedings by Andrea da Santa Croce; the official acts have gone missing), the Greek Acts (or Praktika, accompanied by a Description

of 700 Orthodox delegates, of whom 29 were bishops and Metropolitans, together with the Patriarch and the Emperor. Nor did anyone, either, oppose the burial of Patriarch Joseph II, who died on June 10, 1439, in the Dominican Church of Santa Maria Novella. The inscription on his tomb, on the contrary, demonstrated in three languages the unanimous recognition by Christians of unity in the European Church: *Unus ut Europae cultus et una fides.*

At Constantinople, the reception of the Council of Florence was not, as the polemicist Doukas would have us believe, a negative one. The historians Joseph Gill and Vitalien Laurent have shown that, in contrast to what happened after the Council of Lyon in 1274, there were neither mass demonstrations, nor any organized resistance. True, Emperor John did not immediately announce the Union upon his return, but this was above all because the news of his wife's death had demoralized him. George Scholarios[48] himself wrote in 1439 that the Union was popular.[49] The man who, out of opportunism and hurt pride, according to Joseph Gill,[50] took an oath to defend the cause of his former teacher Mark Evgenikos in June 1445, was already in 1440 or 1441 authoritatively rejecting the

---

by a Greek scribe, John Plousiadenos, probably taken from a text by Dorotheos of Mytilene, as well as some documents which are almost certainly authentic) and the Memoirs of Sylvester Syropoulos. The reliability of these sources is discussed at length by Joseph Gill in his monograph The Council of Florence (Cambridge: Cambridge University Press, 1959).

48 George Kourtesios, called Scholarios, was a fervent disciple of Thomas Aquinas, and acknowledged the Pope as the "pastor of the universe." At Florence, he publicly defended the union by holding that the Latins had been able to prove their orthodoxy. He left Florence with the despot Demetrius and with George Gemistus Plethon on June 25. After the Emperor's death, he became a monk in 1450 and took the name Gennadios. After having promised Mark Evgenikos that he would defend his cause, he defended wherever he could Evgenikos's "fidelity to the ancestral faith and to orthodox doctrine." He became Patriarch on January 6, 1454, by the will of the Sultan, who entrusted the seals to him, as the Emperors had previously done, in the Church of the Holy Apostles, because Hagia Sophia had become a mosque. He left his role two years later, but was twice recalled by the Sultan. He ended his life in a monastery, where he wrote several treatises, among them a summary of Aquinas's Summa Contra Gentiles. He died after 1472. For Joseph Gill, some of Gennadios's subscriptions to letters bear witness to his excessively well-developed ego, and to his pride, that had been wounded by his not having been sufficiently recognized by the Emperor and by the Patriarch at the Council of Florence, in contrast to Bessarion. He signed himself "universal master of the Church of the orthodox, the humble monk Gennadios." Mark Evgenikos knew how to appeal to this brilliant monk by flattering his pride. Joseph Gill, Personalities of the Council of Florence, chapter 7, "George Scholarius," 86.
49 Georges Scholarios, Œuvres, Migne, Patrologia Graeca, 155, coll. 396 and 397.
50 Gill, Personalities of the Council of Florence, 79–94.

anti-unionist bishop's *Syllogistic Chapters against the Latins*. Marie-Hélène Blanchet, a researcher at the CNRS, believes that the Greek historian Th. Zèzès has not produced any convincing arguments to show that Scholarios was not the author. Moreover, the new Patriarch elected in the place of Joseph on May 4, 1440, Metrophanus of Cyzicus, favored the union, as did his successor Gregory Mammas, elected in 1443. The pro-unionist Emperor Constantine XI Palaiologos (1405–1453), who became *basileus* after John VIII's death on October 31, 1448, was greatly preferred by the people to his brother Demetrios, who was an anti-unionist. Thirteen years later, despite the agitation led by the Grand Duke Luke Notaras, by Demetrios Palaiologos, and by Gennadios Scholarios, the act of Union was proclaimed on December 12, 1452, in Hagia Sophia in Constantinople, with the participation of Latin and Byzantine prelates, among whom were ten Metropolitans, and a numerous crowd.

In Eastern Europe, Metropolitan Isidore, who had also become an apostolic delegate for Rus and the lands around it, was also favorably welcomed to Buda and then to Kiev. As Florent Mouchard and Bernard Marchadier have reminded us,[51] panegyrics of the period also show that the Council of Florence was at one time accepted by Boris, the Grand Prince of Tver, the adversary of the Grand prince of Moscow, Vasily II, called "the Blind." As for Novgorod, it did not at first display its hostility to the Council of Florence, but did not hesitate to align its position with that of Moscow.[52] At Buda, Isidore signed an encyclical on March 5, 1440, in which he declared:

> You, therefore, Christians Latin as well as Greek, and all of you who come from the Ecumenical Church of Constantinople, that is, Russians, Serbs, Romanians, and other Christian nations, receive this most holy union with great veneration and rejoicing of spirit. I ask you at once, in the name of our Lord Jesus Christ who oversupplies us with benefits, no longer to permit any division between yourselves and the Latins. For you are the servants of our Lord Jesus Christ, and you have been baptized in His name.

---

51   Florent Mouchard, "'Le métropolite de Kiev revint du concile de Rome': Le concile de Florence et sa réception dans la Rus" (Novgorod, Pskov, Tver', Moscou, 1439–1461); Bernard Marchadier, "Isidore de Kiev," in Arjakovsky and Hallensleben, *Le concile de Florence*.

52   The principality of Novgorod would be added by force to Muscovy in 1478. Traditions of links to the West nevertheless remained lively there, since when Archbishop Gennady of Novgorod (who occupied his See between 1484 and 1504) undertook to have the whole of the Bible translated into Church Slavonic, he appointed to his team to work on the Latin Vulgate three Catholics, among whom was a certain Benjamin, a Croat Dominican.

And you, Latin nations, accept sincerely and without reservation all those who profess the Greek faith. All have been baptized, and their baptism is holy and true and has been approved by the Roman Church as valid and of equal value. Reject, therefore, any point of difference between you on these questions; the Latins must learn, like the aforementioned Greeks, to treat the Church made by this union as shared between them. And when the Greeks live in Latin countries, or when there is a Latin church in their countries, let them take part in the holy liturgy, and let them contemplate in faith the Blessed Sacrament, with the same marks of respect and of a contrite heart as they show in their own churches. What is more, they can confess their sins to Latin priests, and receive from them the Body of Christ. The Latins, for their part, must go into the Greek churches and take part in the divine services, in order to worship with one burning faith the Body of Jesus Christ; for it is truly the Body of Jesus Christ, whether it is consecrated by the Greek priest with leavened bread or by the Latin priest with unleavened bread. It is therefore correct to retain both rites, whether with unleavened or leavened bread. Let the Latins also confess their sins to Greek priests and let them take communion with them, for there is no difference in value between the two sacraments. Thus determined the Council in solemn session held in the glorious divine Church of the city of Florence on the sixth day of June 1439.[53]

Certainly, despite Isidore of Kiev and Avraam of Suzdal signing the Act of Union, Grand Prince Vasily II of Moscow rejected the Union of Florence in 1441. The latter was already involved in a full war of succession, and feared the opening of a new front to the West. In 1448, after the victory of the Sultan at Varna on November 10, 1444 over the European armies, he claimed to be the sole remaining defender of the Orthodox Church. He imprisoned Isidore, who managed only with difficulty to escape from Muscovy. Vassily even broke with the Patriarch of Constantinople by having Metropolitan Jonas elected as Metropolitan of Kiev and of all Russia. As John Meyendorff writes, from this moment on, the Muscovite Church became dependent on the arbitrary, and more and more secular, power of the Tsars.[54]

---

53   Gill, The Council of Florence, 2–4. The original Greek text of this encyclical has disappeared. Only a version in Church Slavonic is extant.
54   John Meyendorff, "Was there an encounter between East and West at Florence?" in Alberigo, Christian Unity, 174.

Sylvester Syropoulos's *Memoirs* devoted to the Council of Florence were written in 1444 – 1445.[55] They reveal the limits of the political consciousness of some of the representatives of the Byzantine Church. It is well known that Eusebius of Caesarea was strongly influenced by the First Ecumenical Council and its debates — which had remained, for him, unresolved — on the relation between the Father and the Son within the Trinity. This Council of Nicaea had, as we have already seen, had an influence on his definition of orthodoxy as correct truth and on his political representation of the history of the Church. He separated the life of the world from the life of the Christian community, while unifying them by the figure of the *basileus*.[56] Eleven centuries later, Sylvester Syropoulos's inability to accept the conciliar decisions of the Council of Florence of 1438 – 1439 is characteristic of this essentially nomo-canonical and political vision of orthodoxy. But if Eusebius became the thurifer of Caesaro-Papism, Syropoulos went so far as to choose, with the other intellectuals of his generation, to privilege "the turban over the tiara."[57] At the beginning of this period in Church politics, when devotion and doctrine were beginning to become separated from each other, Eusebius was the historian of record. He was the man who had been able to narrate the ecclesial path from the first apostles to the Imperial Council of Nicaea. The Bishop of Caesarea had been able to have Constantine accepted as the representative of God on earth. At the end of this period, at the moment when, in the West, the nation-states were beginning to combine against the power of the Pope, and when, in the East, the Church was discovering the brutal reality of a Muslim state, Sylvester was the memoirist of the short term, the last witness of the so-called "symphonic" model of medieval Orthodoxy.

The personality, and the major work, of the Grand Ecclesiarch of the Church of Constantinople, are known to us thanks to the work of the Assumptionist Vitalien Laurent. The latter was a scholarly researcher at the CNRS and an expert adviser to the Congregation for Faith and Doctrine at the Vatican.[58] As Laurent has shown in his translation, Syropoulos's

---

55 Vitalien Laurent, *Les Mémoires du grand Ecclésiarque de l'Eglise de Constantinople Sylvestre Syropoulos sur le concile de Florence* (1438 – 1439) (Rome: Institut Pontifical Oriental, 1971).

56 Arjakovsky, *What is Orthodoxy?*.

57 This is the famous expression that the chronicler Doukas put in the mouth of Luke Notaras before the Fall of Constantinople. Cf. Vasile Grecu, ed. *Michael Ducas, Istoria turco-bizantină* (1341 – 1462) (Bucharest, 1958).

58 Syropoulos was born around 1400 into a famous family of ecclesiastics attached to the Great Church of Constantinople. After studying theology, he became a Patriarchal administrator rather than a true theologian. Around 1430 he became the Grand

Memoirs were transcribed by Theodore Agallianos, himself an archon and a friend of the author's. Laurent says of Agallianos that he was an "uncompromising Orthodox of the first order." The memoirs were published in Leyden in 1660. They were very soon severely criticized by Catholic historiographers, and praised to the skies in a monolithic fashion by Orthodox historians such as George Koressios (d. 1660), Patriarch Dositheos of Jerusalem (d. 1707), and Adamantios Diamantopoulos.[59] Vitalien Laurent's analysis is in marked contrast with all these. If he shows the great value of Syropoulos's testimony as a protagonist and direct witness of the events described, the French historian cannot not note the approximations, lacunae, and excessive subjectivity of Syropoulos's account. Syropoulos pleaded the cause of those who had had the weakness to sign the decree of Union before the integralists of his time, who were opposed to it. He devotes only fifteen pages out of more than 250 to the public sessions of the Council of Florence. And above all, because of the many snubs he incurred in his own circle for having been a signatory, he does not hesitate to insert untruths, which have been authoritatively exposed both by Laurent and by Joseph Gill. When there is a conflict between the *Memoirs*

Ecclesiarch, one of the highest roles in the Patriarchal Byzantine curia. In 1438 – 1439 he participated actively in the Council of Florence, and signed the decree of Union. Despite what the Byzantine historian Doukas said about the matter, there were no mass demonstrations over, nor any organized resistance to, the Council's decisions in Constantinople in the years that followed. Certainly, there were anti-Unionists, with Mark Evgenikos as their captain. Syropoulos, who, upon his return, regretted having signed the Act of Union, wrote in 1444 – 1445 his Recollections or Memoirs of the Council in order to justify his approach. But as Vitalien Laurent writes, "the opposition movement did not, on the eve of the Turkish conquest, have the breadth of support that is attributed to it by the polemical literature which has come down to us." It does, however, seem that the consideration with which the new Emperor Constantine XII (1449 – 1453) treated the anti-Unionists precipitated the anti-Unionist turn of Scholarios, one of the chief protagonists of the Council. The latter retired from his positions as a judge and first secretary in the Patriarchate, and became a monk, Gennadios, in 1450. Syropoulos, guessing that the political situation would soon change, also abandoned his positions. But on December 14, 1452, ten Metropolitans and a large group of clerics still participated in a service in Hagia Sophia proclaiming the decree of Union in the presence of the Emperor and the ruling bodies. After the Fall of Constantinople, the sources differ on Syropoulos's fate. Some historians believe that he died during the seizure of the city. But Vitalien Laurent points out that a Patriarch with the name of Sophronios Syropoulos appears in the years after the Fall of Constantinople (doubtless between summer 1463 and July 1464) and believes it to be highly likely, in view of a synodal document of 1488, that this is our chronicler. He seems to have died, probably after having been dismissed by the Synod, in a "tragic fall" at the age of sixty-five.

59 Adamantios Diamantopoulos, "Guennadios Scholarios," *Hellenika*, IX (1936), 285–308. He had previously published a book on Mark Evgenikos in Athens in 1899.

and the *Acts* of the Council, Joseph Gill privileges the latter account, and explains why.[60] For Laurent, the partisan character of Syropoulos's narrative is "undeniable":

> The accuracy of the facts is indeed usually irreproachable; it is only their presentation and interpretation which cause difficulty, not only for a Catholic reader, but for any completely non-denominational scholar.[61]

Syropoulos's *Memoirs* are above all characteristic of a paradigm of Orthodoxy which, in linking sound doctrine to *raison d'état*, led to the effective submission of the spiritual to the political power. The justification Syropoulos gives for his having signed the decree of Union, even though it was written five years after the events, is telling in this respect:

> Since this is the order given by our master, the Emperor, and in view of the fact that everyone believes that this is in the interest of the City and for the unity of Christians, I do not wish to seem not to love or not to desire the preservation and growth of my country, nor to be opposed to its greater good, to its progress, to what will be useful to Christians, or to all the other benefits which are expected from this for the City. As a result, I shall, by necessity, follow the majority in complying with the order and the will of the Emperor, but I protest even now that it is neither by conviction nor by free choice that I shall express an opinion that what has happened represents the sound doctrine of our Church. God knows, indeed, the preferences of my soul, that I do not accept the thing, and do not accept with a good will. Let the matter remain with God's mercy! I act thus for the present, but it will still be open to me later to act, so far as I am concerned in the matter, as I wish.[62]

The Council of Florence could have succeeded. The spirit of the Renaissance, which Gemistus Pletho (1355/60 – 1452) partly embodied, and the

---

60   Gill, *The Council of Florence*, viii–xv, and *Personalities of the Council of Florence*, 176–77: "Syropoulos' Memoirs do not purport to be a continuous narrative of even all the official or semi-official occurrences. The table given above shows that he records practically nothing of the relations with the Latins in the last months at Florence. They are recollections, and recollections almost entirely of inter-Greek relations. (. . .) The historian, therefore, when the sources are opposed, should prefer the 'Acta,' remembering, however, though never fully trusting, Syropoulos' description of the situation behind the scenes."
61   Laurent, *Mémoires de Syropoulos*, 32.
62   Ibid., 493.

demand for the unity and truth of Christian consciousness, represented by Nicholas of Cusa (1401 – 1464), were strongly manifested at the Council in 1439. In 1453 the German cardinal-priest Cusa, who had taken part in the Council of Florence, was still writing his De Pace Fidei. In this utopia, he imagined a universal council of all nations and all religions with the aim of working out a plan for perpetual peace.

This vision did not materialize, mainly because of the collapse of the Byzantine Empire, but also because of an erroneous political theology that was defended for many centuries by the representatives of the Churches. After 1453, the Byzantine patriarchs lost all their independence, and took their lead from then until the twentieth century from the Sultan.[63] On the Roman side, meanwhile, it was the neo-Platonic philosophy of Marsilio Ficino (1433 – 1499) that began to spread, with its dream of a universal religion with foundations that were more Platonic than Christian — to the point that Pope Clement VIII (1535 – 1605) wished to overcome the division of opinion in the age of the Reformation by founding a Chair in Platonism at the Sapienza University of Rome. But Cardinal Robert Bellarmine (1542 – 1621), a member of the Sacred Congregation of the Roman Inquisition, dissuaded him from promoting in this way "the cloud of error."[64]

The whole history of metaphysics was overturned. Father Henri de Lubac explained in his book Surnaturel in 1946 that Cardinal Bellarmine, after the Council of Trent, hypothesized the existence of a realm of "pure nature" in order to uphold the absolute gratuity of grace by which man is elevated to a supernatural condition. Subsequently, to the same end, theologians, in ever greater numbers, set themselves to presenting a "system" of "pure nature," according to which man is naturally ordered towards an end proportioned to his nature, that is, a natural end. By pure gratuity, however, it was added, God could lift man out of this natural state to a supernatural end. Man no longer possessed, in his vision of his own freedom, the fact of the inalienable character of his divine image. As George Chantraine explains, Thomists, Scotists, nominalists, Suarezians, and Molinists alike all saw in this teaching the shared thought of the Catholic Church, without which it was feared that the gratuity of the divine offer of salvation would be compromised. It was only in the twentieth century, thanks to the work of Henri de Lubac, and to patristic renewal and ecumenical dialogue, that Catholic theology was able to measure the

---

63   Lina Muhr Nehmé, 1453, Mahomet II impose le schisme orthodoxe.
64   Magnard, Pourquoi la religion?, 182.

extent of the forgetting of Being in modern theologians such as Jansen, Suarez, and Bellarmine.

> The system of "pure nature" is not traditional, contrary to the usual opinion of theologians until about halfway through the present century; it falsifies, indeed, the texts of St Thomas and St Augustine, and it goes against the teaching of Revelation as it has been received in the Church until our own day; because of this system, theology cut itself off from philosophy, and prepared the way for a separate philosophy, as we find in Descartes in the seventeenth century; furthermore, this system also showed evidence of a secularization that was already underway and that deprived Christians of a way to discriminate between secularization and engagement with the world.[65]

Yet as late as 1930, Pope Pius XI, who was hostile to the ecumenical movement, canonized Robert Bellarmine, and declared him, the following year, a Doctor of the Church. It was necessary to wait for the Second Vatican Council in 1961 for the memory of ecumenicity to be reborn in the ecclesial consciousness.

THE DENOMINATIONAL CONSCIOUSNESS OF THE CHURCH

The denominational consciousness of the Church is the result of a complex phenomenon marked by the victory of political Islam over Byzantine political theology, the promotion in Central and Western Europe of the principle that "the religion of the prince is the religion of the state," the consolidation of a clerical vision of the Church's action, the growing separation between philosophy and theology giving rise to affirmations of faithful memory, and the coming of a new form of missionary universalism that gave rise to deep ruptures between the different denominations, which had become dependent on secular interests.

The main explanation usually invoked is that religions entered, in the sixteenth and seventeenth centuries, into a cycle of violence so intense that it required an intervention on the part of the secular power to bring them back to reason by making them dependent on a pacifying secular state. But this very notion of a "war of religions" presents problems from a historical point of view, all the more so because it had been applied for

---

65   Georges Chantraine, "La théologie du surnaturel selon Henri de Lubac," *Nouvelle Revue Théologique*, 2: 119 (April, 1997), 227.

four centuries by historiographers and modern political scientists, whose work is questioned more and more today. This kind of explanation was also sharply criticized by the American theologian William Cavanaugh in a book called *The Myth of Religious Violence*:

> What I call the "myth of religious violence" is the idea that religion is a transhistorical and transcultural feature of human life, essentially distinct from "secular" features such as politics and economics, which has a peculiarly dangerous inclination to promote violence. Religion must therefore be tamed by restricting its access to public power. The secular nation-state then appears as natural, corresponding to a universal and timeless truth about the inherent dangers of religion. In this book, I challenge this piece of conventional wisdom, not simply by arguing that ideologies and institutions labeled "secular" can be just as violent as those labeled "religious," but by examining how the twin categories of religious and secular are constructed in the first place.[66]

Cavanaugh mentions a whole series of facts that invalidate the usual explanation, according to which the chaos of the wars in Europe in the sixteenth and seventeenth centuries was a peculiarly ecclesial phenomenon. He points in particular to the fact that the "Catholic" Kings of France allied themselves with Protestant sovereigns, and even with sultans, in order to combat the German Emperors, who, however, were also Catholic. There is insufficient space in this brief history of ecumenical consciousness to set out all these facts and to give an account of all Cavanaugh's arguments. I shall limit myself to quoting his conclusion:

> I argue that there is no transhistorical and transcultural essence of religion and that essentialist attempts to separate religious violence from secular violence are incoherent. What counts as religious or secular in any given context is a function of different configurations of power. The question then becomes why such essentialist constructions are so common. I argue that, in what are called "Western" societies, the attempt to create a transhistorical and transcultural concept of religion that is essentially prone to violence is one of the foundational legitimating myths of the liberal nation-state. The myth of religious violence helps to construct and marginalize a religious Other,

---

66   William T. Cavanaugh, *The Myth of Religious Violence: Secular Ideology and the Roots of Modern Conflict* (Oxford: OUP, 2009), 10.

prone to fanaticism, to contrast with the rational, peace-making, secular subject.[67]

This conclusion is of the highest interest for the present study, insofar as it allows us to understand that the rise of denominational consciousness in the modern age was the result, in the first place, of the victory of a new theology of salvation, that of the modern State, over the Papo-Caesarist and Caesaro-Papist conceptions of classical consciousness. It is well known, indeed, that the so-called secular conception of sovereignty was theorized in France by Jean Bodin. In 1576, Bodin published *The Six Books of the Republic*, a work in which the sovereignty of the state is presented as unique, absolute, indivisible, and non-transferable. There is here an obvious reprise of the divine sovereignty of classical theology, but now awarded to the secular power. Christianity's theology of politics had, however, shown to the men and women of the Renaissance all its limitations, and especially its failure to match the theology of the Gospel.

This is why Jean Bodin himself sought to conceive a new model for encounters between the various European religions. Between 1587 and 1593 he wrote the *Colloquium heptaplomeres de abditis rerum sublimium arcanis*, or *Colloquium of the Seven about Secrets of the Sublime*.[68] This work presents a dialogue between seven scholars belonging to three different religions (Judaism, Christianity, and Islam) concerning the respective merits of those religions. It finishes with a conclusion that is of the greatest interest here, insofar as the French jurisprudentialist proposes to establish a balance between the different symbolic and religious universes by acknowledging that they all share the same compass. The four poles of this compass are glory (piety), memory (mutual charity), the law (benignancy), and justice (Justice). The text refers to an edict of the Emperor Jovius (332–364), which it presents as paradigmatic for the new concord that is to be created:

> Curtius: ... Even better is the statement of Emperor Jovianus. After he proposed an edict of union, which he called Henoticon, to gather together the Pagans, Christians, Arians, Manichaeans, Jews, and almost two hundred sects in harmony, he constantly urged speakers to use restraint, lest they confound the people and

---

67 Ibid., 11.
68 *Colloque entre sept scavants qui sont de differens sentimens des secrets cachets des choses relevees*, ed. F. Berriot (Genève: Droz, 1984); *Colloquium of the Seven about Secrets of the Sublime*, trans. Marion Leathers Daniels Kuntz (Princeton, NJ: Princeton University Press, 1975).

the order of the state by seditious gatherings, but he urged them
to challenge the people to piety, uprightness, and mutual love. [69]

The very idea that the modern secular state might possess an absolute
sovereignty presents a problem not only to post-modern philosophers
such as Michel Foucault or Giorgio Agamben, but also to the new spiritual
theology of politics. But before broaching the topic of contemporary
reflection on the major event of the victory of the secular state in the
modern age, it is important to consider the three other major causes of
the rise of denominational identity.

THE INCURSION OF POLITICAL ISLAM INTO EUROPEAN ECUMENICAL CONSCIOUSNESS

The victories of Sultans Murad II and Mehmed II in the 1440s over
the Byzantine Empire, and the Fall of Constantinople in 1453, obliged
the Byzantine patriarchs to recognize new, Koranic laws, and to submit
to the sultans. The second Rome's entry into a condition of servitude
prompted the Church of Muscovy to reject the Council of unity at Florence (even though it has been supported by Metropolitan Isidore of
Kiev) in 1441, to proclaim itself autocephalous in 1448, and to regard
itself as the Third, and last, Rome. The Patriarch of Constantinople did
not recognize this Church until 1589. But on January 14, 1721, Peter
the Great suppressed the Patriarchate of Moscow, and replaced it with a
holy synod of bishops under his own control. The Russian Church had
to submit to the Tsars until 1917.

For his part, the Patriarch of Constantinople or Istanbul possessed,
under the system of Ottoman government, authority over the Churches
of Antioch, Jerusalem, Alexandria, and Cyprus. It had been given precedence in the Church — after the See of Rome — since the Fourth Ecumenical Council, a precedence which had, since the rupture with the
Roman Church in 1484, taken the form of Petrine oversight (the right
to convoke councils, the right of appeal, the right to recognize statutes
of autocephaly, and so on). [70] Patriarch Jeremias II of Constantinople
was, after a historic journey to Moscow, nevertheless forced to recognize
the autocephaly of the Church of Muscovy in 1589. The Patriarchate of
Constantinople nevertheless retained its authority over the Church of

---

69   Bodin, *Colloquium of the Seven*, 471.
70   The Ecumenical Patriarchate has granted autocephaly to the Churches of Moscow
(1589), Greece (1850), Serbia (1879), Romania (1885), Poland (1924), Albania (1937),
Bulgaria (1990), and the Czech Republic (1998).

Kiev for a further century. After the entry of Muscovite troops into Kiev, the see of Constantinople in 1686 granted the Patriarchate of Moscow the power temporarily to appoint the Metropolitan of Kiev, but on the condition that whoever was appointed should acknowledge the Patriarch of Constantinople as his primate.[71]

In the sixteenth century, on the initiative of Philip Melanchthon, a correspondence began between some German Protestants from Tübingen and the Byzantine Church.[72] Analyzing the letters exchanged between the group around Jacob Andrea and Martinus Crusus and the chancellery of Patriarch Jeremias II Tranos (1536 – 1595) shows the limits of the denominational logic that had been set up.[73] Patriarch Jeremias II read with care the copy of the Greek translation of the Augsburg Confession (1530) that had been sent to him. This text emphasized the faithfulness of the Reformers to "the ancient faith" in matters of doctrine concerning God, original sin, the Son of God, sanctification, the ministry of preaching, the Church, the holy Supper, baptism and confession, faith and works, and the cult of the saints.

In his reply, the Greek patriarch drew out eight points of agreement: 1. The authoritative and inspired character of Holy Scripture, and the need to translate it into the language of the people, contrary to the practice of the Roman Church of the period, which confined itself to Latin. 2. The Triune character of God. 3. The existence of original sin and the origin of evil do not come from God. 4. The existence of two natures in the unique Person of Christ. 5. Christ, and not the Pope, is alone the head of the Church. 6. A common belief in the second coming of Christ and in the Last Judgement. 7. Communion in two kinds, both in bread and in wine. 8. A rejection of the Roman doctrines concerning merits, indulgences, the treasure of the saints, purgatory, and clerical celibacy.

---

71   It was this decree which was annulled in 2018 by the Holy Synod of Constantinople after the latter confirmed not only that the Metropolitan of Kiev no longer recognized the Patriarch of Constantinople as primate, but also that a religious conflict of more than thirty years' duration had seen Ukraine torn up among three different Orthodox Churches. Constantin Vetochnikov, a researcher at the Collège de France, showed this in a conference paper: "La "concession" de la métropole de Kyiv au patriarche de Moscou en 1686: Analyse canonique," "Proceedings of the 23rd International Congress of Byzantine Studies, Belgrade, 22 – 27 August 2016," https://credo.press/221236/.

72   N. Kazarian, "La Chrismation dans la correspondance du Patriarche Jérémie II et des Luthériens de Tübingen (16e siècle)," *Chrismation et confirmation. Questions autour d'un rite post-baptismal* (Rome: Edizioni Liturgiche, 2009), 291–303.

73   Father Cyrille Argenti, *Histoire de l'Eglise en Orient et en Occident*, chapter 2, booklet no. 28 (Paris: Radio-Dialogue, 2009).

But the points of disagreement he raised prevented any possibility of a later rapprochement. 1. The importance of the apostolic tradition, that is to say, not the *sola scriptura* [Scripture alone] of the Lutherans, but the transmission of Scripture and of faith by the Tradition. 2. The procession of the Holy Spirit: the Lutherans, in contrast to Protestants today, had adopted the Roman doctrine of the *filioque*, and Jeremias II argued against it at length. 3. Free will, a refutation of the doctrine of predestination. 4. The sacraments: Jeremias II agrees with Catholics on their number, while Lutherans limit them to two. 5. The importance of baptism by immersion, contrary to the Catholic and Protestant practice of baptism by aspersion. 6. Confirmation and first communion on the same day as baptism, in order to enter the Church. 7. The Eucharistic mystery is truly the transformation of bread and wine into the body and blood of Christ, contrary to the Lutheran doctrine. 8. On this topic: the use of leavened bread, and not of unleavened bread, a practice which the Lutherans shared with the Roman Catholics. 9. The infallibility of the Church and the Ecumenical Councils. 10. The importance of feast days, prayers to the Virgin Mary and to the saints, prayers for the dead, the veneration of icons and relics, and the custom of fasting.

In 1629, wishing to develop these first inter-denominational exchanges, Patriarch Cyril Loukaris published an *Eastern Confession of the Christian Faith* whose aim was to bring about a synthesis between Eastern theology and Calvinist theology. In it, he affirmed, in particular, that "we believe that man is justified by faith and not by works."[74]

The Orthodox Church of Kiev, despite its rupture with the main body of the Church in 1596, remained faithful to the spirit of the Council of Florence until the seventeenth century, through the figure of Metropolitan Peter Mogila. The latter wished, as late as the 1640s, to reunite his Church with Rome.[75] This fact had a considerable influence on all the Orthodox Churches assembled at the synods of Jassy.[76] Metropolitan Peter Mogila

---

74   The Patriarch of Alexandria, Metrophanes Critopoulos (1589 – 1639), a Greek former monk from Mount Athos, who was close to Loukaris, also composed a confession of faith with a view to a synthesis. For him, the Church, as the Bride of Christ, could not be identified with an association having a legal status. This conception of the Church witnesses to the fact that the apophaticism of Eastern theology was becoming more and more incapable of communicating a conception of the Church as a constituted institution.
75   Antoine Arjakovsky, "Towards a Future Collaboration of Byzantine Catholics and Byzantine Orthodox Christianity," in *Arriving at a Common Narrative: The 'Lviv Sobor' of 1946 and Its Aftermath to the Present*, ed. Daniel Galadza (Vienna: University of Vienna/Stiftung Pro Oriente, 2021).
76   James Likoudis, "Testimony to the Primacy of the Pope by a 17c. Russian Orthodox Prelate," https://web.archive.org.

of Kiev, who had received the title of exarch from the throne of the Apostolic See of Constantinople, published, in reply, in 1640, a Latin *Orthodoxa confessio fidei catholicae et apostolicae Ecclesiae Orientalis.* This confession of faith began with the words: *Homo christianus orthodoxocatholicus ut unitam eternam assequatur, quaue obseruare debet?* *Fidem rectam et bona opera* [What must Christian Catholic-Orthodox man observe in order to attain eternal unity? Correct faith and good works].[77] One can see that the Eastern Christian identity was still understood in a pre-denominational way. For the Metropolitan of Kiev, the Eastern conception of sanctification/justification was closer to the Catholic tradition than to the Calvinist. His "Confession" received the approbation of a pan-Orthodox synod held at Iasi in 1642, and then again in 1643, by the four Eastern Patriarchs. A series of councils held at the initiative of Patriarch Dositheus thirty years later, in 1672, at Constantinople, then at Jerusalem, and then again at Constantinople in 1691, elicited a consensus of the Orthodox Churches around this Confession of Faith. That is why Father Georgij Florovsky acknowledged in 1936 that, despite the Catholic influences on it, Mogila's Confession of Faith contained no errors in relation to the Orthodox Christian tradition.

Mogila's Confession was not acceptable to the "Protestant" world because of the fact that it considered charitable works as a source of sanctification. But it was also unacceptable to the "Catholic" world insofar as it rejected any juridical primacy for the Roman Popes. The Oriental Patriarchs declared in 1848 that the supreme authority in the Church was neither the Pope, nor even the Ecumenical Council, but the "consciousness of the Christian people."[78] As Jaroslav Pelikan writes, "neither the biblical spiritualism of the Protestant view nor the juridical institutionalism of the Roman Catholic view could do justice to the Eastern understanding of the authority of the fathers in its dynamic relation to Scripture and the councils."[79] The political ruptures had become ecclesial ones too.

Nicolae Iorga (1871–1940), a Romanian historian and politician, gave a nostalgic account of this period in his book *Byzantium after Byzantium*. He showed that the hopes of a cultural and religious resurrection of the Byzantine universe that had been raised in the Mediterranean, especially in the sixteenth-century Balkans and Greece, by the fact of the Ottoman Empire's weakness, had no lasting foundation:

---

77 Antoine Malvy and Marcel Viller, eds., *La confession orthodoxe de Pierre Moghila* (Rome: Orientalia Christiana, 10), 1.
78 "Encyclique des Patriarches orientaux," *Orthodoxie en Abitibi* (abitibi-orthodoxe.ca).
79 Jaroslav Pelikan, *The Spirit of Eastern Christendom* (600–1700) (Chicago: University of Chicago Press, 1974), 289.

The ecumenical patriarch ... came to take the place of the vanished empire by cooperating with the existing empire. A trend of union of all the Churches from Cairo to Moscow to Venice appeared in Ancona, Crete, in the sixteenth century, and for a while it was believed that the legacy of Constantine the Great, of Justinian, and of the Comnenus family would be passed on to the one who had a court similar to that of the old emperors and who, on his vestment of coarse black wool, was wearing the Imperial eagle. Through commerce, taking on lease even the revenues of the Ottoman Empire, the Byzantine aristocracy, which, to protect itself from conversion to Islam, had remained in hiding for a time, rose again. Proving themselves worthy of their great name, these "archons" understood how to gain through the Church, but also outside of the Church, supreme authority over things. The tolerance of Selim II, the first sultan of the Turkish decline, made possible, in the same sixteenth century, the epoch of Michael Cantacuzenus, the clever and arrogant businessman whom one of the viziers nicknamed "the son of Satan." (...) But it was these "Phanariots" who brought about the end of Byzantium. As dragomans of the Porte, as informers in the capitals neighboring free Christianity, they became impregnated with a double state of mind, harmful for Byzantium, able to resist all dangers until then .... This represented, at the dawn of the nineteenth century, the death of Byzantium. It had survived for almost four centuries in its imperial Christian form, after it had survived for one thousand years in its previous Roman form.[80]

A spiritual revival did appear in Eastern Christianity in the eighteenth and nineteenth centuries, with the publication of the *Philokalia of the Neptic Saints* in Venice by Nicodemus the Hagiorite (1782), and then with its diffusion into the Balkan and Slav lands. Against the rationalist conception of the world of the Enlightenment, the *Philokalia* showed that human rationality was fulfilled, after a combat with the passions, in a meeting with the divine Spirit. As the Orthodox priest Cyril Argenti (1918 – 1994) wrote, this work of faith-intelligence, this quest for *nepsis*, that is, for sobriety of soul and heart, is indissociable from the Orthodox Christian conception of Trinitarian life.

---

80   Nicolae Iorga, *Byzantium after Byzantium*, trans. Laura Treptow (Iasi, Oxford, and Portland: Center for Romanian Studies, with the Romanian Institute of International Studies, 2000), 27–30.

Life in Christ, orthodoxy, is a union with Christ, a union that is possible and necessary not only for great saints and mystics, but for each Christian. When Christ prays to his Father, on the eve of his own death, He prays "that they may be one in Me, I in them and they in Me, as I am in Thee, Father, and Thou art in Me" (John 17:21). The goal of the Christian life is "life in Christ," that is, to be grafted on to Christ, to be united to Him so that he can pass on to us the sap of his Holy Spirit, when we become a single plant with him, when we are the shoots of a vine of which He is the stem. It is this "life in Christ" that, from generation to generation, the holy Fathers have lived especially intensely, so that each of us may, little by little, come to participate in it. Each time we take communion, when we unite our body and soul to the body and blood of Christ, we are united with Him, we become one flesh with Him, we inaugurate this "life in Christ," which we feed by daily communion, by reading Scripture, by prayer.[81]

The *Philokalia* was translated into several languages, and gave rise to a spiritual revival.[82] But this spiritual revival was also contested by Russian religious philosophy. There was in hesychasm a particular method of attaining to individual deification.[83] This involved a rejection of the world, an apophatic conception of the divine mysteries, and a reluctance to associate the powerful vision of the divine energies present in creation with ways of transforming society and economic and political life. Moreover, as François Thual writes, the "dowry of Byzantium" consisted above all in the transformation of a Constantinian conception of the Empire-Church into a multitude of autocephalous nation-state-churches putting themselves forward as the legitimate heirs of the Empire-Church.[84]

AFFIRMATIONS OF MEMORY

As well as the incursion of political Islam into European civilization, and the identitarian retreat of Eastern Christian spirituality, other factors

---

81   Argenti, *Histoire de l'Église*. The King James Version text of the relevant part of John 17:21 is as follows: "That they may all be one; as thou, Father, art in me, and I in thee, that they may also be one in us . . . ."

82   The *Philokalia* was translated into Church Slavonic in St Petersburg in 1793, then into Russian in 1877, Romanian in 1946, English in 1951, and German and French after 1953. Paisius Velichkovsky (1722–1794) translated the Philokalia into Church Slavonic and Russian at Neamts, in Moldova.

83   Hiéromoine Élisée, *Le monachisme d'Orient* (Paris: Cerf, 2017).

84   François Thual, *Le douaire de Byzance* (Paris: Ellipses, 1998).

also put an end to the medieval conception of universality, beginning with the rupture between the discourse of faith and that of reason. Let us begin by mentioning the rise of a new philosophical relationship to the world initiated by humanism and nominalism. William of Ockham (c. 1285 – 1347) held that universal concepts were only words, without any substantial reality. This put in question the intellectual premises of traditional theology. Thanks to printing, these new ideas enjoyed widespread dissemination. On February 23, 1455, Gutenberg produced at Mainz the first Bible printed with moveable type.

The discovery of new worlds also overturned existing representations. On October 12, 1492, Christopher Columbus disembarked on an island in the Bahamas, thus beginning the European conquest of America. The desire for expression in vernacular languages came into conflict with the universality of Latin Christianity. Francis I's Ordinance of Villers-Cotterêts, in 1539, made the use of French in all legal acts, notarized contracts, and official legislation compulsory. To these revolutions we may add the coming, in Europe, of a certain cultural *estrangement*, to use Yves Congar's term, between East and West.[85] As a result, the men and women of the Renaissance felt the need to assert their identity by adopting new confessions of faith, at Augsburg in 1530, at La Rochelle in 1571, at Jassy in 1642, and at Westminster in 1646.

Three main spiritual types then appeared and were, gradually, defined as "Orthodox," "Catholic," and "Protestant." Among the latter are found denominational subdivisions, linked to the figures of Martin Luther and John Calvin, but also to schisms and revival movements. All belonged to the same level of consciousness, according to which the Orthodoxy of faith is characterized above all by a faithful memory (whether faithful to the Councils, to the Pope, or to Scripture).[86] This rupture between faith and reason led to many controversies. For a faithful memory can also become a repetitive memory when it is not in accord with the eschatological pole of glory.

It suffices to mention the major disagreement between Christians over the mystery of the Eucharist. As Yves Krumenacker has shown in his biography of John Calvin, patristic sophiological thought had become foreign to the Genevan reformer. In his *Institutes of the Christian Religion*,

---

85   Yves Congar, *After Nine Hundred Years: The Background of the Schism between the Eastern and Western Churches* (New York: Fordham University Press, 1959), 1 – 6. ("Estrangement" is in English in the original text. — *Translator.*)
86   Arjakovsky, *What Is Orthodoxy?*.

published in 1650, Calvin speaks of divine wisdom as a "labyrinth" from which man can find no way out (IVC, III, XXI, 1). Calvin did not hesitate to dissociate the two natures of Christ, divine and human:

> For Calvin, since the Ascension, Christ is in the Kingdom of God, and his human nature is no longer in the world (this is why, strictly speaking, the bread of the Supper cannot be the "body of Christ"), and divine presence cannot in any way be found in the world.[87]

In anticipation of the five hundredth anniversary of the Reformation in 2017, the Lutheran-Roman Catholic Commission on Unity prepared a historical and theological report aimed at throwing light in an ecumenical way on the reasons for the divergences in the sixteenth century between Catholic and Reformed Christians. In particular, the Commission sought to recover a differentiated consensus on a shared understanding of the sacrament of the Eucharist.[88] The essence of their conclusions can be summarized as follows. Luther's main objection to the Catholic doctrine of the Eucharist concerned the understanding of the mass as a sacrifice. The eschatological approach of the primitive Church, which re-actualized the unique sacrifice of Christ by means of *anamnesis*, the narrative of the fulfillment of the Passion, and by *epiclesis*, the invocation to the Father to send the Spirit upon the gifts of bread and wine, was no longer understood, to the point where, for many, the celebration of the mass was itself a further sacrifice. Now, the Eucharist was not, for the German reformer, a "good work," because this would be to transform a divine gift into a human work. The Commission admitted that Catholics had difficulties recognizing eucharistic sacrifice as the unique sacrifice of Jesus Christ.

On the Catholic side, Luther's rejection of the concept of transubstantiation provoked doubts as to whether the doctrine of the real presence of Christ had been fully acknowledged in his theology. It was established, however, that even if Luther considered the distinction made between substance and accidents as too philosophical, he did not doubt the real presence of Christ "in, and under the kinds of, the bread and wine." This

---

87   Yves Krumenacker, *Calvin. Au-delà des légendes* (Paris: Bayard, 2009), 490. This position has to be qualified, in Martin Hoegger's view, because for Calvin it is the Holy Spirit which makes us communicate "really and truly in the body and blood of Christ" (Institute IV. 17. 33).

88   Lutheran-Roman Catholic Commission on Unity, *From Conflict to Communion: Lutheran-Catholic Common Commemoration of the Reformation in 2017* (Leipzig: Evangelische Veranstalt, 2013).

exchange of properties was for him analogous to the union of the divine and human natures in Christ. Advances in theology in the twentieth century, as well as in the ecumenical movement, have, nevertheless, allowed Catholic and Lutheran theologians to restore the notion of anamnesis to a place of honor, and thus to take their distance from the theology of supernatural grace. In 1978, in a document called "The Eucharist," the Catholic and Lutheran theologians affirmed that:

> The Lutheran tradition affirms the Catholic tradition that the consecrated elements do not simply remain bread and wine but rather by the power of the creative word are given as the body and blood of Christ. In this sense Lutherans also could occasionally speak, as does the Greek tradition, of a "change" ("The Eucharist," 51). Both Catholics and Lutherans "have in common a rejection of a spatial or natural manner of presence, and a rejection of an understanding of the sacrament as only commemorative or figurative" ("The Eucharist," 16).[89]

The progress made in 2017, however, consists in understanding that the rationale of faithful memory alone was insufficient. Only a purified metaphysical intelligence, that is to say a metaphysics that is eschatological, personalist, sapiential, and participative, would be in a position to grasp the sacramental event in an orthodox manner. Moreover, Luther criticized the Catholic practice which forbade lay people to receive communion under the two kinds of the body and blood of Christ. But it was admitted that the difference was more a practical than a theological one. The Commission judged that "Catholics and Lutherans are at one in the conviction that bread and wine belong to the complete form of the Eucharist."[90] It is thus that, after four centuries of polemics, Catholic and Lutheran theologians managed to overcome the great rupture of the sixteenth century.

Some contemporary Catholic theologians, however, had a less conciliatory approach. In 1962–1965, the Catholic theologian Hans Küng took part in the Second Vatican Council. This universal council proposed an *aggiornamento* with reference to the modern period of the Roman Church. His unaccommodating, but also un-nuanced definition of the denominational consciousness of the Catholic Church in the modern era testifies to the wounds inflicted in the course of the ages within the Roman Church itself:

---

89 From *Conflict to Communion*, 58.
90 "The Eucharist," 64, quoted in From *Conflict to Communion*, 60.

Down to the Second Vatican Council (1962 – 1965), the Western Church essentially retained the form that it had taken in the high Middle Ages. Indeed, some Catholics fixated on Rome still remain imprisoned in this medieval paradigm. But this Roman system clearly contradicts the gospel. For the church of the New Testament is: — not centralized: but the Ecclesia Romana claims to be the 'mother,' with the pope as 'father'; — not legalistic: but the pope wants to be executive, legislative, and judiciary at the same time, supported by a canon law which he himself has fabricated, the interpretation of which requires a science of canon law; — not politicized: but the Roman Church sets itself up alongside the state power as an independent institution of government with an international status, a diplomatic service, and special rights; — not clericalized: but a patriarchal hierarchy and a clergy of celibate males set above the people clearly dominates the laity; — not militarized: but over the centuries a militant church has manifested itself in 'holy' wars of conversion, wars against heretics, crusades (even against fellow Christians) and wars of religion, and also in persecutions of Jews, burnings of heretics and witches.[91]

The Churches' self-understanding, beginning with that of the Catholic Church in the Counter-Reformation period, was very different. Moreover, the different spiritual types that emerged with the change in consciousness were, to begin with, not completely fixed. In 1523, the Catholic priest Erasmus of Rotterdam, in his treatise, *Spongia Adversus Aspergines Hutteni* [A sponge for von Hutten's aspersions], imagined a faith common to all Christians based on a few fundamental points (the existence of God, the immortality of the soul, the resurrection of Christ, and so on), in which the question of knowing whether the college of Cardinals was an indispensable limb of the Church was not considered as an article of faith. As Stefan Zweig wrote, Erasmus was one of the first European intellectuals. He approached humanism in an ecumenical manner, as an antidote to ecclesial fanaticism, and as a renewal of the spirit of chivalry.

> So far as Erasmus was concerned, there existed neither a moral nor an unbridgeable antagonism between Jesus and Socrates, between Christian teaching and the wisdom of classical antiquity, between piety and ethics. He, an ordained priest, accepted the heathen into his intellectual paradise; and in the same spirit of

---

91   Küng, *Tracing the Way*, 221.

tolerance he took his place side by side with the Fathers of the Church. Philosophy, so far as he was concerned, was just as pure a method of the search for God as was theology. . . . [92]

This is why, even so late as April to May 1541, at the Colloquy of Regensburg presided over by Emperor Charles V, it was possible to believe that a reconciliation could be found between the "Catholics" and the "Protestants" in the Holy Roman Empire. But the exchanges between John Calvin, Philip Melanchthon, and Martin Bucer, on the one hand, and, on the other, Gasparro Contarini (the Pope's legate), Johannes Eck, and Johannes Gropper did not yield any result. So the Emperor ended up imposing his own will on the Empire in 1555 with the Peace of Augsburg, which recognized an equality of rights among Lutherans and Catholics.

In France, the Colloquy of Poissy called by Catherine de Medici in September–October 1561 bore no tangible fruit, despite the presence of humanists such as the Chancellor of France, Michel de l'Hôpital, and the Protestant theologian Théodore de Bèze. The edict of tolerance of January 1562 was swept away by war between the various noble families who were contesting power, especially after the massacre of Wassy on March 1, 1562. At the same time, royal authority was changing from a feudal to an absolutist type. [93] King Henry IV imposed an edict of tolerance in 1598, but it was respected for only a few decades. The separation between denominations became institutionalized in Europe after the Treaty of Westphalia in 1648, and in France, in 1685 with the revocation of the Edict of Nantes by Louis XIV. As a result of these decisions, the princes ended up fixing denominational types by imposing their law: *Cujus regio ejus religio*, "the prince's religion is the religion of the realm."

There then began the denominational era of ecclesial consciousness. True, each of these spiritual types continued to evolve through to the twentieth century. Eminent personalities in each of the denominations retained the memory that their Church was attached to the one Church of Christ — personalities such as, to mention only a few, the French Catholic scholar Guillaume Postel (1510 – 1581), the German Lutheran mystic Jakob Boehme (1575 – 1624), the German Lutheran theologian Georg Calixtus (1586 – 1656), the Orthodox Metropolitan of Moldavia Peter Mogila (1596 – 1646), the Spanish Franciscan Christobal Spinola (1626 – 1695), the

---

92   Stefan Zweig, *Erasmus: The Right to Heresy*, trans. Eden and Cedar Paul (London: Souvenir Press, 1979), 4.

93   Noël Valois, "Les essais de conciliation religieuse au début du règne de Charles IX," *Revue d'histoire de l'Église de France*, 31 (119) (1945), 237–76.

suffragan bishop of Trier, Johann Nikolaus von Hontheim (Febronius) (1701 – 1790), the German Protestant theologian Friedrich Schleiermacher (1768 – 1834). All of these sought to recover the underlying friendship uniting those baptized in Christ. The denominational paradigm of the age, however, was against them.

This new ecclesial consciousness consisted in identifying the Church of Christ with the theological, juridical, and sacramental borders of one's own denomination. It gave rise to new ecclesial institutions such as the Lutheran Church and the Reformed Church, or, again, the Church of England, institutions which themselves fractured into several other ecclesial communities, such as the puritan Baptists and the Mennonites (disciples of Menno Simons, 1496 – 1561). John Wesley (1703 – 1791), while remaining faithful to the Church of England, proposed a new way of opening oneself to the divine Spirit [l'Esprit divin]. This way was inspired by the *devotio moderna* of Thomas à Kempis and by the Moravian Pietists. It stirred up a spiritual revival movement that gave rise to the formation of Methodism. In 1743, Wesley drew up a series of "general rules" of discipline for the "bands" that he had created and that multiplied in England, but also in the United States and across the world. Later, a dynamic of "re-awakenings" founded on the personal conversion of individuals convinced that they had been saved by grace, and that it was necessary to be reborn in the Spirit, characterized the Anglo-Saxon world. This was so far true that in the nineteenth century inter-denominational rapprochements began within the new family of Protestant Christians calling themselves "Evangelicals."[94]

Such a denominational consciousness also gave rise to the Catholic Counter-Reformation (or Catholic Reformation) after the Council of Trent was brought to completion in 1563, the creed of a triumphalist religion that led directly to heaven and wished to lead all the faithful with it. The Roman Church's watchword became "No salvation outside the Catholic Church!" This is why the Papacy endowed itself with new institutions and new administrative organs such as the *Sacra Congregatio de Propaganda Fide* (Congregation for the Evangelization of Peoples) in 1622.

The historian Jean Delumeau believes that the Catholic Reformation had deleterious consequences on a spiritual level. According to Delumeau, the Counter-Reformation "misused ideas of guilt, defined mortal sin with an inhuman rigidity, and aroused in the most delicate and fragile souls

---

94   Timothy J. Demy and Paul R. Shockley, *Evangelical America: An Encyclopedia of Contemporary American Religious Culture* (Santa Barbara, CA: ABC-CLIO, 2017).

an unhealthy obsession with moral scruples." Delumeau holds that the Counter-Reformation legitimized persecutions of Protestant minorities in France until the 1780s.[95] Moreover, it confused Christianity with Latin culture, and did not attempt to understand non-European civilizations, even to the point of remaining silent for a long while about the slave trade.

Nevertheless, Delumeau acknowledges that this Catholic Reformation gave rise to new forms of creativity, such as Baroque art. New figures of great sanctity appeared such as the Basque-Spanish theologian Ignatius of Loyola (1491 – 1556), the founder of the Society of Jesus, Carlo Borromeo (1538 – 1584), the Italian Archbishop of Milan, Cardinal Filippo Neri (1515 – 1595), the Italian founder of the Oratory, the Spanish Carmelite priest and mystic John of the Cross (1542 – 1591), and the French nun and mystic Marguerite-Marie Alacoque (1647 – 1690).

In such a state of affairs, attempts at inter-denominational rapprochement were doomed to failure. This is what emerges from the correspondence that began between the Lutheran philosopher and mathematician Gottfried Wilhelm Leibniz (1646 – 1716) and Jacques-Bénigne Bossuet (1627 – 1704), the Catholic bishop of Meaux and the tutor of the Dauphin, the future Louis XV. The politician and member of the Académie Française Charles Rémusat in 1861 wrote as follows on the subject of their non-dialogue:

> One need not study the authentic documents for long before noticing the lack of sympathy and the fundamental conflict that forever divides the Protestants and the Catholics, Leibniz and Bossuet. One sees instantly that for the first group, this is a negotiation which must bring the two parties into agreement without humiliating or wounding the pride of either of them; for the second, it is a controversy, from which one of the two must emerge victorious. A negotiation has to end in a deal; a controversy has to end in a conversion. What Leibniz wants is peace; what Bossuet wants is victory.[96]

A trend towards "reasonable orthodoxy" can, however, be seen with the beginning of the Republic of Letters, a trend that included eminent intellectual figures such as Descartes, Bayle, Leibniz, Locke, and many others. From 1833 onwards, under pressure from Evangelical Protestants, Great Britain abolished slavery, which also had worldwide repercussions.

---

95 "Les Églises sous Louis XV (de 1724 à 1760)," https://www.museeprotestant.org/.
96 Charles de Rémusat, "Leibniz et Bossuet, d'après leur correspondance," *Revue des Deux Mondes* (second series) 31 (1861), 386 – 411.

MISSIONARY CONSCIOUSNESS AND SCHISMS

ECCLESIAL UNIVERSALISM AND CO-TERRITORIALITY

The denominational consciousness of the whole Christian world in the modern era led to a movement for the expansion of ecclesial institutions beyond their traditional territories. This movement was to the detriment of local churches that had already existed for several centuries in lands considered as virgin by the new denominations. For the Orthodox theologian Grigorios Papathomas, the new universalist ecclesiology came into conflict with the fractal and Eucharistic ecclesiology of the first millennium, for which there could only be one bishop in any given city. This new universalist and pastoral ecclesiology was born at the moment of the Crusades in the thirteenth century. It privileged the pastoral bond of the bishop with his church over the Eucharistic bond of the faithful gathered together in the same place.

Stimulated by the phenomenon of the verticalization of ecclesial power, the new attitude gave rise to an ecclesiology of co-territoriality. This phenomenon did not exist in the first millennium, because of the power of the Empire. Drawing encouragement from the secular powers from the sixteenth to the twentieth centuries, the ecclesiology of co-territoriality was pursued alongside the expansion of all the churches, to the point of forming the main basis of colonialism. This also gave rise to an "ethno-phyletist" Orthodox ecclesiology insofar as, according to Papathomas, "the jurisdiction of these churches is exercised knowingly and above all over *persons*, as in Reformation ecclesiology":

> This *double co-territoriality*, which resulted from the political situation created by the Crusades, was imposed and perpetuated with this homogeneous structure until the Reformation. In other words, from the thirteenth to the sixteenth century we have, on one hand, an ecclesiastical *mono-territoriality* and *mono-jurisdiction* in Western Europe, in the territory of the Roman patriarchate, while, on the other hand, this same patriarchate is also encouraging an *ecclesiastical co-territoriality*, and, later, the exercise of a *cross-border (multi-)jurisdiction (hyperoria)* in the territories of the other churches of the East, where, henceforth, there begins to be a *co-territoriality* at once *exterior (outside the communion)* and *interior (inside the communion)*. In these newly-born ecclesiological idioms, it was also possible to detect the premises of the

113

universalist ecclesiology that developed later, especially just after the Reformation . . . . [97]

Protestant Pietism rejected the idea of a state church. Jean de Labadie (1610 – 1674) in France, Philipp Jakob Spener (1635 – 1705) in Alsace, August Hermann Francke (1663 – 1727) in the Margraviate of Brandenburg, and Count Nicolaus Ludwig von Zinzendorf in Moravia (1700 – 1760) regarded the Augsburg Confession as an ecumenical confession of faith.[98] This began a new period of Christian ecumenical consciousness. The Danish-Halle Mission was set up with the aim of spreading the knowledge of God all round the world and of building a *spiritual fellowship*, a "universal Church." It was no longer doctrine which was the heart of Christian faith but its capacity to extend across the whole planet.

The expansionist missionary movement concerned all the churches because, at the end of the nineteenth century, missions of the Russian Church can be found in California, missions of the Anglican and Baptist Churches in India, and those of the Moravian Brothers all around the world. Nicolaus Ludwig, Count von Zinzendorf (1700 – 1760) is a major figure in the German Protestantism of the eighteenth century: a Lutheran pastor, a bishop of the Moravian Church, and an *ordinarius* (superior) of the communities of the Brothers of Unity (*unitas fratrum*). The Moravian Brothers formed a community which was founded in the fifteenth century in the Kingdom of Bohemia, and which was forced to go into exile in Saxony in 1722 as a result of persecution. During the years 1719 – 1720, Zinzendorf made a study visit to France and the Netherlands: he then bound himself in friendship to people of other denominations, and began to think about the possibility of a union between the Churches. Among Catholic personalities, Zinzendorf had close relations with the Cardinal de Noailles, to whom he had wished to dedicate the French translation of Johann Arndt's *Four Books of True Christianity*. In August 1727, he founded the Herrnhut community, and dedicated himself thereafter to proclaiming the Gospel and to dialogue between the different Christian churches, undertaking a great many journeys and missions. He was ordained as a bishop of the Moravian Brethren in Berlin on May 20, 1737. He set up missionary colonies in the Antilles (1732), in Greenland (1733), among the North American Indians (1735). By the time of Zinzendorf's death, the

---

97 Grigorios Papathomas, "Au temps de la post-ecclésialité," Istina 51.1 (2006), 64–84.
98 Ruth Rouse, ed., A History of the Ecumenical Movement, Volume One, 1517–1948 (Geneva: World Council of Churches, 1954), 101.

Moravian Brethren had sent missionary colonies from Herrnhut into Livonia, and to the north coast of the Baltic Sea, to South Carolina, to Surinam, to several regions of South America, to the East Indies, to the Egyptian Copts, to the Inuits of Labrador, and to the west coast of South Africa.

The British Baptist minister William Carey (1761 – 1834), meanwhile, published in 1791 *An Enquiry into the Obligations of Christians to Use Means for the Conversion of the Heathens*. This book gave rise to the creation of the Baptist Missionary Society, as well as that of the Serampore Theological College, which was in the nineteenth and twentieth centuries a nursery for Baptist missionaries in India. Carey himself left for India in 1793. In Carey's lifetime, the Bible was translated into no fewer than forty-two languages and dialects, beginning with Sanskrit and Bengali. These missions greatly contributed to European colonialism around the world.

The limitations of this political conception of the universality of the Church appeared very early on, as soon as the sixteenth century, but especially with the Thirty Years' War in the Holy Roman Empire between 1618 and 1648.

THE UNIAT QUESTION AND THE CASE OF THE KIEVAN CHURCH

According to Jean Delumeau, it was in the eighteenth century, above all, that the Roman denominational conception of universality displayed its limitations:

> The Catholic Reformation, by means of its doctrinal clarifications, its enrichment of religious language, its artistic innovations, its consolidation of the training of the faithful, and its educational and charitable initiatives, contributed to the emergence of Western modernity, as, in a parallel way, the Protestant Reformation did too. It was not a backwards-looking enterprise. It was instead only when, in the eighteenth century, it lost its dynamism that it became enclosed in an over-insulated clerical world from which the new scientific and technological culture was excluded.[99]

This point of view could be disputed by reminding ourselves that all Churches since the end of the sixteenth century, including the Roman Church, had moved away from the ecclesiology of the Council of Florence. After that time, indeed, the competition to which the new missionary Churches devoted themselves led to the breaking-off of communion between the Churches. Because the "Uniat question" remains one of the

---

99   Jean Delumeau, *Un christianisme pour demain* (Paris: Hachette, 2003 [1977]), 328.

main subjects of tension among the Churches today, it is well to return to the history of the chief of these unified Churches, that is, the Church of Kiev.[100]

Between the thirteenth and the fifteenth centuries, within the Metropolitante of Kiev, after the partition of Rus into two political entities, two Orthodox Churches were progressively constituted as the legitimate heirs of the See of the city. That of Kiev-Halych lived under the domination of the Kingdom of Poland from 1350 onwards, then of the Grand Duchy of Lithuania from 1385 onwards. Until the sixteenth century it was in communion both with Constantinople, its Mother Church, and with Rome, following the decisions of the Council of Florence. The second Church, that of Kiev-Moscow, had its seat in Moscow after the removal of Metropolitan Pyotr of Kiev and all Rus to Vladimir and then to Moscow in 1325. Neither the Church at Halych nor that at Moscow was an autonomous church. This is why the Church of Kiev was still represented at the Council of Florence by a single Metropolitan for a double entity, the Greek Metropolitan Isidore, whom the Patriarch of Constantinople named as Metropolitan of Kiev and all Rus. The latter supported the decisions of the Council. As is well known, Grand Prince Vasily II rejected the decisions of the Council of Florence and declared the Church of Kiev and Moscow autonomous from Constantinople in 1448.

The Church of Kiev-Halych thus remained the only Orthodox Church present at the Council of Florence not to have rejected the reconciliation with Rome. Pope Pius II (1458 – 1464), on September 3, 1458, signed a bull, Decens reputamus et congrutum, addressed to Isidore's successor, Metropolitan Gregorios of Kiev-Halych (1458 – 1472) to document the fact that the Orthodox Metropolitanate of Kiev was divided into two parts: the upper part lying in the Grand Duchy of Moscow, and the lower part, which was made up of the Polish-Lithuanian state. The Church of Kiev supported the formation of the Union of Lublin in 1569 between the

---

100   M. Tchoubaty, Istoria Hrystianstva na Rusi-Ukrainy, 2 vols (Rome: UCU, Neo Eboraci, 1976), I.1; Ukrains'ka tserkva: Narisi z istorii Ukrains'koi Pravoslavnoi Tserkvi K, 2 vols (Kiev: Ukraina, 1993); Ivan Ogienko: Ukrains'ka tserkva (litopys.org.ua); Borys Gudziak, Crisis and Reform: Kievan Metropolitanate, the Patriarchate of Constantinople and the Genesis of the Union of Brest (Cambridge, MA: Harvard University Press [Harvard Series in Ukrainian Studies], 1996); J. Meyendorff, A. Papadakis, L'Orient chrétien et l'essor de la papauté (Paris: Cerf, 2001); Vladimir Vodoff, Naissance de la chrétienté russe (Paris: Fayard, 1988); Andreas Kappeler, Petite Histoire de l'Ukraine (Paris: IES, 1997). (The "Uniat" Churches are those of Eastern Christendom in communion with Rome that nevertheless keep their own languages, rites, and canon law. See Cross and Livingstone, Oxford Dictionary of the Christian Church, "Uniat Churches."— Translator.)

Kingdom of Poland and the Grand Duchy of Lithuania. This republic of two nations can be thought of as anticipating the post-modern model of the European Union, in which two states agree to share a certain number of aspects of their sovereignty.

The Church of Moscow, for its part, held that, after the Fall of Rome in 410 and the Fall of Constantinople in 1453, it had become "the third Rome." In 1589, under pressure from the regent, Boris Godunov, but also for internal reasons, Patriarch Jeremias II of Constantinople decided formally to recognize the autocephaly of the Muscovite church. Metropolitan Job of Moscow was raised to the title of Patriarch of "Moscow and all Rus." This decision preceded by several years the beginning of the Time of Troubles in Muscovy, a period of anarchy that came to an end only in 1613 with the rise of the Romanov dynasty.

The Orthodox bishops of the Church of Kiev-Halych were distrustful towards Muscovy, a state in the process of formation that claimed authority over the Church of Kiev. This state had expanded considerably under Tsars Ivan III (1440 – 1505) and Ivan IV, "the Terrible" (1530 – 1584). The bishops of Kiev-Halych turned towards Rome. But Pope Clement VIII did not regard the Church of Kiev-Halych as a church capable of setting its own conditions (thirty-three articles had been drafted in 1595 and sent to the Pope), but as an *ecclesia dissidens*. The Orthodox bishops of the Kiev-Halych Metropolitanate had no choice but to submit. The era of Roman ecclesiological exclusivism had returned: "no salvation outside the Roman Catholic Church." In 1596, six of the eight bishops of the Church of Kiev-Halych decided to place themselves under the jurisdiction of the Patriarchate of Rome at the Council of Brest.[101]

This provoked a negative reaction from two bishops who decided to re-establish their membership of the community of Eastern Churches through the Patriarchate of Jerusalem. A third Church of Kiev appeared, declaring itself independent of both Rome and Moscow. This new Church resisted the ascendancy of the Church of Kiev-Moscow until the end of the seventeenth century. Around 1630, the Orthodox Metropolitan of Kiev, Peter Mogila, wrote a confession of faith so close to Catholic doctrine that in 1640 – 1648 it formed the basis of a local agreement with the Bishop of Kiev who was united to Rome, Veniamin Rutsky. The Orthodox Metropolitan of Kiev sent a memorandum to Rome in 1644 suggesting that

---

101 Oscar Halecki, *From Florence to Brest (1439 – 1596)*, 2nd ed. (Hamden, CT: Archon Books, 1968); Ihor Mončak, *Florentine Ecumenism in the Kyivan Church* (Rome: Ukraïns'kij Katolic'kij Universitet im. Sv. Klimenta Papi, 1987).

the Orthodox and Catholic Churches should be re-united. But the text received no reply. After the Treaty of Westphalia in 1648, which consolidated the new denominational representation of sovereignty, the times were no longer favorable to dialogue.

In 1654, by the Treaty of Pereyaslav, the Russian Empire secured Kiev and the left bank of the Dnieper. The Metropolitan of Kiev was forced to submit to the Patriarchate of Moscow in 1686. Furthermore, the Popes were no longer of the same mind that had presided over the Council of Florence. Their main objective was now that of the Counter-Reformation. A vast operation was put in train between the seventeenth and nineteenth century of Latinizing the Church of Kiev-Halych and bringing it into conformity with Roman canons. When Pope Benedict XIV (1740 – 1758) proclaimed the principle of *Praestanti Ritus Latini*, the liturgical rite of many Eastern "Catholics" became unrecognizable to their "Orthodox" brothers. It was then that the terms "Catholics" and "Orthodox" began to be used to distinguish the Churches by means of their different rites. Moreover, the republic of two nations was dissolved between 1773 and 1795 by the Russian and Austrian Empires and the Kingdom of Prussia, which put a stop to any attempt at reconciliation between the Orthodox and Catholic Churches. The united Church of Kiev-Halych, which passed into Austrian control after the first partition of Poland in 1773, nevertheless benefited from a higher degree of recognition of its sovereignty.[102]

The missionary zeal of the Counter-Reformation Roman Church, founded on a denominationalist understanding of the Church's universality, became dominant. At the beginning of the eighteenth century a number of churches united to Rome were born, in Transylvania in 1700 and in Antioch in 1724, churches whose members had often previously belonged to the Orthodox Churches of Romania and Antioch. This provoked, in return, the Patriarch of Constantinople's decision no longer to recognize Catholic baptisms as valid. In 1755 a synod was convened at Constantinople for the purpose of ordering the re-baptism of Catholics who had converted to the Orthodox Church.[103] This rule, which is still invoked in the twenty-first century by some Greek hierarchs,[104] was not overturned until 2016, at the Pan-Orthodox Council of Crete. The latter

---

102   Arjakovsky, *En attendant le concile de l'Église Orthodoxe.*
103   Father George Dragas, "The Manner of Reception of Roman Catholic Converts into the Orthodox Church," orthodoxinfo.com.
104   Metropolitan Hierotheos Vlachos, "Third Letter to the Holy Synod of Greece concerning the Draft Documents Prepared for the Upcoming Pan-Orthodox Council," *Orthodox Christianity*, March 5, 2016, http://orthochristian.com/.

returned, indeed, to the more ecumenical practice of the primitive Church and to the decision of the synod of 1484 which, citing the Council of Florence, recognized baptism in the Roman Church as valid.[105]

THE RISE OF THE DEIST CONCEPTION OF UNIVERSALITY

The Canadian philosopher Charles Taylor has described at length in several of his books the characteristics of modern and denominational consciousness. The latter was founded, in Western Europe, on a reason which was disinterested, abstract, and conceptual.[106] John Locke's *Reasonableness of Christianity* is a treatise that does not call man to participate in divine action in the world, since, according to Locke, such a cooperation has become impossible. God can no longer do any more than to shed light on the nature of the intangible law. The role of grace tends to disappear, while the process of glorification through works, when separated from faith, is judged unworthy.

> If the good of man that God calls to becomes more and more available to human rational scrutiny, it also becomes more and more encompassable with human powers.[107]

The blossoming of Deism in the Enlightenment was a reaction to a Lutheran, and then hyper-Augustinian conception, for which human will is so corrupted by original sin that men need a grace which will "save" them, that is to say, which will extract them from a nature that is taken to be radically fallen.

In combatting this flight from the world, deism was inspired by a naturalistic conception of grace. "The good that God wills comes more and more to centre on natural good alone. Even eternal reward comes to be seen as just a lot more of the same — and distributed so as to support the production of natural good down here."[108]

The Christian East wished to remain faithful to an anthropology that placed the center of identity not in intelligence, but in a rationality united with the heart. The Cartesian intellectual method consists in a detachment. Intelligence must get rid of the world in order to reconstruct it starting from its own *cogito*. Hesychastic spirituality, rediscovered thanks to the publication of the *Philokalia of the Neptic Fathers* by Nicodemus the

---

105   George Demacopoulos, "Innovation in the Guise of Tradition," *Public Orthodoxy*, March 22, 2016, https://publicorthodoxy.org.

106   Taylor, *Sources of the Self*.

107   Ibid., 245–46.

108   Ibid., 247.

Hagiorite in Venice in 1782, proposes to the intelligence a quite different path. This collection is inspired, in particular, by Nicephoros the Solitary, who wrote the Treatise on Watchfulness and the Guarding of the Heart at the end of the thirteenth century, and by the Methodos (twelfth century), a text that puts forward a method of thought based on a combat. This struggle consists in attaining to a transparency between one's deep self and its thoughts. Man must struggle against his passions, against the desire for possessions, for domination, and for luxury. It is a matter of attaining the level of watchfulness, of nepsis, capable of locating the point at which forgetting, neglect, and ignorance emerge. This struggle has the outcome of bringing about either a suffocation in the desire for oneself, or a union between intelligence and the "heart." "At this last stage," writes Olivier Clément, "fleshly desire — epithumia — can be transformed into an eros for God."[109] Nous, the cerebral intelligence, finds its root in the heart. The virtues — faith, fear of God, abstinence, tenderness, hope — allow us to attain to the stage of impassibility and peace (hesychia). By means of a work of humility, the human heart approaches the divine heart, all the way through to a state of deification and a vision of God. The Gospel, indeed, assures pure hearts that they "shall see God" (Matt. 5:8). Thus the rationality of Easter Christianity had remained symbolic, and faithful to the Athonite monastic tradition. But as Jacques Lison has shown for Gregory Palamas's pneumatology, this tradition was more and more weakened by its aversion to any form of positive theology or philosophical conceptualization.[110] Hostile to any way of imagining a personal form of action in the world on the part of the divine energies, this tradition ended up masking stoical representations of the all-powerfulness of a divine fatum behind the haze of apophatic theology, as is the case in the famous prayer of the fathers of the Russian monastery of Optina Pustyn'.[111]

Christian consciousness, unable to maintain the syntheses that had been outlined at the Council of Florence, split more and more between the sixteenth and eighteenth centuries, in both the East and the West. In the East, the intellectual revival of hesychast spirituality, cut off from its dialogue with Western scholastic theology, led to the de facto abandonment of reflective knowledge to Western philosophy, and the spread of a pietistic kind of spirituality, hostile to the Catholic and Protestant worlds. The

---

109   Olivier Clément, "Introduction," La Philocalie. Les écrits fondamentaux des pères du désert aux pères de l'Eglise (IVe–XIVe siècles) (Paris: DDB, J.-C. Lattès, 1995), 18.

110   Jacques Lison, L'Esprit Répandu (Paris: Cerf, 1994).

111   Antoine Arjakovsky, Voyage de Saint-Pétersbourg à Moscou. Anatomie de l'âme russe (Paris: Salvator, 2018).

canon law handbook of the Greek Orthodox Church, the Pidalion, published in 1791 by Nicodemus the Hagiorite, anticipated that all Christians who wanted to become "Orthodox" would stand in need of re-baptism.

In the West, a deist belief in a supernatural God withdrawn from the affairs of the world and in a rationality restricted to the natural space-time of the *saeculum* replaced the ancient paradigm of faith-truth. The action of the Wisdom of God in the world was limited by deist consciousness to an enigmatic "invisible hand." This fracturing of the horizons of the Kingdom in Europe coincided (except in the case of the Holy See) with a move on the part of the Churches towards submission to the dominant political powers. At Rome, this movement gave rise to the construction of a singular juridical universe under the rule of the *jus divinum* and radically distinct from the secular world.

These developments promoted the rise of a radical scientism, founded in a Utilitarian ethics, in all communities that privileged the principle of egalitarian universalism. This new spirituality brought with it the Enlightenment. From François-Marie Arouet, known as Voltaire (1694 – 1778) to Gotthold Ephraim Lessing (1729 – 1781), European intellectuals argued in favor of toleration, appealing to the idea of freedom of conscience. Lessing, in *Nathan the Wise* (1779), recounted the parable of a father who wanted to pass on to his three sons a ring that possessed a secret power to make whoever wore it, and was animated by this belief in toleration, pleasing to God and men alike. For Lessing (who was a Freemason) this was a way of saying that God loves Judaism, Christianity, and Islam equally, whereas these three religions argue with each other and each claim to possess the truth, instead of imitating the love the Father has shown towards them.

The spiritual and intellectual movement of the Enlightenment led to a de-denominationalization of political life in Europe. In 1721, Tsar Peter I set up the Holy Synod, which subordinated the Church to the State. In France, in 1787, the Edict of Toleration granted Protestants civil rights, the right to register marriages and births before magistrates, but Protestant public worship was still prohibited. It was necessary to wait for August 26, 1789, and the Declaration of the Rights of Man and the Citizen for liberty of conscience and of worship to be proclaimed in France. Very soon, relations between the National Assembly and the Pope became strained. In 1790 the French Revolution proclaimed the Civil Constitution of the Clergy, which made priests employees of the state.

PART THREE

The Inter-Denominational Period in the Consciousness of the Church (1789–1995)

INTRODUCTION

THE PERIOD OF HARDENING ATTITUDES

The secularization of European courts brought with it differing reactions from different churches. The Orthodox Church, whose Patriarchate had been suppressed by Peter the Great, merged its own interests together with those of the Tsars. The Holy Synod of the Russian Church justified imperial politics, including when it was necessary to integrate some rebel churches by force, as in the case of the Greek Catholic Church of Belarus in 1839 or the Ukrainian Greek Catholic Church in 1946. But despite a reforming Council held *in extremis* in 1917, the Russian Church lost its privileged status after the Bolshevik revolution of October 1917, and was harshly persecuted.

The Roman Catholic Church lost its Papal States with the coming of the Italian nation-state in 1870. It managed, however, to sign a certain number of concordats with European states, such as that with Napoleonic France in 1801, which enabled it to maintain its temporal independence. This was only consolidated, however, in 1929, with the Lateran Treaty, in which the Italian state officially recognized the Vatican as a state and conferred upon it a territory of forty-two hectares in Rome. The struggle for the institutional survival of the Church brought with it an increased verticalization of power within it. At the First Vatican Council, the Roman Church proclaimed the dogma of pontifical infallibility on July 18, 1870, in the dogmatic constitution *Pastor Aeternus*. This provoked a schism with the Old Catholic Church, as well as increased hostility on the part of the other Christian denominations.

A marked hardening of attitudes also came about in the Bishop of Rome's relations with other churches. On January 6, 1848, in his letter

In *Suprema Petri Apostoli Sede*, Pope Pius IX formulated the principles of Uniatism as it had been practiced in the eighteenth and nineteenth centuries. The Eastern Churches were invited to return to the fold by tidying up their liturgy and recognizing the unconditional primacy of the See of Rome. The Eastern Patriarchs of Constantinople, Alexandria, Antioch, and Jerusalem, which were all under Ottoman control, defended their spiritual autonomy all the more bitterly. They reacted vigorously on May 6, 1848, with a theological statement explaining why the faith of Peter could not be separated from the See of Peter. For the Orthodox Patriarchs, the mission of the Bishop of Rome could not be distinguished from the mission of any other bishop.[1] And above all, the Eastern Church defended its own "faithful memory." It congratulated itself on having "kept its former countenance unaltered" in matters of dogma. But the Patriarchs' defense of Orthodox theology was itself strongly impregnated with Platonic philosophy, which, when all was said and done, had little to do with the Gospel, and which could not be satisfactory to the Westerners.[2] Moreover, the Eastern Church's refusal to acknowledge even the possibility of the Spirit's blowing in the life of the world prevented it from seeing the emergence of national identities as a legitimate desire for harmonization between a state, a culture, and a language. The Patriarchate of Constantinople clumsily condemned any form of emergence of a local church and a national identity. The Bulgarian Church's demand for autocephaly was

---

1   "Encyclique des Patriarches Orientaux, en Réponse à une Lettre Encyclique du Pape Pie IX aux Chrétiens d'Orient," *Orthodoxie en Abitibi*, abitibi-orthodoxe.ca.

2   "Nor can we pass over the following circumstance in silence: that the Romans, when they draw arguments from the holy Fathers, often and always wrongly confuse the idea of the eternal procession of the Holy Spirit with that of its temporal mission, that is to say, the supernatural gifts of the Holy Spirit which emanate from the Father and are distributed by the Son. It is the same with the two different ideas expressed by the two Greek words οὐσία and ὑπόστασις, which the ancient Latin words expressed by a single word, substance; in this, the medieval and modern theologians confuse two different ideas with each other, and they understand substance (ὑπόστασις) where it is a question of essence (οὐσία), and they understand essence (οὐσία) where it is a question of substance (ὑπόστασις). The Eastern Church believes and confesses that the Holy Spirit has the same essence (οὐσία) as the Father and the Son, but it denies that the Holy Spirit personally or hypostatically (ὑπόστασις) proceeds from the Father and from the Son, and rejects this innovation as a groundless and blasphemous doctrine. — This is how the Westerners, not wishing to deepen the difference between substance and essence (ὑπόστασις καὶ οὐσία), stray from the true theology. This is their whole matter of dissent from us; this is what established the schism and their disagreement with the Eastern Church." A. P., trans., *Réponse de l'Église orthodoxe de l'Orient à l'encyclique du pape Pie IX, adressé par S. S. aux Chrétiens orthodoxes grecs en janvier 1848* (Paris: Librairie Friedrich Klincksieck, 1850), 3–35.

condemned in 1872 by the Patriarchate of Constantinople. The demand was identified with "phyletism" pure and simple, that is, with a retreat into one's own ethnic group.

Denominational hardening of positions thus affected both the Catholic and Orthodox Churches equally in the nineteenth century, and that despite the setting up in Paris in 1856 of the association and bulletin Œuvre des Écoles d'Orient, under the direction of the future cardinal Lavigerie. Since the end of the Crimean War in 1856, under the terms of the treaty of Paris, France had become the protectress of the Christians of the Ottoman Empire. The association was mobilized in order to promote education and charity in the Middle East, particularly in 1860, after the massacres of Christians by the Druzes in Mount Lebanon.

Nevertheless, in 1894, in his apostolic letter *Orientalium dignitas*, Pope Leo XIII took account of the replies received from Constantinople and formulated the new principle of "unionism," in place of a proselytizing "uniatism." This "unionism" did not bring up once more the question of the "universal" jurisdiction of the Roman See. Moreover, it was addressed only to the Eastern Churches united to Rome. But, following the lead of the Council of Florence, it asked the bishops of the Latin rite to put themselves in the service of the Patriarchs of the Church of the East on the canonical territory of the latter:

> We single out this directive from among them as their funda-
> mental condition for success: Latin rite priests are to be sent
> to those regions by the Apostolic See only for the purpose of
> assisting or helping the Patriarchs or Bishops there. The former
> are to be careful not to use the faculties granted them for acting
> in a way prejudicial to the Patriarchs or Bishops or for reducing
> the number of their subjects. By the force of these laws, evidently,
> the duties of the Latin clergy are to be kept within their proper
> limits in their relations with the Eastern rite hierarchy. [3]

This denominational conception of universality is also found in the new code of canon law adopted in 1917 by the Roman Catholic Church. It still rested on the idea which had originated in the Counter-Reformation that the Roman Catholic Church was "in its kind, and in law, the perfect society, " as Pope Leo XIII had written in his encyclical *Immortale Dei* in 1885. At least until 1943, the date of Pope Pius XII's encyclical *Mystici*

---

3   Pope Leo XIII, "Orientalium Dignitas — On the Churches of the East," www.
papalencyclicals.net.

Corporis, the Catholic Church identified itself wholly and exclusively with the mystical Church of Christ. Here is what the Catholic theologian George Tavard writes on the subject of this code of canon law:

> Now a perfect society should have a perfect legal system. In the system that was embodied in the code, the Church is in fact highly clerical. No section is devoted to the laity, which appears in it incidentally, in connection with the tasks of the clergy: the lay faithful are receivers of the sacraments and possible candidates for ordination, for interdict and excommunication, and eventually for canonization. [4]

If the Pope's magisterium acquires such a normative place in the Catholic Church, on the Lutheran side it is the notion of justification by faith that serves as the metalanguage of reference. In the classical world of the Reformation, as well as the classic reference to the Word of God, the believer's individual experience of the Holy Spirit becomes decisive. Conversely, in the Eastern Churches, the central criterion of denominational consciousness is that of fidelity to the patristic consensus crystallized by the seven Ecumenical Councils and put into practice by the liturgy.

Finally, most states became separate from their churches, as in France in 1905, with some notable exceptions such as the United Kingdom. The gradual end of the Constantinian era of the Church came with the fall of empires in the First World War (1914 – 1918). The end of this era nevertheless prompted new reflection on the history of the Church and on ecclesiology. [5] This new current of reflection had been anticipated, from the end of the eighteenth century onwards, by Romantic thought. By virtue of its rejection of what had become the strictly-drawn borders of Christian denominations, Romanticism contributed to the rise of the "ecumenical movement" in the modern sense of the term.

THE ROMANTIC MOMENT

The rise of the new, so-called inter-denominational conception of the *oikouménē* began at the start of the nineteenth century. It was initiated by European Romantic thinkers, as the French philosopher Georges Gusdorf (1912 – 2000) convincingly demonstrated in his book *Du Néant à Dieu dans le savoir romantique* [From Nothingness to God in Romantic Knowledge]. Romanticism was initially defined as a new metaphysics inspired by the

---

4   George H. Tavard, *Vatican II and the Ecumenical Way* (Milwaukee, WI: Marquette University Press, 2006), 12.
5   Arjakovsky, *What Is Orthodoxy?*.

development of German philosophy between 1780 and 1830. The names of Kant, Fichte, Schelling, and Hegel proclaimed a new age of universal philosophy:

> All the great Romantic writers, beginning with Novalis, Coleridge, and Chateaubriand, and through to Schelling and Victor Hugo, are religious thinkers, whose freely conceived ideas, myths, and imaginings are attempts to negotiate the relations between humanity and divinity. The nineteenth century is the century of the de-denominationalization and the declericalization of religion; and since the churches as institutions make for dogmatic rigidity and fixed traditions, the religious domain is characterized by destabilization, by putting the elements that make up religious consciousness back into play again. Freed from dogma, the sense of the sacred inspires a new attentiveness to the whole realm of what is human. It is as if, suddenly, religions and metaphysical systems appeared to be screens and obstacles, barring the way to the absolute of which they were the guardians.[6]

In Romanticism, the poet and the artist have a sacred mission to awaken souls, to act as prophetic proclaimers of a truth that escapes ordinary men. In 1797, the poet Friedrich Hölderlin (1770 – 1843), in his *Hyperion*, proclaimed the birth of a "new Church" gathering together all men of good will in truth:

> You ask me when this will be ? When time's favourite, the youngest and most beautiful daughter of time, the new Church, shall emerge from these tarnished forms which have grown old; when the awakened feeling of the divine shall return to humankind its own divinity, and to its breast its fair youth; when — I cannot announce it, since I barely have an intimation of it, but it is quite certainly coming.[7]

Two years later, the poet Novalis (Friedrich von Hardenberg) (1772 – 1801) dreamed in *Die Christenheit oder Europa* (Christendom, or, Europe) of "a prophetic, a wonder-working [wunderthätige] and a wound-healing [wundenheilende] age, a consoling age that will spark the flame of eternal life."[8] For Novalis, it was not a matter of going backwards so as to lead the

---

6   Georges Gusdorf, *Du néant à Dieu dans le savoir romantique* (Paris: Payot, 1983), 132.
7   Friedrich Hölderlin, "Hyperion, oder der Eremit in Griechenland," in *Hölderlin: Werke, Briefe, Dokumente*, ed. Pierre Bertaux (München: Winkler, 1969), 244–45.
8   Novalis, *Werke, Tagebücher, und Briefe Friedrich von Hardenbergs*, ed. Hans-Joachim Mähl and Richard Samuel, 3 vols (München: Carl Hanser, 1978), 2: 745.

separated Churches into the bosom of the ancient Church. An ecumenical Christianity had to bring humanity together in a new spiritual space:

> Christianity must become living and effective again, and must again form a visible Church without regard to territorial borders, a Church which will welcome into its bosom all those souls who thirst for the supernatural, and will gladly become the mediatrix between the ancient and the modern world.[9]

The Church to come had to be authentically universal, for "the other continents of the world are waiting for Europe's reconciliation and resurrection in order to join it and to become co-citizens of the Kingdom of heaven."[10] The text ended with a profession of faith: "It is coming; it must come, the holy time of eternal peace, in which the new Jerusalem will be the capital of the world...."[11]

One of the deepest impulses of the Romantic era was a faith in dialogue, understood as an autonomous and non-dogmatic source of truth, and as something which no dogma could replace. The German Protestant theologian and philosopher Friedrich Schleiermacher (1768 – 1834) regarded the ineffable character of individuality and dialogue as the pillars of a new universal hermeneutics. A friend of Friedrich Schlegel's, he was appointed in 1810 to the chair of theology at the University of Berlin alongside Wilhelm von Humboldt. In his treatise On Religion: Speeches to its Cultured Despisers (1799), Schleiermacher defined religion as an intuitive contemplation and a feeling. Religious consciousness is thereby situated at the very origin of self-consciousness, beyond rational thought and ethical action, which themselves proceed under the inspiration of religious consciousness. The proper place of religious consciousness, therefore, is at the very origin of being, there where knowing and acting, subject and object, self-consciousness and awareness of God meet, because they have not yet become separated from each other. At this zero point of consciousness, self-consciousness is included within awareness of God, as the finite is included in the infinite: this is the meaning of the feeling of absolute dependence. Moreover, for Schleiermacher, who was a Protestant pastor educated by the Moravian Brethren, it is also just as true to say that awareness of God is included within self-consciousness, because it is a matter of "an experience of the infinite which man brings about through

---

9   Novalis, Werke, 3:750.
10   Ibid.
11   Ibid.

finite things." At the heart of fundamental religious experience, there is, then, an intuition of the universe, that is to say, of the One and All. This intuition itself constitutes the union of subject and object, the (mystical) fusion of the one who reflects and of the object reflected upon. And this means, for Schleiermacher, "the annihilation of the self, an annihilation that is the only means of realizing the divine within oneself."[12]

The Romantic movement suffered from its proximity to the pantheist current in European metaphysics going from Spinoza to Hegel and Schelling. But it also benefitted from the renewed quest in French and German mysticism for created Wisdom. The French poet Victor Hugo associated created Wisdom with Jacob's ladder. This ladder, for Hugo, "ascending through millions of leagues, links the constellations with the blue legions of the air; it peoples the top, the bottom, the edges and the middle, and, in the depths, it vanishes in God!" This is why its temporal expression cannot be grasped if it is thought of simply as an impersonal cosmic cycle. The world, according to the Book of Revelation, only has meaning if divine Wisdom encounters earthly Wisdom. That is why this ladder is also the promise of a new beginning. At the end of time, "the terrible storm-tossed chasm will cease to be mute, and will stammer out 'what do I hear?' Sorrows shall cease in all the darkness: an angel will shout: 'the beginning!'" Thus for Victor Hugo, "everything is a voice, and everything is a fragrance; everything, in the infinite, says something to someone."[13] This deep and invisible reality, present at the heart of the universe, can only be reached by the poet's "mouth of shadow" in an eschatological manner. This experience of Wisdom, undergone by most of the Romantics, was that of a broken Wisdom, separated from the breath of the Spirit. "Spirit! spirit! spirit! I cried out, frantically. The spectre pursues me without having heard me." In Hugo's *Contemplations*, Wisdom appears as dark and terrifying.[14] And nevertheless, Romantic consciousness was certain of one thing: no single institution could make Wisdom its own property.

---

12   Jean Richard, "Anthropologie religieuse et théologie. À propos d'un récent ouvrage de Michel Meslin," *Laval théologique et philosophique* 46 (3) (1990), 383–402.
13   Victor Hugo, "Ce que dit la bouche d'ombre" [What the mouth of shadow says] (1855), from *Les Contemplations*, in Hugo, *Œuvres Poétiques*, ed. Pierre Albouy (Paris: Gallimard [Éditions de la Pléiade], 1967), 801–22, 802.
14   "Et l'on voit tout au fond, quand l'œil ose y descendre, / Au delà de la vie, et du souffle et du bruit, / Un affreux soleil noir d'où rayonne la nuit!" "And right at the bottom, when the eye dares to go down there, / Beyond life, and breath, and noise, / There is seen a terrible black sun from which the night shines out!" "Ce que dit la bouche d'ombre," 806.

Following his conversion to Christianity, Paul Verlaine was able to give a name to the unknown woman who appeared to him in his strange and affecting dreams, "a woman who is never quite the same each time, nor entirely different, and who loves me and understands me." This woman, as he later writes, is no other than Wisdom. In his poem entitled "Sagesse" [Wisdom], he transcribes the words he heard from her:

> "J'étais née avant toutes causes
> Et je verrai la fin de tous
> Les effets, étoiles et roses. (. . .)
> "Qui je suis ? me demandais-tu.
> Mon nom courbe les anges même. . . ."
>
> I was born before all causes/ And I shall see the end of all effects, stars, and roses. Who am I, you were asking? My name makes the very angels bow down. . . . [15]

This rediscovery of Wisdom, and, still more, of the sense of mystery, contributed, according to Georges Gusdorf, to a transition from an understanding of faith as faithful memory to a discovery of faith as fair knowledge:

> The Romantic period is not marked by static repetition or by retrospection, but by growth, in which meaning unfurls over the whole extent of its duration. Ecumenism is situated within this process of Romanticism's coming into being, each spiritual persuasion following the path of its own loyalties, while asking the others to be faithful to theirs. The mystery of God remains the final destination, since no participant can in advance attribute to itself possession of the last word. The progress of the whole movement takes place not by subtraction, but by the addition of further participants. It is for each to wait in the patience of faith for another revelation when the final consummation arrives. Ecumenism can exist in its intention, from now on, as a prophetic truth, trusting to the unfathomable design of Providence, the mistress of human destinies. [16]

Johann Wolfgang von Goethe (1749 – 1832) reveals a darker aspect of Romanticism in his *Faust* of 1832, a work that has become legendary in the collective mentalities of the modern age. The story goes back to

---

15   Paul Verlaine, *Sagesse*, II, in Paul Verlaine, *Œuvres Poétiques Complètes*, ed. Yves-Gérard Le Dantec, rev. Jacques Borel (Paris, Gallimard [Éditions de la Pléiade], 1962), 241 – 43.
16   Gusdorf, *Du néant à Dieu*, 567 – 68.

a thirteenth-century manuscript which was rediscovered in Lutheran circles. It portrays a destitute deacon selling his soul to the devil using a Jewish magician as intermediary. This secret pact contracted with the devil grants, in a fleeting way, knowledge of the secrets of the universe and omnipotence. The immanence of the contract with a tangible Lucifer becomes preferable to the sacramental void of any relationship with a distant God. But as Emmanuel Reibel writes, this new vision of the world can only terminate in further alienation:

> Far removed from the divine logic resting on gift and forgiveness, the diabolical give-and-take offers no more than omnipotence for a limited time. The paradox is thus that the iconoclastic freedom which Faust flaunts puts itself in fetters in the very act through which it expresses itself: the contract with the devil is, indeed, at once the apex of freedom and the height of alienation. [17]

ROMANTIC CONSCIOUSNESS AND THE INTER-DENOMINATIONAL MOVEMENT

From 1815 to 1995, denominational consciousness, shaped by this Romantic renaissance, ascended three steps of ecclesial consciousness. The so-called "unionist" moment lasts from 1815 to 1919, that is to say, from the rise of the Holy Alliance to the collapse of the old international order. This was a period in which the denominational paradigm was strongly dominant; in the course of the period, the Catholic, Protestant, and Orthodox powers combined to block the path to the forces of secularization. Nevertheless, during this period, with such figures as Vladimir Solovyov (1853 – 1900), Johann Adam Möhler (1796 – 1838), John Henry Newman (1801 – 1890), and John Mott (1865 – 1955), there appeared the first inklings of an awareness of the limits of a strictly denominational conception of the Church.

The pan-institutional moment of ecclesial consciousness concerns the period between 1920 and 1965. In the course of this period, the ecumenical movement tries to give itself a structure, first by means of conferences, and then by means of institutions, with the creation, in Amsterdam, of the World Council of Churches in 1948, and of the Secretariat for Promoting Christian Unity in Rome in 1960. The aim was to allow a restored faith in the one, holy, catholic and apostolic Church creatively to combine the vertical axis of order and transmission with the horizontal axis of life and work.

---

17   Emmanuel Reibel, Faust. La musique au défi du mythe (Paris: Fayard, 2008), 17.

The following period, from 1965 to 1995, can be characterized as a more pastoral and more theological period, even if, in the course of these years of "peaceful coexistence," the ecumenical movement also positioned itself critically towards ideologies. The Church is no longer understood as the *societas perfecta*, as in the epoch of the dominant denominational paradigm, but as the people of God and the Body of Christ. This period of doctrinal and social re-centering is sometimes thought of as the moment of the three glorious decades of theological ecumenism: thirty years in the course of which dozens of bilateral and multilateral ecumenical agreements were signed, and in which important texts were published, such as John Paul II's encyclical Ut *unum sint* (1995).

This period was followed, as we shall see below, by a phase of crisis. The upheavals in the world order at the beginning of the 1990s, beginning with the extension of the neo-liberal paradigm across the whole planet, choked off the Romantic spirit of the ecumenical movement. The ecumenical movement was more and more associated with globalization, irrespective of denominational and regional identities. A rebalancing of forces within ecumenical institutions was demanded by these trends, but also by the churches, who were worried about losing their identity.

Nevertheless, the end of the Cold War was also the sign of a victory for the spiritual paradigm over capitalist and communist ideology. This victory, prepared for within certain ecclesial institutions such as the Conference of European Churches, lent a certain daring to the Churches. Thus, for example, the great agreement on justification by faith between Catholics and Protestants, the question which had given rise to the Reformation in the sixteenth century, was signed in 1999. This agreement had been prepared and ripened in the course of the preceding period. But the enthusiastic atmosphere of the 1990s made it possible for most of the Churches involved to sign it. A deep questioning of inter-denominational consciousness prompted both a redisposition of representations and identities and a spiritual renaissance of ecumenical consciousness.

These chronological boundaries are only indicative. They vary, indeed, with the levels of consciousness, the space-times, and the spiritual types within each ecclesial community. Nevertheless, they do make it possible to grasp an overall dynamic in Christian consciousness at the moment when this consciousness, along with the phenomenon of the mediatization and digitization of the means of communication, became truly global.

THE UNIONIST MOMENT (1815–1919)

IMPERIAL POLITICAL THEOLOGY AND THE EMERGENCE OF CHRISTIAN DEMOCRACY

In 1815, the European powers were concerned with putting in place a new international political theology capable of thwarting the messianic ideology of the Enlightenment, which was perceived as anti-religious. A new model, called the Holy Alliance, was conceived by the chancelleries of the Orthodox Russian empire, the Catholic Austrian empire, and the Lutheran Kingdom of Prussia. By the treaty of September 26, 1815, signed at Paris, the empires which had triumphed over Napoleon's armies agree that

> conformably to the words of the Holy Scriptures, which command all men to consider each other as brethren, the Three contracting Monarchs will remain united by the bonds of a true and indissoluble fraternity, and considering each other as fellow countrymen, they will, on all occasions and in all places, lend each other aid and assistance; and, regarding themselves towards their subjects and armies as fathers of families, they will lead them, in the same spirit of fraternity with which they are animated, to protect Religion, Peace, and Justice.[18]

Austria, Prussia, and France are "members of one and the same Christian nation." The three princes of the allied nations are "designated by Providence to govern three branches of the One family." Even if this alliance was rejected by some states, including the Papal states, it prompted a decisive development of the denominational paradigm.

This, however, did not prevent deist and scientistic philosophy from spreading more and more strongly in the nineteenth and twentieth centuries, especially with the rise of the great masters of suspicion, August Comte (1798 – 1857), Charles Darwin (1809 – 1882), Karl Marx (1818 – 1883), Friedrich Nietzsche (1844 – 1900), and Sigmund Freud (1856 – 1939). The new secular religion of humanity, the new theory of evolution, the new philosophy, and the new science of the depths of the human unconscious provoked a vigorous reaction from the Catholic Church. After the national revolutions of 1848, there was more and more talk of the benefits of Christian Democracy in Europe. In France, Father Lacordaire's paper *L'ère nouvelle* [The New Era] called in 1848 for an alliance of the people with Jesus Christ to bring together social preoccupations and liberal aspirations.

---

18   "The Holy Alliance Treaty," https://www.napoleon-series.org/.

In Germany, in 1871, after the Proclamation of the German Empire, the Catholic party, created in 1852, was transformed under the guidance of Ludwig Windhorst and Mgr Wilhelm Emmanuel von Ketteler into a party of the constitution (the *Zentrum* [center]). It was able to welcome non-Catholics into its ranks. Elsewhere in Europe, at the end of the nineteenth century, political parties came into being that defined themselves as Christian, as in Austro-Hungary, in Belgium, and in Switzerland. But Rome long resisted this modernity. Pope Pius IX was opposed both to the movement for unity and to the liberal state, since neither of the two, in his view, felt themselves bound to any obligation towards God. Moreover, for the Italian pontiff, neither the state nor the nation were ends sufficient to themselves. Their mission was to allow men and women to go towards God through a whole series of intermediary bodies, beginning with the family and ending with the Church.

The election in 1878 of Leo XIII, as well as the rise of an intransigent and anti-individualist Catholicism after the First Vatican Council, changed the situation. The new Pope, a doctor of theology and of law, was the scion of a very old aristocratic family. He possessed solid diplomatic experience as a former nuncio to Belgium. A former Archbishop of Pérouse, he had been present when the Papal states were dissolved in 1870. He was thus conscious of the need for a reform of the political theology of the Holy See. Ten years after being elected, he published an important encyclical entitled *Libertas*. In it, he rejected secular freedom insofar as the latter was reduced to individual choice. But he recognized such freedom insofar as it was understood as the human being's capacity to follow the voice of his or her conscience, and the right to follow the will of God. Aspiring towards a new Christianity, the Pope also acknowledged that the modern state possessed a certain legitimacy if it worked towards the common good. This led certain radical Catholics to oppose the Pope. In some regions, such as in Belgium, Catholic political parties wanted to free their societies from the tutelage of the state. But the encyclical of 1892, *Inter sollicitudines* [Amidst Concerns] invited Catholics to recognize republican institutions. A further encyclical of Leo XIII's, *Graves de communi re* [Serious Discussions] made explicit the Pope's position by promoting Christian Democracy against social democracy. Thus, by giving its support to the recognition of democratic states and by legitimizing the notion of Christian Democracy, the Vatican contributed to the gradual rise of Christian Democracy all across Europe.

Moreover, on May 15, 1891, Pope Leo XIII opened a new chapter in the magisterium's reflection on the economic and social life of the peoples in his encyclical *Rerum novarum*. His condemnation of liberal capitalism, as well as of Marxist ideology, is irrevocable. On the latter, he writes as follows:

> It is clear that the main tenet of socialism, community of goods, must be utterly rejected, since it only injures those whom it would seem meant to benefit, is directly contrary to the natural rights of mankind, and would introduce confusion and disorder into the commonweal. The first and most fundamental principle, therefore, if one would undertake to alleviate the condition of the masses, must be the inviolability of private property.[19]

The Pope held that it was the doctrine of the Gospel which should mold and govern the state. In France, the Le Chapelier law had in 1781 dissolved the corporations, and, with them, a whole stack of legal codes that protected the professions by drawing on some of the principles worked out by theologians such as St Thomas Aquinas. These principles, in particular, protected private property, but in setting such property in relation to the common good. With the revolution, all citizens possessed the same rights, but they also found themselves alone and isolated in the face of the state. This is why the Pope encouraged Christians to form themselves into corporations or syndicates on a basis which would not necessarily be denominational. The essential thing was that this basis should not cut itself off from the spiritual foundations and aims of work:

> We may lay it down as a general and lasting law that working men's associations should be so organized and governed as to furnish the best and most suitable means for attaining what is aimed at, that is to say, for helping each individual member to better his condition to the utmost in body, soul, and property. It is clear that they must pay special and chief attention to the duties of religion and morality, and that social betterment should have this chiefly in view. . . . [20]

In France, this development in the Holy See prompted the creation of the Semaines Sociales de France [French Social Weeks] on August 1, 1904, a movement of young lay people initiated by Marius Gonin in Lyon and Adéodat Boissart in Lille.[21] True, in 1905, a law concerning

---

19 "Rerum Novarum. Encyclical of Pope Leo XIII on Capital and Labor," vatican. va, section 15.

20 Ibid., section 57.

21 Jean-Dominique Durand, ed., *Les Semaines Sociales de la France: cent ans d'engagement social des catholiques français, 1904–2004: actes du colloque international d'histoire, 13–16 octobre 2004, Université Jean-Moulin-Lyon 3* (Paris: Parole et Silence, 2006).

the separation of church from state put an end to the regime of the *concordat*, abrogated the notion of "recognized worship," and made churches into private associations. Moreover, article 4 arranged for the goods of public establishments for worship to be devolved from worship associations. In response, Pope Pius X denounced this unilateral abrogation of the concordat. Hesitant, like his predecessors, in the face of any kind of modernism, Pope Pius also in 1910 condemned the Sillon [The Furrow], Marc Sangnier's pro-democratic social movement, which he accused of mixing religion with politics.

The First World War was the disastrous consequence of the new separatist political theology of the secular powers. It overturned previously existing European attitudes, and brought about a realization that even the most glittering civilizations were mortal. It prompted an increase in revolutionary, communist, and fascist ideologies. From the point of view of ecclesial consciousness, the recognition of a non-denominational Christian syndicalism thus became indispensable.[22] On November 1, 1919, the Confédération Française des Travailleurs Chrétiens [French Federation of Christian Workers] was created in Paris. Its basis was, as in the case of the German Christian syndicates, a "lay" one, that is, one that was free and independent with respect to any church or party. This also meant, in conformity with the encyclical *Singulari quadam* (1912),[23] that the confederation was open to all, beginning with Catholics and Protestants, as long as they adhered to Christian social principles as they had been presented in *Rerum novarum*, as was specified in article 1 of the Federation's statutes.

A third external factor contributed to the development of the denominational paradigm towards a more inter-denominational conception of the universality of the Church and of the world. This was the question of migrations. In the nineteenth century this was a question of interest only to a few people, such as the Orthodox Russian prince, Ivan Gagarin, who had become a Jesuit in 1843, and who lived in France until 1882, where he founded the journal *Études* [Studies], and even to a few communities (the number of European migrants to the United States in the nineteenth century is estimated at sixty million, of whom almost half, in 1850, were

---

22   Joseph Thouvenel, CFTC [*Confédération française des travailleurs chrétiens*]: 100 ans de syndicalisme chrétien et après? (Paris: Téqui, 2019).

23   "We do not deny that Catholics, in their efforts to improve the workers' living conditions, more equitable distribution of wages, and other justified advantages, have a right, provided they exercise due caution, to collaborate with non-Catholics for the common good." "Singulari Quadam: Encyclical of Pope Pius X on Labor Relations," vatican.va, section 5.

Irish). But the movement broadened in the twentieth century, especially, after the First World War, with the surge into Western Europe and the United States of many East Europeans fleeing the rise of communist and fascist totalitarian regimes.

The Catholic, Protestant, and Orthodox Churches had already developed exclusive narratives founded on self-centered, homogeneous, and continuous genealogies from the beginnings to the present day. International political developments, and pressure from the empires, impelled them, however, to think about the impasses inherent in the existing model. At the same time, theologians and historians within each of the denominations proposed new narratives that could imagine the universality of the Church in a new way. Subsequently, these new representations of the Church gave rise to a huge movement for inter-denominational rapprochement, first in the Protestant and Anglican world, and then in the Catholic and Orthodox ones. If the history of the Church's ecumenicity before the nineteenth century is still little known, it has, on the other hand, been much discussed by many authors for the period from 1815 to the present.[24] Some of the main lines of this discussion will be introduced here.

THE PROTESTANT DYNAMIC

Romanticism's messianic hope was not a reprise of the universal consensus of the medieval period, but a new culture, born of the religious synthesis of new times. In Germany, Protestants and Catholics were in contact with each other. The Romantic movement stimulated mutual recognition between denominations that had been indifferent or hostile neighbors. The Catholic Tübingen school of theology benefited from this. It produced new reflections on the Church thanks to Johann Adam Möhler, who, in 1825, published *Unity in the Church, or, The Principle of Catholicism*. But the dynamic of inter-denominational gathering-together displayed itself mainly in the Lutheran and Anglican Reformed world.

In 1838, William Palmer, an Anglican theologian at Oxford, conceived in his *Treatise on the Church of Christ* a new way of representing the history

---

24   This history of the Church's ecumenicity has so far been the subject only of short studies. Thus the huge history of the ecumenical movement published by the World Council of Churches, which comprises four volumes and several thousand pages, devotes only twenty-six pages to the history of the Church between the first and the sixteenth centuries! This period is even completely absent from the Dictionary of the Ecumenical Movement. This is why the topic of the history of relations between the Churches in the first and second millenniums has been on the agenda of the Joint Commission for Theological Dialogue for several years now.

of the Church, in which each of the great denominations was thought of as a branch of the same ecclesial trunk. This new history of the Church, despite its limitations, made new ecumenical initiatives possible. In 1844, the English philanthropist George Williams, an Anglican who had become a Congregationalist, wanted to spread the Gospel by means of sport. He founded the Young Men's Christian Association, and then, ten years later, its female equivalent — the YWCA. The purpose of both organizations was to proclaim Jesus Christ as God and Savior according to the Gospel, as well as the propagation of virtue among young people by means of the promotion of sporting activities. In 1855, the world association of YMCA was founded in Paris.

Among the ten signatories of the Charter of the YMCA was found the young Franco-Swiss Calvinist Christian Henry Dunant (1828 – 1910). In 1862, Dunant published *Recollections of Solferino*, a pacifist manifesto that called for the creation of emergency aid services for the war-wounded. Dunant had personally lived through the "European disaster" of the battle of Solferino, on June 24, 1859.[25] Dunant was influenced by two women, each belonging to a Christian denomination other than his own: Florence Nightingale, a British Unitarian who pioneered nursing in England, and the Grand Duchess Elena Pavlovna of Russia, a member of the Orthodox Church, who had also distinguished herself in the service of the wounded during the Crimean War. In his book, Dunant is already imagining the organization that would go on to receive three Nobel Peace Prizes in the twentieth century:

> Why should we not profit from a period of relative tranquility and calm to study, and to try to resolve, a question of such great and universal importance, both from the point of view of humanity and from that of Christianity?[26]

The following year, Dunant created the International Committee of the Red Cross, whose mission was at once universalist, personalist, and pacifist. On August 22, 1864, with the support of the main European states, the international Geneva Convention established the principle of neutrality for those caring for the wounded in wartime, which represented a revolution in the international law that had emerged from the Treaty of Westphalia. In 1901, Dunant himself received the first Nobel Peace Prize.

---

25 Henry Dunant, *Un souvenir de Solférino* (Paris: Comité de la Croix-Rouge française, 2014 [1862]), 99.
26 Ibid., 109.

In his memoirs, he relates how his idea of creating a flag of peace, the famous red cross on a white background, was born of his desire to put in place "a new kind of truce of God."[27]

These ecumenical commitments on the part of the YMCA and the Red Cross prompted the creation, three decades later, of the World Student Christian Federation, at the castle of Vadstena in Sweden in 1895, by the American Methodist John Mott (1865–1955), the itinerant secretary of the YMCA,[28] and the Swedish Lutheran Karl Fries.[29] The objectives of the WSCF were even broader than those of the YMCA and YWCA. Its goals, indeed, were "to shape students so as to make them aware of their responsibility for critical thinking and constructive transformation of our world by offering a space for prayer and celebration, for theological reflection, for the study and analysis of social and cultural processes, and for solidarity and action beyond the borders set in place by culture, gender, and ethnicity."[30]

The Evangelical Alliance was created in London in 1846, in the presence of around eight hundred Christians belonging to fifty-two different denominational churches. Once again with the support of Henry Dunant, it put in place an "ecumenical union of all believers" beyond denominational and national borders. But this common wish to recover the orthodox tradition of the faith of the first Christian centuries also prompted many individual conversions, as in the case of the Anglican priest John Henry Newman (1801–1890), who became a Roman Catholic in 1845. This is why this first phase of the renewal of ecumenical consciousness is called "unionist." The time was not yet ripe for the wish to be enriched by otherness and by differences in the interpretation of the apostolic faith. True, the end of the nineteenth century saw the first Anglo-Catholic conversations between Lord Halifax, a British Anglican, and Father Fernand Portal, a Lazarist French Catholic. These discussions bore upon the eventual recognition by Rome of ordinations performed by the Church of England. In 1896, Rome rejected any such recognition, in the bull *Apostolica curae*.

The international Lutheran alliance was born in 1868, a year after the first Lambeth Conference, a pan-Anglican synod. In 1875, in London, sixty-four delegates representing twenty-one churches founded the Alliance

---

27   Henry Dunant, *Mémoires*, ed. Bernard Gagnebin (Paris: L'Age d'Homme, 1971), 46.
28   C. Howard Hopkins, *John R. Mott* (Grand Rapids, MI: Eerdmans, 1979).
29   Suzanne de Dietrich, *Cinquante ans d'histoire: La Fédération universelle des associations chrétiennes d'étudiants* (1895–1945) (Paris: Semeur, 1948).
30   "The Federation: History," http://www.wscf.ch.

of Reformed Churches, adopting the Presbyterian system and thus putting an end to three centuries of fission in Reformed Protestantism, and signing up thenceforth to an ecumenical rationale. In 1881, it was the turn of the Ecumenical Methodist Conference to see the light of day, before that of the Congregationalist churches (1891) and the Baptist World Alliance (1905).

In the United States, a Unitarian Christian, Jenkin Lloyd Jones, launched the Parliament of Religions in Chicago in 1893 at the World's Columbian Exposition. For the first time, representatives of the Eastern and Western religions gathered together. The intervention of Swami Vivekananda (1863 – 1902), an Indian philosopher and Hindu *sannyasi* (ascetic) was particularly remarked upon, and was greeted by the public with prolonged applause. The disciple of Ramakrishna, Gadadhar Chattopadhyay (1836 – 1886), the Bengali Hindu mystic, proposed a gnosis that would bring the Gospel together with the non-dualist doctrine of the Vedanta. His work later influenced Romain Rolland and Mahatma Gandhi.

From the other direction, but still within the American Protestant family, at the beginning of the twentieth century the Pentecostal movement was born on the initiative of Charles Fox Parham (1873 – 1929), a Methodist preacher from Kansas, who ended up by rejecting denominational borders in the name of a movement for holiness, and William Joseph Seymour (1870 – 1972), an African-American disciple of Parham's, who, with Neely Terry and Lucy Farrow, founded the "Apostolic Faith Mission" community in 1906, based at 312 Azusa Street in Los Angeles. Open to both black and white Christians — a feature of which Parham disapproved — the community experienced charismatic events shortly before the Los Angeles earthquake of April 18, 1906.[31] The heirs to the tradition of the "great awakenings," these communities experienced primitive forms of the effusion of the Spirit such as the phenomenon of "speaking in tongues" or glossolalia, or cures linked to baptism in the Spirit. Organized into Assemblies of God from 1914 onwards, these communities were part of a logic of a rediscovery of the spiritual sources of the Christian faith, rather than of a logic of inter-denominational dialogue. Nevertheless, they came in the twentieth century to grasp that their rediscovery of the theology of the Holy Spirit represented a specific gift which was present in the other Christian traditions, and which demanded to be shared. This missionary dimension of the Pentecostalist awakening led this family of communities

---

31   Robert Owens, *The Azusa Street Revival: Its Roots and its Message* (Lanham, MD: Xulon Press, 2005); Vinson Synan, *The Century of the Holy Spirit: 100 Years of Pentecostal and Charismatic Renewal, 1901–2001* (Nashville: Thomas Nelson, 2001).

to number more than five hundred million followers by the end of the twentieth century.

For his part, John Mott, the president of the Young Men's Christian Association, and the Secretary-General of the World Student Christian Federation, was one of the initiators, together with Joseph H. Oldham (1874–1969), a Scottish layman from the United Free Church of Scotland, and Robert Gardiner (1855–1924), an American Episcopalian layman, of the celebrated World Missionary Conference of 1910 in Edinburgh. Many of the leading ecumenical figures of the twentieth century took part in this event, which influenced a whole generation of Christians, notably Charles Brent (1862–1929), a Canadian Episcopalian bishop who later became the first president of the Faith and Order Commission in Lausanne, but also the promoter of the World Alliance for Promoting International Friendship through the Churches.[32]

The international work towards friendship and peace was also a source of commitment to the ecumenical movement. In the same year as the Edinburgh conference took place, the former British soldier, Robert Baden-Powell (1857–1941) decided to found the Scouting movement, shortly after his sister Agnes had begun setting up the first Girl Guide groups.[33] Similarly, Pierre de Coubertin, a former pupil of the Jesuits, decided to found the modern Olympic movement. De Coubertin was a Parisian Catholic married to an Alsatian Protestant, Marie Rothan. They married in 1895 at the St Pierre de Chaillot church in Paris, a marriage which was followed by a ceremony in a Reformed church. The following year, on de Coubertin's initiative, the first modern Olympic games were

---

32 John Mott was elected President of the World Methodist Council on this occasion.
33 Baden-Powell's religious convictions were also ecumenical, because he saw to it that the Scouting movement was set up outside Anglican auspices. His spiritual testament to the young, composed shortly before his death, is often quoted: "I believe that God put us in this jolly world to be happy and enjoy life. Happiness does not come from being rich, nor merely from being successful in your career, nor by self-indulgence. One step towards happiness is to make yourself healthy and strong while you are a boy, so that you can be useful, and so can enjoy life when you are a man. Nature study will show you how full of beautiful and wonderful things God has made the world for you to enjoy. Be contented with what you have got, and make the best of it, look on the bright side of things instead of the gloomy one. But the real way to get happiness is by giving out happiness to other people. Try and leave this world a little better than you found it, and when your turn comes to die you can die happy in feeling that at any rate you have not wasted your time but have done your best. Be Prepared in this way, to live happy and to die happy, stick to your Scout Promise always even after you have ceased to be a boy and God help you to do it. Your friend, Baden-Powell." https://www.scout.org/node/19215.

held at Athens. De Coubertin became president of the International Olympic Committee, and was often called "the apostle of sporting ecumenism."[34] Later, de Coubertin met Robert Baden-Powell, to whom he was introduced by Nicolas Benoît (1875 – 1914), a naval officer who founded the Éclaireurs de France, a French Scouting association, and who contributed to the introduction of Scouting into France. But de Coubertin, guided more by the secular version of the Olympic movement than by Baden-Powell's religious conception, refused to introduce the principle of respecting young people's religious opinions. This produced the first rupture in French Scouting, between the Éclaireurs de France and the Éclaireurs Français.

In England, the Christian Social Union was created in 1889 at the initiative of Edward White Benson (1829 – 1896), the Archbishop of Canterbury. In Germany, in 1890, the Evangelisch-Sozialer Kongress (Evangelical Social Congress) was set up by Friedrich Naumann. In Switzerland, the pastor and Zürich University theologian Leonhardt Ragaz (1868 – 1945) also developed activity dedicated to a social and pacifist Christianity. Some of these initiatives were inspired by the ideas of Christoph Friedrich Blumhardt (1842 – 1919), a German Evangelical pastor and theologian, the son of Johann Christoph Blumhardt, an influential pietist pastor. Others were influenced by the American Baptist theologian Walter Rauschenbusch (1861 – 1918). In New York, in 1892, Rauschenbusch set up the Christian association of the Brotherhood of the Kingdom, whose mission was to put the Social Gospel into practice beyond denominational borderlines. In 1907, he published *Christianity and the Social Crisis*, and, in 1917, *A Theology for the Social Gospel*, which rallied many Protestant and Evangelical Churches to his cause. His works advocating the Social Gospel later greatly influenced the Protestant Martin Luther King and the Catholic Dorothy Day.

THE ORTHODOX DYNAMIC

As far as the Orthodox Church was concerned, in 1902 Joachim III, the Patriarch of Constantinople, wrote an encyclical addressed to the other Orthodox Patriarchs on the topic of Christian unity and of his ardent desire for union with all those who share faith in Christ. If he underlined the difficulty presented to the achievement of such unity by the doctrinal positions of the various Western Churches, he also explained that the attitude of the Orthodox denominations towards the ecumenical process was strongly marked by this desire for unity. In order to overcome the difficulty, it was necessary, therefore, in his view, to endeavor to discern

34   https://fr.wikipedia.org/wiki/Pierre_de_Coubertin.

what it was that made "differences" (*diaphora*) of a practical order into "divisions" (*diairesis*) that were a perversion of these differences.

On the Russian Orthodox front, the intellectuals played a dominant role in promoting an open ecclesial consciousness. The philosopher, poet, and theologian Alexei Khomyakov (1804–1860) was one of the leaders of the Slavophile movement. His main doctrine was that of *sobornost'* (conciliarity), a principle according to which the authentic freedom of humanity was realized not in individualism, but in catholicity, that is to say, in practicing social life following the model of the whole of the life of the Trinity. The result of this was to rehabilitate the priesthood of all believers at all levels of the Church, and the commitment of citizens at all levels of the social hierarchy. His views about Western Christians were riddled with prejudices. Nevertheless, he published an important text, *The Church Is One*, in which he helped his contemporaries to free themselves from a narrow denominationalism:

> The grace of faith is inseparable from holiness of life, and neither a single specific community nor a single pastor can be acknowledged as the guardian of the entirety of the Church's faith, nor can a single community nor a single pastor be held to represent the entirety of the Church's holiness.[35]

As Nikolai Berdyaev noted in his 1911 essay on him, Khomyakov was one of the first Russians to use the term ecumenism. Khomyakov showed solidarity with the Eastern Patriarchs when the latter responded in 1848 to Pope Pius IX's encyclical *In suprema Petri sede*.[36] Like them, he thought that "infallibility resides in the ecumenism of the Church united by mutual love, and that the immutability of dogma and the purity of the rite were both consigned to the guardianship not only of the Church hierarchy but of the whole people of the Church, which is the Body of Christ."[37]

Just like Khomyakov, the Russian Church historian Vasily Botolov (1853–1900), in the *Introduction to the History of the Church* he wrote in 1896, shortly before his death, explained that the Orthodox Church believed in the conciliar [*sobornaya*] Church, that is to say, in the catholicity of the Church (a catholicity ecumenically, rather than denominationally, understood). Bolotov, a professor at the St. Petersburg Theological Academy, added that the question of the procession of the Holy Spirit from

---

35 A. S. Khomiakov, "L'Église est une," https://kalomiros.blogspot.com.
36 "Encyclique des Patriarches Orientaux," *Orthodoxie en Abitibi*, abitibi-orthodoxe.ca.
37 Khomyakov quoted in Nikolai Berdyaev, *Khomiakov* (Lausanne: L'Age d'Homme, 1988), 65.

the Father through the Son, adopted at the Council of Florence by all the Churches, could be regarded as a valuable theological opinion.

The Russian philosopher Vladimir Solovyov (1853 – 1900), like Bolotov, lived only to the age of 47. Like Bolotov, he was one of the generation of Russian intellectuals who rediscovered the meta-denominational catholicity of the Church. While remaining faithful to his Orthodox Christian faith, he agreed to take communion at the hands of a Greek Catholic priest, Father Nikolai Tolstoy. Although he then refrained from this, his ecumenical vision remained characterized by a unionist and theocratic consciousness. In his letter of September 21, 1886 to the Croat bishop of Djakovo, Josip Juraj Strossmayer (1815 – 1905), Solovyov explains the connection that exists between the ministry of the Pope as defined by the First Vatican Council, and the teaching contained in the 1848 encyclical of the Eastern Patriarchs on conciliarity. In 1889, in *Russia and the Universal Church*, he suggests that a "moral and intellectual" — and thus post-denominational and post-diplomatic — bond should be established between the consciousness of the Russian people and the Universal Church:

> The profoundly religious and monarchic instinct of the Russian people, certain prophetic events in its past history, the enormous and compact bulk of its empire, the great latent strength of the national spirit in its contrast to the poverty and emptiness of its actual existence — all this seems to indicate that it is the historic destiny of Russia to provide the Universal Church with the political power it requires for the salvation and regeneration of Europe and the world.
>
> Great tasks cannot be accomplished with small means. It is not a matter of religious compromise between two hierarchies, nor of diplomatic negotiations between two governments. It is primarily a moral and intellectual bond that must be forged between the religious conscience of Russia and the truth of the Universal Church . . . . [38]

THE PAN-INSTITUTIONAL MOMENT (1920–1965)

The First World War left more than eighteen million dead, of whom more than nine million were civilians. It put an end to the Ottoman, German, Austro-Hungarian, and Russian Empires. It overturned the European geopolitical balance of power, especially because of the redistribution of

---

38   Vladimir Soloviev, *Russia and the Universal Church* (London: Geoffrey Bles, The Centenary Press, 1948), 31.

German colonies, the imposition of heavy war reparations on Germany, and the creation of new states such as Poland, Czechoslovakia, and Yugoslavia; but also, in 1922, of the USSR. Most historians agree in recognizing that the separatist logic that presided over the inaptly named Peace Conference (January to August, 1919) only prompted the rise of totalitarianisms and prepared the way for the Second World War. Moreover, the Democratic President of the United States, Thomas Woodrow Wilson (1856 – 1924), a fervent Presbyterian Christian and the son of a pastor, was unable to have his liberal and democratic vision of international relations adopted, nor to have the Treaty of Versailles ratified by the Senate (the Treaty provided for the creation of a League of Nations).

Following the carnage of the War, which had extended right around the planet, the churches realized that they must change their political and economic theology. They did this, however, in a disorganized way and according to different rhythms, which prevented them from bringing any pressure to bear on the decisions of the Congress of Versailles and the train of events which it set in motion. There existed, nevertheless, a third way in Europe, a way between secularism and denominationalism, thanks to the commitment of the Catholic, Orthodox, Anglican, Lutheran, and Reformed churches.

THE POPES' COMMITMENT TO A SOCIAL DOCTRINE AND THEIR OPPOSITION TO ECUMENISM

Spurred on by Pope Leo XIII's encyclical, *Rerum novarum*, many others followed, notably Pius XI's encyclicals of the 1920s and 1930s against nationalism, fascism, Nazism, and communism. In particular, *Quadragesimo anno*, in 1931, called for the rebuilding of professional bodies and for a social order founded on the principle of subsidiarity. A common personalist front was gradually formed in Europe to oppose the rise of atheism and of totalitarian ideologies. It brought together eminent thinkers such as Nikolai Berdyaev (1874 – 1948), Jacques Maritain (1882 – 1973) and Emmanuel Mounier (1905 – 1950) in France, Maria Montessori (1870 – 1952) in Italy, the Italian exile Luigi Sturzo (1871 – 1959), and Alfred North Whitehead (1861 – 1947), who lived in Great Britain and then in the United States.

Political parties describing themselves as Christian came together in Paris in 1925 to form a Secrétariat International des Partis Démocratiques d'Inspiration Chrétienne [International Secretariat of Democratic Parties Inspired by Christianity]. The Italian Popular Party was founded by Father Luigi Sturzo and by Alcide de Gasperri, and the Popular Action Party by

Angel Herrera Oria in Spain. The Popular Democratic Party in France was driven by personalities such as Robert Schuman and Emmanuel Desgrée du Lou, and so on. Some of these parties had only a brief existence, but they then re-appeared in other forms. But if Christians contributed to the democratization of institutions and to the extension of universal suffrage, including votes for women (first in the Protestant and Orthodox world, and then in the countries with a Catholic tradition, as in France in 1944 under the influence of General de Gaulle), they did not manage to overcome the national rivalries between countries. To further complicate matters, Pope Pius XI discouraged the ecumenical movement. The man who presided over the destiny of the Catholic Church between 1922 and 1939 preferred Catholic Action, understood as the participation of lay people in the hierarchical apostolate of the Church, beyond the "narrow borders of a party." Christian political parties therefore had a limited influence before the end of the Second World War.

The Catholic Church was not as visionary in matters concerning the institutional reform of the Church as it was in questions of social commitment. Nevertheless, in 1919, in Continental Europe, after the carnage of the First World War, the churches could not remain immoveable. In Galicia, Metropolitan Andrei Sheptytsky sought to revive the Eastern sources of the Ukrainian Greek Catholic Church.[39] Interdenominational conversations between leading Catholic and Anglican figures initiated at the end of the nineteenth century were continued in the Malines Conversations. These were presided over by Cardinal Mercier between 1921 and 1926. In the course of the fourth conversation, the Belgian cardinal read out a memorandum entitled "L'Église anglicane unie et non absorbée" [The Church of England United and Not Absorbed] which, by itself, symbolized the beginning of a new era. As Raymond Loonbeck and Jacques Mortiau relate, Dom Lambert Beauduin, a Belgian Benedictine monk, had composed this report in January 1925. In it, he suggested that the Archbishop of Canterbury should receive investiture from the Pope by the imposition of the pallium, and should obtain in this way liturgical and canonical autonomy. Lambert Beauduin's suggestions were particularly bold:

> Pursuing its position to its logical conclusion, the memorandum recommends that all the historic Anglican Sees should be retained, and once underway, that the Catholic Sees whose establishment had been decided upon by the Pope on September

---

39   Peter Galadza, *Unité en division* (Paris: Parole et Silence, 2009).

29, 1850 should be suppressed. Pius VII, the author reminds us, demanded that all titular French bishops — who numbered more than a hundred — should resign in order to make possible the Concordat of 1801. In this new situation, the Archbishop of Canterbury would take fifth place in the rank order of Patriarchs, behind the holders of the ancient Sees of Constantinople, Alexandria, Antioch, and Jerusalem, but ahead of the cardinals![40]

But Cardinal Mercier died in 1926. He left a testament, however: "To be united, it is necessary to love each other; to love each other, it is necessary to know each other; to know each other, it is necessary to meet each other." At the time of the discussions themselves, the method of dialogue employed was comparative (an inventory was made of current agreements and disagreements), selective (discussions were limited to certain points of contention), and then prospective and pragmatic (an attempt was made to imagine the consequences of any eventual recognition of Anglican orders on the part of the Catholic church). For his part, Dom Lambert Beauduin founded the Abbey of Amay sur Meuse in 1925 (which later moved to Chevetogne) with the participation of Metropolitan Andrei Sheptytsky (1865–1944), a Polish-Ukrainian Catholic of the Byzantine rite. This Benedictine community was able to celebrate the Eastern Latin rite, and devoted itself to a coming-together of Eastern and Western Christians. The Catholic abbey celebrates two rites alongside each other [bi-rituelle], and its journal, Irenikon, is the symbol of a new mode in which Christians can come together, a mode that aims to put peace and friendship at the basis of all inter-denominational rapprochement.

The encyclical Mortalium animos of January 6, 1928, however, put a stop to all Catholic initiatives of a unionist kind. The Pope, indeed, reaffirmed in this text the unionist doctrine of the Roman Catholic Church:

> [T]he teaching authority of the Church, which in the divine wisdom was constituted on earth in order that revealed doctrines might remain intact for ever, and that they might be brought with ease and security to the knowledge of men, and which is daily exercised through the Roman Pontiff and the Bishops who are in communion with him, has also the office of defining, when it sees fit, any truth with solemn rites and decrees, whenever this is necessary either to oppose the errors or the attacks of heretics,

40 Raymond Loonbeck and Jacques Mortiau, Un pionnier, Dom Lambert Beauduin (1873–1960). Liturgie et Unité des chrétiens, 2 vols (Louvain la Neuve: Éditions de Chevetogne, 2001), 1:481.

or more clearly and in greater detail to stamp the minds of the faithful with the articles of sacred doctrine which have been explained. But in the use of this extraordinary teaching authority no newly invented matter is brought in, nor is anything new added to the number of those truths which are at least implicitly contained in the deposit of Revelation, divinely handed down to the Church: only those which are made clear which perhaps may still seem obscure to some, or that which some have previously called into question is declared to be of faith. So, Venerable Brethren, it is clear why this Apostolic See has never allowed its subjects to take part in the assemblies of non-Catholics: for the union of Christians can only be promoted by promoting the return to the one true Church of Christ of those who are separated from it, for in the past they have unhappily left it.[41]

It therefore became dangerous for the clergy, and even for Catholic intellectuals like Jacques Maritain in Paris, openly to pursue their ecumenical commitments. There were, however, a few notable exceptions. One can mention the Semaines pour l'unité des chrétiens [Weeks for Christian Unity] started by Abbé Paul Couturier (1881 – 1953)[42] in Lyon in 1933, or the publication by the Dominican father Yves Congar with the publishing house Cerf of the book Chrétiens désunis. Principes d'un "œcuménisme" catholique [Christians disunited: principles for a Catholic "ecumenism"] in July 1937.

THE IMPETUS GIVEN BY THE ECUMENICAL PATRIARCHATE AND THE PARIS SCHOOL

In January 1920, when the Ottoman Empire found itself isolated after its defeats at the hands of the Allies, and after the genocide of Armenians in 1915 had demonstrated the devastating power of the Young Turks, the Metropolitan Dorothée of Brussels, the locum tenens of the Patriarchate of Constantinople, published an encyclical addressed "to the churches of Christ around the world," and so to the oikouménē of the churches:

> Our own church holds that rapprochement between the various Christian churches and fellowship between them is not excluded by the doctrinal differences which exist between them. In our opinion such a rapprochement is highly desirable and necessary.

---

41 "Mortalium animos: Encyclical of Pope Pius XI on Christian Unity," sections 9 – 10: https://www.vatican.va.

42 Maurice Villain, L'abbé Paul Couturier: apôtre de l'Unité chrétienne; souvenirs et documents (Tournai: Casterman, 1957).

It would be useful in many ways for the real interest of each particular church and of the whole Christian body, and also for the preparation and advancement of that blessed union which will be completed in the future in accordance with the will of God. We therefore consider that the present time is most favourable for bringing forward this important question and studying it together.[43]

The synod of Constantinople proposed the creation of a League of Churches, comparable to the League of Nations that had just been created at Versailles in 1919, with the aim of protecting the interests of all the Churches in the wake of the collapse of the kingdoms and empires which had protected them before the First World War.

The Russian revolution of February 1917 separated Church and State, which made possible not only the holding of the Council of Moscow in 1917–1918, and the re-establishment of the Patriarchate, but also the first ecumenical advances on the part of the Russian Church towards the Church of England. However, after 1927, the Russian Church, once more stripped of patriarchal authority by the Bolsheviks after the death of Patriarch Tikhon in 1925, swore allegiance to the Soviet state.[44] But some members of this historic council of the Russian Orthodox Church, like Metropolitan Evlogy Georgiyevsky, fled to Paris. There, in 1925, they founded the Institut St Serge [St Sergius Institute], which became one of the main drivers of the ecumenical movement in the twentieth century, thanks to a number of its teachers such as Sergij Bulgakov, Georgij Florovsky, and Nicholas Afanasiev.[45] Metropolitan Evlogy struck up friendly relations with Father Couturier. He reminded him of the famous words of Metropolitan Platon of Kiev, that "the walls which separate us do not reach as far as heaven." They both took part in the creation of the ecumenical movement, and in 1929 created with some Anglicans the Fellowship of St Alban and St Sergius. An Anglican priest of the Brotherhood of St Alban and St Sergius affirmed the following in 1936:

---

43   "Unto the Churches of Christ Everywhere," Encyclical of the Ecumenical Patriarchate, 1920: www.oikoumene.org.

44   Stalin re-established the Patriarchate in 1943, and encouraged the holding of a Pan-Orthodox conference in Moscow in 1948, with the aim of bringing all Orthodox Churches under its control. The effort collapsed in the absence of the Ecumenical Patriarchate, but the Soviet state exercised tight control over the Russian Orthodox Church as well as the Orthodox Churches of the Central European countries until 1991.

45   Antoine Arjakovsky, The Way: Religious Thinkers of the Russian Emigration and their Journal, 1925–1940 (Notre Dame, IN: University of Notre Dame Press, 2013).

I believe that the Russians in Paris are performing an even greater service than that of conserving its faith for the Russia of tomorrow. They have brought something to the West, and they are receiving something from it. If there were at once an intensification of Anglican mystical devotion under the contact with Russian mysticism, and a broadening of the Orthodox vision on the social and economic side implied by the Gospel and the sacraments under the contact with Anglican social thought, then from this abyss of suffering and sorrow there would have been born something of considerable importance for God's Church as a whole. [46]

After nearly ten years of carefully building ties in the Anglo-Russian Fellowship, Father Sergij Bulgakov and Bishop Gore declared themselves, between 1933 and 1936, in favor of reciprocal Eucharistic hospitality among Orthodox and Anglican Christians. The plan was not put into practice, because of resistance from one side (Georgij Florovsky) and the other (O. Clarke). [47] Both Father Sergij and Gore were deeply spiritual men, and both contributed to a situation in which all Orthodox Churches gradually came to belong to the World Council of Churches in the twentieth century. [48] The pan-Orthodox and ecumenical initiatives of the Paris School were recognized by the Ecumenical Patriarchate, from which most of the Russian emigrés in Paris came, when, in September 1961, a pan-Orthodox synaxis was held at Rhodes by Patriarch Athenagoras. All the Orthodox Churches participated in this meeting, as well as representatives of the non-Chalcedonian Churches of the World Council of Churches. It was called in order to react in a concerted way to the announcement of the Catholic Second Vatican Council. A wind of reform was blowing. The Orthodox Churches were unanimous in their support for the World Council of Churches. In a talk that has remained famous, Mgr Konstandinis de Myre affirmed that the Orthodox Church "refuses to let itself be defined by the narrow frameworks of the past, and to be thought of as the Church of the first eight centuries, the first seven Ecumenical Councils, and of the Fathers of the fourth and fifth centuries." [49]

But in the face of resistance from some bishops, the Orthodox Churches understood that it was necessary for them first to resolve some internal problems before they could speak with one voice. In 1964, Patriarch

---

46 Irenikon 13 (1936), 64.
47 Arjakovsky, The Way, 369–70.
48 After 1998, the Orthodox Churches of Bulgaria and Georgia left the WCC, while continuing to participate in some of its activities.
49 Konstandinis de Myre, Lumière et Vie (1961), 139.

Athenagoras took the decision to create the Pan-Orthodox Center of Chambésy, a few kilometers away from the headquarters of the WCC in Geneva. He went to Chambésy in 1965 after his historic visit to Rome and to Canterbury. The Chambésy center was inaugurated in June 1966, and formed a base for organizing the talks that would prepare for the Pan-Orthodox Council. But the ecumenical enthusiasm of the 1960s soon ran dry. The Orthodox Church did not take part in the Second Vatican Council, as some people had at first hoped. Only the Russian Church and the Institut St Serge in Paris sent a few representatives to act as observers.

THE COMMITMENT OF THE ANGLICAN CHURCH AND OF THE PROTESTANTS

The Ecumenical Patriarchate of Constantinople's idea for a League of Churches comparable to the League of Nations was taken up again with the calling of the Lambeth Conference in October 1920. The British bishops were inspired by the famous Lambeth Quadrilateral, itself inspired by William Reed Huntington and adopted by the Episcopalian Church at Chicago in 1886, and then, in 1888, by the Church of England, at the third Lambeth Conference. In it, Anglican doctrine was synthesized into four points with a view to making reconciliation with other Christian churches possible. The four pillars are: Holy Scripture, which contains everything necessary to salvation and which forms the last recourse in matters of faith; the Niceno-Constantinopolitan Creed and the Apostles' Creed, which are sufficient expositions of Scripture; the sacraments instituted by Christ himself (baptism and the Eucharist); and the historic episcopacy, adapted to local conditions. This stripped-down conception of Anglican identity led to numerous internal discussions, especially with the so-called "high Church" group of Anglicans which recognized five, rather than two, sacraments. The fourth pillar, of the episcopacy, was also contested from different directions by the Catholic Church and by Congregationalist communities. But this synthetic, flexible, and open approach forged the resolutely ecumenical identity of the Anglican Church in the twentieth century, which defined itself as at once catholic, reformed, and orthodox. In October 1920, the Anglican bishops of the whole world proposed a new ecumenical and eschatological conception of the catholic Church:

> We acknowledge all those who believe in our Lord Jesus Christ, and have been baptized into the name of the Holy Trinity, as sharing with us membership in the universal Church of Christ which is his Body. We believe that the Holy Spirit has called us

in a very solemn and special manner to associate ourselves in penitence and prayer with all those who deplore the divisions of Christian people, and are inspired by the vision and hope of a visible unity of the whole Church. We believe that God wills fellowship. By God's own act this fellowship was made in and through Jesus Christ, and its life is in his Spirit. We believe that it is God's purpose to manifest this fellowship, so far as this world is concerned, in an outward, visible, and united society, holding one faith, having its own recognized officers, using God-given means of grace, and inspiring all its members to the world-wide service of the Kingdom of God. This is what we mean by the Catholic Church. We do not ask that any one Communion should consent to be absorbed into another. We do ask that all should unite in a new and great endeavour to recover and to manifest to the world the unity of the Body of Christ for which he prayed.[50]

This declaration served as a basis for the Anglican church's ecumenical commitment, which gave rise in 1948 to the World Council of Churches. It also gave support to the creation of the Church of South India in September 1947, on the eve of Indian independence. This Indian church managed to reunite the Anglican church, the British Methodist church, and some Congregationalist and Reformed churches. Today it represents one of the most numerically significant Christian churches in India, after the Roman Catholic church.[51]

During the inter-war period, the questioning of denominational consciousness was the work above all of the Protestant, Anglican, and Orthodox communities. The Parliament of Religions which assembled in 1893 in Chicago did not manage to turn itself into an institution. Nevertheless, the meeting prompted, in the following century, an extension of the ecumenical movement, towards inter-religious dialogue. In July 1936, the World Congress of Faiths was held in London, on the initiative of the British explorer and settler Francis Younghusband (1863–1942).

---

50 "The Lambeth Conference: Resolutions Archive from 1920": https://www. anglicancommunion.org/media/127731/1920.pdf, resolution 9, in which the Anglican Church distinguishes between the historical Church and the universal Church, and proposes an ecumenical and eschatological definition of the catholic Church.

51 The Christian churches can count around twenty-eight million followers in India, or 2.3% of the population (2011 figures). The churches with the largest numbers of faithful are the Catholic Church (11 million), the Assemblies of God (5 million), the Lutheran church (4.2 million), the Church of South India (4 million), the Syro-Malabar Church (4 million) and the Syro-Malankara Catholic Church (2.5 million).

Among the speakers at this Congress were D. T. Suzuki, one of the first Zen Buddhist scholars to write in English, the Confucianist S. I. Hsiung, the Muslim Yusuf Ali, the Hindu Sarvepalli Radhakrishnan, who later became President of India, the Jewish professor J. L. Magnes, the Sikh Sirdar Mohan Singh, and the Baha'i leader Shoghi Effendi. Alan Watts, who later moved to America and became the Zen Buddhist guru of the "beat generation" in the 1950s, was also present at the Congress. Later on, in the 1960s, Juliet Hollister (1916 – 2000) created the "Temple of Understanding" with the support of personalities such as Eleanor Roosevelt, with the same goal of creating a more just and more peaceful world by means of inter-religious education.

The Edinburgh conference of 1910 also prompted, after the First World War, the creation of the International Missionary Council in 1921 at Lake Mohonk, New York. The IMC organized conferences at Jerusalem (1928) and at Tambaram, near Chennai (Madras) in 1938, at the instigation of John Mott. The movement for "practical Christianity," Life And Work, was formed in Stockholm in 1925, with 661 delegates and 37 nations represented, from 31 Christian churches, and then continued at Oxford in 1937 (when 44 nations attended), at the instigation of the Archbishop of Uppsala and primate of Sweden, Lars Olof Jonathan Söderblom (1866 – 1931). The latter received the Nobel Peace Prize in 1930 "for his efforts to involve the churches not only in the work towards ecumenical union, but also that towards world peace." Finally, the Faith and Order movement, begun at Edinburgh in 1910, was created starting with two large conferences, at Lausanne in 1927 (400 delegates from 108 churches) and then at Edinburgh in 1937 (122 churches), under the oversight of the English Archbishop William Temple. The ecumenical movement positioned itself very clearly against any form of racism or anti-Semitism, especially at the Oxford conference of 1937. From the very beginning of the institutionalization of the ecumenical movement, a tension appeared between those who, like Nathan Söderblom, the Lutheran Archbishop of Uppsala, held that the word "ecumenical" meant "that which concerns the life of the Church as a whole," and those for whom, like Father Georgij Florovsky, ecumenism consisted first of all in recognizing together the truth of faith. The synthesis between the two came from Willem Visser't Hooft (1900 – 1985), a young Dutch Reformed theologian, who had been influenced by Karl Barth and who was noticed in the 1920s by John Mott and John Oldham. Visser't Hooft later became the first Secretary General of the WCC (from 1948 – 1966) thanks to his ecumenical vision:

An ecumenical movement that interests itself only in doctrine remains hanging in the air. An ecumenical movement that interests itself only in action loses its identity as a movement centered on Christ, and thus becomes the tool of forces set up against each other in the social and political domain.... The ecumenical movement has a future only if it resists the temptation to choose between the unity of the Church and the unity of humanity, and learns in its turn to become more and more aware that the Lord gathers his people together so that they may be the light of the world.[52]

THE DYNAMIC OF CONVERGENCE AFTER THE SECOND WORLD WAR

The Second World War, starting with the Molotov-Ribbentrop pact on August 23, 1939 in Moscow, ended in the surrender of the Nazi regime on May 8, 1945 and the surrender of Japan on September 2, 1945. It was the most murderous conflict in history, with more than sixty million dead, of whom at least forty million were civilians. In this sense, it represents the most striking failure ever of modern secular and denominational consciousness.

The Successes of Christian Democracy

After the war, thanks to their commitment to the resistance to totalitarianism, Christian Democrats took power in Europe and contributed, between 1945 and 1965, to four major advances: the re-establishment of a state possessing the rule of law and democracy; a political reconciliation between nations that had been at war for centuries; the creation of the European Economic Community; and the movement for the decolonization of the European empires. A succession of popes, from Pius XII to Paul VI, went along with this movement. This is not the place to tell the story of the popular republican movement, of the CDU (Christian Democratic Union) and the CSU (the Bavarian party, the Christian Social Union) or of the Italian Christian Democrat party, whose fates were very different from each other. The history of the role of Christians in the re-establishment of democracy, in reconciliation, in the creation of European institutions, and in the decolonization movement have been the subject of many studies.[53]

---

52   Ans J. van der Bent, "W. A. Visser't Hooft (1900–1985), a biographical presentation," in W. A. Visser't Hooft, *pionnier de l'œcuménisme Genève-Rome*, ed. Jacques Maury (Paris: Cerf, 2001), 37.
53   Corine Defrance and Ulrich Pfeil, Histoire Franco-Allemande, vol. 10, *Entre Guerre froide et Intégration européenne. Reconstruction et Rapprochement, 1945–1963*

We shall give only three examples of the major contribution of Christians to this process.

It was a Catholic convert from Alsace, of Jewish and Protestant heritage, Joseph Rovan (1918 – 2004), who published a programmatic article in favor of reconciliation in Emmanuel Mounier's journal *Esprit* on October 1, 1945, entitled "L'Allemagne de nos mérites" [The Germany We Deserve]. Even before he was a naturalized French citizen, while he was still exiled in France with his family, Rovan had enlisted in the Resistance, and had been arrested and sent to Dachau, where he had met Edmond Michelet. The latter, who became General de Gaulle's defense minister after the war, entrusted to Rovan the task of looking after German prisoners of war in French hands. Rovan was one of the great builders of the policy of twinning French and German towns with each other. Chancellor Helmut Kohl later made him his advisor on Franco-German relations.

The second example is that of European reconstruction, which was possible only thanks to the political reconciliation between France and Germany. It was again a Christian, Robert Schuman, who, as the French government's minister for foreign affairs, announced on May 9, 1950, the creation of the European Coal and Steel Community, after having received support from the leaders of the governments of the six member states. This was, for one who had spent part of the war in the sanctuary of La Salette, a way of putting into practice the vision expressed by the prophet Isaiah: "they shall beat their swords into plowshares, and their spears into pruning-hooks: nation shall not lift up sword against nation, neither shall they learn war any more" (Is. 2:4). On July 8, 1962, a mass for peace in Reims Cathedral, in which General de Gaulle and Chancellor Konrad Adenaeur took part, sealed the Franco-German reconciliation. This mass was one of the origins of the Treaty of Paris in 1963.

It is also well-known — and this is our third example — that General de Gaulle played a decisive role in making France decolonize upon his return to power in 1958. We will content ourselves, therefore, with noting, along with the historian Jean-Marie Mayer, the ecumenical spirit that presided after the war over the success of the Christian Democrat leaders:

(Villeneuve d'Ascq: Presses du Septentrion, 2012); Wolfram Kaiser, *Christian Democracy and the Origins of the European Union* (Cambridge: Cambridge University Press, 2007); Pierre Letamendia, *La démocratie chrétienne* (Paris: Presses Universitaires de France, 1993); Maurice Vaussard, *Histoire de la démocratie chrétienne* (Paris: Seuil, 1956). See also the website europe-infos.eu on the role of Christians in the formation of the European Union.

In the Resistance, a *de facto* rapprochement was affirmed among different denominations, as well as a search for ecumenism. From then on, it became possible to found a party calling itself "Christian" without arousing from the outset the suspicion of clericalism; and it became possible to bring together Catholics and Protestants in one organization, giving life to Windthorst's old dream.[54]

The Creation of the World Council of Churches

Just as the League of Nations was created shortly before the great conferences on Work and Life and on Faith and Order, the World Council of Churches was created shortly after the adoption of the United Nations Charter in San Francisco on June 26, 1945. The charter upheld the fundamental rights and dignity of each human person. It created a new international institutional foundation in the United Nations Organization.

The double movement, both social and institutional, on the part of Anglican, Protestant, and Orthodox Christians between the two world wars converged in the creation of the World Council of Churches on August 23, 1948. The assembly was held at Amsterdam in the presence of 147 Christian denominations coming from 44 countries. The Council set for its goal the service of the universal Church by the creation of a "fraternal association of churches that accept Our Lord Jesus Christ as God and Savior." In their closing statement, the Anglican, Lutheran, Reformed, Methodist, and Orthodox signatories announced that "in forming the WCC, we have bound ourselves to a new obligation towards Him, and we have bound ourselves one to another. We have decided to remain together." Visser't Hooft then found this historic phrase: "It was one of those moments when God seems to gather up the whole history of the past so as to bring it to fulfillment in a flash of lightning."

The International Missionary Council merged with the WCC in Delhi in 1961. The bishop of the Church of South India, Lesslie Newbiggin (1909 – 1998), then became the first director of the WCC's Commission on World Mission and Evangelism. Today the WCC, whose offices are in Geneva, brings together around 350 churches and church communities, representing over 500 million Christians from more than a hundred of the world's countries.[55]

---

54 Jean-Marie Mayeur, *Des partis catholiques à la démocratie chrétienne* (Paris: Armand Colin, 1980), 195.
55 https://www.oikoumene.org.

At the Amsterdam meeting, Christians trusted in their ability to reconcile the social principle with the liberal principle. The founding assembly of 1948 had the theme "The World's Disorder and God's Plan." It opened the floor to speakers such as the Swiss Reformed theologian Karl Barth (1886 – 1968) and the British Biblical scholar C. H. Dodd (1884 – 1973). On a more political level, it invited John Foster Dulles (1888 – 1959), an American Presbyterian who was a diplomat and who had taken part in setting up the United Nations, to contribute, as well as the Reformed Czech theologian Josef Hromadka (1889 – 1969). The latter, a militant anti-Nazi who had returned to Prague in 1947, represented the voice of the Christians of the socialist world, before the Cold War set in. His debate with John Foster Dulles, an anti-communist Republican, confirmed the world's division into two large ideological groupings identified by Winston Churchill in his speech at Fulton on March 5, 1946.

In January 1953, Dulles became Secretary of State in the United States, and, until 1959, implemented the policy of "containment" of communist regimes on behalf of President Eisenhower. He could count on the support of his brother Allen Dulles, the director of the CIA. The Reformed theologian and socialist Hromadka, for his part, set up the Christian Peace Conference in 1958. But he resigned from the organization after Soviet troops entered Czechoslovakia in 1968.

The WCC continued its pre-war efforts to bear common witness on behalf of the churches on the burning issues that concerned the people of the world. In 1948, it declared itself in favor of the creation of the State of Israel. This first, striking decision of the new assembly was the first of many political positions which the WCC took, whether on the question of possible paths to reconciliation between Israelis and Palestinians in the Middle East, [56] or on other issues linked to justice, peace, and the protection of the environment. [57]

The WCC also decided to add a new dimension to its activities, in addition to theological and political reflection, as well as social action and missionary work: ecumenical education. The castle of Bossey, twenty kilometers from Geneva, in Switzerland, which had first been used in 1946 by W. Visser't Hooft to host ecumenical training courses, became the base for a great deal of training activity in ecumenical thought for the younger generations of the various churches. It was led, in particular, by the Greek

---

56   Ibid.
57   World Council of Churches, "Care for Creation and Climate Justice," https://www.oikoumene.org.

Orthodox theologian Nikos Nissiotis, and then by John Samuel Mbiti, a Kenyan Anglican philosopher who was regarded as "the father of modern African theology," but also, latterly, by one of his former pupils, the Orthodox Romanian priest Ioan Sauca, who, in 2020, became the acting Secretary General of the WCC. Sauca was at the heart of the WCC's educational strategy after the setting-up, in 1969, of an education department. In the 1970s and 1980s the department was especially influenced by the work and personality of Paolo Freire (1921 – 1997), a Brazilian pedagogue who was close to liberation theology, and the Archbishop of Recife, Dom Helder Camara (1909 – 1999).

The founding assembly of Amsterdam was also marked by shared prayers, which represented a decisive development with regard to the first meetings in the 1930s. From 1948 onwards, all the main poles of the ecumenical movement could be found brought together: the pole of reflection on the institutional order, the cultic pole, the pole of social justice and evangelization, and, lastly, the pole of education. The whole subsequent history of the World Council of Churches, and with it of the ecumenical movement, was marked by the relations between these four poles of the Christian faith.

At the second assembly, in Evanston, near Chicago, in 1954, 163 churches from 48 countries gathered again around the theme, "Christ, the only hope of the world." In the new charter it adopted, the WCC specified that it was a "fraternal association of churches which accept Our Lord Jesus Christ as God and Savior."[58] In 1961, in New Delhi, at the third General Assembly, the member churches of the WCC, to which were added, in particular, the Orthodox Churches of the Eastern nations, took a step further. They defined themselves as "a fraternal association of churches that confess Lord Jesus Christ as God and Savior according to the Scriptures, and that are endeavoring to respond together to their shared vocation for the glory of God alone, Father, Son, and Holy Spirit."[59] At a moment when the events unfolding in Rome were on everyone's lips, the united churches of India affirmed that at the WCC they were in a "permanent state of council." The Catholic Church sent observers to New Delhi. It was not a member of the WCC, but, given the launch of the Second Vatican Council, it decided to take part, in particular through the Faith and Order Commission. This Commission organized a gathering of more than five hundred participants

---

58   https://www.oikoumene.org.
59   Jean-Paul Willaime, "Le Conseil œcuménique des Eglises," in Jean-Marie Mayeur, ed., Histoire du christianisme, vol. 13, Crises et renouveau (Paris: Desclée, 2000), 147.

in Montreal in 1963. At this assembly, Christians found a shared language to understand the Tradition, with a capital T, as "the Gospel itself handed down from generation to generation in and through the Church, Christ himself present in the life of the Church." Tradition with a small t was, meanwhile, understood as the denominational form of tradition, marked by the history of different churches. Denominational conceptions of the foundation of the church were able to encounter each other without fear. Three years later, in 1966, a conference devoted to the theme "Church and Society," this time initiated by the Commission for Life and Work, was held in Geneva. Its mission was to discern the movements of the Spirit within various theological and ideological trends, such as the theology of revolution. From 1964 onwards, a "Joint Working Group" of the Roman Catholic Church and the World Council of Churches was put in place.

Thus the WCC represents, together with the Pontifical Council for Promoting Christian Unity, one of the main institutional vectors of the ecumenical movement, thanks to its global assemblies, which are held every seven years,[60] thanks also to its Ecumenical Institute in Bossey, to its publications, to its Commissions for ecumenical and inter-religious dialogue, and to its mission and social justice initiatives.

The Catholic Revolution

In 1928, the Catholic Church had rejected the ecumenical movement in the name of its unionist conception of unity. But the Lyonnais Catholic priest Paul Couturier, Father Yves Congar, author of the 1937 book *Chrétiens désunis* — *Principes d'un "œcuménisme" catholique* [Christians Disunited — Principles of a Catholic "Ecumenism"], Dom Lambert Beauduin, and other Catholic pioneers of ecumenism in Europe did not despair. They originated a spiritual and post-unionist conception of ecumenism. After the Second World War, this conception strongly influenced Brother Roger Schütz (1915 – 2005) and Mother Geneviève Micheli (1883 – 1961), the two Protestant founders of the men's community, Taizé, in France, and the women's community of Grandchamp, in Switzerland.[61] All these people were aware of the link between the Franco-German wars of the nineteenth and twentieth centuries and the "break-up of Christianity" in the medieval

---

60   Amsterdam, 1948; Evanston, 1954; New Delhi, 1961; Uppsala, 1968; Nairobi, 1975; Vancouver 1983; Canberra, 1991; Harare, 1998; Porto Alegre, 2006; Busan, 2013. The eleventh General Assembly was postponed until August–September 2022 in Karlsruhe because of the coronavirus pandemic. www.oikoumene.org.
61   "Tiers-Ordre de l'Unité," Communauté de Grandchamp, https://www.grandchamp.org.

era. They had been influenced by the Liturgical Movement initiated at the end of the nineteenth century by figures such as Dom Prosper Guéranger, on the Catholic side, and Jules Amiguet, on the Protestant.[62] They also acknowledged the power of reconciliation emanating from Andrei Rublev's icon of the Trinity.[63] Brother Roger, before beginning a life in community at Taizé in 1949, had welcomed Jews hunted by the Nazis to his hermitage, and then, after the war, had done the same for German prisoners of war. Since the thirties, Paul Couturier, who was a friend of the Russian Orthodox Metropolitan Evlogy Georgiyevsky and of the Reformed pastor Wilfred Monod, disseminated tracts calling for prayers for Christian unity[64] and for the formation of an "invisible monastery":

> If, every Thursday evening, in a weekly commemoration of Holy Thursday, an ever greater multitude of Christians of every denomination were to form themselves into something like a giant network enveloping the whole earth, like a vast invisible monastery in which all would be absorbed in prayer to Christ for Unity, would not this be the dawn of Christian unity breaking upon the world? Is it not this attitude of sincere, deep, and ardent spiritual emulation for which the Father is waiting in order to make real the visible unity of the body of the Church, in order to accomplish all the necessary miracles to reunite in his visible Church all those who love him, and who have been visibly marked by his baptismal seal?[65]

The Taizé community subsequently became the spearhead of the ecumenical movement among young Europeans, to the point of hosting each year tens of thousands of young people in Burgundy, and organizing large

---

62   André Bardet, *Un combat pour l'Église. Un siècle de mouvement liturgique en Pays de Vaud* (Lausanne: Bibliothèque historique vaudoise, 1988).

63   Sœur Minke, "La catholicité vécue à la Communauté de Grandchamp. Une expérience de spiritualité œcuménique," *Vers une catholicité œcuménique* (Fribourg: Academic Press, 2013), 259 – 66.

64   Paul Couturier's prayer is as follows: "Lord Jesus, who, the night before you died for us, prayed for all your disciples to be perfectly one, as you are in your Father, and as your Father is in you, make us feel the pain of the unfaithfulness of our disunity. Give us the loyalty to recognize, and the courage to reject, that which is hidden in us of indifference, of mistrust, and even of mutual enmity. Grant us to meet each other in you, so from our souls and from our lips there shall ascend without ceasing your prayer for the unity of Christians, as you will it, by the means which you will. In you, who are perfect charity, make us find the path which leads to unity, in obedience to your love and to your truth."

65   Villain, *L'abbé Paul Couturier*, 73.

gatherings of young people in and beyond Europe for the New Year as well.[66] After Brother Roger's tragic death in 2005, Brother Aloïs became the prior of a community comprising a hundred brothers coming from all around the world. The Orthodox theologian Olivier Clément paid homage to this at once Catholic and Protestant community, which is able to celebrate the Eucharist jointly. In his book, he reveals the secret of Taizé:

> At Taizé [the young people] are attracted because of its universality, yet, at the same time, the identity of each is preserved. Nobody is asked to give up his or her national or denominational allegiance; on the contrary, these allegiances enrich each other, and learn to accept each other. Young Christians can thus live out unity in diversity.... At Taizé there is a concrete universal together with undisguised particularisms, which communicate with each other.[67]

The Focolare movement was also born during the Second World War, at Trento in 1943. Its foundress, Chiara Lubich, seeing the disaster of the bombing of her city, decided to turn to God to rebuild civilization, beginning from God's promise of friendship to His disciples. Later, she will write:

> It is 1943. War is raging, in Trento as elsewhere. Ruins, debris, and many dead. For various reasons, I get together with other young people of my own age. One day, I find myself with my new friends in a dark cave, with a lit candle and the Gospel in my hands. I open the book and I read Jesus's prayer: "Father... that they may be one" (John 17:11 – 21). This is not an easy text, for we are hardly ready for this, yet these words seem to become clearer one by one, and they put in our hearts the conviction that we were born for this page of the Gospel.[68]

In May 1944, Lubich set up the first *focolare*, meaning "hearth," with several other young women. Little by little, the group expanded, and in 1945, it numbered more than five hundred. In 1948, Chiara Lubich got to know Igino Giordani, a writer and journalist, and then a Christian Democrat deputy. He becomes the first married *focolarino*, and an ardent promoter of the Focolare movement, facilitating its rapid spread in Europe,

---

66   One can also add the Pomeyrol Community of Saint Étienne du Grès in the Gard region, which has adopted the Taizé office and has given rise to a Third order.
67   Olivier Clément, *Taizé, un sens à la vie* (Paris: Bayard/Centurion, 1997), 26.
68   Chiara Lubich, *Pensée et spiritualité* (Paris: Nouvelle Cité, 2003), 44.

and then to other continents. The Focolare movement is today an inter-national ecumenical community, made up mostly of women, and with statutes approved by the Holy See. The movement, led since 2008 by Maria Voce, is one of the main lay communities in the world, with roots in 180 countries, more than 140,000 members, and two million sympathizers. From 2021, its president is Margaret Karram, a Catholic Arab Israeli born in Haifa. The movement is especially committed to inter-religious dialogue and to the theme of the economy of communion. It has inspired several hundred firms to share part of their profits with the very poorest in soci-ety. The movement also has a university, Sophia University, led by Piero Coda. The university is based in the experimental city of Loppiano, near Florence, one of the twenty-four small cities founded by the movement.[69]

All these ecumenical initiatives, to which one can also add the Semaines liturgique œcuméniques [Ecumenical Liturgical Weeks] at the Institut Saint Serge in Paris from 1953 onwards, prepared the way for the great turn taken by the Catholic Church at the beginning of the 1960s. Pope John XXIII relaunched the ecumenical commitments of the Roman Church by the announcement on January 25, 1959, at the end of the celebration of the week of prayer for Christian unity, of the convocation of the Second Vatican Council. In June 1960, he set up the Pontifical Secretariat for Promoting Christian Unity, whose presidency was entrusted to Cardinal Bea. The Secretariat was the project of Mgr Jan Willebrands, a Dutchman who in 1952 had organized, with Frans Theissen, a Catholic conference on ecumenical issues.

The Council opened on October 11, 1962, with a mass and a speech by John XXIII, *Gaudet Mater Ecclesia*. The fathers of the Council soon acknowledged that the Catholic Church stood in need of purification and renewal. The Council took an unexpected turn on October 13, thanks to an intervention by Cardinal Liénart of Lille, demanding a postpone-ment of the votes to appoint the members of the commissions. He was immediately supported by Cardinal Frings, the Archbishop of Cologne, known for his opposition to the Nazi regime. The meeting immediately applauded both Liénart and then Frings. "Two minutes and thirty seconds" then elapsed before Mgr Felici, the Italian who was the Secretary of the Council, agreed to let the fathers take the Council into their own hands. Liénart later related that he had taken the decision to speak up during the mass that preceded the meeting. By means of this *coup de théâtre*, and this first symbolic victory, the Council allowed the reforming and ecumenical

---

69   "L'université Focolare Sophia en audience chez le pape," https://www.focolare.org/.

current of opinion among the bishops to gain the upper hand over the conservative side, which was then in the majority in the curia.[70]

In the course of its work, the Council drew a distinction between those who had been involved in the origin of the divisions and the Christians who had been born into a situation of division, and who could not be held responsible for those divisions, nor obliged to display any loyalty towards them. This approach freed history from the yoke of the past. After the death of Pope John XXIII on June 3, 1963, and the election of Paul VI, the latter opened the Second Session of the Council on September 29, 1963, with these words, which bore witness to the spirit of continuity wished for by the new Pope: "This, then, is a Council of invitation, of expectation, and of trust in a wider and more fraternal participation in its authentic ecumenicity."

The Council adopted some documents which must briefly be introduced: the dogmatic constitution on the Church, *Lumen Gentium* ("Christ is the light of the nations"); the decree on the Eastern Catholic Churches, *Orientalium Ecclesiarum*, and the decree on ecumenism, *Unitatis Redintegratio* ("The restoration of unity"), promulgated by Paul VI on November 21, 1964.[71] These documents afforded a first definition of the Catholic principles of ecumenism. The great step forward made by the Council was to acknowledge that the one Church of Christ was present in the Catholic Church, while ceasing to identify the borders of the Church of Christ with the borders of the Catholic Church alone.[72] This made it possible to

---

70 Catherine Masson, "L'intervention du cardinal Liénart au concile Vatican II le 13 octobre 1962," in Guillaume Cuchet and Charles Mériaux, *La dramatique conciliaire de l'Antiquité à Vatican II* (Villeneuve d'Ascq: Septentrion, 2019), 385–404.

71 *Lumen Gentium* (vatican.va); *Orientalium Ecclesiarium* (vatican.va); *Unitatis Redintegratio* (vatican.va).

72 "Christ, the one Mediator, established and continually sustains here on earth His holy Church, the community of faith, hope, and charity, as an entity with visible delineation through which He communicated truth and grace to all. But, the society structured with hierarchical organs and the Mystical Body of Christ, are not to be considered as two realities, nor are the visible assembly and the spiritual community, nor the earthly Church and the Church enriched with heavenly things; rather they form one complex reality which coalesces from a divine and a human element. For this reason, by no weak analogy, it is compared to the mystery of the incarnate Word. As the assumed nature inseparably united to Him, serves the divine Word as a living organ of salvation, so, in a similar way, does the visible social structure of the Church serve the Spirit of Christ, who vivifies it, in the building up of the body. This is the one Church of Christ which in the Creed is professed as one, holy, catholic and apostolic, which our Saviour, after His Resurrection, commissioned Peter to shepherd, and him and the other apostles to extend and direct with authority, which He erected for all ages as 'the pillar and mainstay of the truth.' This Church

recognize other churches and other types of ecclesiality within the mystic borders of the Church, just as the decree Unitatis Redintegratio recognized the baptism of all Christians (Unitatis Redintegratio, 3). In distinguishing between full and imperfect communion, the Council understood ecumenism not as a capacity to create an association of Churches, but as the capacity to recognize a communion, which signified a rejection of the previous models of reciprocal absorption or of fusion.[73] Nothing, therefore, which was not necessary (Acts 15:28; Unitatis, 18) ought to be imposed in order to re-establish unity. For the first time since the Council of Florence in the history of the Catholic Church, it was affirmed that "the canonical structure of the Orthodox Churches does not need to be changed," a point which later pleased the Greek Orthodox Metropolitan John Zizioulas.[74]

Peter de Mey, a professor at the Catholic University of Leuven, has, however, noted that the document on the Eastern Catholic Churches did not possess the same ecumenical opening as the other two documents drawn up by different commissions. In particular, the Belgian theologian, Gustave Thils, played a decisive role in drafting Lumen Gentium's section 13, which recognized legitimate forms of plurality within the Catholic Church.

> Within the Church particular Churches hold a rightful place; these Churches retain their own traditions, without in any way opposing the primacy of the Chair of Peter, which presides over the whole assembly of charity and protects legitimate differences, while at the same time assuring that such differences do not hinder unity but rather contribute toward it. (Lumen Gentium, 13)[75]

But in Orientalium Ecclesiarum, these Eastern Churches, which are certainly recognized in their specificity as local churches in communion with

---

constituted and organized in the world as a society, subsists in the Catholic Church, which is governed by the successor of Peter and by the Bishops in communion with him, although many elements of sanctification and of truth are found outside of its visible structure. These elements, as gifts belonging to the Church of Christ, are forces impelling toward catholic unity" (Lumen Gentium, 8).

73   Walter Kasper, "Le décret sur l'œcuménisme. Une nouvelle lecture après 40 ans," in Rechercher l'unité des chrétiens: actes de la conférence internationale organisée à l'occasion du 40e anniversaire de la promulgation du décret "Unitatis redintegratio" du Concile Vatican II, Rome, 11–13 novembre 2004 (Paris: Nouvelle Cité, 2006), 33.

74   John Zizioulas, "Unitatis redintegratio, une rélexion orthodoxe," in Rechercher l'unité des chrétiens, 53.

75   Peter de Mey, "Gustave Thils and Ecumenism at Vatican Council II," The Belgian Contribution to Vatican II (Leuven: Peeters, 2005), 389–413.

the Church of Rome, are nevertheless asked to submit themselves to the Bishop of Rome's decisions:

> The patriarchs with their synods are the highest authority for all business of the patriarchate, including the right of establishing new eparchies and of nominating bishops of their rite within the territorial bounds of the patriarchate, without prejudice to the inalienable right of the Roman Pontiff to intervene in individual cases. (*Orientalium Ecclesiarum*, 9)

The Second Vatican Council did not dare to take the step of distinguishing more clearly the level of ecumenical consciousness from the level of catholic consciousness. This can be understood according to a binary and non-inclusive logic. The conciliar documents therefore identified the Roman Catholic Church with the visible, hierarchical part of the one Church of Christ. It is the Church of Christ "as a constituted and organized society in this world" which subsists in the Catholic Church. The opposite would have been more logical, given the fact that according to the Gospel, the Father's house has "many mansions" (John 14:2), which makes the Church of God a broader space-time than that of the Roman Catholic mansion. But because of its conception of the Roman Catholic Church as the visible part of the Church of Christ, the Second Vatican Council made possible — as indeed happened in 2000, with the declaration *Dominus Iesus* — a stricter reading of the documents adopted, a reading in which the universal Church tends to be identified with the Roman Catholic Church.[76]

Other texts adopted at the Second Vatican Council also had a bearing on ecumenism. The constitution *Dei Verbum*, adopted in 1965, made it possible to bring Catholic, Protestant, and Orthodox Christians more firmly together, by proposing a more balanced relationship between Scripture and Tradition. As Bernard Sesboüé summarizes the matter, Scripture and Tradition were now at last understood as a single reality, the same Word of God consigned to us in writing and through the apostolic tradition.

The declaration *Dignitatis Humanae*, on religious freedom, adopted on December 7, 1965, was also important for ecumenical rapprochement. Inspired by the Jesuit theologian John Courtney Murray, it firmly defended freedom of conscience, because "every human person has the right to religious freedom." This right, which also extended to social groups and to families, had still been disputed by the Vatican before the Council, which

---

76 *Dominus Iesus*, August 6, 2000, www.vatican.va.

refused to give moral permission for error in legitimating freedom of choice. But it was at last possible to acknowledge this right insofar as it had its foundation in the very dignity of the human person. The foundation of law is therefore not subjective. It resides in the very nature of man, which makes it possible to meet in advance any accusation of indifferentism or subjectivism. This declaration therefore rests on a juridical and canonical deepening of the primacy of human consciousness:

> On his part, man perceives and acknowledges the imperatives of the divine law through the mediation of conscience. In all his activity a man is bound to follow his conscience in order that he may come to God, the end and purpose of life. It follows that he is not to be forced to act in a manner contrary to his conscience. Nor, on the other hand, is he to be restrained from acting in accordance with his conscience, especially in matters religious. (Dignitatis Humanae, 3)

The Council also saw the Catholic Church entering into inter-religious dialogue. On October 28, 1965, Pope Paul VI published the declaration Nostre Ætate, "on the Church's relations with non-Christian religions." Article 2 of the declaration was sensational, in that for the first time for a long time, the Catholic Church was open to the truth of the Jewish religion, of Islam, of Hinduism, and of Buddhism:

> The Catholic Church rejects nothing that is true and holy in these religions. She regards with sincere reverence those ways of conduct and of life, those precepts and teachings which, though differing in many aspects from the ones she holds and sets forth, nonetheless often reflect a ray of that Truth which enlightens all men. Indeed, she proclaims, and ever must proclaim Christ "the way, the truth, and the life" (John 14:6), in whom men may find the fullness of religious life, in whom God has reconciled all things to Himself. The Church, therefore, exhorts her sons, that through dialogue and collaboration with the followers of other religions, carried out with prudence and love and in witness to the Christian faith and life, they recognize, preserve and promote the good things, spiritual and moral, as well as the socio-cultural values found among these men. (Nostra Ætate, 2)

The French academic Louis Massignon was one of the main protagonists, together with Father Charles de Foucauld, in the establishment in the twentieth century of a dialogue between Islam and the Catholic Church.

According to Massignon, the few lines dedicated to Islam in *Nostra Ætate* made it possible to launch many initiatives and dialogues in its wake:

> The Church regards with esteem also the Moslems. They adore the one God, living and subsisting in Himself; merciful and all-powerful, the Creator of heaven and earth, who has spoken to men; they take pains to submit wholeheartedly to even His inscrutable decrees, just as Abraham, with whom the faith of Islam takes pleasure in linking itself, submitted to God. Though they do not acknowledge Jesus as God, they revere Him as a prophet. They also honor Mary, His virgin Mother; at times they even call on her with devotion. In addition, they await the day of judgment when God will render their deserts to all those who have been raised up from the dead. Finally, they value the moral life and worship God especially through prayer, almsgiving and fasting. Since in the course of centuries not a few quarrels and hostilities have arisen between Christians and Moslems, this sacred synod urges all to forget the past and to work sincerely for mutual understanding and to preserve as well as to promote together for the benefit of all mankind social justice and moral welfare, as well as peace and freedom. (*Nostra Ætate*, 3)

According to the historian André Kaspi, the passages of the declaration that concern the Jewish religion owe a great deal, for their part, to the work done by the French historian Jules Isaac in the Amitié Judéo-chrétienne de France [French Jewish-Christian Friendship Association] after the Second World War. The part played by the Judeo-Christian Friendship Association of Florence, at the initiative of the Christian Democrat Giorgio La Pira, can also be mentioned. On June 13, 1960, Pope John XXIII had a decisive conversation with Jules Isaac. The latter, as André Kaspi relates, set out his request in the following way:

> Pagan anti-semitism was inconsistent; Nazi anti-semitism was also inconsistent, but what horrors it had committed. "Between the two of them, the only consistent anti-semitism, and the only one that had had any leverage, was the anti-semitism produced by a particular Christian theology, under the pressure of circumstances, because the Jewish denial of Christianity was the main obstacle to Christian propaganda in the pagan world." It was not enough to take a step back from teaching disdain. The voice of the head of the Church must make itself felt. How? It would be fitting to create a subsidiary sub-commission charged

with studying this question. The Pope expressed his agreement. Moreover, he showed understanding and sympathy for what his visitor was saying throughout.[77]

Both men died in 1963, and did not see the fruit of their labors. But the declaration Nostra Ætate encouraged mutual respect between Jews and Christians, and explicitly recommended that Christian teaching should be strictly in conformity with the Gospel. Later, in 1993, this text formed the basis of the Vatican's recognition of the state of Israel.

> Furthermore, in her rejection of every persecution against any man, the Church, mindful of the patrimony she shares with the Jews and moved not by political reasons but by the Gospel's spiritual love, decries hatred, persecutions, displays of anti-semitism, directed against Jews at any time and by anyone. (Nostra Ætate, 4)

Father Claude Jeffré, a French Dominican specializing in inter-religious dialogue was pleased that Nostra Ætate proposed "an ethics of dialogue with other religions." He was also pleased that, with its decree on missionary activity in the Church, Ad Gentes, proclaimed by Paul VI on December 7, 1965, the Council invited believers to respect "the seeds of the Word" present in non-Christian religions (Ad Gentes, 11). Moreover, the role of the Holy Spirit in human history, beyond religious borders, was recognized: "Doubtless, the Holy Spirit was already at work in the world before Christ was glorified" (Ad Gentes, 4).

The pastoral constitution Gaudium et Spes on "The Church in the Modern World," proclaimed in December 1965, also made it possible to imagine that men could be saved outside the visible borders of the Church. It declared, indeed, that "the Holy Spirit in a manner known only to God offers to every man the possibility of being associated with this paschal mystery" (Gaudium et Spes, 22). Starting from this point, one can therefore hold that these elements, as a preparation for the Gospel, played and still play a providential role in the economy of salvation. In recognizing this, the Church felt impelled to enter into dialogue and collaboration. The Trinitarian beginning of the conciliar text quickly became famous:

> The joys and the hopes, the griefs and the anxieties of the men of this age, especially those who are poor or in any way afflicted, these are the joys and hopes, the griefs and anxieties of the

---

77   André Kaspi, Jules Isaac, historien, acteur du rapprochement judéo-chrétien (Paris: Plon, 2002), 234.

> followers of Christ. Indeed, nothing genuinely human fails to
> raise an echo in their hearts. For theirs is a community composed
> of men. United in Christ, they are led by the Holy Spirit in their
> journey to the Kingdom of their Father and they have welcomed
> the news of salvation which is meant for every man. That is why
> this community realizes that it is truly linked with mankind and
> its history by the deepest of bonds. (*Gaudium et Spes*, 1)

But this acknowledgement, and this beginning, for Geffré, did not
supply a theological foundation clearly justifying the dialogue encouraged by the Church. This first theology of inter-religious dialogue was
placed under the sign of the theology of fulfillment. According to the
latter, non-Christian religions played the role of "preparing for the Gospel." Whatever was correct and good in other religions was understood
only as an inferior version, or, at best, as a distant preparation for what
was found in full in Christianity. Thus, for example, for Jules Monch-
anin, Hinduism continually oscillated between the heresy of modalism
(three aspects in God: Being, Knowledge, and Blessedness) and that of
tritheism (Brahma, Vishnu, Shiva). That is why Father Geffré, during the
post-conciliar period, developed, for his part, together with other Christian scholars like Jacques-Albert Cuttat and Olivier Clément, a theology
of religious pluralism recognizing the otherness of other religious traditions in their irreducible difference.[78] The post-modern age of Christian
theology was thus beginning.

Gaudium et Spes, nevertheless, had the great merit of giving a new
impetus on a global scale to the Church's social teaching. In particular,
it suggested that the notion of *cooperation* between states and religions
should be added to the traditional principle of separation between the
kingdom of Caesar and the Kingdom of God:

> The Church and the political community in their own fields
> are autonomous and independent from each other. Yet both,
> under different titles, are devoted to the personal and social
> vocation of the same men. The more that both foster sounder
> cooperation between themselves with due consideration for the
> circumstances of time and place, the more effective[ly] will their
> service be exercised for the good of all. For man's horizons are not
> limited only to the temporal order; while living in the context
> of human history, he preserves intact his eternal vocation. The

---

78   Elodie Maurot, "Claude Geffré expose 40 ans de dialogue interreligieux," *La
Croix*, June 6, 2007, www.la-croix.com.

> Church, for her part, founded on the love of the Redeemer, con-
> tributes toward the reign of justice and charity within the borders
> of a nation and between nations. By preaching the truths of the
> Gospel, and bringing to bear on all fields of human endeavor
> the light of her doctrine and of a Christian witness, she respects
> and fosters the political freedom and responsibility of citizens.
> (*Gaudium et Spes*, 76)

The whole question at issue, however, is whether this development of
the Catholic Church towards the political world, the role of lay people,
and ecumenism, did not arrive a decade too late.

DOCTRINAL AND SOCIAL ECUMENISM (1965–1995)

CHRISTIAN POLITICAL COMMITMENT

The sixties, right around the world, were years of rebellion against a
too-vertical vision of authority. A whole new generation wished to free
itself from excessively authoritarian representations of paternity and of
political and religious power, representations which it considered archaic.
Fewer and fewer of the faithful considered real reform and authentic
declericalization of the institutional Church possible. More and more
believers were turning away from a strictly denominational conception
of faith, understood merely as a form of "belonging," as Grace Davie
put it.[79] It was the deep belief of the American rabbi Abraham Joshua
Heschel, born in Warsaw in 1907, that believers had to stop adopting an
overbearing position in the name of their faith:

> When faith is completely replaced by creed, worship by discipline,
> love by habit; when the crisis of today is ignored because of the
> splendor of the past; when faith becomes an heirloom rather
> than a living fountain; when religion speaks only in the name
> of authority rather than with the voice of compassion — its
> message becomes meaningless.[80]

This type of conviction reflected the spirit of the new generation. It
prompted Rabbi Heschel to enter into dialogue with the great spiritual

---

79   Grace Davie, "Believing without Belonging: Is This the Future of Religion in
Britain?" *Social Compass* 37 (4) (1990), 455–69.
80   Abraham J. Heschel, *God In Search of Man: A Philosophy Of Judaism* (London:
John Calder, 1956), 3.

figures of his time, such as the African-American Baptist pastor Martin Luther King, in order to envisage new forms of governance more centered on people. But mindsets developed more abruptly towards more horizontal and more "neutral" forms of governance. This prompted the transition from an inter-denominational conception of relations between states and churches towards a more secular, even *laïciste*, vision of these relations.

Christian unions and Christian Democratic parties bore the brunt of this change. They experienced, indeed, a slow erosion of their membership and of their influence. Thus in France, for example, article 1 of the statutes of the CFTC (French Christian Workers' Association) was disputed. A painful split in the union ensued between, on the one hand, the heirs of the lay Christian vision of the CFTC, like Gaston Tessier, and, on the other, the founders, such as Jacques Delors and Edmond Maire, of the Confédération Française Démocratique du Travail (CFDT) [French Democratic Confederation of Labor], which was closer to the Socialist party. The situation in Germany was the same; in 1969, after two decades in power, the CDU-CSU [Christian Democratic Union and Christian Social Union] had to surrender the reins of power to a social-liberal coalition. In Italy, after many splits and scandals, the Christian Democrat party was dissolved in 1994.

The history of Christian Democracy was not over, however. Christian Democrats returned to power at various times in the various countries mentioned, especially in Germany and at the level of the European parliament. In 1976, the European People's Party was set up; the party was a federation of Christian Democrat parties in the European Union. It was made up of twelve parties from seven countries, such as the German CDU and CSU, the three faith parties of the Netherlands, the two Christian parties from Belgium, the Social Christian party of Luxembourg, the French CDS [Centre Des Démocrates Sociaux (Social Democrat Center Party)], the Italian Christian Democrats, and so on . . . It was presided over by the Belgian Prime Minister Léo Tindemans. The EPP's program in 1979 called for treaties to be modified so as to strengthen the power of the executive in the Community and extend the powers of the European Parliament. The party helped to elect presidents of the European Commission of a Christian persuasion like Jacques Delors (1985–1995) and his successors from 1995 and 2004, Jacques Santer, Romano Prodi, José Barroso, Jean-Claude Juncker, and Ursula von der Leyen. The EPP's president since 2019 has been Donald Tusk, a Catholic Christian and a former president of the European Council.

Nevertheless, it is certainly the case that, from the 1960s onwards, a new wind was blowing in Europe, marked by a more and more secular conception of society. The EPP's manifesto of 2012 testified to this development within Christian Democracy, moving from explicit reference to a personal, all-creating God to an anthropocentric and eclectic discourse open to all spiritual horizons and founded on "values."[81] This was so far the case that on November 9, 1982, at Santiago de Compostela, Pope John Paul II offered a somber description of the spiritual landscape of Europe:

> In the civil domain, Europe is divided. Artificial fractures deprive its peoples of the right for all to meet each other in a climate of friendship, and of the right freely to bring together their efforts and their creativity in the service of a peaceable social life, or in that of a solidary contribution to resolving problems that affect other continents. Civil life finds itself influenced by the consequences of secularized ideologies, which extend from the denial of God or restrictions on religious freedom to the overwhelming importance given to economic success in relation to human values of work and production; ideologies of materialism and hedonism, which undermine the values of the family of the one and many, values such as that of life's beginning at conception and the moral protection of young people; all the way through to a "nihilism" that incapacitates the will to confront crucial problems such as that of the new poor, emigration, ethnic and religious minorities, good use of means of information, whilst at the same time it provides weapons to terrorism.[82]

This is why, before an audience made up of the King and Queen of Spain, the rectors of the European Catholic universities, the members of the Council of Europe, and representatives of the European episcopacies, the Polish Pope appealed to Europeans as follows:

> I, Bishop of Rome and pastor of the universal Church, from Santiago de Compostela, cry out to you, old Europe, full of love:

---

81 "Manifesto: EPP Statutory Congress," October 17–18, 2012: "We put the human being at the centre of our convictions. We human beings have an inherent natural dignity, which makes us unique. This is valid both for those of us who believe in God as the source of truth, justice, good, and beauty, as well as those who do not share this faith but respect the same universal values as arising from other sources. We recognize Greek and Roman heritage, Judeo and Christian values, as well as the Enlightenment, as being the roots of our civilisation." https://epp/eu.

82 "'Europe, retrouve-toi toi-même', l'appel du pape Jean-Paul II en 1982," La Croix, www.la-croix.com.

> Find yourself again. Be yourself. Discover your origins. Revive
> your roots. Revisit those authentic values which have made your
> history a glorious one, and your presence on other continents a
> beneficial one. Reconstruct your spiritual unity, in a climate of
> complete respect for other religions and for authentic freedoms.[83]

This development in European societies, at once political and religious, contributed to the crisis of denominational consciousness. It prompted a gradual withdrawal on the part of the churches, sometimes of their own volitions, and sometimes under pressure from states and societies, to a more theological and self-centered conception of the ecumenical movement.

THE CONSEQUENCES OF VATICAN II

The churches, nevertheless, sought for a long time to avoid this development by agreeing to open themselves to modernity. Even if one can reasonably wonder whether the Holy See did not act too late, the Second Vatican Council was able to grasp "the joys and sorrows" of its time. That is why it had such a great resonance and was the occasion for so many ecumenical and inter-religious vocations. The Pontifical Council for Promoting Christian Unity was tasked from the beginning with overseeing relations with the Jewish world. Imperceptibly, the inter-denominational conception of ecumenism was transformed into an inter-religious vision.

The situation was the same among the laity. The American Cistercian monk Thomas Merton was committed to inter-religious dialogue, especially among the various monastic traditions:[84] Hinduism, Buddhism, the Zen tradition, Shintoism and Sufism. But the author of *The Seven Storey Mountain* died on December 10, 1968, electrocuted in his hotel bedroom, when he had been taking part in an inter-religious colloquium in Bangkok. His work helped to bring about the establishment in Kyoto in 1970 of the World Conference on Religion and Peace,[85] which today acts as a consultative body for Unesco and Unicef, and which has branches in several countries, France among them.[86] For its part, the Vatican organized from 1978 onwards an inter-religious dialogue between Buddhist and Catholic monks. The Pontifical Council for Interreligious Dialogue's document of 1984 went on to suggest four forms of dialogue situated at

---

83   Ibid.
84   http://www.monasticinterreligiousdialogue.com/.
85   "Religions for Peace," https://rfp.org/.
86   "Religions pour la paix — France," http://religionspourlapaix.org/.

the four poles of religious consciousness, those of law, justice, memory, and glory:

a) The dialogue of life, in which people force themselves to live in a spirit of openness and good neighborliness, sharing their joys and their sorrows, and their problems and human preoccupations;

b) The dialogue of works, in which there is collaboration with a view to the integral development and total emancipation of man;

c) The dialogue of theological exchanges, in which specialists attempt to deepen understanding of their respective religious legacies, and to arrive at an appreciation of the spiritual values of each other's traditions;

d) The dialogue of religious experience, in which people rooted in their own religious traditions share their spiritual riches, for example concerning prayer and contemplation, concerning faith, and concerning ways of seeking God or the Absolute.

The writer André Chouraqui (1917 – 2007), who was present at the Second Vatican Council in Rome had the idea, together with Father Jean Daniélou (1905 – 1974) of an association that could spread a reciprocal and respectful knowledge of the three monotheist religions, Judaism, Christianity, and Islam. Soon joined by the Jesuit Michel Riquet, the man of letters Jacques Nantet, and the rector of the Grand Mosque of Paris, Hamza Boubakeur, they founded the Brotherhood of Abraham (1967). [87] In its *Manifesto*, the Brotherhood sets out the following basis for its work of building a fraternal world:

> Three great religions, three monotheisms — Judaism, Christianity, and Islam — explicitly refer to the same patriarch, Abraham. Whether this is by tradition, as with Ishmael's and Israel's descendants, or whether the line of descent is purely spiritual, as with the Christians, all three consider themselves to be the sons of Abraham. Saint Paul says that "they which are of faith, the same are the children of Abraham" (Gal. 3:7). Thus millions of believers agree in the memory of one and the same man, the father of their peoples, but also a model of faith in the one God, a faith that is essential to all three religions. The Koran offers Abraham as "a paragon of piety, an upright man obedient to God. He was no idolater. He rendered thanks for His favors, so

---

87   "Fraternité d'Abraham," http://www.fraternite-dabraham.com/.

that He chose him and guided him to a straight path."[88] That is why, in a world that is divided, and that is threatened and too often is actually torn apart by the mutual rivalry and enmity of peoples, it seems more than ever the right moment to bring together in one brotherly and peaceful line all those who share at least the faith of Abraham, and consider themselves as his sons, heirs of the promise that God made him: "in thy seed shall all the nations of the earth be blessed" (Gen. 22:18).[89]

A few years later, in 1977, the Groupe de recherche islamo-chrétien [Islamic-Christian Research Group] was created in Paris. This also has branches in the Arab world, such as that in Tunis. In 1993, the former Algerian minister and philosopher Mustafa Cherif, together with the White Father Michel Lelong, set up an Islamic-Christian Friendship Group. These initiatives, and others, were prompted by Pope John Paul II's journeys to Muslim countries, such as his trip to Kaduna in Nigeria in 1982, and that to Casablanca, in Morocco, in 1985. After these, in 1988, the Vatican created the Pontifical Council for Interreligious Dialogue. The Catholic Church in France also has the SRI, the Service de relations avec l'Islam [Islamic Relations Service]. In Rome, the Pontifical Institute for Arabic and Islamic Studies was set up, and in Egypt the Dominican Institute for Oriental Studies. In France, several institutes of religious studies and theology were set up, particularly in Paris, and in Marseille at the initiative of Father Jean-Marc Aveline, who later became Archbishop of Marseille. Mgr Aveline was close, together with Christian Salenson, to Father Christian de Chergé and the monks of the Atlas Abbey of Tibhirine in Algeria. Among the large number of journals dedicated to Islamic-Christian dialogue, we can point to the excellent journal *Oasis*, published in Venice by the Oasis Foundation and started by Cardinal Angelo Scola.

Staying in France, Father René Beaupère, a disciple of Father Paul Couturier whose courses Beaupère took in Lyon, was also one of the first promoters of the ecumenical movement from the Catholic side. The Dominican René Beaupère went with many ecumenical cruises to Israel and to Greece from the beginning of the 1960s onwards. He also set up the Centre œcuménique Saint Irénée [Saint Irenaeus Ecumenical Center] in Lyon and founded two journals, *Foyers Mixtes* [Mixed Households] and *Chrétiens en Marche* [Christians On The Move].[90] The Mixed Household

---

88 *The Koran*, trans. N. J. Dawood (Harmondsworth: Penguin, 1990), 196 (16:122).
89 "Le manifeste fondateur," http://www.fraternite-dabraham.com/.
90 https://unitedeschretiens.fr/Rene-Beaupere.html.

movement notably secured, in 1970, the Roman *motu proprio Matrimonia mixta*, which granted dispensations permitting inter-faith marriages.[91]

In Italy, Enzo Bianchi took the decision on the last day of the Second Vatican Council to retire to the hamlet of Magnano to lead a life of prayer. Three years later, men and women came to join him to set up the monastic community of Bose. This Catholic community, made up of Christians belonging to different denominations, is today devoted to Christian unity. It has played a decisive ecumenical role for several decades in bringing the Orthodox churches closer together with the Catholic and Protestant churches, but also with each other. Today it is made up of more than eighty members and extends into a number of brotherhoods scattered throughout Italy.[92]

After the Council, the Catholic Church committed itself to many bilateral dialogues, especially with the Orthodox Church and the Anglican communion (ARCIC [Anglican-Roman Catholic International Commission]). After a preliminary document adopted in Malta in 1968,[93] the Anglican-Roman Catholic Commission published in 1971 a document on the doctrine of the Eucharist, and then, in 1973, a document on "Ministry and ordination," followed by several declarations on authority in 1976 and 1981.[94] But the Congregation for the Doctrine of the Faith expressed reservations about the points of consensus arrived at. The make-up of the Commission changed, on both sides. Between 1983 and 2011, several documents were published on the doctrine of salvation (1990), on communion (1993), on doctrinal authority (1999), and on the Virgin Mary (2004). Thanks to the Pro Oriente foundation, set up in Vienna in 1964 by Cardinal König, the Catholic Church also arrived at important agreements on Christological topics with the Eastern Churches: with the Syriac Church in 1971, with the Coptic Church in 1973, and with the Assyrian and Chaldaean Churches in 1994. In France, the Groupe des Dombes, which had been started after the war by Father Couturier, launched a series of consultations between Catholic and Protestant theologians, and perfected an extremely fruitful method for ecumenical convergence. This led to many important convergence documents, such as that of 1999 on

---

91 Maurice René Beaupère, *Nous avons cheminé ensemble, Un itinéraire œcuménique: entretiens avec Béatrice Soltner* (Lyon: Olivétan, 2012).

92 "Monastero di Bose," https://www.monasterodibose.it/.

93 Anglican/Roman Catholic Joint Preparatory Commission, "The Malta Report," http://www.prounione.urbe.it/.

94 Anglican/Roman Catholic Joint Preparatory Commission, "The Final Report," http://www.prounione.urbe.it/.

the figure of the Virgin Mary, entitled *Marie dans le dessein de Dieu et la communion des saints* [Mary in God's Plan and the Communion of Saints].[95]

Pope John Paul II was behind the interreligious gathering in Assisi on October 27, 1986. Two months later, before the Roman Curia, the Pope recalled this event in order to make explicit its full significance, and to dispel fears of syncretism, on one hand, and of proselytism on the other:

> It is in this great plan of God's concerning the humanity of the Church that the Church finds its identity and its task of a "universal sacrament of salvation" by being precisely a sign and instrument both of a very closely knit union with God and of the unity of the whole human race. (*Lumen Gentium*, 1) This means that the Church is called to work with all its forces (evangelization, prayer, and dialogue) so that the fractures and divisions among people, which distance them from their principle and their goal, and which make them hostile to each other, should be repaired; it also means that the whole of humankind, in the infinite complexity of its history, and with its various cultures, is "called to be the new people of God" in which the blessed union of God with man and the unity of the human family is healed, strengthened, and uplifted: "All men are called to be part of this catholic unity of the people of God, which in promoting universal peace presages it. And there belong to or are related to it in various ways, the Catholic faithful, all who believe in Christ, and indeed the whole of mankind, for all men are called by the grace of God to salvation." (*Lumen Gentium*, 13)

This double definition allows it to be understood that the spiritual and interreligious epoch of Christian consciousness does not weaken denominational consciousness, but, on the contrary, strengthens it. The Pope links the two definitions of the Church by the decisive expression "self-consciousness":

> In this sense, it must also be said that the identity of the Catholic Church and the consciousness which it has of itself were strengthened at Assisi. The Church, indeed — that is, we ourselves — have in the light of that event better understood the true meaning of the mystery of reconciliation and unity which the Lord entrusted to us, and which he put into practice for the first time when he offered his life "not for that nation only, but

---

95 Groupe des Dombes, *Marie dans le dessein de Dieu et la communion des saints* (Paris: Bayard/Centurion, 1999).

that also he should gather together in one the children of God that were scattered abroad." (John 11:52)[96]

This event was subsequently taken up annually and organized by the Community of Sant' Egidio which had been set up in Rome in 1968 by Andrea Riccardi immediately after the Second Vatican Council. This community committed itself to prayer, to peace, and to the poor in 74 countries. Presided over today by Marco Impagliazzo, the Community of Sant' Egidio brings together more than sixty thousand lay people.[97] Moreover, in 1988, the Council for a Parliament of the World's Religions (CPWR) was formed. Its objective was "to cultivate harmony among the world's religious and spiritual communities to achieve a just, peaceful and sustainable world."[98] The CPWR sponsored inter-denominational parliaments in 1993, in Chicago (for the centenary of the first conference), in 1999 in the Cape, in South Africa, in Barcelona in 2004 (with more than a thousand speakers and four hundred and thirty workshops), in Melbourne, Australia, in 2009, in Salt Lake City in 2015, and in Toronto in 2018 (with more than eight thousand participants).[99] We may also add the setting-up in 1995 of the Organisation des Religions Unies [United Religions Organization] in 1995 (the United Religions Initiative [URI] from 2000 onwards) by the Episcopalian priest William Swing, the former Soviet president Mikhail Gorbachev, and several other personalities. The announcement of the new organization was made at a service held at the Grace Episcopal Cathedral of San Francisco on June 25, 1995, in order to commemorate the fiftieth anniversary of the signature of the United Nations Charter. The URI has operated since then in more than 108 countries.[100]

Pope John Paul II came back to this topic of the Church's relations with other religions in his encyclical *Redemptoris Missio* in 1990:

> Moreover, the universal activity of the Spirit is not to be separated from his particular activity within the body of Christ, which is the Church. Indeed, it is always the Spirit who is at work, both when he gives life to the Church and impels her to proclaim

96 Ibid.
97 "Sant' Egidio," https://www.santegidio.org/.
98 "Council for a Parliament of the World Religions," https://charterforcompassion.org/.
99 "Parliament of the World's Religions: 2018 Toronto," https://parliamentofreligions.org/.
100 "Celebrating 20 Years of URI's Journey," https://uri.org/.

Christ, and when he implants and develops his gifts in all individuals and peoples, guiding the Church to discover these gifts, to foster them and to receive them through dialogue. Every form of the Spirit's presence is to be welcomed with respect and gratitude, but the discernment of this presence is the responsibility of the Church, to which Christ gave his Spirit in order to guide her into all the truth (cf. John 16:13).[101]

This ecumenical, interreligious, and post-denominational turn in Catholic consciousness was judged to be an irreversible one by Pope John Paul II. In the encyclical Ut Unum Sint, published in 1995, ecumenism is defined as "the way of the Church." Neither a supplement nor an appendix, ecumenism is part of the essence of the Church and of its traditional activity (Ut Unum Sint 7 and 20). The Polish Pope wanted his role of primate in the Church to be the topic of a world-wide discussion, so as to bring to light new ways of exercising his ministry that would be acceptable to the whole Christian world. He formulated this request in paragraphs 95 and 96:

> For a whole millennium Christians were united in "a brotherly fraternal communion of faith and sacramental life . . . . If disagreements in belief and discipline arose among them, the Roman See acted by common consent as moderator." In this way the primacy exercised its office of unity. When addressing the Ecumenical Patriarch His Holiness Dimitrios I, I acknowledged my awareness that "for a great variety of reasons, and against the will of all concerned, what should have been a service sometimes manifested itself in a very different light. But . . . it is out of a desire to obey the will of Christ truly that I recognize that as Bishop of Rome I am called to exercise that ministry . . . . I insistently pray the Holy Spirit to shine his light upon us, enlightening all the Pastors and theologians of our Churches, that we may seek — together, of course — the forms in which this ministry may accomplish a service of love recognized by all concerned."
>
> This is an immense task, which we cannot refuse and which I cannot carry out by myself. Could not the real but imperfect communion existing between us persuade Church leaders and their theologians to engage with me in a patient and fraternal dialogue on this subject, a dialogue in which, leaving useless controversies behind, we could listen to one another, keeping

---

101 "Redemptoris Missio: On the Permanent Validity of the Church's Missionary Mandate," https://www.vatican.va/.

before us only the will of Christ for his Church and allowing ourselves to be deeply moved by his plea "that they may all be one . . . so that the world may believe that you have sent me" (John 17:21)?[102]

PROGRESS MADE BY THE WORLD COUNCIL OF CHURCHES

This spectacular deepening of ecumenical consciousness on the part of the Catholic Church, driven forward by the Second Vatican Council, was also made possible by the progress made by the World Council of Churches in the course of this same period — the years from 1965 to 1995. In July 1968, the WCC meeting at Uppsala in Sweden was on the theme of the following eschatological verse from the book of Revelation: "Behold, I make all things new" (Rev. 21:5). William Visser't Hooft had already passed on the baton of acting as Secretary General of the WCC to the American Presbyterian pastor Eugene Carson Blake (1906 – 1985). In his farewell speech, Visser't Hooft returned one last time to the universality of ecumenical consciousness:

> When it is said that God makes all things new this means above all that through Christ God re-creates humanity as a family united under his reign. Mankind is one, not in itself, not because of its own merits or qualities. Mankind is one as the object of God's love and saving action. Mankind is one because of its common calling. The vertical dimension of its unity determines the horizontal dimension . . . . It must become clear that church members who deny in fact their responsibility for the needy in any part of the world are just as much guilty of heresy as those who deny this or that article of the faith. The unity of mankind is not a fine ideal in the clouds; it is part and parcel of God's own revelation.[103]

There was thus an attempt to forge links between the deepening of doctrine and social commitment. In 1972, the Methodist pastor Philip Potter was elected Secretary General of the WCC. He devoted himself to organizing the Council's General Assembly in Nairobi, Kenya, in 1975, devoted to the theme "Jesus Christ frees and saves." The WCC was at that time strongly mobilized in defense of human rights around the world, and supported great political figures such as president Luiz Inacio "Lula"

---

102   "*Ut Unum Sint*: On Commitment to Ecumenism," https://www.vatican.va.
103   Willem Visser't Hooft, "The Mandate of the Ecumenical Movement," *The Ecumenical Review* 70.1 (March, 2018), 113 – 14.

da Silva in his struggle against the Brazilian dictatorship, and Nelson Mandela in his struggle against apartheid.[104] In 1998, President Mandela went to Harare, to the General Assembly of the WCC, devoted to the theme "Let us turn towards God in the joy of hope," a theme influenced by the work of Jürgen Moltmann, to pay emphatic homage to the organization:

> To us in South and Southern Africa, and indeed the entire continent, the WCC has always been known as a champion of the oppressed and the exploited. On the other hand, the name of the WCC struck fear in the hearts of those who ruled our country and destabilized our region during the inhuman days of apartheid. To mention your name was to incur the wrath of the authorities. To indicate support for your views was to be labeled an enemy of the state. Precisely for that reason, the vast majority of our people heard the name of the WCC with joy. It encouraged and inspired us. When, thirty years ago, you initiated the Programme to Combat Racism and the Special Fund to support liberation movements, you showed that yours was not merely the charitable support of distant benefactors, but a joint struggle for shared aspirations. Above all, you respected the judgment of the oppressed as to what were the most appropriate means for attaining their freedom. For that true solidarity, the people of South and Southern Africa will always remember the WCC with gratitude.[105]

One of the most celebrated successes of the Faith and Order Commission of the WCC in respect of theological rapprochement was the document entitled, "Baptism, Eucharist, Ministry" adopted in Lima in 1982, which demonstrated substantial convergence between the Churches, at least where the first two sacraments were concerned. The document was presented to the WCC meeting in Vancouver in 1983, a meeting that was conceived at Lima by Max Thurian, a Taizé brother, and presided over by Robert Runcie, the Archbishop of Canterbury, with the participation of Protestant, Orthodox, and Catholic Christians (the two latter families of Churches abstained from joint communion, however). All the participants recited

---

104   "President Lula asks Assembly to 'keep alive the flame' of solidarity," https://www.oikoumene.org/.
105   "Together on the Way: Address by President Nelson Mandela to the WCC on the occasion of its 50th Anniversary, Harare, 13 December 1998," http://www.wcc-coe.org/.

the Niceno-Constanitopolitan Creed as a sign of their common faith. In the daring final litany not only were the Virgin Mary, the patriarchs, the prophets, the apostles, and the martyrs celebrated, but also Maximilian Kolbe, Dietrich Bonhoeffer, Martin Luther King, Oscar Romero, and Bishop Samuel of Egypt, the leader of those looking after ecumenism in the Coptic Church, who had just died (1920 – 1981). Subsequently, these documents were the subject of a lengthy process of reception within individual local churches.

But something had seized up in the ecumenical movement during the 1990s. Despite the meeting devoted to it at Bossey in 1995, the Lima Liturgy was called into question thereafter.[106] Let us, however, remember that ecclesial consciousness in the years between 1960 and 1990 was greatly affected by the fact that Christians suffered from the same persecutions, which brought them together beyond their doctrinal or jurisdictional differences. The Ukrainian Greek Catholic Cardinal Josyf Slipyj, after having spent eighteen years in the Gulag, published in 1980 a report entitled The Church of Martyrs, in which he invited ecumenists to take account of this new reality.[107] But when this Church came out of the catacombs in 1989, and when the churches freed themselves from the oppression of persecutory states, the unifying testimony of the witnesses of the faith was soon forgotten.

Between 1965 and 1995 the WCC encouraged the organization of regional ecumenical assemblies on all continents (Conferences of the Churches in Europe, in Latin America, in the Middle East, in the Pacific, in Asia, in Africa, and in the Caribbean).

In Europe, the Conference of European Churches [CEC] was set up in 1958, with the participation of Orthodox and Protestant Churches from the whole of the continent on both sides of the Iron Curtain. This organization greatly contributed to encouraging links between Christians living under communist regimes and Christians living in liberal democracies. In association with the Council of European Bishops' Conference, an organization of Catholic bishops in Europe, the CEC convoked an assembly in Basel in 1989, and then others at Graz in 1997 and at Sibiu in 2007. In 2001, in Strasbourg, it adopted the Charta œcumenica. These meetings were at the time the occasion of moments of joy, thanks to the reunions

---

106   Thomas F. Best and Dagmar Heller, Eucharistic Worship in Ecumenical Context. The Lima Liturgy and Beyond (Geneva: World Council of Churches, 1998).
107   See Kirche in Not / Ostpriesterhilfe. Special number of The Mirror 2, Königstein im Taunus (March 1981), 14.

between Christians from East and West after the fall of the Berlin Wall in 1989. The Basel assembly was focused on the theme "Justice, Peace, and the Integrity of Creation," and received a strong influx of delegates from East Germany. It gave rise to powerful propositions such as the demand for a debt amnesty for the poorest developing countries, the implementation of international conventions on the rights of man, and drastic limits on the consumption of polluting energy.[108]

There were also some clarifications. In 1992, at the tenth assembly of the CEC in Prague, thirty-five signatures of Charter 77, the dissident movement led by Vaclav Havel, addressed a letter to the member churches. They reproached them with having been blind to the real sufferings of Christians opposed to the communist regimes. "Your efforts towards *détente* between East and West were founded on erroneous conceptions; they have been harmful, because they encouraged immoral regimes and prolonged their existence."[109] These gatherings nevertheless contributed to the churches' renouncing competitive evangelization, and to their deciding to cooperate closely with each other.

Each of the regional economic conferences could on its own form the topic of a long narrative, as is shown by the eight-hundred-page history of the ecumenical movement in Asia written by Ninan Koshy, a Christian of the Church of South India. Koshy was the secretary general of the student Christian movement in India, and then the director of the Commission of the Churches on International Affairs at the WCC.[110] The vast fresco which he makes of the history of the ecumenical movement in Asia culminates with the reflections of Ahn Jae Woong, the secretary-general of the Christian Conference of Asia, in support of a rediscovery of the "radical meaning of ecumenism." Instead of an idea of ecumenism that is too focused on the "people of God," and that sometimes risks becoming too denominational, the Korean theologian, one of the pioneers of the democratic movement in Seoul, prefers a broader sense of the idea of universality:

> I prefer to emphasize this wider meaning through three coined words — theo-ecumenics, eco-ecumenics, geo-ecumenics. By

---

108   The meeting of the WCC on the same theme at Seoul, by contrast, prompted the expression of feminist, anti-capitalist, and anti-racist slogans, but without being in a position to transform these expressions of anger into realistic programs for action.
109   Quoted in Jean-Paul Willaime, "Le Conseil œcuménique des Eglises," 165.
110   Ninan Koshy, A History of the Ecumenical Movement in Asia, 2 vols (Hong Kong: CCA, WSCF, YMCA, 2004).

theo-ecumenics I mean that our ecumenical mission should have a theocentric emphasis on God as source and creator, protector and liberator of the world. By eco-ecumenics I mean that our ecumenical mission should be eco-friendly and must involve the whole of God's creation. By geo-ecumenics I mean that our ecumenical task should be geo-contextual — where Asia's unique plurality of religions, cultures, races, languages, peoples, creeds, and colors are affirmed and helped to flourish.[111]

Ecumenical ecclesial consciousness reached a first apogee in the years 1990 – 2000, so far as relations between Catholics and Protestants were concerned. Several new institutions played a decisive role, such as, for example, the Strasbourg Ecumenical Institute, set up in 1965, or the *Societas Œcumenica*, founded in 1978.[112] We might also mention the *Centro pro Unione* brought into being in Rome in 1968 by the Franciscan Friars of the Atonement, a community founded by Father Paul Wattson (1863 – 1940).[113] Wattson was an American Episcopalian priest. With the nun Lurana White, he had co-founded the octave for the unity of the Church in 1908, and was converted the following year to the Catholic Church.

The participation of Orthodox Christians in the ecumenical movement benefited from the support of the Russian Church from 1961 onwards. But despite the efforts of Metropolitan Nicodemus of Leningrad in support of Christian unity, this Church's links with Soviet power made its position ambiguous. Father Gleb Yakunin (1934 – 2014) in 1965 condemned the Russian Church's compromises with the KGB in an open letter to the Russian Patriarch, Alexis I.[114] Moreover, the Patriarchate of Moscow, already compromised among its elites by its duplicity towards the Kremlin and the Western churches, was careful not to promote the ecumenical movement among its faithful.

This is why the real commitment of the Orthodox Church to the ecumenical movement was above all a Western phenomenon. With the creation in the 1950s of Syndesmos, the World Fellowship of Orthodox Youth, of the Orthodox brotherhood for Western Europe, and of the journal *Contacts*, a whole constellation of Orthodox theologians such as Father Boris Bobrinskoy, Olivier Clément, Elisabeth Behr-Sigel, and Nicolas Lossky, actively contributed to the integration of ecumenical theology into the

---

111   Koshy, *Ecumenical Movement in Asia*, 1:352.
112   http://www.societasœcumenica.net/.
113   "Centro Pro Unione" 96 (Fall, 2019), https://www.prounione.it/.
114   https://ru.wikipedia.org/wiki/Якунин,_Глеб_Павлович.

Orthodox Church.[115] In France and in the United States, joint national commissions for theological dialogue between Catholics and Orthodox were set up. In 1996, the Saint Vladimir Seminary in Crestwood, New York, published a book providing a synthesis of the fifty consultations of the American commission that had taken place between 1965 and 1995 with the texts of the eighteen resolutions, extending from convergence on the mystery of the Eucharist to the document on the shared rejection of any form of proselytism.[116]

In addition, the Joint International Commission for Dialogue between the Catholic Church and the Orthodox Church published several consensus texts: on the mystery of the Church and of the Eucharist in the light of the mystery of the Holy Trinity (Munich, 1982); on "Faith, Sacraments and Church Unity" (Bari, 1987); on "the Sacrament of Order in the Sacramental Structure of the Church" (Valamo, 1988); and on Uniatism, past methods of union, and the present search for full communion (Balamand, 1993).[117] One had to wait until the year 1986 for the pre-conciliar conference dedicated to the topic of Christian unity to pronounce in favor of the ecumenical movement. This monumental work made it possible thirty years later, at the Pan-Orthodox Council of Crete, to adopt a resolution favorable to the ecumenical movement (without the participation of the Sees of Moscow, Antioch, Tbilisi, and Sofia, but with their preliminary agreement, given at Chambésy in January 2016). The Orthodox Church from this point onwards gave full official recognition to "the historical name of other non-Orthodox Christian Churches and Confessions that are not in communion with her."[118]

---

115 See, in particular, Sarah Hinlicky Wilson and Aikaterini Pekridou, *A Communion in Faith and Love: Elisabeth Behr Sigel's Ecclesiology* (Geneva: World Council of Churches, 2017).

116 John Borelli and John H. Erickson, *The Quest for Unity, Orthodox and Catholics in Dialogue* (Crestwood, NY: St Vladimir's Seminary Press, 1996).

117 "Documents Episcopat sur la Semaine de prière pour l'unité des Chrétiens," https://unitedeschretiens.fr/.

118 "The Orthodox Church, which prays unceasingly 'for the union of all,' has always cultivated dialogue with those estranged from her, those both far and near. In particular, she has played a leading role in the contemporary search for ways and means to restore the unity of those who believe in Christ, and she has participated in the Ecumenical Movement from its outset, and has contributed to its formation and further development. Moreover, the Orthodox Church, thanks to the ecumenical and loving spirit which distinguishes her, praying as divinely commanded that all men may be saved and come to the knowledge of the truth (1 Tim. 2:4), has always worked for the restoration of Christian unity. Hence, Orthodox participation in the movement to restore unity with other Christians in the One, Holy, Catholic and Apostolic Church is in no way foreign to the nature and history of the Orthodox Church,

PROPHETIC SPIRITUAL GESTURES

As we have seen, the history of the ecumenical consciousness of the Church has been marked by four great periods: the eschatological period (characterized by a fractal conception of the universal); the political (structured by an analogical and Christocentric relationship between the earthly order and the celestial city); the denominational period (marked by a rupture between faith and reason); and, finally, the inter-denominational period (which ceases to identify the visible borders of the Church with those of the Kingdom). In the course of this last, extremely fruitful, period, the Church came no longer to appear as a static reality, but as a living body animated by spirit. The shared rediscovery of the Fathers of the Church and of the Gospel has allowed the Church to be rediscovered as a ship on a pilgrim voyage between the "already there" and the "not yet" of the Kingdom. The logo adopted by the World Council of Churches is, precisely, the boat of Christ's apostles.

In the course of this inter-denominational period, powerful gestures were made that would have been unthinkable at the beginning of the nineteenth century. It is enough to mention the mutual accord on Eucharistic communion between the Roman Catholic Church and the Syrian Orthodox Church signed in 1984 by Pope John Paul II and Patriarch Ignatius Zakka I Iwas. Here is an extract from that agreement:

> Our identity in faith, though not yet complete, entitles us to envisage collaboration between our Churches in pastoral care, in situations which nowadays are frequent both because of the dispersion of our faithful throughout the world and because of the precarious conditions of these difficult times. It is not rare, in fact, for our faithful to find access to a priest of their own Church materially or morally impossible. Anxious to meet their needs and with their spiritual benefit in mind, we authorize them in such cases to ask for the Sacraments of Penance, Eucharist and Anointing of the Sick from lawful priests of either of our two sister Churches, when they need them. It would be a logical corollary of collaboration in pastoral care to cooperate in priestly formation and theological education. Bishops are encouraged to promote sharing of facilities for theological education where they judge it to be advisable. While doing this we do not forget that we must still do all in our power to achieve the full

---

but rather represents a consistent expression of the apostolic faith and tradition in a new [sic] historical circumstances." See www.holycouncil.org.

visible communion between the Catholic Church and the Syrian Orthodox Church of Antioch and ceaselessly implore our Lord to grant us that unity which alone will enable us to give to the world a fully unanimous Gospel witness. [119]

This remarkable period culminated in 1991, amid the enthusiasm surrounding the fall of the Berlin Wall, in the publication of a joint text on a shared understanding of the Niceno-Constantinopolitan Creed (381), entitled *Confessing the One Faith*. [120] It was signed by all the Churches, Catholic, Orthodox, and Protestant, in the Faith and Order Commission of the World Council of Churches. With a preface by the great Catholic ecumenist Jean-Marie Tillard, it proclaimed the faith of all these Churches in Christ, truly God and truly man, in one God, Father, Son, and Holy Spirit, and in the Church as a reality that is one, holy, catholic and apostolical. It was an important text for the Orthodox Church, which had previously affirmed on several occasions, particularly at its pre-conciliar conferences, that an ecumenical agreement on the Niceno-Constantinopolitan creed would bring about an agreement for its part to recognize the Western churches as authentic sister churches. The theologians of the Church of the East defended the veracity of the proclamation on the procession of the Holy Spirit from the Father, whereas many churches affirmed even in the 1980s that the text of 381 declared that the Holy Spirit proceeded from the Father *and from the Son*. But in Munich in 1982 a major advance took place. The Catholic and Orthodox Churches, informed by the renewal of personalist, sapiential, and Trinitarian theology of the Paris School, affirmed the following point:

> Without wishing at this point to resolve the difficulties between East and West on the topic of the relationship between the Son and the Holy Spirit, we can already say together that this Spirit who proceeds from the Father (John 15:26) as from the only origin within the Trinity, and who has become the Spirit in our filiation (Romans 8:15), since he is also the Spirit of the Son (Galatians 4:6), is communicated to us, particularly in the Eucharist, by this Son on which the Spirit reposes, in time and in eternity (John 1:32). [121]

---

119 "Common Declaration of Pope John Paul II and the Ecumenical Patriarch Moran Mar Ignatius Zakka I Iwas of Antioch," www.vatican.va.

120 World Council of Churches, *Confessing the One Faith: An Ecumenical Explication of the Apostolic Faith as it is Confessed in the Nicene-Constantinopolitan Creed (381)* (Eugene, OR: Wipf and Stock, 2010 [Faith and Order Paper, 153]).

121 Joint Catholic-Orthodox Commission for Dialogue, *Le mystère de l'Eglise et de l'Eucharistie à la lumière du mystère de la Sainte Trinité : Munich, 30 juin– 6 juillet* (Le

This new theology prepared the way for a broader consensus. The Faith and Constitution document of 1991 specifies that "both Western and Eastern Christians have wished to be faithful to the affirmation of the Niceno-Constantinopolitan Creed that the Spirit proceeds from the Father, and both agree today that the intimate relationship between the Son and the Spirit is to be affirmed without giving the impression that the Spirit is subordinated to the Son. On that affirmation all Christians can agree, and this enables an increasing number of Western churches to consider using the Creed in its original form."[122]

The Catholic Church even agreed in September 1995 to publish a clarification of its doctrine on the *filioque*, recognizing that the Niceno-Constantinopolitan Creed (without the *filioque*) represented the most authentic faith of the Church. But the reception of this document in the Roman Catholic Church was difficult. The theologian Emmanuel Durand accepted the Roman position on the condition that it should be specified that "The Spirit proceeds from the Father, who is Father only in relation to the Son."[123] While such a level of convergence should have pushed the churches publicly to proclaim their shared faith and forms of reciprocal sacramental recognition linked to this convergence in faith about essential matters, nothing of the kind took place. The fifth world conference on Faith and Order which took place in 1993 in Santiago de Compostela implored the churches to show boldness in recognizing each other's sacraments of baptism, Eucharist, and ordination.[124] At this conference held in Spain, some theologians even pointed to the possibility of organizing an Ecumenical Council with the help of a structure bringing together the Pontifical Council for Christian Unity and the Faith and Order Commission. But the hopes born of the end of the Cold War were soon disappointed. The idea was rejected at Harare in 1998. Fifty years after the creation of the World Council of Churches in Amsterdam, the ecumenical movement was entering a new period of its history.

Mesnil saint Loup: Éditions du Livre Ouvert, 1994), 28.

122 *Confessing the One Faith, An Ecumenical Explication of the Apostolic Faith as it is confessed in the Nicene-Constantinopolitan Creed*, Faith and Order 153 (WCC: Geneva, 1991), 78.

123 Jean Yves Brachet and Emmanuel Durand, "La réception de la 'Clarification' de 1995 sur le 'Filioque,'" *Irenikon* 78, 1/2 (2005), 47–109.

124 "Message from the Fifth World Conference on Faith and Order, 1993." See https://www.oikoumene.org/.

PART FOUR

The Crisis of Christian Inter-Denominational Consciousness Since 1995

I N THE MIDDLE OF THE 1990S, JUST AS THE ECU-menical movement was bearing fruit for reconciliation among the churches, and also for reconciliation among political and ideological systems, fruits which would have been unimaginable a decade earlier, Christian consciousness unexpectedly underwent a crisis that showed itself, over the course of several years, to be more and more serious. Schematically, we can say that the new stage of globalization of exchange and communications brought about a short circuit between the space-times of churches that did not possess the same levels of ecumenical consciousness. The pre-existing tensions between the different levels of consciousness—classical, modern, post-modern, and spiritual—became enflamed. The communities of North and South, of East and West, did not always possess sufficiently strong shared reference points to allow them to trust each other. Moreover, the preceding phase of inter-denominational progress had in most cases been achieved by the different churches' elites and theological hierarchies. These had not always taken the time clearly to explain the results of the progress they had made to their churches' members, while at the same time a new surge of secularization pushed a growing number of the world's citizens away from the well-defined parameters of modern denominational consciousness.

The result of these developments was twofold. On the one hand, we have witnessed since 1995 a radical refiguration of the ecclesial landscape, with the transition from the "inter-denominational" paradigm to the "trans-denominational" paradigm. This development can be understood as part of a very modern desire for the reassurance given by political and religious identities at one of the four poles of religious consciousness. From another point of view, we have also seen over the last twenty years growing evidence of a radicality in spiritual questions, whose main characteristic is the desire to reaffirm, this time in a post-modern way, the power of religious consciousness, including in its atheist version, with respect to secular consciousness. This double development indicates, in my view, that contemporary ecumenical consciousness cannot be reconciled nor blossom otherwise than at a new level of consciousness, that of spiritual consciousness, which is found at the crossroads between the four poles of glory, memory, law, and justice.

We will examine the concomitant development of modern identities (chapter four) and post-modern identities (chapter five) in two separate chapters, while gauging the extent to which the post-denominational remaking of identities and the desire for radical spirituality are mingled between them. In chapter four, devoted to the crisis of Christian inter-denominational consciousness, we will first introduce the chief successes in the area of reconciliation between the churches, but also the first signs of the crisis in consciousness which the churches have undergone since the middle of the 1990s. Then we will introduce the four new trans-denominational constellations that emerged alongside denominational identities in the course of this period, marked by the growing influence of post-modern ideas. Lastly, we will use the concept of the churches' self-understanding to explain the deep-lying causes of the crisis of confidence that took hold of the ecumenical movement at the turn of the millennium. Chapter five will be reserved to the recent history of the emergence of radical identity, and of its possible transformation within ecumenical consciousness, within spiritual consciousness. This consciousness is not new, since, as we have been able to see, there have always been thinkers, prophets, mystics, and saints who have been able to place themselves where paths cross. It remains severely threatened today by its internal imbalances and by the way in which, in various religious traditions, it is being reclaimed by violent sects. Nevertheless, it will be seen that this spiritual consciousness manifests itself today in a more meaningful way, to the point of being in a position to claim that it will one day become paradigmatic.

THE DYING EMBERS OF INTER-DENOMINATIONAL ECUMENISM AND THE ECUMENICAL WINTER

The grand period of theological ecumenism was not arrived at in a single day, nor in a homogeneous fashion. The progress of the years 1965 – 1995 continued to bear fruit in the course of the following period. Thus the famous agreement of 1999 between Lutherans and Catholics on the doctrine of justification was the result of more than thirty years of dialogue, as the text of the declaration explains (point 3):

> Special attention should be drawn to the following reports: "The Gospel and the Church" (1972) and "Church and Justification" (1994) by the Lutheran-Roman Catholic Joint Commission, "Justification by Faith" (1983) of the Lutheran-Roman Catholic dialogue in the USA and "The Condemnations of the Reformation Era — Do They Still Divide?" (1986) by the Ecumenical Working Group of Protestant and Catholic theologians in Germany. Some of these dialogue reports have been officially received by the churches. An important example of such reception is the binding response of the United Evangelical-Lutheran Church of Germany to the "Condemnations" study, made in 1994 at the highest possible level of ecclesiastical recognition together with the other churches of the Evangelical Church in Germany.[1]

All this work led to an agreement (which will be discussed below) at the very end of the twentieth century. On October 31, 1999, in Augsburg, Cardinal Edward Cassidy, representing the Catholic Church, and Bishop Christian Krause, the President of the World Lutheran Federation, signed a major agreement on justification by faith. This differentiated consensus, later adopted by the World Methodist Council in 2006 and by the World Communion of Reformed Churches in 2018, made possible a shared understanding of the salvation of man "by divine grace alone through faith in Christ." The Catholic and Protestant Churches managed in this way to heal one of the principal wounds which had appeared in ecclesial consciousness in the sixteenth century.

Similarly, the *Charta Œcumenica*, adopted by all the European Christian churches in Strasbourg in 2001, was the fruit of more than forty years of exchanges between European theologians of the East and West. It was publicly signed by all the Christian churches of Germany on the ecumenical *Kirchentag* [Church Day] of May 2003 in Berlin. It is preceded by the following declaration:

> As the Conference of European Churches (CEC) and the Council of European Bishops' Conferences (CCEE) we are, in the spirit of the Messages from the two European Ecumenical Assemblies of Basle (1989) and Graz (1997), firmly resolved to preserve and

---

1 "Joint Declaration on the Doctrine of Justification by the Lutheran World Federation and the Catholic Church," www.vatican.va.

develop the fellowship that has grown up among us. We give thanks to the Triune God for guiding our steps towards an ever deeper fellowship through the Holy Spirit. Various forms of ecumenical co-operation have already proved themselves. Christ's prayer is ". . . that they may all be one. As you, Father, are in me and I am in you, may they also be in us, so that the world may believe that you have sent me" (John 17 : 21). If we are to be faithful to this prayer, we cannot be content with the present situation. Instead, aware of our guilt and ready to repent, we must strive to overcome the divisions still existing among us, so that together we may credibly proclaim the message of the Gospel among all people. Listening together to God's word in Holy Scripture, challenged to confess our common faith and to act together in accordance with the perceived truth, let us bear witness to the love and hope which are for all people. Europe — from the Atlantic to the Urals, from the North Cape to the Mediterranean — is today more pluralist in culture than ever before. With the Gospel, we want to stand up for the dignity of the human person created in God's image and, as churches together, contribute towards reconciling peoples and cultures. In this spirit, we adopt this charter as a common commitment to dialogue and cooperation. It describes fundamental ecumenical responsibilities, from which follow a number of guidelines and commitments. It is designed to promote an ecumenical culture of dialogue and cooperation at all levels of church life, and to provide agreed criteria for this.[2]

As well as multilateral ecumenism and bilateral ecumenism, the inter-denominational period of ecclesial consciousness also saw a vigorous period of ecumenical reconciliation within each large family of churches. The Reformed and Lutheran Protestant Churches came closer to each other in a very significant way during this period after the Concord of Leuenberg (Switzerland), which was signed in March 1973. The latter contributed to the creation of unified Protestant Churches throughout Europe, as in 2013 in France. Since 2004, the Concord of Leuenberg has become the Communion of Protestant Churches in Europe (CPCE), that is to say, more than fifty million Protestants, and numbers 107 member Lutheran, Methodist, Reformed, and United Reformed Churches, from more than thirty countries in Europe and South America.

---

2 "Charta Oecumenica: Guidelines for the Growing Cooperation among the Churches in Europe," www.ceceurope.org.

Reconciliation between Protestants and Anglicans was also the fruit of several decades of a long labor of dialogue and the building of trust and friendship between communities. At Porvoo in Finland, on October 13, 1992, Anglicans and Lutherans shared the Eucharist a week before they signed a common statement. This accord concerns the Anglicans of Great Britain and Ireland and the Lutherans of the Scandinavian and Baltic countries. It bears on a shared conception of the episcopacy, mutual Eucharistic hospitality and the welcoming by each Church of the other's members, the recognition and reciprocal exchange of ministers (bishops, priests, and deacons), participation in ordinations in other churches, especially episcopal churches, and shared conciliar consultations on points touching on faith and order in the Church. The Reuilly Declaration, made in Paris on July 1, 2001, follows the Porvoo Agreement and the Meissen Agreement of 1988. It establishes a full communion between the Anglican, Reformed, and Lutheran Churches which signed it:

> We, the Church of the Augsburg Confession of Alsace and Lorraine, the Evangelical-Lutheran Church of France, the Reformed Church of Alsace and Lorraine, the Reformed Church of France, the Church of England, the Church of Ireland, the Scottish Episcopal Church, and the Church in Wales, on the basis of our fundamental agreement in faith, our common understanding of the nature and purpose of the Church, and our convergence on the apostolicity of the Church and the ministry contained in Chapters II–VI of the Reuilly Common Statement, make the following acknowledgements and commitments, which are interrelated. (i) We acknowledge one another's churches as churches belonging to the One, Holy Catholic and Apostolic Church of Jesus Christ and truly participating in the apostolic mission of the whole people of God. (ii) We acknowledge that in all our churches the word of God is authentically preached, and the sacraments of baptism and the eucharist are duly administered. (iii) We acknowledge that all our churches share in the common confession of the apostolic faith. (iv) We acknowledge that one another's ordained ministries are given by God as instruments of grace for the mission and unity of the Church and for the proclamation of the word and the celebration of the sacraments. (v) We acknowledge one another's ordained ministries as possessing not only the inward call of the Spirit but also Christ's commission through the Church, and look forward to the time when the fuller visible unity of our churches makes possible the interchangeability

of ministers. (vi) We acknowledge that personal, collegial, and communal oversight (*episkope*) is embodied and exercised in all our churches in a variety of forms, as a visible sign expressing and serving the Church's unity and continuity in apostolic life, mission and ministry. [3]

Despite these agreements, in the course of the 1990s an ecumenical winter settled over the Christian churches, signifying the end of a period in which the Christian denominations had drawn closer together. This phenomenon has several causes, both external and internal to the Churches.

When the Soviet regime collapsed, the Orthodox churches understood that they now had more freedom, but also that they had to distance themselves from their previous ecumenical commitments. Post-Soviet public opinion suspected, indeed, that these commitments had been inspired by the Kremlin for propaganda purposes or in order to infiltrate the churches, and, through them, Western democracies. The Orthodox churches then seized upon the slightest pretext to disassociate themselves from the ecumenical movement. At the Canberra assembly in Australia in 1991, devoted to the theme "Come, Holy Spirit, renew all creation," a presentation in the medium of dance by a Korean theologian shocked many Orthodox participants. This put a stop to any possibility of concelebration, which was still being experimented with at the preceding assembly in Vancouver. At the subsequent assemblies of the WCC at Harare (1998), Porto Alegre (2006), and Busan (2013), there was no longer any question of it. In its place, non-Eucharistic celebrations were proposed to the participants in these assemblies.

The term of office of Emilio Castro (1927–2013), a Uruguayan Methodist pastor, as Secretary General of the WCC (1985–1992) was also a source of growing divisions, particularly at Seoul in 1990, on the occasion of the meeting on "Justice, Peace, and the Integrity of Creation." At a moment when the world was racked with many tensions marking the end of the confrontation between the capitalist and communist blocs, the voice of liberation theology had become problematic. On one hand, most liberal communities supported this liberation theologian in his political and pacifist conception of ecumenism. On the other, a minority of more conservative communities preferred to insist upon the spiritual dimension of the ecumenical movement. This minority also rejected the very idea of Eucharistic hospitality defended by Castro. From 1998 onwards,

---

3   "The Reuilly Declaration," www.churchofengland.org.

Orthodox Christians for their part disputed more and more publicly the decision-making process of the WCC, inspired by a classic parliamentary model. The latter was regarded as too secular and as establishing the domination of the larger churches over the rest of the member churches. At the end of the 1990s, the Orthodox churches persuaded the new Secretary general, Konrad Raiser, to set up a special Commission allowing decisions to be taken by the method of differentiated consensus (for all topics apart from budgetary matters and those related to personnel). Raiser was a Reformed German pastor, a former assistant to Philip Potter, who served between 1993 and 2003 before handing over responsibility to the Kenyan Methodist pastor Samuel Kobia (2004–2009). Kobia's term of office was also heavily disputed on all sides, which compelled him to give up his post at the end of the single term which was all he served.

Moreover, some of the ecumenical advances agreed upon by the churches in the 1990 at the international level had not been integrated by the signatory institutions into their internal organizations. Thus the English Catholic theologian Paul Murray lamented that the agreements of 1998 between the Catholic and Anglican churches on the question of authority, which bore particularly on the place of the Bishop of Rome, had not led to the churches' coming any closer together on a sacramental level.[4] The Anglican Church's decision to ordain women to the priesthood from 1992 onwards, and then to the episcopacy from 2013, blocked any possibility of reconciliation on the Roman side. Conversely, the creation of the Ordinariate by Pope Benedict XVI in England in 2009, so as to allow "High Church" Anglicans to join the Catholic Church, was displeasing to Canterbury.

Another brake on progress had symbolic significance. In 1995, an ecumenical initiative on the part of the Christians of the East, although promising, was stopped in its tracks. Pleased with the success of the Balamand accords in 1993 between the Catholic and Orthodox Churches on the Uniat question,[5] Mgr Elias Zoghby, the Melkite Archbishop of Baalbek in Lebanon suggested in February 1995 that joint communion between Catholic and Orthodox Christians had now been made possible, provided only that a profession of faith was made beforehand. This profession consisted only of the two following points:

---

4   Anglican-Roman Catholic International Commission, "The Gift of Authority (Authority in the Church III)." See www.ewtn.com.
5   Pontifical Council for Promoting Christian Unity, "Uniatism, Method of Union of the Past, and the Present Search for Full Communion," www.vatican.va.

(1) I believe in everything taught by the Eastern Orthodox faith.
(2) I am in communion with the Bishop of Rome as the first
among the bishops, within the limits recognized by the holy
Fathers of the East in the course of the first millennium before
the separation.

This initiative was supported by twenty-four of the twenty-six bishops
of the synod of the Melkite church in July 1995. It was also supported by
the Orthodox Metropolitan of Mount Lebanon, Met. Georges Khodr, who
signed the following declaration: "I hold that this profession of Mgr Elias
Zoghby's fulfills the necessary and sufficient conditions for re-establishing
the unity of the Orthodox churches with Rome." Mgr Zoghby also received
support from the French Orthodox theologian Olivier Clément, as well
as from Abp. Vsevolod (Maidansky), the Orthodox Archbishop of the
Ecumenical Patriarchate residing in Chicago.

But neither the Orthodox Church of Antioch nor the Roman Catholic Church looked with favor on this initiative. In October 1996, the
Orthodox Church of Antioch was the first to declare that "regarding
inter-communion now, our Synod believes that inter-communion cannot be separated from the unity of faith. Moreover, inter-communion
is the last step in the quest for unity and not the first."[6] For their part,
Cardinals Joseph Ratzinger, Achille Silvestrini, and Edward Cassidy replied
to the Greek Melkite Patriarch Maximos V (Hakim) on June 11, 1997, to
the effect that it was necessary to avoid "premature unilateral initiatives
or eventual outcomes that would not have [been] pondered sufficiently."[7]

The Russian Orthodox Church also blocked any progress in ecumenical
dialogue at the Joint International Commission for Theological Dialogue
Between the Catholic Church and the Eastern Orthodox Church. Exploiting
bad memories of a former Roman "Uniatism" or even of a "Catholic proselytism" presented as having gone on for many centuries, memories that
still lingered in some Orthodox Churches, the Russian Church rejected the
idea that the Greek Catholic or Melkite Churches could live in a double
communion with both Rome and Constantinople. The ecumenical movement as a whole was criticized by the Orthodox Churches at a synaxis held
at Thessalonika in 1998. Despite the efforts of the WCC to put in place
more inclusive decision-making processes, especially after the General

---

6   Quoted in "Letter to his Beatitude Maximos V. Hakim," https://web.archive.org.
7   Joseph Ratzinger, Achille Silvestrini, and Edward Cassidy, "letter to His Beatitude
Maximos V Hakim, Greek-Melkite Patriarch of Antioch and of all the East, of Alexandria and of Jerusalem," June 11, 1997, orthocath.files.wordpress.com.

Assembly at Porto Alegre, two Orthodox Churches (those of Bulgaria and Georgia) left the WCC in 1998. Several other Orthodox Churches (Serbia, Romania, Greece)[8] took their distance from the ecumenical movement for reasons of internal discipline (fear of a reconciliation between Greek Catholics and Orthodox)[9] and also for external reasons (a rejection of "Papism" and of the "pan-heresy of ecumenism," etc.).[10]

The change of atmosphere was felt even within the families of the Anglican, Catholic, and Orthodox Churches. The Anglican communion has no longer gathered in synod since 2008 because of the risk of schism among its members. At the last Lambeth Conference of 2008, only three quarters of the bishops were present because of persistent disagreements, especially within the Anglican Church of Nigeria, on the topic of whether it was possible for members of the clergy to live proudly and openly as homosexuals. The question of the ordination of women to the episcopacy is also a source of dispute.

The Catholic Church also became aware of the limits of a rather vertical organizational model, emphasized during the papacy of John Paul II by certain powerful communities such as Opus Dei or the Legionaries of Christ. This model was not yielding as many fruits as it had in the past, especially where evangelization was concerned. The condemnation of liberation theology in the 1980s by the Vatican, now recognized as too sweeping, singularly weakened the Catholic Church in Latin American from the 1990s onwards.[11] With the genocide of the Tutsis in Rwanda in April to July 1994 by the Hutu government, the Church became aware of a failure of Christianity. As an anonymous cardinal acknowledged when interviewed by the journalist Olivier Le Gendre, "when a religion that calls itself Christian puts the love of God and of my neighbor at the center of its message, it is right to wonder whether genocides that take place in a Christian country are not a sign that this religion has failed in its mission."[12] This is why the same cardinal began a campaign calling for a Church closer to the poor and organized on a less institutional and denominational model. Conversely, during the pontificate of Benedict

---

8   "Synaxis of Greek Clergy and Monastics against Ecumenism held in Thessaloniki," December 2017, www.orthochristian.com.
9   Mircea Pacurariu, *The Uniatism in Transylvania* (Bucharest: Romanian Orthodox Church Bible and Mission Publishing House, 1991), www.orthodoxhistory.info.
10   "Greek Orthodox Bishops denounce Pope Francis, Church of Rome, and Ecumenism as Antichrist Plan of Freemasons," www.cogwriter.com.
11   "Qu'est-ce que la théologie de la libération," *La Croix*, https://croire.la-croix.com/.
12   Olivier Le Gendre, *Confessions d'un Cardinal* (Paris: Lattès, 2010).

XVI, inter-denominational reconciliation was understood as needing to allow a new acknowledgement of the communities set up by Mgr Marcel Lefebvre (1905–1991), communities that had been in a state of schism since 1988. In 2007, the Vatican published a *motu proprio* authorizing the use of the Latin mass according to the liturgies of the Council of Trent, so as to facilitate a rapprochement with the Fraternity of Saint Pius X. On February 5, 2008, Benedict XVI modified the prayer for the conversion of the Jews contained in the Tridentine Missal, by removing the disputed appeals to "lead that people out of their darkness" and to remove their "blindness," but by continuing to invite prayers "that God and our Lord illuminate the heart" of the Jews and that they "come to know Jesus Christ." The Jewish community made its unhappiness clear.

In the Orthodox Church, the tensions between Moscow and Constantinople, situated on opposite sides of the Berlin Wall, had been acute between 1946 and 1976, with a first rupture of communion in 1970, the year in which Moscow recognized the autocephaly of the Orthodox Church in America. The resumption of the pre-conciliar discussion process took place in 1976 after the Helsinki Agreement was signed on August 1, 1975, at the Conference on Security and Cooperation in Europe. The Churches were subject to strong political pressure, especially in the countries of the socialist bloc, all the way through the Cold War. When tensions eased at the beginning of the 1990s, and when the countries of the East confronted their communist past, a whole series of inter-Orthodox and inter-denominational disputes was revived. The tension within the Orthodox world particularly increased the pressure on inter-denominational relations, especially on the question of the persecution of the Greek Catholic Churches by the Patriarchate of Moscow, and on that of the accusation of proselytism which was leveled in the other direction by Moscow against Rome. The Catholic Church's presence in Russia and Belarus was subjected to very strict controls. Once again there was a rupture in communion between Moscow and Constantinople in 1996, this time over the Estonian affair. The tension reappeared in 2014 as a result of the Russo-Ukrainian war, which was supported by the Patriarchate of Moscow and condemned by that of Constantinople. In June 2016, the refusal of Patriarch Kirill of Moscow to attend the Pan-Orthodox Council of Crete, despite the promise which he had reiterated at Chambésy in January 2016 a few months before taking office, and which led the churches of Moscow, Georgia, Bulgaria, and Antioch to suspend their participation in the Council, was regarded by Patriarch Bartholomew of Constantinople as a failure to acknowledge his leadership.[13] The Orthodox Church has been in a state of schism since the Patriarchate of Moscow forbade its members from celebrating the Eucharist together with those of the Patriarchate of Constantinople, because of Patriarch Bartholomew's recognition of the Ukrainian Orthodox Church.[14]

It is clear that phenomena like these have contributed to the ecumenical winter. But it is also necessary to consider the wider context of ultra-liberal globalization that has gripped the planet since the 1990s. The wave of secularization of the years 1960 – 1990 consisted in the decoupling of faith from allegiance. It has been summarized by some sociologists with the phrases "believing without belonging," or "spiritual but not religious," or even "Jesus Yes, church No." This phenomenon testifies to a deep desire of the world's peoples to exit from the modern shackles of the *cujus regio ejus religio* model ("the prince's religion is the religion of the realm").

But if faith seeks to free itself from any kind of institutional expression, it can also fragment when neo-liberal, scientistic, and consumerist ideology anaesthetizes consciousnesses and frees individuals from any feeling of responsibility for the common good. Moreover, the Church is the place where social circles that would not otherwise come into contact with each other can meet. It too, however, can become fragmented if the institutions that structure it are no longer able to count among their number members who are ready to enter into dialogue with each other and ready to support the Church.

The globalization of the years 1990 – 2000 was accompanied by a movement of expansion of post-modern philosophy represented by thinkers such as Jacques Derrida, Richard Rorty, and Slavoj Zizek.[15] This anti-modern or post-modern philosophy offered a critique of rationalist universalism. But it also freed itself from an epistemology founded on the value of truth. As Zygmunt Bauman recognized, moreover, it was becoming more difficult to love one's neighbor in an age in which "everything was becoming fluid."[16] Noting "the dissolution of forms," the post-modern level of consciousness promoted new hybrid and multi-cultural societies, without taking account

---

13   See "Vers la réconciliation et le schisme au sein de l'Église Orthodoxe," www. cath.ch.

14   Antoine Arjakovsky, "La reconnaissance de l'Église de Kiev par Constantinople est une décision sage," *La Croix*, www.la-croix.com.

15   Martin Lloyd Thomas, "Postmodernisation and the Formation of a Postmodern Political Disposition," https://www.sheffield.ac.uk/polopoly_fs/1.71453!/file/thomas.pdf.

16   Zygmunt Bauman, *Liquid Love: On the Frailty of Human Bonds* (Cambridge: Polity Press, 2014).

of the reality of differing levels of consciousness. At its most extreme, this development of ecclesial consciousness gave birth to a new post-modern religious profile which the Americans called "Emerging Church."[17] But this new period of globalization also fostered a better acquaintance on the part of Christians with the life of churches other than their own. New rapprochements have taken place through and sometimes beyond traditional attachments to people's communities of origin. What has been called the winter of ecclesial consciousness does not, therefore, signify an absence of life, but the remaking of the ecclesial landscape.

THE FOUR NEW CONSTELLATIONS OF TRANS-DENOMINATIONAL CONSCIOUSNESS

The ecumenical winter, then, prompted a radicalization of ecclesial consciousness, which was itself reinforced, as we shall see in more detail below, by the radicalization of minds on a global scale as a result of developments in ideology. Since the end of the 1990s, we have witnessed the formation of four vast trans-denominational constellations, beyond the allegiance of religious currents in the churches of origin, and animated by the four major expressions of faith, that is, law and justice, memory, and praise: an ecumenism centered on virtue and the protection of the family; an ecumenism of justice, organized along the axis of social justice and ecology; an ecumenism of tradition, attentive to the reception and transmission of truth in its different modes of expression; and, lastly, a mystical ecumenism, oriented first of all towards the new manifestations of the Holy Spirit that emerge through shared prayer, the witness of the saints, and artistic creation. The Pontifical Council for the Promotion of Christian Unity has made the same finding in its *vademecum* entitled "The bishop and Christian unity," published in 2020. The Catholic theologians of the Holy See use slightly different categories. They call the ecumenism of virtue a "dialogue of charity," the ecumenism of justice "dialogue of life," mystical ecumenism "spiritual ecumenism," and the ecumenism of tradition they call a "dialogue of truth":

> The ecumenical movement is one and indivisible and should always be thought of as a whole. Nonetheless it takes various forms according to the various dimensions of ecclesial life. Spiritual ecumenism promotes prayer, conversion and holiness

---

17   https://en.wikipedia.org/wiki/Emerging_church.

for the sake of Christian unity. The Dialogue of Love deals with encounter at the level of everyday contacts and cooperation, nurturing and deepening the relationship we already share through baptism. The Dialogue of Truth concerns the vital doctrinal aspect of healing division among Christians. The Dialogue of Life includes the opportunities for encounter and collaboration with other Christians in pastoral care, in mission to the world and through culture. These forms of ecumenism are here distinguished for clarity of explanation, but it should always be borne in mind that they are interconnected and mutually enriching aspects of the same reality. Much ecumenical activity will engage a number of these dimensions simultaneously. For the purposes of this document distinctions are made in order to help the bishop in his discernment. [18]

What is more, the Vatican ecumenists treat some spheres of ecumenical activity as belonging to different categories from those I have set out. So, for example, the Pontifical Council places the work of memorial reconciliation in the category of spiritual ecumenism, while for me it belongs to the effort of faith-reason in support of a shared historical narrative, which places it within the ecumenism of living tradition. Similarly, Rome places "pastoral ecumenism" solely within "the dialogue of life," whereas for me it integrates all the axes of ecumenical commitment. Lastly, Rome integrates interreligious dialogue within the ecumenism of life, whereas I consider that interreligious dialogue belongs at a distinct level of consciousness and covers all four of the poles of faith. But these differences are relative in comparison to the shared observation that ecumenical work usually possesses in each case a particular orientation of the Christian faith beyond any strictly denominational rationality, an orientation which is moral or ethical, meditative or incarnate, and which in each case tends to marginalize the other axes of Christian life.

THE ECUMENISM OF VIRTUE

The neo-conservative movement of ecclesial consciousness centered on personal and family morality was started by Cardinal Ratzinger when he was Prefect of the Congregation for the Doctrine of the Faith. On August 6, 2000, he published a statement entitled *Dominus Iesus*, in which he proposed a restrictive interpretation of the development of ecclesial consciousness

---

18   Document of the Pontifical Council for Promoting Christian Unity, "The Bishop and Christian Unity: an ecumenical vademecum," December 4, 2020, www.vatican.va.

that had taken place at the Second Vatican Council. Indeed, he once more identified the *Una Sancta* with the Roman Catholic Church alone.

> With the expression *subsistit in*, the Second Vatican Council sought to harmonize two doctrinal statements: on the one hand, that the Church of Christ, despite the divisions which exist among Christians, continues to exist fully only in the Catholic Church, and on the other hand, that "outside of her structure, many elements can be found of sanctification and truth," that is, in those Churches and ecclesial communities which are not yet in full communion with the Catholic Church. But with respect to these, it needs to be stated that "they derive their efficacy from the very fullness of grace and truth entrusted to the Catholic Church."[19]

This official text of the Catholic Church, moreover, in wishing to oppose relativism in religious matters and in seeking to refute theological eclecticism, religious subjectivism, and theological agnosticism, had the effect of putting a stop to all the progress made in interreligious dialogue led by the Catholic Church since Vatican II. The French Orthodox theologian Olivier Clément had published in 1997 a text on the possible ways to reconciliation between the Orthodox Church and the Catholic Church. But three years later, he reacted vigorously against *Dominus Iesus*:

> It is not possible to say, as Cardinal Ratzinger maintains, that Christianity, in the institutional sense of the term, is the only path to salvation. There are undeniably several divine economies, and the Holy Spirit blows everywhere. That it should be Christ who, in the last instance, carries within Himself all men, why not? But He does so within various non-Christian traditions themselves, and not exclusively through the Church.[20]

But one trend within Orthodox Christian thought was itself inspired by the new radical spirit. Patriarch Kirill of Moscow, elected in 2008, clearly invoked the crisis in ecumenical consciousness to justify his attachment to a neo-traditional Christianity.[21] Regarded by some as an ecumenist as a result of his commitments in the WCC in the 1980s, the Patriarch has nonetheless severely criticized the ecumenical movement, which he

---

19 Congregation for the Doctrine of the Faith, "Declaration 'Dominus Jesus' on the Unicity and Salvific Universality of Jesus Christ and the Church," www.vatican.va/.
20 "Paris: Vive réaction orthodoxe à la déclaration 'Dominus Iesus' du cardinal Ratzinger," La Croix, September 6, 2000, www.cath.ch.
21 "En Russie, le tsar et le patriarche," Le Monde, December 18, 2015.

considers too liberal, for the last thirty years.[22] Thus he has in this way, for example, justified his Church's leaving the Conference of European Churches in 2008, but also the annexation the year before that of the Russian Church overseas, known for its anti-ecumenical positions, to the Moscow Patriarchate.

This post-interdenominational and neo-conservative current is today attracting to itself Christians belonging to various ecclesial families throughout the world. Apart from certain currents in the Catholic and Orthodox Churches, a large number of currents within the Protestant churches are also found among them, particularly American churches such as the Southern Baptist Convention, the Evangelical churches, the Pentecostal Assemblies of God, and the Seventh Day Adventists. The latter have come out strongly against the recognition of civil marriages between homosexual couples, authorized by the Supreme Court of the United States on June 26, 2015.[23]

A recent book by Rod Dreher, *The Benedict Option: A Strategy for Christians in a Post-Christian Nation* (New York: Sentinel, 2017), itself symbolizes this convergence of a post-denominational viewpoint on the "family values" of the different denominational traditions. Its author, an American from Louisiana, born in 1967, and coming from the Methodist church, went over to the Catholic Church in 1993, finally joining the Russian Orthodox Church in 2006, after the sexual scandals which rocked the Roman Catholic Church in the United States. His successive different attachments are all linked to his quest for a world made up of traditional values, a world he considers as having been swallowed up today. For Dreher, Christians who want to keep their faith must separate themselves as much as possible from secular society, which Dreher regards as becoming more and more distant from traditional Christian values, especially those concerning sex, marriage, and gender.

One can also observe rapprochements between the Orthodox churches in the United States and the Evangelical churches coming out of the *Fundamentals* movement (1910 – 1915), and out of the renewal of theology led after 1945 by Billy Graham.[24] Some groups, not only in the United States but also in Israel, are influenced by the work of John Darby (1800 – 1882). They profess the same "dispensationalist" theses, according to which God

---

22   "His Holiness Patriarch Kirill: Inter-Christian relations are in a protracted crisis, as polarization of Christians' opinion on liberal or traditional reading of Christian message was added to classical differences among confessions," www.mospat.ru.

23   Erwin W. Lutzer, "The Great Divide: Same-Sex Marriage And The Evangelical Christian," 2015, www.moodymedia.org.

24   James J. Stamoolis et al., *Three Views On Eastern Orthodoxy and Evangelicalism* (Grand Rapids, MI: Zondervan, 2010).

sovereignly governs the world through dispensations, or progressive phases of revelation of his divinity. These stages, in contrast to traditional doctrine, cannot be affected by any interpretation made by differing levels of ecclesial consciousness. It is this group of Christians who aim to conquer political leaders who present themselves as Christian such as Donald Trump and Vladimir Putin.

THE ECUMENISM OF JUSTICE

In the face of this new ecumenical alliance between neo-conservative churches, characteristic of the consciousness of zealots, a new type of ecumenical alliance is also found between currents in different churches that are attached to the "prophetic" or "contestatory" model. This model was promoted by Konrad Raiser, the former Secretary General of the World Council of Churches, and by Lewis S. Mudge, the American author of the book *The Church as Moral Community* (WCC, 1998). Among ecumenical currents oriented primarily towards questions of a sustainable economy, justice, and peace, one can mention the Focolare Community, or, again, the Iona Community founded in 1938 by a pastor of the Church of Scotland, George MacLeod.[25] In 1997, the WCC published a text called *Costly Obedience*, which aimed to transform the ecumenical movement into a "moral community" whose principal objective would be to struggle against the weaknesses of the churches in respect of ethnic, nationalist, and economic violence, and to reflect on the socio-political implications of their baptismal and Eucharistic life. The terms justice and peace have the mission of gathering the faithful, beyond their denominational allegiances, and of mobilizing them to struggles such as that against apartheid or that for the liquidation of the poorest countries' debts to the great economic powers.

In a book entitled *For A Culture Of Life*, published in 2002 by the World Council of Churches, Raiser, a disciple of the German Reformed theologian Jürgen Moltmann, defends a catholicity founded on a broadened conception of the *oikouménē*, understood here as the "household of life," the place in which all life dwells. The Church is here understood above all as the Father's house. This changes the ecumenic model. The objective of the ecumenical movement becomes conviviality, a companionship within a single house founded on the reciprocal recognition of baptisms. This rules out any exclusions, apart from fundamentalist positions. This ecological vision is opposed to an ultra-liberal conception of the *oikouménē*. Unlike liberal globalization centered on the removal of customs barriers,

---

25   https://en.wikipedia.org/wiki/Iona_Community.

ecumenical and ecological ecclesiology holds that the goal of the economy is first of all to put itself at the service of life. This obliges political leaders to protect local communities before thinking of integrating them into commercial markets and global financial systems. One can link the work carried out by Hans Küng with the Parliament of the World's Religions with this current. The Parliament, indeed, adopted in 1993 a text entitled "Universal Declaration of Human Responsibilities," proposing a culture of non-violence and respect for life, a culture of solidarity and a just economic order, a culture of tolerance and of life in total truthfulness, a culture of equality of rights and of partnership between men and women. [26]

In the Orthodox world, Ecumenical Patriarch Bartholomew has also specially committed himself to mobilizing Christians of different denominations beyond the Orthodox churches. He has organized several colloquiums with the support of Prince Philip, the Duke of Edinburgh, particularly around the issue of the world's great bodies of water, inviting experts and contributors from many different fields. [27] These nine interdisciplinary meetings took place between 1995 and 2018, on the Mediterranean, the Black Sea, the Danube, the Arctic, the Mississippi, and the Sporades. He has also organized several ecumenical seminars in support of ecological education.

Pope Francis has also devoted his energies to the support of ecology in his encyclical *Laudato Si'* in 2015, by appealing to the conscience of the world's peoples well beyond Christian consciousness. The Archbishop of Canterbury, Justin Welby, has also shown his support for an ecclesiology centered primarily on the pole of justice. Together with Pope Francis, he also has the objective of promoting peace-building in South Sudan. [28]

THE ECUMENISM OF TRADITION

The Church is for Christians not only the Ark of alliance, as for the promotors of the ecumenism of virtue, nor only the House of the Father, as for the defenders of the ecumenism of justice. It is also the Body of Christ.

Paul Murray, a British lay Catholic who teaches systematic theology at Durham University, observed a crisis in the ecumenical movement at the beginning of the 2000s. He shares the viewpoint of the Princeton

---

26   Hans Küng, *A Global Ethic for Global Politics and Economics* (New York: Oxford University Press, 1988), 111.
27   "Bartholomew and the Environment: Nature, Orthodoxy, and Global Leadership," www.blogs.goarch.org.
28   "Archbishop of Canterbury: May Christians face pandemic in unity," Vatican News, November 17, 2020, www.vaticannews.va.

Proposal for Christian Unity (*In One Body Through the Cross*) written in 2003 by sixteen theologians from different denominations. This suggests that questions of faith must have a visible expression and must not be dependent on a social agenda. Inspired by the book *The Ecumenical Future* published in 2004 by Carl E. Braaten and Robert W. Jenson, but also by the work of David S. Yeago and William G. Rush on the major part that reception plays in the progress of ecumenical consciousness, Paul Murray encouraged from 2006 onwards a new kind of ecumenical assembly that he has himself called *Receptive Ecumenism*, which one might call "neo-traditional." One of the major points of this movement is to call "the churches to grow together in a visible way in a structural and sacramental unity with the Triune God." It aims to strengthen ecclesial institutions by allowing them to bring together the best of the ecumenical movement and by thus giving them a new evangelizing vigor.

This current is fundamentally pragmatic. Paul Murray, indeed, influenced by the Pittsburgh philosopher Nicholas Rescher, born in 1928, has spoken in favor of a so-called "realist" ecclesiology that takes account of the impossibility of the churches' moving further towards ecumenical reconciliation "in the short to medium term," but aims nevertheless to keep alive the prophetic flame of the coming union of the churches. In his article "Receptive Ecumenism and Catholic Learning," he explains that the work of faith is not to subject oneself to questioning by the different beliefs of others. It consists, rather, in "becoming more fully, more richly, what we already are."[29] For Murray, from the Roman Catholic perspective, for example, this much-needed process of ecclesial growth, conversion, and maturing through receptive ecumenical learning is not a matter of becoming *less* Catholic but of becoming *more* Catholic precisely by become more appropriately Anglican, more appropriately Lutheran, more appropriately Methodist, more appropriately Orthodox, etc.[30] This does not mean either abandoning ecumenical dialogue or throwing oneself, as Konrad Raiser suggests, into social or ecological mission, which for Murray have little chance of success without structural unity and catholicity. It is matter of suggesting to the churches that they should integrate "the ecumenical legacy," as the Catholic Church began to do with the publication in 1993 of a *Directory for the Application of Principles and Norms on Ecumenism*.

---

29   Paul D. Murray, ed., *Receptive Ecumenism and the Call to Catholic Learning* (Oxford: Oxford University Press, 2008), 6.
30   Murray, ed., *Receptive Ecumenism*, 16.

For the late Catholic theologian Margaret O'Gara, Professor of Ecumenical Theology at the University of Toronto, this current of an ecumenism of reception takes the question of truth seriously. But it seeks to add an emotional dimension to the purely intellectual quest for truth:

> In the Princeton Proposal for Christian unity, *In One Body through the Cross*, a group of ecumenical scholars criticizes the ecumenical movement for sometimes giving in to a kind of "liberal indifference," leading others to react with "divisive sectarianism." Wanting to avoid an indifferent relativism, some churches focus on older formulations to define their identity over against other churches. But, in fact, the Princeton Proposal argues, both liberal indifference and divisive sectarianism are often marked by a shift away from the question of truth and towards the question of identity: "The question 'Is it true?', that is, faithful to the divine revelation, was implicitly equated with 'Is it authentically Catholic?', 'Is it Evangelical?', 'Does it express the mind of Orthodoxy?', 'Is it congruent with the dynamics of the Reformation?'" (Princeton Proposal, section 41) The Proposal continues, "This shift from truth to identity reflects a kind of tribalization of Christian communities" that can play into the hands of secular nationalism, ethnic conflict, or consumerist dynamics. (42)
>
> Such reflections raise the need for repentance before any exchange of gifts is possible. It was a spirit of repentance that animated the US Lutheran–Roman Catholic Dialogue statement on *The Church as Koinonia of Salvation* when it used the language of "woundedness" to describe the situation of each church. Rather than only mutual affirmations or exchange of gifts, the agreement asks Lutherans and Roman Catholics for a mutual recognition that the ordained ministries and communities of each are wounded because of the lack of full communion. [31]

By receiving the gifts of other churches, each local church is able to progress spiritually, and sometimes to heal its own wounds. It is a matter, therefore, of a new type of intra-denominational ecumenism which does not seek to convert others, and which refuses any apologeticism of the kind displayed by neo-conservative ecumenism, but which consists in defending the truth of one's church while integrating the best of other ecclesial traditions. This question of the apprenticeship of "the heart's

---

31   Margaret O'Gara, "Receiving Gifts in Ecumenical Dialogue," in Murray, ed., *Receptive Ecumenism*, 26–39, 30.

reason" [*la raison du cœur*] and of good education is therefore central for receptive ecumenism. It is participating in a project of the democratization of ecumenism, thanks to a more simple methodology. The latter consists in asking oneself what positive elements each believer can receive from the other churches. This explains the significant number of high-level academic conferences organized by this movement since 2006 in Europe, in America, and also in Australia. Durham University's website lists many theological studies and publications linked to this movement of receptive ecumenism.[32]

If this movement was born in the Catholic Church, we have seen that it was inspired by theologians belonging to different Christian traditions like William G. Rush and David Yeago of the Lutheran church. It has welcomed eminent personalities from different Christian traditions and significant contributions from Nicholas Sagovsky of the Anglican church, Metropolitan Kallistos Ware of the Orthodox Church (Constantinople) and Father Andrew Louth (Orthodox Church, Moscow).

The Dutch Reformed theologian Anne-Marie Reijnen uses the symbol of the house to make heard the ways in which a faithful memory can help each denomination to rediscover its own identity, and, with it, its hospitality towards others:

> God meets each one of us when we have entered into our "closet" (Matt. 6:6), the patristic *cubiculum cordis*, at the same time as *together* we meet God in his house or in his body, which is the Church. The house lends itself both to solitude and to solidarity. Carl Gustav Jung had recourse to the image of the house to explain the task of the psychologist; we borrow the image from him to speak of the churches. Here is what Jung said about the "terrestrial conditioning" of the soul, described in terms of architecture and archaeology: "We have to describe and to explain a building the upper story of which was erected in the nineteenth century; the ground-floor dates from the sixteenth century, and a careful examination of the masonry discloses the fact that it was reconstructed from a dwelling-tower of the eleventh century. In the cellar we discover Roman foundation walls, and under the cellar a filled-in cave, in the floor of which stone tools are found and remnants of glacial fauna in the layers below."[33] Gaston

---

32   https://www.dur.ac.uk/theology.religion/ccs/projects/receptiveecumenism/publications/.
33   C. G. Jung, *Contributions to Analytical Psychology*, trans. H. G. and Cary F. Baynes (New York: Harcourt, Brace, 1928), 118–19. This passage is taken from the essay

Bachelard quotes this passage from Jung in his *Poetics of Space* in order to develop his intuition: "not only our memories, but the things we have forgotten are 'housed.'"[34] Allow me to repeat: "not only our memories, but the things we have forgotten are housed!" Later, Bachelard says of the cellar that "it is first and foremost the *dark entity* of the house . . . ."[35] And again, in the words of the poet Joë Bousquet (1897 – 1950): "He was a man with only one story: he had his cellar in his attic."[36] You can see where I am going with this. Before we can heal and practice exorcism in the wake of Him who healed and who expelled the demons, we would do well to take the measure of what our ecclesial houses are, what memories and what forgettings dwell in them, and on which floor of our dwellings we are speaking to those in adjoining apartments.[37]

MYSTICAL ECUMENISM

Finally, there is a fourth constellation in the present ecumenical movement which defines the Church above all as the Temple of the Holy Spirit. It has certain points in common with the ecumenism of reception, as is shown by the commitment of some Catholic monasteries, at Chevetogne in Belgium, and at Bose in Italy, to the Churches' better comprehension of the theology of other sister churches. Cardinal Kasper invites us to harvest the fruits of all the ecumenical dialogues between Catholics, Lutherans, the Reformed, Anglicans, and Methodists.[38] The American Catholic theologian Jeffrey Gros has called us to the same work by publishing in four volumes all the ecumenical agreements of the past half-century (*Growth In Agreement*).[39]

But as Antonia Pizzey has shown in a dissertation for the Catholic University of Australia, this fourth current of spiritual ecumenism must

---

entitled "Mind and the Earth." Quoted in Gaston Bachelard, *Poetics of Space*, trans. John R. Stilgoe (Boston, MA: Beacon Press, 1994), xxxvii.

34 Bachelard, *Poetics of Space*, xxxvii.

35 Ibid., 18.

36 Joë Bousquet, *La neige d'un autre âge*, quoted in Bachelard, *Poetics of Space*, 26.

37 Anne-Marie Reijnen, "Comment habiter sa propre demeure tout en édifiant la maison commune: quelques remarques," *Actes des colloques sur le concile de Florence* (forthcoming).

38 Walter Kasper, *Harvesting the Fruits: Aspects of Christian Faith in Dialogue* (London: Bloomsbury, 2013).

39 All the texts of the ecumenical agreements are accessible on the "Faith and Order Papers digital edition" web page: https://archive.org/details/faithandorderpapersdigitaledition.

be distinguished from the movement for institutional ecumenism.[40] Led today by Cardinal Kasper, the author of a *Handbook of Spiritual Ecumenism*, this current is above all the heir of the movement started at the beginning of the twentieth century and taken up in the 1930s by abbé Paul Couturier, then by the World Council of Churches, the Pontifical Council for Promoting Christian Unity, and the Semaines de prières pour l'unité des chrétiens [Christian Unity Prayer Weeks]. The latter take place every year in the third week of January between the feasts of the apostles Peter and Paul. Closest to Cardinal Kasper's heart, in his own words, is the "spiritual *oikouménè*":

> It is the heart of the *oikouménè*. By this I mean the *oikouménè* of prayer and of conversion. Without prayer, and without conversion, there is no *oikouménè*. But with prayer and conversion, much — everything even — is possible, in the words of Jesus.[41]

Cardinal Kasper is of course the first to insist on the need to "harvest the fruits" of decades of theological consensus agreements signed over more than fifty years. But this spiritual ecumenism finds its framework in the celebration of the liturgical year.[42] It appeals in particular to the martyrs of the Church so as to receive the support of the saints of the Church, because they believe firmly in their beneficent action in the world, whether we think of Father Alexander Men, of Martin Luther King, or of Mother Theresa.[43] This ecumenism recalls the words of Christ: "where two or three are gathered together in my name, there am I in the midst of them" (Matt. 18:16). The Church, from this point of view, is understood above all as the Temple of the Holy Spirit. Attention to art is important to this current of ecumenical consciousness, whether we think of the icon, as a window into the invisible, or of painting, as an experience of epiphany.[44]

Even if institutional work is indispensable to making the unity of the Church visible, beginning with the work of education *ad intra* and of dialogue *ad extra*, spiritual ecumenism also, as Kasper writes, demands

---

40 Antonia Pizzey, "Heart and soul: Receptive ecumenism as a dynamic development of spiritual ecumenism," PhD dissertation, Australian Catholic University Research Bank, 2015.

41 http://www.vatican.va/roman_curia/pontifical_councils/chrstuni/lutheran -fed-docs/rc_pc_chrstuni_doc_20091031_greeting-kasper_fr.html.

42 Kasper, *Harvesting the Fruits*, 63.

43 "A Cloud of Witnesses: Opportunities for Ecumenical Commemoration," Monastery of Bose, October 29 to November 2, 2008, *Faith and Order Paper* 209, https:// archive.org/.

44 Gennadios Limouris, *Icons: Windows on Eternity* (Geneva: WCC Publications, 1990 [Faith and Order Paper, 147]).

a "'change of heart and holiness of life,' arising from Jesus' call to conversion."[45] This is why it grants a place of particular importance to inter-denominational couples in bringing about the Kingdom of God on earth. Convinced that the Church is one, the ecumenism of prayer is perfectly aware of the fact that there exist several different levels of consciousness in the Church. Cardinal Kasper therefore invites Christians to do everything possible, commensurate with their actual extent of mutual communion, to discover the reality of this unity which is already present in the Church:

> Though not in full communion with the Catholic Church, other Churches and Ecclesial Communities retain in reality a certain communion with it, in varying degrees. This ecclesiology of communion is the context for understanding and nurturing ecumenism, directed to *"making the partial communion existing between Christians grow toward full communion in truth and charity."*[46]

Such an approach therefore invites us to go beyond the framework of official inter-denominational ecumenism, since God addresses human beings as his friends. Like Cardinals Bea[47] and Koch,[48] the former and current leaders of the Pontifical Council for Promoting Christian Unity, Kasper believes in the opportunities offered by an ecumenism of friendship. This ecumenism of friendship gave rise to the creation in 2004 of the Institute for Ecumenical Studies in Lviv, Ukraine, the only ecumenical Institute currently existing within the former USSR.[49]

This type of ecumenism not only is not limited to official dialogues, but also questions the Churches' tendency to institutionalize the ecumenical movement. Met. John Zizioulas, the Metropolitan bishop of Pergamon, has shown the limitations of the decision taken by the central committee of the WCC in Toronto in 1950 that the World Council of Churches did not constitute a "super-church."[50] As Zizioulas laments, this decision has led the member churches to content themselves with an inter-denominational conception of the *Una sancta*. As a result, since the WCC does not possess

---

45   Walter Kasper, *A Handbook of Spiritual Ecumenism* (New York: New City Press, 2007), 11.

46   Ibid., 14–15.

47   "Text of Cardinal Bea's Speech on Ecumenical Friendships," in "Vatican II: 50 years ago today," https://vaticaniiat50.wordpress.com.

48   "Cardinal Koch on the Week of Prayer for Christian Unity," in "Ecumenism: A Network of Friendship (Part 1)," https://zenit.org/.

49   See www.ecumenicalstudies.org.ua.

50   "Toronto statement," https://www.oikoumene.org/.

a single legal personhood, the documents which it adopts have no force other than as they are received by each of the Council's member churches. This process of reception is often long, never complete, and not very transparent. This is why rank-and-file Christians seldom know whether their churches have accepted this or that ecumenical agreement. In 1995, the decisive year for the reversal in ecumenical consciousness, Zizioulas gave an important talk entitled "The Self-Understanding of the Orthodox and their Participation in the Ecumenical Movement," which ended with the following words:

> The Orthodox participate in the Ecumenical Movement out of their conviction that the unity of the Church is an inescapable imperative for all Christians. This unity cannot be restored or fulfilled except through the coming together of those who share the same faith in the Triune God and are baptized in His name. The fellowship that results from this coming together on such a basis and for such a purpose cannot but bear an ecclesiological significance, the precise nature of which will have to be defined. [51]

SELF-UNDERSTANDING, A KEY FOR EXPLAINING THE CRISIS IN THE ECUMENICAL MOVEMENT

This remaking of the Church's ecumenical consciousness cannot be understood unless one first acknowledges — this is my first point — the limits of the inter-denominational approach; and, second, unless one sees the matter from the perspective of spiritual self-understanding, in which each level of reality perceived is linked to a corresponding level of consciousness. All this is needed so as, in a third part, to bring to light the impasses of denominational ecclesiology.

The spiritual level of consciousness can be grasped through the concept of the churches' self-understanding of themselves. Participation in the life of the Church requires ideas of what the Church at bottom really is, rather than a socio-political attachment to particular denominations. On a theological level, this means that the Church is one in its diversity, because it reflects the Trinitarian nature of God. The Orthodox bishop John Zizioulas has used the expression "personhood" to signify the One — Father, Son,

---

51   John Zizioulas, "The Self-Understanding of the Orthodox and their Participation in the Ecumenical Movement," The Ecumenical Movement, the Churches, and the World Council of Churches: An Orthodox contribution to the reflection process on "The Common Understanding and Vision of the WCC," ed. G. Lemopoulos (Geneva: WCC-SYNDESMOS, 1995).

and Holy Spirit — which is relation. As the Niceno-Constantinopolitan Creed affirms, the unity of God is personal and relational. The realization of the spiritual, personal, and relational character of the life of the Church has given birth, in the work of Nikolai Berdyaev as in that of Denis de Rougemont and Jacques Maritain, to the philosophical current of personalism, the conception of the person as microcosm and macrocosm. From this perspective the person is defined by his capacity to acquire different levels of consciousness in the image of the divine tri-hypostatic Person.[52]

Let us take three examples, from the Orthodox, Catholic, and Protestant churches respectively, of this development in the course of the twentieth century of the realization that if God is relation, then the Church is also relational.

THE REALIZATION IN THE ORTHODOX CHURCH

As we showed when discussing Orthodox Christian consciousness[53] with the help of the main historians of the two thousand years of the Church, four great definitions of the Church, but also of God, have, historically, constituted four types of ecclesial consciousness, which each have different degrees of radicality: the building, or proselytizing, type, for the representation of the Church as Body of Christ; the liturgical, or aesthetic, type, for the representation of the Church as Temple of the Holy Spirit; the ascetic, or zealot, type, for the representation of the Church as Ark of Salvation; the committed, or disputatious, type, for the representation of the Church as the House of the Father. These four ecclesial profiles can be disposed along two axes, the vertical axis (spiritual to proselytizing), and the horizontal axis (moral correctness to knowledge of justice).[54]

In this spiritual representation of ecclesial faith, the role of mediators, who are not always clergy as in the denominational schema, is decisive. In this case, in the Orthodox world, the Paris School played an important role in the twentieth century in bringing to light a fifth and more mystical conception of the Church as the Bride of the Lamb.[55] In this conception, the Church is understood as divine-humanity *in actu*, a desiring and receptive community, united and committed, in which the marriage of the human and the divine takes place. Several very different people, such as

---

52 Antoine Arjakovsky, *Essai sur le père Serge Boulgakov (1871–1944), philosophe et théologien chrétien* (Paris: Parole et Silence, 2006).

53 Arjakovsky, *En attendant le concile.*

54 Arjakovsky, *What Is Orthodoxy?*

55 Bulgakov, *The Bride of the Lamb.*

Father Sergij Bulgakov, Nikolai Berdyaev, Georgij Fedotov, and Mother Maria Skobtsova have defended such a representation of the Church. They contributed to forging this fifth type of ecclesial consciousness, which one might call sapiential. They were among the first to participate, in France, in the first inter-denominational meetings since the Reformation, and, in Europe, in the meetings that led to the formation of the World Council of Churches. From 1935 onwards, they declared themselves to be in favor of communion between the Orthodox and the Anglican Churches.

Father Sergij Bulgakov, in his famous dispute with Father Georgij Florovsky, affirmed that ecumenical ecclesial consciousness differed from denominational ecclesial consciousness in the fact that it did not believe that the unity of the Church had to be absolutely homogeneous. Christ Himself adapted his speech and his attitudes according to the people whom he was addressing, taking account of the different kinds of consciousness existing among the apostles and the disciples, among the Pharisees and the Sadducees. It is a scientistic belief to think that truth must be identical and homogeneous, always the same and susceptible of being tested by everyone. Christian faith holds, on the contrary, that participation in the truth is, above all, an event of communion. Bulgakov added that the practice of the primitive Church rested in particular on the adage attributed to St Vincent of Lérins: *in necessariis unitas, in dubiis libertas, in omnibus caritas.*[56]

THE REALIZATION IN THE CATHOLIC CHURCH

This new, typological, and post-denominational representation of Christian consciousness has epistemological and, initially, sociological repercussions. The ecclesial consciousness of French Catholics was the subject of a deep-level sociological study in 2016 on the basis of an Ipsos poll.[57] The study questions the myth of the growing secularization of attitudes in France. This myth rested on an identification of Christian consciousness with the liturgical spiritual type. According to Yann Raison du Cleuziou, only 5% of French people go to mass regularly, while 53% of the French population consider themselves to be Catholics, and almost fifteen million of them (or 23% of French people) consider themselves to be committed Catholics. It is therefore important to open our eyes to a reality which sociological consciousness did not manage to discern.[58]

---

56   Unity in necessary things, freedom in doubtful things, charity in all things.

57   "Qui sont vraiment les catholiques de la France?" *La Croix,* January 12, 2017, www.la-croix.com.

58   I myself (in 2011) proposed a new typology of Orthodox consciousness, close to that of Yann Raison du Cleuziou for Catholicism: see Arjakovsky, *En attendant le concile.*

The first circle of Christians is made up, according to du Cleuziou, of "occasional cultural Christians" [*festifs culturels*] — a very prominent type among the Orthodox — "the observant" (ascetic type), "visionaries and charismatics" (liturgical type), and the "solidary and emancipated" [*fraternels ou emancipés*] (committed type). Raison du Cleuziou has detected, amid these families of Catholics, a fifth type that one can call "conciliar" (sapiential type) and that is divided by its sociology as well as by its positioning between the different constituents of the Catholic church.[59] This, in brief summary, is how the Christians of France define themselves.[60]

For the "occasional cultural Christians" (45% of committed Catholics), Jesus, the founder of their religion, is a God of love. Often coming from among the working classes, these believers are not regular churchgoers. They claim attachment to the Church through their baptism. Influenced by a godmother or a grandmother, they are interested in the cultural aspect of Christianity, as well as in its traditions. Their political commitment is often towards the right of the political spectrum. They represent most of the Catholics in France.

For "observant" Catholics (7%), Jesus is the Son of God who died on the cross and was resurrected from the dead to offer salvation to humanity. For them, to be a believer is to seek to be worthy of this salvation by means of a personal and ascetic effort of rectification. Admiring Pope Benedict XVI, they love solemn masses with a certain hieratic quality: incense, deep silence after communion, contemplative chants and Latin prayers, although strict traditionalists are in a minority among them. The "observant" Catholics share in the conviction that they enjoy a privileged relationship with religious truth and that they belong in some respects to an elite minority. As a minority within the Church, the "observant" Catholics have to conform, in their diocesan practice, to the Roman magisterium. As a minority in matters of morals, they defend the Catholic family model, are heavily committed to opposing same-sex marriage, and condemn all infringements on human life.

For the "visionaries" (4%) or "charismatics," Jesus is a person with whom they are familiarly acquainted. For them to be a believer is to allow Jesus to enter every part of one's life. Most of the time, charismatics have grown up in a Catholic family, but have one day had the experience of

---

59   Yann Raison du Cleuziou, "La structuration interne du catholicisme français: une description sociologique en deux enquêtes successives," *Bulletin de littérature ecclésiastique* 473, January–March 2018, 9–37.
60   "Quelles sont les six familles de catholiques en France?" *La Croix*, November 1, 2017, www.la-croix.com.

an encounter with Jesus, after which their previous faith life comes to seem artificial to them. These people have often changed their place of worship. They gather in communities of converts (such as Emmanuel or Chemin Neuf [New Way]), admire personalities such as Father Daniel-Ange de Maupeou d'Ableiges, and like to participate in collective praise and silent meditation. What often distinguishes them is a wish to take up an explicitly faith-oriented political approach.

For "solidary" [fraternels] Catholics (26%), Jesus is He who includes everyone. He transgressed the social order of his time in order to make God's mercy manifest. He cares for the leper and pardons the woman taken in adultery. For these Catholics, to be faithful to Jesus is to adopt, like Abbé Pierre (Henri Marie Joseph Groués, 1912–2007), a position of hospitality and compassion. They like mass to be a time of hospitality and communion in which everyone can find a place: men and women, divorcees who have remarried and homosexuals, French people and foreigners. Claiming the heritage of Vatican II, they admire Pope Francis and recognize themselves in his definition of the Church as a "field hospital." This group is associated with a second, narrower, circle, those of the "emancipated" (4%). For emancipated Catholics, Jesus struggles against servitude and calls people to take up their freedom in the service of their neighbors. To be a believer, for them, is to be conscious of the collective consequences of one's actions, and, consequently, to become committed, like Guy Aurenche, to social and political struggle against injustice.

Lastly, for the "conciliar" Catholics (4%), Jesus is He who witnesses to God's mercy by breaking down borders that exclude people. Fervent admirers of Pope Francis, they are hostile to the Latin mass, and defend the heritage of Vatican II. They are receptive to the Gospel's account of the woman taken in adultery and of Christ's meeting with the good Samaritan.

THE REALIZATION IN THE PROTESTANT CHURCH

It can be seen that the lines of division among Christians are less and less of an institutional or denominational kind, and that they must be understood in a spiritual way. In the Protestant world, in France (the "Attestants" [Witnesses], the "Fraternité de l'Ancre" [Brotherhood of the Anchor]), in Switzerland (the "R3" and the "Landeskirchen Forum"), in Belgium ("Unio Reformata"), in the Netherlands ("Evangelisch Werkverband"), and at a European level ("Ensemble Pour L'Europe"), new "faith" networks have emerged in recent years around this same desire to go beyond historic forms of religious disposition and to witness to a living faith in God the Trinity in a less institutional way.[61] The "Blue Manifesto" of the "R3" (Rassemblement pour un Renouveau Réformé [Gathering for Reformed Renewal])[62] written between 2013 and 2016 by a number of Swiss Reformed pastors and lay people, among them Shafique Keshavjee and Martin Hoegger, testifies to this renewal.[63] It reveals in particular that spiritual renewal consists in moving from a denominational and pyramidal ecclesiology to an ecclesiology in tension, in the service of communion. This new representation and practice of the Church must be capable of uniting the pole of the law (and therefore of witness) with that of justice (and service), the pole of glory (and celebration) with that of memory (and formation).

> We want to broaden fraternal communion with other churches (Evangelical, Catholic, Anglican, Lutheran, Orthodox, and migrant churches), communities, and movements. Hence our refusal to give in to discouragement and defeatism, to authoritarianism or sectarianism. Convinced that the Church needs a management which corresponds to its nature, we seek a form of leadership and governance which embodies the values of the Church. We set ourselves apart from the tendency to center everything on pastoral ministry, which is contrary to the Biblical foundation of the diversity of ministries and the vocation of every baptized person as "prophet, king, and priest." In particular, we are standing up for a Church in which the Bible will be received as a living Word of God, in which each person will be valued, together with his or her charisms, and in which a diversity of ministries will be acknowledged. We are convinced that only a simultaneous strengthening of all five of these dynamics of the Church — koinōnia (communion), leitourgia (celebration), diakonia (service), didachē (education), and marturia (witnessing) — will

---

61   See "Préface," *Hokhma* 117 (February 2020), https://www.croirepublications.com/hokhma/.

62   The "Blue Manifesto" is available at https://www.ler3.ch/wp-content/uploads/2018/11/Manifeste-Bleu.pdf.

63   In the R3, Reformed Christians who see themselves as "confessing," "evangelical," "charismatic," "orthodox," "Calvinist," "ecumenical," or "former freethinkers" learn to pool their various resources. The movement, which some have called "an Evangelical movement within the Reformed Church" is in reality influenced by several revivals (Biblical, spiritual, liturgical, intercultural, interecclesial) within the churches that came out of the Reformation (in the North and in the South) and that have often lived in dialogue with other churches (the ecumenical movement, the Evangelical movement, charismatic and monastic renewal movements). See Martin Hoegger's article "Dix signes d'un renouveau de l'Église," *Hokhma* 110 (2016), 45–59.

allow the Church, in the power of the Spirit, to grow and to build itself in love (Ephesians 4: 14 – 16). This is why we want to strengthen these five dynamics. ("Blue Manifesto")

We can take an example to illustrate this realization of the limits of the inter-denominational ecumenical model. For what we can see happening at the European level can also be seen at the global level of the Reformed churches. Odair Pedroso Matteus, a pastor in the Independent Presbyterian Church of Brazil, himself defended an analogous analysis in a book entitled *Beyond Confessionalism: Essays on the Practice of Reformed Ecumenicity* (Sao Paolo: Emblema, 2010). Since 2015, Matteus has led the Faith and Order Commission of the World Council of Churches. An acknowledged expert in ecumenism, Matteus contributed in 2010 to the transformation of the World Alliance of Reformed Churches into a World Communion of Reformed Churches (with a hundred million believers, the third largest communion of churches in the world). Aware of the limitations of a denominational self-understanding, Matteus calls on the churches to choose an ecumenical path, following John the Baptist. Just as the friend of the Bridegroom did two thousand years ago, Matteus invites the churches to "decrease" so that the Church of Christ can be revealed in all its fullness.

Matteus is influenced by the Swiss reformer Philip Schaff (1819 – 1893), a church historian who taught in New York and who contributed to the setting-up of the Parliament of Religions in Chicago in 1893. Schaff held that the history of the Church is that of the new life which Christ introduced into human nature. After this, the history of the world becomes that of the coming of the Kingdom of God on earth. The history of the Church can no longer be that of denominations which seek to perpetuate themselves. As Matteus reminds us, the reformers did not want to create a new church, but to clarify and restore the faith and life of the Church in faithfulness to the word of God. This is why, according to him, the Westminster Confession of Faith (of 1846, taking up that of 1646) must be a basis for, not an end-point of, the life of the Reformed church.[64]

It is here that Matteus introduces the decisive concept of "ecumenical self-understanding" in order to redefine interecclesial relationships today. With this concept, Matteus shows that a number of different currents can be found within the Reformed world: an inter-denominational ecumenical

---

64 *The Humble Advice of the Assembly of Divines now by Authority of Parliament sitting at Westminster* (London, 1647); Robert Shaw, *An Exposition of the Confession of Faith of the Westminster Assembly of Divines* (Philadelphia: Presbyterian Board of Publication, 1846).

current, an intradenominational ecumenical current, a denominational current which wants to recover and purify its own religious tradition, and lastly a current supporting "global unity among sectarian groups." The unity of the Church is a gift as much as a task. Thus Matteus reminds us that "the visible unity of the Church is not identical with its unity." This is why he holds that the balance between these four currents must be realized by means of a fifth level of median consciousness convinced that the unity of the Church rests on reciprocal Eucharistic hospitality. For Matteus, indeed, God's action in the world to make his Kingdom come must take priority over ecclesiastical arrangements. He is therefore pleased that the World Alliance of Reformed Churches, at the instigation of the Scottish Presbyterian John A. Mackay, a professor at Princeton from 1948 onwards, should have sought to exit from denominational definitions of itself and instead to promote a "Reformed, Evangelical, and Catholic theology." Neither "ecclesiastical tribalism" nor "democratic centralism," the Church was, for Mackay, a living body that must live in its plurality while remembering that these structures do not come from its own essential nature. The World Alliance of Reformed Churches declared as follows in 1945: "We believe that we dare not refuse the sacrament to any baptized person who loves and confesses Jesus Christ as Lord and Saviour."[65]

THE CRISIS OF THE DENOMINATIONAL PARADIGM

Ecumenical science allows one to understand some of the limitations of the denominational theology of this period. It notes that church leaders committed to ecumenical dialogue are usually motivated only by some of the poles of religious consciousness. It also makes clear that the ecumenical winter of the years 1990 – 2020 concerns the classical, modern, and post-modern levels of consciousness. Let us, therefore, return to the terms of the debate on the notion of ecclesial consciousness.

THE CRISIS OF THE DENOMINATIONAL PARADIGM IN THE ORTHODOX WORLD

On the side of the Orthodox Church, the years between 1990 and 2020 have shown that the traditional model of a unity of the fourteen auto-cephalous churches (and the autonomous churches attached to them) was no longer suited either to the universal Church nor even to pan-Orthodox

---

65   Matteus, *Beyond Confessionalism*, 111.

conciliarity. Whereas in the 1990s the evangelical model of *koinonia* was still presented as the trademark of the Orthodox Church, today, after nearly a century of discussions on this topic, the inability of the churches all to gather together in council has put an end to the belief of Orthodox Christians themselves in the superiority of their own ecclesiology.[66]

Father Cyrille Argenti was one of the promotors of ecumenism in the Orthodox Church in Marseille, where he founded the series of interreligious programs on Dialogue Radio, in France, where he worked on the Joint Commission for Dialogue with the Roman Catholic Church, and worldwide (he took part in the WCC assembly in Nairobi). In these different settings, he used to present three models of ecclesial unity that existed in the ecumenical movement: the "Catholic model," which he defined as juridical and as (too) vertical; the "Protestant model," which rested, for him, on an excessively broad tolerance towards doctrinal variations; and lastly, the "Orthodox model," which he defined in the following way:

> The third model of unity, which is the Orthodox one, is what one could call a conciliar model. It is the idea that there can be geographical, but not doctrinal, diversity, and that, as a consequence, each local church can have its own culture, its own language, its own administration, but that they must maintain a total unity in faith with the other churches, by means of listening to each other and periodic meetings of church leaders within the framework of local, regional, and universal councils. For the Orthodox, there is no distinction between doctrine and the unity of faith.[67]

This model, therefore, distinguishes the diversity of the faith, as a variable geographical reality, from the unity of faith, as an atemporal and intangible one. The same separation between history (diversified) and doctrine (unitary) is found in another introduction to the Orthodox Church, *The Church of the Seven Councils*, by Met. Kallistos Ware. But this model has been brought into question in the last thirty years by a phenomenon with two aspects.

On the one hand, the globalization of exchanges and information has, in a half-century, transformed the planet into a small village. Societies

---

66   Antoine Arjakovsky, "Comment sortir de la crise actuelle de l'Église Orthodoxe?" *Le Blog d'Antoine Arjakovsky*, December 15, 2018, http://arjakovsky.blogspot.com/.
67   Cyrille Argenti, *Quelle Église pour l'unité chrétienne?* 2 (La Bastide d'Engras: Radio Dialogue, 2009).

have become more and more mixed, because of the phenomenon of huge migrations. In Paris and in New York once can find representatives of the Bulgarian and Antiochene, Serbian and Greek, and Russian and Romanian churches. Although Orthodox Christians have celebrated Easter on different dates for decades, their inability to celebrate Easter together now appears as the height of anachronism. Differences that passed unnoticed fifty years ago, such as the "rebaptism" by churches in the Greek tradition of heterodox Christians who wish to enter the Orthodox Church, have become inadmissible for most Christians in other denominations. Similarly, the serious interecclesial conflicts, frozen in position during the period when individual political powers dominated the churches, can no longer be ignored in the contemporary era. The Russian Orthodox Church's elimination of the Ukrainian Greek Catholic Church in 1946 in Lviv (all the bishops of this church were arrested by the Soviet regime, while the Patriarchate of Moscow declared that this church was "freely attaching" itself to the Patriarchate of Moscow), a church with more than five million members, could no longer be hidden in 1991 at the moment when this Catholic Church, which was the heir of the old Church of Kiev, was able to emerge from the catacombs. Relations between the Orthodox Churches and the Greek Catholic Churches have, moreover, brought into question the idea, inherited from the Hellenistic era, that in the global era each single territory should take charge of a single church. It is the very notion of homogeneity between physical and pastoral space that has been put in question by the century of migrations.[68] The idea, then, that the geographical diversity of religious practices was acceptable in return for unity of faith was put in question. This was all the more the case because the pre-conciliar meetings revealed that the various Orthodox Churches were not all ready to communicate from the same cup. By dint of living out an ecclesiology of *sobornost* excluding any pan-Orthodox personal primacy, the Orthodox Churches came into conflict over the question of

---

68 In 2001, the Catholic Church also supported an agreement between the Chaldaean and the Assyrian churches of the East which made reciprocal admission to Eucharistic hospitality possible when necessary. These agreements imagined that when Chaldaean Christians took part in a celebration of the Assyrian Eucharist, the Assyrian priest would be invited to insert the words of consecration into the anaphora. This was accepted by the Assyrian Church, but it is not prescriptive. As Peter Neuner writes, "it therefore seems that it is possible to legislate for individual churches within the Catholic communion in ways which are not necessarily also valid for the universal Church. This corrects what is sometimes said to be the case, that is to say, that something is not possible in one place if it cannot also be brought into force in the universal Church." Peter Neuner, *Théologie œcuménique*, 238.

primacy and of diptychs — that is to say, the question of the order of precedence of local churches — a question so thorny that no consensus has been found after fifty years of dialogue on the topic.[69]

The Russian Church, which was not affected by the break-up of the USSR, believed at the beginning of the 1990s that it must once more become an imperial church, and that its mission was to restore the myth of Moscow as the "third Rome." In a 2013 text on the question of primacy in the universal Church, the Patriarchate of Moscow assured readers that the *power* of the bishop was equal to the *authority* of God, and that the authority of the Bishop of Rome as the successor of Peter had no foundation in the Gospel:

> The bishops of Rome, who enjoy the primacy of honour in the Universal Church, from the point of view of Eastern Churches, have always been patriarchs of the West, that is, primates of the Western Local Church. However, already in the first millennium of church history, a doctrine on a special divinely-originated magisterial and administrative power of the Bishop of Rome as extending to the whole Universal Church began to be formed in the West. The Orthodox Church rejected the doctrine of the Roman Church on papal primacy and the divine origin of the power of the first bishop in the Universal Church. Orthodox theologians have always insisted that the Church of Rome is one of the autocephalous Local Churches with no right to extend her jurisdiction to the territory of other Local Churches. They also believed that primacy in honour accorded to the bishops of Rome is instituted not by God but men.[70]

This position of the Patriarchate of Moscow's, too vague, historically, to be correct, does not correspond with the position defended by Olivier Clément in his book You Are Peter [Rome Autrement]. For Clément, the Church, drawing on Scripture and Tradition, had in the first millennium several different antennae for hearing what the Spirit wished to say to it:

---

69 "The lists of names of living and departed Christians for whom special prayer is made in the Greek and Latin Eucharistic Liturgies. Though until recently read secretly in the West, in early times the diptychs were recited publicly, and the inclusion or exclusion of a name was held to be a sign of communion or excommunication. The term is derived from the two-leaved folder (Greek δίπτυχον) within which the lists were written." (Cross and Livingstone, Oxford Dictionary of the Christian Church, "diptychs.") — Translator.

70 "Position of the Moscow Patriarchate on the problem of primacy in the Universal Church," 2013: https://mospat.ru/en/.

— The council as an expression of universal communion.

— The pope as being charged with care for this communion and watching over the Petrine and Pauline correctness of the faith.

— But also the *utilitas* of the people of God, its "sense of the Church," which can express itself in times of major crisis through the witness, the martyrdom, of a lone prophet.[71]

The Patriarchate of Moscow also affirms that the authority of the Patriarch of Constantinople in the Orthodox Church is only a matter of form:

> The source of primacy in honour on the level of the Universal Church lies in the canonical tradition of the Church fixed in the sacred diptychs and recognized by all the autocephalous Local Churches. The primacy of honour on the universal level is not informed by canons of Ecumenical or Local Councils. The canons on which the sacred diptychs are based do not vest the primus (such as the Bishop of Rome used to be at the time of Ecumenical Councils) with any powers on the church-wide scale. The ecclesiological distortions ascribing to the primus on the universal level the functions of *governance* inherent in primates on other levels of church order are named in the polemical literature of the second millennium as "papism."[72]

The Ecumenical Patriarchate, for its part, had a tendency to wish to defend its domain, but on the basis of medieval authorities, which led some hierarchs, such as Abp. Elpidophoros Lambrianidis, to advocate strange theories. On March 16, 2009, the Secretary of the Holy Synod of Constantinople declared that "the whole Orthodox diaspora, that is, the whole Orthodox population living outside the traditional borders of its church of origin, must be subordinated to Constantinople." This was simply to cross out the many attempts to build local churches by Orthodox Christians who had for several generations no longer defined themselves as members of a diaspora.[73] Subsequently he went so far as to assert that if the archbishop of Constantinople is one among equals, as Ecumenical Patriarch he is *"primus sine paribus."* This text of February 12, 2014, is still posted on the website of the Ecumenical

---

71   Olivier Clément, *You Are Peter: An Orthodox Theologian's Reflection on the Exercise of Papal Primacy*, trans. M. S. Laird (New York: New City Press, 2003), 54–55.

72   "Position of the Moscow Patriarchate on the problem of primacy in the Universal Church," https://mospat.ru/en/.

73   Sebastian Rimestad, *Orthodox Christian Identity in Western Europe* (London: Routledge, 2020).

Patriarchate today.[74] The other churches have preferred to believe that the organization of the Church is autocephalous, by imagining that this nineteenth-century invention went back to the earliest Christian centuries, which is incorrect, as John Erickson has shown in his book *The Challenge of Our Past*.

On May 11, 2019, European Orthodox Christians, members of the Orthodox Brotherhood, of the Institut St Serge, of the Action Chrétienne des Étudiants Russes/Mouvement de Jeunesse Orthodoxe [Russian Christian Student Action/Orthodox Youth Movement], of Syndesmos (the World Fellowship of Orthodox Youth), of the journal *Contacts*, and of several European Orthodox parishes, published an open letter asking the churches to move from a phyletic, nationalist, and autocephalist ecclesiology to a baptismal, Eucharistic, and pastoral one:[75]

> It is therefore necessary first of all that church institutions should show evidence of a spirit of self-criticism and repentance; it is a matter of urgency to rediscover the spirit of the Council of 1917, which proposed a new ecclesiology which must be understood not as a vertical and therefore clerical reality, in which lay people must act only in obedience to their bishops, but rather as a baptismal, Eucharistic, and pastoral reality; to work, that is, in a much more daring fashion towards ecumenical commitment.[76]

---

74 https://www.patriarchate.org/.

75 The first signatories were Antoine Arjakovsky, Sophie Clément-Stavrou, Alexandra de Moffarts, Georges El Hage, Jean-Jacques Laham, Daniel Lossky, Olga Lossky-Laham, Jean-Claude Polet, Noël Ruffieux, Cyrille Sollogoub, Michel Stavrou, Bertrand Vergely, and André Veriter.

76 The French text of the letter can be found at https://arjakovsky.blogspot.com/2019/; the English text, at https://www.wheeljournal.com/blog/2019/5/25/letter-from-the-europe. The latter continues: "The time has come, for example, for the Christians of the Patriarchate of Moscow to explain to their Orthodox brothers and sisters why their Church is so much in solidarity with the State and its decisions, even the anti-Christian ones. Those who are responsible in the Patriarchate of Constantinople should equally revise their difficulties in effectively directing the Pan-Orthodox ecclesial life in the world. For our part, we are convinced that the actual Orthodox Church in Western Europe is, in spite of its limitations, capable of organizing debates on these matters. A strictly vertical approach will not, in fact, bring about anything other than a bit more disorder and division. Along these lines, it is necessary to recognize the visionary character of the decisions of the 1917–1918 Council of Moscow which revalorized the complementarity and co-responsibility of lay people, men and women, clergy and hierarchs. To deny this heritage would be not only harmful but illusory. It is equally urgent to rediscover the sacramental dimension of life in the Church. According to such an ecclesiology, largely developed by the most eminent theologians of the 20th century, the Eucharist makes the Church and, simultaneously, the Church manifests

Elsewhere, within the Orthodox Church itself, thinkers appeared at the end of the nineteenth century who were able to explain that the faith of the Church was not a monolithic reality, that it had evolved over time. Vladimir Solovyov showed in 1886 in his book *The Dogmatic Development of the Church and the Question of Church Unity* that non-Biblical terms such as "hypostasis" and "homoousios" had been used creatively by the Fathers of the Church. What is more, eminent Orthodox theologians such as Father Sergij Bulgakov have explained that the history of the Church is made up of debates between thinkers with particular opinions, *theologoumena*, and different interpretations of this or that article of faith. The conciliar structure is not by itself sufficient to "make truth." The intervention of a council to impose one interpretation instead of another can sometimes be salutary, but it can also lead to ruptures that are damaging to the life of the Church. In other words, there is no conciliar infallibility. Only a sophiological conception of the Church, which understands the latter at once as people of God and as Bride of the Lamb, makes it possible to bring to light the living Tradition of ecclesial consciousness. Such was the main teaching of the book *Living Tradition* published by teachers at the Institut Saint Serge in response to the criticisms made by several hierarchs and theologians in 1935–1936 of the sophiological doctrine of Father Sergij Bulgakov.[77] Father Thomas Hopko, who was the Dean of St Vladimir's Orthodox Theologican Seminary at Crestwood, NY, from 1992 to 2002 also, in 1985, denounced the myth of the vitality and unity of faith in the Orthodox Church. At a meeting on the Lima Document on Baptism, Eucharist, and Ministry, Hopko, a disciple and friend of Father Schmemann, painted a somber and sorrowful picture of an Orthodox Church made up of "self-centered ethnic ghettoes" hostile to the world and concerning themselves only with questions concerning fossilized rituals.[78]

---

the common Kingdom in this world. By reassembling in unity 'the children of God scattered throughout the world,' does not the Eucharistic offering give, to those who communicate in it, the possibility of uniting themselves with one another and mutually enriching themselves with their spiritual, national, historical and cultural diversities? Finally, this community, brought together into a territory by the Eucharist, cannot disassociate itself from the history of peoples. It is therefore necessary to assure a link among the Churches of origin and the Orthodox faithful who are installed or who sojourn in the West; to open their eyes on what the Orthodox share with the other Christian Churches; and, above all, before roundly and irrevocably condemning, to see the potentials of holiness in the elements of the world which still await the divine light."

77 See Arjakovsky, *The Way*.

78 Thomas Hopko, "Tasks facing the Orthodox in the Reception of BEM [Baptism, Eucharist, Ministry]," in *Orthodox Perspectives on BEM* (Brookline, MA: Holy Cross Orthodox Press, 1985), 135–48.

The tension between unity and diversity is therefore a dynamic intrinsic to Christian doctrine. The adage which consists in affirming that the Orthodox faith is that which has been "believed everywhere, always, and by everyone" runs the risk, when it is poorly understood, of manifesting a monophysite conception of Tradition. From a theanthropic point of view, Vincent de Lérins' adage (*quod ubique, quod semper, quod ab omnibus creditum est*) means instead that the truth of the Gospel crosses centuries and continents through the unceasingly renewed multiplicity of its interpretations. That is why Vincent de Lérins, in his *Communitorium*, explained in 434 that the search for the truth in faith must not rest on a dogmatic corpus.[79] The search for truth in faith therefore consists in opening oneself without ceasing, through the dialogue between God and Men, to the new inspirations of the Spirit that reveal "the parts and forms" of Christian dogma which the Wisdom of the Creator has traced out in advance. As Vincent de Lérins writes, then, no person can freeze the growth of ecclesial consciousness at a given moment.[80]

This depends upon understanding the divine Wisdom not in a scholastic manner, as a divine virtue, but as the very life of God the Trinity. Now, a large number of contemporary Orthodox theologians are ignorant of this sophiological concept of Tradition. Referring chiefly to St Paul, for whom Christ is "the power of God, and the wisdom of God" (1 Cor. 1:24), they

---

79   "But some one will say, perhaps, Shall there, then, be no progress in Christ's Church? Certainly; all possible progress. For what being is there, so envious of men, so full of hatred to God, who would seek to forbid it? Yet on condition that it be real progress, not alteration of the faith. For progress requires that the subject be enlarged in itself, alteration, that it be transformed into something else. The intelligence, then, the knowledge, the wisdom, as well of individuals as of all, as well of one man as of the whole Church, ought, in the course of ages and centuries, to increase and make much and vigorous progress; but yet only in its own kind; that is to say, in the same doctrine, in the same sense, and in the same meaning." Commonitorium (Vincent of Lérins), chapter 23, at www.newadvent.org.

80   "This, then, is undoubtedly the true and legitimate rule of progress, this the established and most beautiful order of growth, that mature age ever develops in the man those parts and forms which the wisdom of the Creator had already framed beforehand in the infant. Whereas, if the human form were changed into some shape belonging to another kind, or at any rate, if the number of its limbs were increased or diminished, the result would be that the whole body would become either a wreck or a monster, or, at the least, would be impaired and enfeebled. In like manner, it behooves Christian doctrine to follow the same laws of progress, so as to be consolidated by years, enlarged by time, refined by age, and yet, withal, to continue uncorrupt and unadulterate, complete and perfect in all the measurement of its parts, and, so to speak, in all its proper members and senses, admitting no change, no waste of its distinctive property, no variation in its limits." Ibid.

are content to identify the Wisdom of God with a faculty belonging to Jesus Christ.[81] In this way, they avoid asking themselves about the many witnesses in the church tradition that associate divine Wisdom with the Holy Spirit.[82] This prevents them, above all, from understanding the divine life in a fully Trinitarian fashion. Hence one can understand why there is a persistent separation among contemporary Orthodox theologians between, on the one hand, a dogmatic corpus that does not go beyond the year 787, the date of the last recognized Ecumenical Council, a corpus considered as untouchable on account of its divinely revealed character, and, on the other, the life of the churches that are supposed each to be free to live autocephalously, since they belong to history, that is to say, to the diversity of the fallen world.

The ability to recover different expressions of faith would, however, allow the Orthodox churches to reform themselves — to accept, for example, the fact that in certain churches one can ordain women to the diaconate. Similarly, an acknowledgement that there are different conceptions of the Church within different Orthodox churches could stimulate theological reflection and an interest in ecumenical dialogue. An Anglican observer has noted that in the matter of the text which set out convergence between the Anglican Church and the Orthodox Church, "The Church of the Triune God," it was difficult to undertake discussion with the Orthodox churches because the latter were less and less capable of speaking in a homogeneous way:

> The Trinitarian approach adopted here reflects an approach to the relation between the Trinity and the Church which has become popular in recent years, almost the house style in the English-speaking world, and it has entered Anglican ecclesiology. Yet the analogy between the life of God and the life of the Church may not be as firmly based as the statement assumes. For example, there is a tension between the discussion of God in the statement and the ecclesiological arguments that are based on this Trinitarian analogy. The first acknowledges that God is "beyond our ken" and that there is therefore a limit to what one can say about the Trinity and the second bases arguments for a way of ordering the Church on the nature of the relations

---

81 Cf., for example, Athanase Jevtitch, *Études hésychastes* (Lausanne: L'Âge d'Homme, 1995).

82 Sergii Bulgakov, *Sophia, The Wisdom of God: An Outline of Sophiology* (Alexandria, VA: Alexander Street Press, 2020).

within the Godhead. It is not clear that these two approaches are compatible.[83]

THE CRISIS OF THE DENOMINATIONAL PARADIGM IN THE CATHOLIC AND PROTESTANT WORLD

The crisis of the Orthodox conciliar model and of the traditional ways of representing the unity of the Church also concerns the other churches. Indeed, the enthusiasm of the World Council of Churches for the *koinonia* (communion/community) model in the years between 1970 and 2000 was somewhat dampened by the excessive polysemy of this term, and the diverging interpretations that were given to it. Moreover, the reform of the Tridentine model by the Catholic Church at the Second Vatican Council made apparent the defects of the pyramidal Catholic model with the figure of the Bishop of Rome at its apex.

In a theological dissertation, François Picart, of the University of Laval, has demonstrated the limitations of the ecclesiology of communion upheld by the ecumenical movement in the years 1960–2010.[84] At the end of the 1950s, the concept of *koinonia* began to be used by some Orthodox, Catholic, and Protestant theologians, such as Nikolai Afanasiev, Jean-Marie Tillard, and Karl Barth. The evangelical conception of communion had the advantage of representing a matrix that could be welcomed by all denominational traditions at a historical moment when, in Lund, in 1952, at the time of the third Faith and Order Conference, these traditions had understood the limitations of the comparative method if one wanted to elaborate a shared theology and to travel together convergently. This reversal was called the Christological method. The Churches all decided "to act together in all things, except where deep differences of belief forced them to act separately." The New Testament understands *koinonia* specifically in terms of participation or communion with the very person and life of Jesus Christ (1 Cor. 1:9) made possible by communion with the Spirit of God (2 Cor. 13:13). Consequently, *koinonia* essentially signifies the intimate unity of the Church with God the Father, mediated by Christ and the Holy Spirit.[85] The term became the

---

83   The Council for Christian Unity: Faith and Order Advisory Group, International Commission for the Anglican-Orthodox Theological Dialogue, "The Church of the Triune God, Briefing Paper for members of the General Synod," www.churchofengland.org.
84   François Picart, "L'unité de communion chez Jean-Marie R. Tillard," doctoral thesis in theology (ICP: Paris, Université de Laval, 2015).
85   Philip Kariatlis, "Affirming Koinonia Theology: An Orthodox Perspective," http://www.sagotc.edu.au/.

main hermeneutic key for half a century in trying to bring the Churches together while retaining respect for each other's differences.[86] In 1991, at the Canberra General Assembly, *koinonia* became the dominant model for describing the unity of the Church.

What is unfortunate, as François Picard explains, is that the use of a concept drawn from the life of the early Church in order to find solutions to the life of the Church twenty centuries later cannot suffice by itself. The life of the Churches has in fact considerably evolved since the moment when the first Christians "continued steadfastly in the apostles' doctrine and fellowship [*koinonia*] and in breaking of bread, and in prayers" (Acts 2:42). The American Catholic theologian Joseph Komonchak also opposes the fluid and sometimes misleading use made of the term *koinonia* by the Dominican theologian Jean-Marie Tillard. This notion, according to him, threatens to vaporize the ecclesial institution in a purely spiritual vision. It also risks being made into a tool to disguise a practice not different from Cardinal Bellarmine's ecclesiology of the "perfect society," which it nevertheless tries to combat. When all is said and done, this ecclesiology of communion, which suggests a practice taking its rationale from the early Church, suffers, for Komonchak, from its disconnection from church practice: "Despite his theological learning and his militant enthusiasm, the Dominican finds it difficult to express the strengthening of the pneumatological and sacramental elements of his theology within the living forms of ecclesial structures."[87]

THE INTERDENOMINATIONAL CRISIS OF THE DENOMINATIONAL PARADIGM

From the 1980s onwards, a conflict appeared within the Catholic Church between faithful memory of the Church, understood as in the first place the Body of Christ, and the desire to glorify God in the Church correctly and liturgically, where the Church is understood above all as the Temple of the Holy Spirit.

> When Jean-Marie Tillard envisages "zones of communion," or when he repeats that we are not in an "all or nothing" situation, when he imagines ties of local communion among separated churches, he does not tackle the question of ties with the *unica*, or relations between local communions and the universal

---

86 "So We Believe, So We Pray: Towards Koinonia in Worship (The Ditchingham Letter and Report)," https://www.oikoumene.org/.

87 Picart, 549.

communion; nowhere does he specify what J. A. Komonchak calls the "formal element." He never indicates how the given facts are contextualized in each generation and in the transition from one to another, according to an approach which would bring together the synchronic and diachronic.[88]

After 1992, Cardinal Ratzinger determinedly opposed Tillard's arguments, especially after the publication of the results of the work of the ARCIC Joint Commission for Dialogue between the Anglican and Roman Catholic Churches.[89] Cardinal Ratzinger reproached the author of the book *Église d'Églises* with having downplayed the significance of the universal ministry of Peter's successors; when this universal ministry was derived from the principle of the local church, it lost its own significance and strength. Similarly, according to the Prefect of the Congregation for the Doctrine of the Faith, the role of bishops as heads of the individual churches was relegated to the second level, behind their participation in a pre-existing universal episcopal college (*motu proprio Apostolos suos*, 1998).[90] This is why this universal Church, identified by Cardinal Ratzinger with the Roman Catholic Church, could have no sister church. Only local churches can consider each other as sisters.

This debate continued between Cardinal Walter Kasper and Pope Benedict XVI on the question of the relationship between local churches and the universal Church. Joseph Komonchak presents the debate as an opposition between an "Aristotelian" and a "Platonist." Whereas the former suggested that the Church of Jerusalem was at once a universal Church and a local church, the latter believed that the originary community of Jerusalem was above all the gathering of the new Israel around the twelve apostles: "she is not a local community that grows gradually," Ratzinger explained in 2001, "but the leaven that is always destined to permeate the whole, and, consequently, embodies universality from the first instant."[91]

To this Cardinal Kasper responded that, if there were singular churches, all nevertheless held themselves to be realizations of the one Church. The

---

88   Ibid., 552.
89   Congregation for the Doctrine of the Faith, "Letter to the Bishops of the Catholic Church on Some Aspects of the Church Understood as Communion," www.vatican.va.
90   John Paul II, Apostolic Letter issued *motu proprio*, "*Apostolos Suos*: on the Theological and Juridical Nature of Episcopal Conferences (1)," www.vatican.va/.
91   Joseph Ratzinger, "The Ecclesiology of the Constitution of the Church, Vatican II, Lumen Gentium," www.ewtn.com; cf. J. Komonchak, "A propos de la priorité de l'Eglise universelle," in *Nouveaux apprentissages pour l'Eglise, Mélanges en l'honneur de Hervé Legrand*, eds. Gilles Routhier and Laurent Villemin (Paris: Cerf, 2006), 256.

development in the second millennium of the ecclesiology for which all authority flows downwards from the Pope has led to the privileging of the universal Church over the local church. Vatican II attempted to restore the ecclesiology of the first millennium to its place of honor by means of its teaching on the local church, on the sacramental character of episcopal ordination, and on the collegiality of the bishops.

In 2002, Cardinal Ratzinger agreed to acknowledge that "the church of Rome is a local church, not the universal Church," but he added that it was "nevertheless a local church with a universal responsibility."[92] For in Roman Catholic ecclesiology, the bishops of the Church are united to each other in a college led by the Bishop of Rome, the successor to the apostolic college led by St Peter (*Lumen Gentium*, 22). This ecclesiology holds that "particular churches" are "fashioned after the model of the universal Church, in and from which churches comes into being the one and only Catholic Church" (*Lumen Gentium*, 23).

This polemic is born of the blindness of the disputants to the double meaning which the very notion of universality possesses, as an eschatological plan and as a historical reality. Consequently, the polemic ended by opposing to each other two Western versions of the ecclesiology of the catholic Church, one privileging the diversity of local churches presented in the first chapter of Revelation, the other insisting on the ontological and chronological primacy of the universal Church, founded at Pentecost, over "particular churches." A few weeks before his death, Georges Tavard provisionally encapsulated the debate in the following way:

> Is the hierarchy that is responsible for Tradition, a hierarchy that
> is necessarily linked to the past whose heritage it is to hand down,
> capable of turning openly towards the future so as to accept and
> finally to make canonical the invention — in the true sense of
> that word — of renewed forms and formulas of faith? To make
> the process easier, it would be necessary to envisage Tradition
> not first of all as the repository of the past, but as an anticipa-
> tory dynamic of the future, under the guidance of the Spirit.[93]

When all was said and done, there were few who were ready to understand the idea of communion, of *koinonia*, in relation to the figure of the Church understood as Bride of the Lamb, a sapiential model that makes it

---

92   Komonchak, "A propos de la priorité de l'Eglise universelle," 260.
93   Georges Tavard, "Vers une ecclésiologie aux dimensions du monde," *Nouveaux apprentissages pour l'Eglise, Mélanges en l'honneur de Hervé Legrand*, eds. Gilles Routhier and Laurent Villemin (Paris: Cerf, 2006), 156.

possible to hold together representations of the Church as Body of Christ and Temple of the Spirit, as House of the Father and Ark of Salvation. This model depends upon understanding the Church as an anticipation of divine-humanity. In the documents preparatory to the Pan-Orthodox Council one can find the following formula:

> [The Orthodox Church] recognizes that the encounter with [the Christian Churches] will take place on a basis whose center is the theandric structure of the Church.[94]

This specific corporeality was heralded in Chapter 21 of the book of Revelation, by the encounter between the heavenly Jerusalem and the earthly Jerusalem. But this conception of the Church no longer figures in ecclesial agendas.[95] Such a conception would make it possible, however, to take account of the reality of the different levels of recognition and communion existing among the churches and within the churches. This at once historical and mystical conception of the Church would also make possible the adoption of a certain pastoral pragmatism, which would authorize, wherever agreed to by communities, suitable and dynamic modes of communion (whether Eucharistic, social, pedagogical, evangelical, and so on).

In any event, during the years between 1990 and 2010, the churches were manifestly not ready to translate symbolic and theological progress into institutional action, either at the level of the Catholic hierarchy or at the level of the hierarchy of the other Churches. The latter were not well placed in general to pass down to their flocks all the ecumenical progress that had been made in the course of more than thirty years. Moreover, certain communities knew nothing of the ecumenical movement; this was especially the case for populations that had lived under communist regimes. On the contrary, this was the moment, for some ecclesiastical structures, to remind the memory of the faithful of old and suppressed wounds, such as the Uniat question. This explains why the churches were at that time preoccupied with this topic, at least until the Balamand meeting in 1993. At the meeting of the Joint Commission for Catholic-Orthodox dialogue in Baltimore in 2000, the Russian Church demanded that the Uniat question should be returned to. Subsequently, the Patriarchate of Moscow pressurized the Roman Catholic Church not to expand in Russia,

---

94 "Grand et saint concile de l'Eglise orthodoxe," quoted by Yves Congar, *Diversités et communion* (Paris: Cerf, 1982), 236.

95 This conception of the Church as Bride of the Lamb does not appear in the different models of the Church described by Peter Neuner in his *Ecumenical Theology*.

because of its political conception of the notion of canonical territory. This confirms the rule according to which, in certain cases, if one ceases to make progress on a spiritual level, one begins to go backwards.

Similarly, when, after the publication of the encyclical *Ut unum sint* in 1995, a certain number of replies were published by eminent personalities in the ecumenical movement, to show that there were a few very simple conditions upon which the figure of the Bishop of Rome could again find his place in a new symphony of the churches,[96] nothing really came of it. On the contrary, the churches threw themselves once again into a new cycle of the decryption of their own divergent interpretations of the nature of the Church, while remaining uninterested in the great issues at stake in the contemporary world and divided over the right balance to maintain between social and doctrinal questions. This process led in 2013 to the publication of a text entitled *The Church: Towards A Common Vision*, which demonstrates that ecclesial ecumenical consciousness had fractured into a sort of interpretative archipelago of divergent viewpoints.[97]

One could multiply examples not only of the lack of boldness shown by church leaders and of the passivity of ecclesial communities, but above all of the methodological gaps in the denominational ecumenical paradigm. The Orthodox and Eastern Churches had arrived in 1989 – 1990 at substantial agreements on their shared faith in Jesus Christ, perfect God and perfect man, after decades of ecumenical dialogue. Simple gestures of trust and mutual recognition could have been made, which would have witnessed to the shared faith of the churches that the life of the Spirit is an incarnate reality. In a prophetic text of 1991, entitled "Pour la conversion des Églises" [Towards the conversion of the churches], the Groupe des Dombes called for gestures of public repentance to be made by the churches and for steps towards conversion.[98] In particular, the group did not hesitate to address the Catholic Church:

> If each denominational church — including, therefore, the Roman Catholic Church, which emerged from the Catholic Reformation of the sixteenth century — bears its part in sinful responsibility for the divisions from which the ecclesial body of Christ is suffering, has not the Roman Church also, in its historical existence,

---

96   In 1997, Olivier Clément concluded his book *You Are Peter* [*Rome Autrement*] by recounting how, after the assassination attempt on John Paul II, the *Pontifex maximus* had become for him the *servus servorum dei*.

97   This text is analyzed below.

98   Groupe des Dombes, *Pour la conversion des Églises. Identité et changement dans la dynamique de communion* (Paris: Le Centurion, 1991).

lost ecclesial plenitude by virtue of the ruptures of the eleventh and sixteenth centuries?[99]

But here too, many pretexts were appealed to for rejecting these gestures of visible communion. Everyone then realized that a new period was beginning. It was hastily described as an "ecumenical winter," but it was really a matter above all of a radical realization that the former denominational and inter-denominational paradigm of ecclesial consciousness had got stuck, and that it was necessary to change the level of consciousness.

CONCLUSION

Since the beginning of the twenty-first century, the landscape of the Church's ecumenical consciousness has, therefore, evolved. The inability of the churches to make prophetic gestures of real, and therefore sacramental, reconciliation, wherever possible, weakened the ecumenical dynamic. On the side of the strictly denominational identities — Catholic, Protestant, Orthodox, Anglican, Reformed, Lutheran, Evangelical, Pentecostalist, and so on — there emerged within Christian ecumenism four great transdenominational constellations of ecumenical consciousness, centered respectively on the notion of moral virtue, on social justice and ecology, on the expression of the truth which founds the Church, and, finally, on the manifestations of the Holy Spirit in shared prayer.

These constellations appeared at the end of a whole series of major inter-denominational rapprochements that took place in the twentieth century. They were also born in conjunction with a crisis that extended across most of the world, although it was expressed in different ways in different places, within the different Christian denominations. The latter, indeed, appeared more and more weakened by the double expansion of secular culture and of fundamentalist currents, as well as by a series of internal scandals and dysfunctions that had appeared within them over the course of thirty years. These crises were further amplified by the emergence of global media and social networks.

One may ask oneself what unites these different ecumenical families, as well as what might be the future of denominational identities in an epoch more and more eroded by a post-modern thought hostile to institutions. These constellations could isolate themselves, and disappear from the general interest of public opinion, as has already happened in Europe. The ecumenical constellations appear to the mainstream media as burial mounds

---

99   Groupe des Dombes, *Pour la conversion des Églises*, 103.

testifying to an old world as yet unacquainted with the delights of 5G and of visa- and barrier-free circulation. The Orthodox Swiss theologian Nöel Ruffieux observes that, as a result, "the globalized *oïkouménē* is no longer listening to the words of self-sufficient and auto-logous churches that care only about their own identities, each talking about itself in its own little corner according to its own rules and its own code of values alone."[100]

These thematic constellations could also be drawn into ideological wars fed by divergent new political currents, as one can see happening in the United States. Thus as Antoine Fleyfel has shown, Zionist Evangelism, a neo-conservative movement made up of several Protestant denominations including the Baptist Church and some Pentecostal currents, numbers today forty million believers, living, in the most part, in the Bible Belt of the USA from Texas to Florida. Convinced that faithfulness to the Bible means supporting the Israeli state in all circumstances, they exert a direct influence on American foreign policy towards Israel, and especially in support of the settlement of Palestinian lands on the West Bank of the Jordan and in Jerusalem.[101] For their part, some church institutions could also enter a cycle of divisions, as the example of the Orthodox communion today shows. Following a synod held on October 15, 2018 at Minsk in Belarus, the Russian Orthodox Church announced a total breaking-off of relations with the Patriarchate of Constantinople because of the latter's recognition of the autocephalous status of the Orthodox Church of Ukraine. "We cannot keep in contact with this Church, which is in a state of schism," affirmed Metropolitan Hilarion Alfeyev, the official in charge of the Patriarchate of Moscow's external relations.

But as sometimes happens when there are great civilizational crises, these transdenominational *oïkouménē* and these weakened church institutions are already being affected by a radical new paradigm. As we shall see below, nothing prohibits this new spiritual paradigm, one which has not yet everywhere been given objective form, from giving rise to a new *type* of ecumenical consciousness able to reconcile and develop the different currents of contemporary religious consciousness. In December 2020, Mgr Tomas Halik, a Czech theologian and sociologist of religion, deeply upset by the struggle that certain ultra-conservative Catholic groups were mounting against Pope Francis, argued that the new ecumenism must go beyond the limits of different denominations, to become an ecumenism of the heart:

---

100   Claude Ducarroz, Noël Ruffieux, and Shafique Keshavjee, *Pour que plus rien ne nous sépare, Trois voix pour l'unité* (Bière: Cabédita, 2017), 258.

101   Antoine Fleyfel, *Les dieux criminels* (Paris: Cerf, 2017), 83.

Is it not time to abandon the pursuit of an ecumenism of "all Christians," and to concentrate instead on the deepening of a fertile ecumenism (sharing, synergy, and mutual enrichment) among sensible people, whether believers or non-believers? True, we recite the same Lord's Prayer and the same creed. Nevertheless, I fear that we live in parallel and irreconcilable universes. The difference is found in people's "hearts."[102]

In the following chapter we will introduce the radicalization of Christian consciousness in the 2000s in comparison to the years when there was a belief in the definitive triumph of secularization, and in which Christianity was understood as the religion "of the end of religion" (Maurice Gauchet). Now, Christianity, while proposing a personal faith in one God, while at the same time being a major source of desacralization in respect of pagan beliefs, is, above all, a religion of incarnation. That is why it takes up with history, and tries to open history to metahistory. Hence the importance of the events of the Jubilee in the year 2000. The Catholic Church asked forgiveness for all its faults, and all the sins which it had committed over the course of its two-thousand-year history. It asked forgiveness, for example, from the Jewish people for the anti-semitism it had promoted for centuries:

> God of our fathers,
> you chose Abraham and his descendants
> to bring your Name to the Nations:
> we are deeply saddened by the behaviour of those
> who in the course of history
> have caused these children of yours to suffer,
> and asking your forgiveness we wish to commit ourselves to
> genuine brotherhood
> with the people of the Covenant.[103]

This sort of declaration allows, if not forgiveness, then at least respect, and, above all, provides the possibility of re-opening dialogue. Very soon, in September 2000, one hundred and seventy rabbis and Jewish scholars met in Baltimore in the United States to declare solemnly that "Nazism is not a Christian phenomenon" and could therefore not be imputed to the Christian faith. The following period of ecclesial consciousness greatly benefited from these symbolic gestures.

102　Mgr Tomas Halik, "La révolution de la miséricorde et un nouvel œcuménisme," *La Croix*, December 3, 2012, www.la-croix.com.
103　"Prayer of the Holy Father at the Western Wall," www.vatican.va.

PART FIVE

The Global Era's Desires for Radicalism and Spiritual Consciousness (from 1995 until the present day)

INTRODUCTION

AT THE TURN OF THE MILLENNIUM A SIGNIFI-cant development took place within what we might call the consciousness of the planet in the era of globalization.

The world has moved — in several phases from the collapse of the USSR in 1991 to the withdrawal of the United States from the Paris Accord of 2019 — from a duopoly to an apolar governance, bringing about instability and injustice. With the acceleration of the globalization of exchange, powerful transnational actors have emerged, whether we think of multinationals capable of exerting pressure on sovereign states, of networks of traffickers, or of terrorist organizations. It is as if the principles that govern international relations, adopted at the Treaty of Westphalia in 1648, and still in force, were showing their limitations.[1] The fragmentation of alliances as a result of successive crises over migrations, including within NATO,[2] provoked a feeling of growing insecurity that gave rise to feelings of anxiety.[3]

---

1   For Pascal Lamy, we need to move to an "alter-national" system of governance, resting on a new conception of sovereignty and founded on the novel community system of the European Union, with principles such as the primacy given to shared values like democracy, subsidiarity, the majoritarian principle, and a monopoly for the Commission on introducing legislative initiatives.

2   Pierre Berthelot, "Relation Turquie–UE–OTAN: sortons de l'ambiguïté," SlateFR, March 17, 2020, http://www.slate.fr/.

3   Manon Nour-Tannous, Xavier Pacreau, Les Relations Internationales, www.vie-publique.fr, September 22, 2020.

We can add to this the worldwide realization that the planet's resources were running out. The Indian intellectual Dipesh Chakrabarty, a professor at the University of Chicago, dates his own intellectual turning-point to 2003, after a fire which devastated Australia. He came to the realization that the whole earth had moved from the Holocene epoch, 11,700 years old, the final geological period of the Quaternary epoch, to the Anthropocene. In the course of this new age, the influence of human beings on the biosphere became so intense that it was itself a major "geological force" capable of influencing geological reality. From this moment on, Chakrabarty's fight for the planet — "this new historico-philosophical entity" — began. [4]

A new and multiform radical spirit appeared, often, but not always, clad in religious apparel. [5] In the many studies of the phenomenon of radicalization in France one sees that four different *types* have to be distinguished from each other within the same profile of consciousness which one can call "violent radicalization": a radicality that soothes existential anxiety; a radicality that allows the radical to pose as a rebel; a radicality brought about by ignorance; and, lastly, a radicality driven by utopianism. [6] The spirit of radicalization is usually, and with good reason, analyzed critically while trying to understand its causes, at a local level, as originating in feelings of a loss of status, of failure, and even of humiliation and anger. [7]

We shall begin by giving three examples from among dozens that illustrate the destructive aspects of this new radical spirit, which is today being propagated on a global scale within the various different political religions. However, despite the obvious risks of this development, we will show that the new radical spirit, understood as a quest for meaning oriented towards the roots of intelligence, also carries positive potential for the future of human consciousness.

THE DANGERS OF RADICALISM

If Islamist terrorism is not a new phenomenon, it is nevertheless certain that the terrorist attacks of September 11, 2001, in New York, and then in other places around the globe, especially in France, with the attacks

---

4 Dipesh Chakrabarty, The Climate of History in a Planetary Age, 77.
5 Laurent Bonelli and Fabien Carrié, Radicalité engagée, radicalités révoltées, enquête sur les jeunes suivis par la protection judiciaire de la jeunesse, www.vie-publique.fr, March 28, 2018.
6 Eric Diard, Eric Poulliat, Rapport d'information sur les services publics face à la radicalisation, www.vie-publique.fr, June 27, 2019.
7 Pierre Conesa, Avec Dieu on ne discute pas, Les radicalismes religieux. Désislamiser le débat (Paris: R. Laffont, 2020).

of 2015, signal a phase of radicalization in Islamism. This radicalization is the sign of a deep rejection not only of what is held to be the abuse of power by the United States in Iraq, but also of the model of civilizational development symbolized by the twin towers.[8] The radical Islamism of Osama bin Laden, the co-founder of al-Qaeda in 1987, or of Abu Bakr al-Baghdadi, who founded Daesh in Syria in 2014, is more of a political than a religious phenomenon. The main Muslim leaders, whether Sunni or Shia, have condemned these organizations in the UN[9] and at the Grozny Islamic Conference in 2016.[10] It is not always easy for modern consciousness, still less for post-modern consciousness, to disentangle political aspects from their religious or mythological substrate, as the debate in France between Gilles Kepel and Olivier Roy over the nature of radicalism has shown.[11] In reality, fundamentalist forces are present in most closed systems, whether secular or religious, Christian or Muslim. In certain Protestant Evangelical circles there can even be seen the promotion of an "ecumenism of hatred."[12]

These forces become even more exacerbated when the self-unknowing religion of the modern secular world is also radicalized. In fact, a new ultra-liberal post-modern mythology, affirming an individual unshackled by any limits (social, national, sexual, or environmental) has developed rapidly for the last twenty years on five continents. In France, a bioethics law was voted through in 2020 giving all women the right to medically assisted reproduction. This law is an authentic "anthropological rupture" for Christians, because it will deprive some children of a father. In January 2020, Mgr Pierre d'Ornellas, the Archbishop of Rennes and the leader of the bioethics group of the conference of French bishops, stood up against this law in the name of the republican principle of fraternity:

> Is not that "fraternity" so dear to the French people damaged by trying to set up an egalitarianism that does not dare to call differences differences — those which are not sources of discrimination? For fraternity demands that the same dignity and the same fundamental rights be acknowledged as belonging to all

---

8   Benjamin Barber, *Jihad vs. McWorld* (New York: Times Books, 1995).

9   Thomas Forquet, "Daesh et l'Iran: un ennemi chasse l'autre," https://www.lesclesdumoyenorient.com/, October 29, 2014.

10   See the Wikipedia entry for "2016 international conference on Sunni Islam in Grozny."

11   In this dispute, Gilles Kepel defined Jihadism as a "radicalization of Islam," while Olivier Roy saw it as an "Islamization of radicality."

12   "Civiltà Cattolica: un œcuménisme surprénant," https://fr.zenit.org/, July 18, 2017.

human beings without distinction of generations. Is such fraternity being respected when the "parenting plan" imposes, with
the force of law, a new "right of power" over the child, while
depriving it of a paternal ancestor? Is that consistent with the
child's dignity? The principle of dignity which, as you well know,
characterizes the French model of bioethics, demands the legal
recognition of the unity of the person in his or her biological,
psychical, and spiritual dimensions. The social contract, as well
as justice, acquire their conciliatory force from respect for this
dignity, from which flows the putting into practice of fraternity. [13]

The radicalization of jihadist beliefs prompted Europeans, in turn, especially after the wave of attacks in Europe in 2015, to question the religious
underpinnings of European civilization. In an essay published in 2018, *La
religion des faibles* [The religion of the weak], Jean Birnbaum showed that
modern Europeans, who believed themselves to have been freed from any
dependence on a transcendent God, were not absolved from all belief. On
the contrary, as Peter Berger and Jürgen Habermas, for example, recognize,
they are discovering that their ways of life — from socializing in cafes to
the experience of municipal swimming pools — are living marks of deep
choices, long since buried in the depths of their collective unconscious, and
whose metaphysical import they must recover as quickly as they can if they
want to preserve and enrich them. Birnbaum reminds us that, as early as
1955, Albert Camus suggested that the task of the intellectuals would be to
give "a content to European values, even if there is no Europe tomorrow." [14]
The difficulty is, as the Christian philosopher Rémi Brague reminds us, that
the "values" of secular beliefs can fluctuate according to collective passions
or the ideological weather, whereas the foundations of religious faith are
secured with bodies of doctrine and interpretative traditions. [15] Fundamentalism, however, whether secular or religious, is chiefly marked by
separating the "truth" from reality, by privileging the civilizational project
at the expense of personal freedom, and of justifying the means by the end.

This is why it is impossible to get rid of "criminal gods," to use Antoine
Fleyfel's expression, by military force alone. [16] In order to counteract
violence, whether that of a caliphate identifying power with God, or
that of the agnostic state, which associates power with conceptual reason,

---

13   "Bioéthique: lettre ouverte de Mgr Pierre d'Ornellas à Edouard Philippe," *La
Croix*, January 27, 2020, www.la-croix.com.
14   Jean Birnbaum, *La religion des faibles* (Paris: Seuil, 2018).
15   Rémi Brague, *Du Dieu des chrétiens et d'un ou deux autres* (Paris: Flammarion, 2008).
16   Antoine Fleyfel, *Les dieux criminels* (Paris: Cerf, 2017).

it is necessary to rediscover the bridges, invisible to the naked eye, that connect, in every sense, religious belief with rational premises. This was the whole point of the celebrated speech given by Pope Benedict XVI at Regensburg in 2006, which was addressed as much to the secular world as to the Islamist world. For Pope Benedict, violence is always the result of a diminution of reason:

> The courage to engage the whole breadth of reason, and not the denial of its grandeur — this is the programme with which a theology grounded in Biblical faith enters into the debates of our time. "Not to act reasonably, not to act with *logos*, is contrary to the nature of God," said Manuel II, according to his Christian understanding of God, in response to his Persian interlocutor. It is to this great *logos*, to this breadth of reason, that we invite our partners in the dialogue of cultures. To rediscover it constantly is the great task of the university.[17]

The "Commissariat à la promotion du genre de vie" [Commissariat for the promotion of ways of life] set up within the European Commission by its president Ursula von der Leyen in 2019, as well as the link put in place the following year by the European Council between the defense of values and the distribution of financial aid, testify to a realization on a European scale that the rediscovery of a rationality open to spirituality and respectful of the dignity of the person can have highly practical political consequences. It would be useful for governments, too, to realize this, and to introduce the teaching of ecumenical metaphysics to university teaching,[18] as well as adopting "deradicalization" policies that could effectively subdue the flames of radicality, without extinguishing them entirely.[19] There is, indeed, in Christian consciousness itself as it is presented in the gospels, a radicality that is not satisfied with conceptual intelligence alone, and that tirelessly seeks the sword — meaning the word that will sever true from false, justice from injustice, law from corruption.[20]

Second, the phenomenon of the radicalization of the populations of the West is also a reaction against neo-liberal globalization and the

---

17   Pope Benedict XVI, "Lecture of the Holy Father," University of Regensburg, September 12, 2006, www.vatican.va.

18   "La théologie a-t-elle sa place à l'université," *The Conversation*, May 11, 2017, www.theconversation.com.

19   "Les limites de la politique actuelle de déradicalisation," *The Conversation*, March 12, 2017, www.theconversation.com.

20   Antoine Nouis, "Le glaive et non la paix?" *La Croix*, October 15, 2018, www.la-croix.com.

delocalization of businesses that have come in its wake. In the face of the exposure of more and more obviously socially unjust situations,[21] resentment has spread, amplified by the media which are more and more present in people's daily lives. The anger of the world's populations, especially of those who live on the periphery of urban centers, has been widely covered in the media and has been translated into resounding protest votes, such as that for Brexit in 2016 by the British people.[22] This resentment, taken up by so-called "populist" parties, thus perceptibly changes not only ways of thinking but also the world's geo-political balance. The rejection of the neo-liberal paradigm has widened to the extent that the world's populations have understood the link between the vagaries of the capitalist mode of development and the crises from which they are suffering, such as that of COVID-19.[23] More and more citizens are campaigning for a radical exit from the neo-liberal economic model. The "Extinction Rebellion" movement has organized civil disobedience actions in sixty or so of the planet's cities to protest against the return to a consumption held to be excessive after lockdown measures were eased in most countries in May 2020.[24] Nicolas Hulot, a former French government minister and the president of an ecological foundation, is gathering a large number of campaigners together to demand that the French government changes its approach. For Hulot, "the world to come is going to be very different from the world of today, whether we like it or not." On May 6, 2020, in the newspaper *Le Monde*, he proposed "beyond urgent measures to ease

---

21   In 2020, Jeff Bezos's net worth was estimated at 200 billion dollars. "COVID-19: les profits de la crise," *Oxfam France*, September 10, 2020, www.oxfamfrance.org.

22   "Les gilets jaunes, reflet d'une crise périurbaine?" *Lumières de la Ville*, December 14, 2018, www.lumieresdelaville.net.

23   To take only a few examples, on May 6, 2020, there appeared in *Le Monde* a manifesto with the title "Non à un retour à la normale" [No to getting back to normal] on behalf of two hundred public personalities from Wim Wenders to Madonna, Muhammad Yunus and Annick de Souzenelle, in favor of a radical reform of objectives, values, and economies: "Consumerism has led us to deny life itself: the life of plants, of animals, and of a great many human beings. Pollution, global warming, and the destruction of natural spaces are bringing the world to a breaking point. For these reasons, together with an ever growing social inequality, it seems to us impossible to imagine 'going back to normal.' The radical transformation that is needed — at all levels — demands boldness and courage. It will not happen without massive determined commitment. When will we act? It is a question of our survival, as well as of our dignity and cohesion." "'Non à un retour à la normale!' de Robert de Niro à Juliette Binoche, l'appel de 200 artistes et scientifiques," *Le Monde*, May 6, 2020, www.lemonde.fr.

24   "Marseille: Rappel à la loi après une manifestation d'Extinction Rébellion," *20 Minutes*, May 12, 2020, https://www.20minutes.fr/justice/.

lockdown, a radical and coherent social, ecological, economic, fiscal, and democratic transformation, whether in terms of tax evasion, placing a higher value on key workers, 'fair exchange,' or the creation of a third Assembly." The former ecology minister added the following:

> This may appear grandiose, but this unbearable world, which creates humiliation, cannot have a peaceful outcome. It must be radical, both in its humanity, and in its solidarity. It is therefore essential to redistribute money, to set limits to incomes and to greed. The time for the regulatory state has returned, but on a democratic basis, with citizens who must participate in articulating these shared rules. (. . .) We are in a radical situation, and I cannot rest content with measures that are not equally radical. [25]

Let us take a third example of the radicalization of minds, from Brazil to New Delhi, through the nationalism or even the imperialism of the state. In India, in the 2000s, the nationalist message of *Hindutva*, "Hindu-ness," which affirms pride in being Hindu, won out over that of the *vedantas*, which extols the unity of all religions and respect for their individual differences. [26] Prime Minister Narendra Modi, the leader of the Bharatiya Janata Party, is a fervent proponent of *Hindutva*. In 2014 he set up a Ministry for Yoga, tasked with the promotion of traditional medicines such as ayurvedic healing. According to Mgr Mascarenhas, the Secretary General of the conference of Catholic bishops in India, the growing persecution of Christians in India is the result of *Hindutva*, which asserts that "Christians are foreigners, enemies of the nation." Some fundamentalist groups declared that from now until 2025, "India would be a Hindu nation, that the Muslims would have to leave for Pakistan and the Christians for the Vatican, or for Christian countries . . . ." [27]

In Russia as in China and in Turkey, the planet's leaders more and more actively whip up popular resentment and play up to popular prejudice by praising the mirage of imperial power. Thus in Istanbul there has for the last twenty years been a vigorous reassertion of neo-Ottomanism. [28] In 2001, Recep Tayyip Erdoğan founded the AKP party, the Justice and

25   "Nicolas Hulot: 'Le monde d'après sera radicalement différent de celui d'aujourd'hui, et il le sera de gré ou de force,'" *Le Monde*, May 6, 2020, www.lemonde.fr.
26   John Micklethwait and Adrian Wooldridge, *God is Back* (New York: Penguin, 2009), 320.
27   Claire Lesegretain, "'C'est une persécution directe contre les chrétiens d'Inde,'" *La Croix*, April 1, 2014, www.la-croix.com.
28   Dorothée Schmid, "Turquie: du kémalisme au néo-ottomanisme," *Institut français des relations internationales*, February 14, 2017, www.ifri.org.

Development Party, an Islamo-conservative party.[29] After winning the general election in 2003, he became Prime Minister from 2003 to 2014, and then President of the Turkish Republic in 2014. Hostile to the Western idea of the rights of man, he openly promotes inequality between women and men, and defends a revisionist conception of history and of science. In 2018, school curricula were changed. All references to Charles Darwin's theory of evolution were suppressed. On a religious level, the AKP proposes a modernized version of the system of *millet*, which governed the hierarchy between communities under the Ottoman Empire and the domination of Islam, which was the religion of the Sultan and of the vast majority of the population. In 2020, against the advice of the world's main religious authorities, the party took the decision to turn the basilica of Hagia Sophia into a mosque.[30]

Thus the new radical paradigm could, in the absence of any objectivation of the phenomenon, lead to new disruptions of the political balance on a national and on an international scale, as anger and resentment heightens. It could also lead to new fissures within traditional denominational identities. The latter have been put under pressure by the phenomena of more and more aggressive secularization, and by the emergence of several large transdenominational groupings which was seen at the end of the twentieth century.

THE POSITIVE POTENTIAL OF THE RADICAL SPIRIT

The historian Louis Manaranche explained in April 2020 that the moment for going backward politically had passed:

> If the real is complex, the reconstruction that is being announced
> will depend upon a certain radicality, in the etymological sense.
> We will only be able to create something that is new and lasting
> by taking the time to go to the root of the problems. This means
> having both patience and courage in the face of other idols that
> will also collapse. And that will allow us to rediscover that rad-
> icality and moderation are not antonyms.[31]

In scientific inquiry, the research of the French physicist Alain Aspect on non-locality is overturning our existing representations of the real and compelling us to return to the roots of science. In 1982, Aspect and his

29   Jean-François Colosimo, *Le sabre et le turban* (Paris: Cerf, 2020).
30   "Débat: Sainte-Sophie transformée en mosquée: comment sortir de l'impasse politico-religieuse?" July 26, 2020, *The Conversation*, www.theconversation.com.
31   *Travaux du Forum du Collège des Bernardins*, April 2020.

team proved that under certain conditions sub-atomic particles, such as electrons, are capable of communicating with each other simultaneously, despite being located at huge distances from each other. The British physicist David Bohm has concluded that despite its apparent solidity, the universe is, at bottom, a gigantic and magnificently detailed hologram. (A hologram is a three-dimensional image all of whose information is distributed to all points of its surface.) This discovery, which had been imagined by Jules Verne, and by the Hungarian Dennis Gabor in 1948, has vertiginous consequences not only on a technological level, but also on the philosophical and ecclesiological levels. According to the American writer Michael Talbot, the capacity of the real to hold the whole of the real in each part of itself allows us to understand the natural order in a new way. In his story, Western science held that the best way of understanding a physical phenomenon was to dissect it and to study its respective parts. But as Talbot explains, the new level of consciousness perceives a more complete vision of the real:

> A hologram teaches us that some things in the universe may not lend themselves to this approach. If we try to take apart something constructed holographically, we will not get the pieces of which it is made, we will only get smaller wholes. [32]

The paradox of the new radical spirit is therefore that it also brings an enrichment of global human consciousness, if only the dynamic that animates it can be freed from some of its blind spots. It is clear that Christians, given their history and the principles of their doctrine, have a role to play in this new period of the purification of intentions, of a new awareness of everyone's positions and weaknesses, and of dialogue between different cultural space-times. Of course, Christians are not the only people who can do this. We have been able to see in the previous volume that these logics of dialogue and synthesis between the different poles of faith were at work in most of the world's religious systems. But given the limits we have set ourselves, the remainder of our account will mainly consider the role of Christian intellectuals and of the churches in this work of getting the new radical spirit under control.

Thus for the American Laurent Cleenewerck, an Orthodox Christian theologian, the return to the sources undertaken by contemporary scientists can help us to imagine a new holographic ecclesiology:

---

32   Michael Talbot, "The Amazing Holographic Universe," December 23, 2005, https://rense.com/.

This paradigm, which replaces the whole-and-part understanding of universalistic ecclesiology, sheds new light on certain liturgical texts, such as the rite of fraction of St John Chrysostom: "The Lamb of God is broken and distributed; broken, but not divided. He is forever eaten yet is never consumed, but He sanctifies those who partake of Him."[33]

Let us add that since 2001 it has been shown, as the physicists Philippe Guillemant and Antoine Suarez report, that these non-local correlations also exist for particles separated in time, and not only for those separated in space.[34] An ecumenical vision of this kind, a quantum and holographic vision of reality, makes it possible to get beyond the aporias of the universalist ecclesiology of the denominational era, and to hold together the two representations of the Church as a mystical reality and as the people of God setting out for the Kingdom of God. It also connects with the vision of Irenaeus of Lyon, the second-century Church father: "where the Church is, there is the Spirit of God; and where the Spirit of God is, there is the Church, and every kind of grace" (*Against Heresies*, III. 24.1). In this way it can be verified that the Spirit is not a principle of anarchy, but a principle of organization. This does not mean, as Nikolai Afanasiev, and, following him, a great many Eastern theologians, believed, that the Church can do without law.[35] The very first decisions of the apostolic college, such as the founding of the diaconate and the adoption of rules for sharing wealth, testify, on the contrary, to the indispensable character of inspired law. The Church is not located outside the history of human beings. It is a holographic and eschatological reality, in three dimensions, unifying created Wisdom and uncreated Wisdom.

To this scientific and ecclesiological discovery we must add a rediscovery of faith as the compass of metaphysical intelligence. The publication in 2013 of Pope Francis's encyclical *The Light of Faith*, co-written with Benedict XVI, is especially significant in this respect.[36] The Pope insists on the need to recover a "correct faith," since the latter "orients reason to open itself to the light which comes from God, so that reason, guided

---

33   Laurent Cleenewerck, "The recovery of eucharistic and holographic ecclesiology," https://www.thefreelibrary.com/.

34   Philippe Guillemant, "Le temps existe-t-il ?" www.guillemant.net.

35   "The primitive Church did not recognize law. . . . It had no need of law because it existed out of that which was its nature, not from that which was alien to its being." Afanasiev, *The Church of the Holy Spirit*, 261.

36   "Encyclical Letter *Lumen Fidei* of the Supreme Pontiff Francis to the Bishops, Priests, and Deacons, Consecrated Persons, and the Lay Faithful on Faith," www.vatican.va.

by love of the truth, can come to a deeper knowledge of God" (*Lumen fidei* 36).[37] For the Pope, the capacity to know the truth is indissociable from the act of loving:

> Through this blending of faith and love we come to see the kind of knowledge which faith entails, its power to convince and its ability to illumine our steps. Faith knows because it is tied to love, because love itself brings enlightenment. (LF, 26)

This rediscovery leads to an openness to a deeper vision of unity in truth:

> All the articles of faith speak of God; they are ways to know him and his works. Consequently, their unity is far superior to any possible construct of human reason. They possess a unity which enriches us because it is given to us and makes us one. (LF, 47)

THE STRENGTHENING OF INTERRELIGIOUS DIALOGUE AS A RESPONSE TO AN UNSATISFACTORY SITUATION

The new condition of a radical spirit, as well as the rediscovery of faith as a source of authentic knowledge, have made possible new syntheses between East and West. In the first place, a phenomenon of *ressourcement* has come about in the very heart of Christian consciousness in recent years, a phenomenon that has made it possible to recover the thought of the Ecumenical Councils of the first millennium as a theology in tension, aiming to hold together the two natures of Christ, divine and human, without attempting to reify his self-consciousness into a synthetic super-nature.

Chinese thought, despite the influence communist ideology still exercises today, is also experiencing a form of renewal, probably as a result of its polar structure, which is especially suited to the current period. China has, moreover, also experienced a growth in its economy and an increase in its standard of living unprecedented in its previous history, to the point where it has become the second most significant economic and political power on the planet. As a result of its entry into globalization, Chinese thought has been prompted to question itself on the difficulty it experiences in thinking transcendence. As François Jullien writes, traditionally, a Chinese thinker seeks neither for the other of the other ("transcendentism" [*transcendentisme*]) nor the same within the other (immanentism). But this wisdom does not allow the integration of the interpersonal encounter found at the root of Western dynamism. François Cheng, a Chinese poet

---

37   www.vatican.va.

and intellectual living in France, has, for his part, managed to penetrate the enigma and to attain to a new level of epiphanic consciousness:

> Today we can see more clearly what was lacking in Chinese thought, and what China must learn from the West. Conversely, as far as aesthetic theory is concerned — regarding the beautiful, and, especially, artistic creation — China seems to have been extremely precocious. This ternary thinking understood from very early on that beauty has, precisely, a ternary character. As we have said, the Chinese are well aware that there exist "objective beauties," and that there is no lack at all of other words to describe them, but in their eyes, true beauty — beauty which comes to be and which reveals itself, beauty which is an appearing-there suddenly touching the soul of the one who catches it — results from the meeting of two beings, or of the human spirit with the living universe. And the work of beauty, always born of a "between," is a third term which, springing from the two in interaction, allows them to exceed themselves. If there is any transcendence, it is in this exceeding.[38]

New syntheses have also appeared in the meeting of Christianity with Judaism and Islam. In the first place, this is because a spiritual renewal has also appeared within these latter religions, to the point at which new dialogues have become possible between Jewish and Muslim intellectuals.[39] Second, the call of Jewish, Christian, and Muslim intellectuals to deconstruct both the imaginary of religious violence and that of Western libertarianism, has spread. It has also prompted a new spirit of mutual trust. Finally, daring religious leaders have been able to take responsibility. Here we need only mention to important declarations. The "Declaration for the Coming Jubilee of Fraternity" was presented by the Chief Rabbi of France, Haïm Korsia to the Archbishop of Paris, Mgr Vingt-Trois, at the Collège des Bernardins in 2015:

> In a step whose sincerity has been tried and tested, the Church has brought about a decisive turning-point with theological

---

38   François Cheng, *Cinq méditations sur la beauté, nouvelle édition* (Paris: Albin Michel, 2008), 146.

39   Here we might mention, for example, the publication during the 2000s of books with Jewish and Muslim co-authors, like Philippe Haddad and Ghaleb Bencheikh's *L'Islam et le judaïsme en dialogue* (Paris: L'Atelier, 2002), or Delphine Horvilleur and Rachid Benzine's *Des mille et une façons d'être juif ou musulman* (Paris: Seuil, 2017), as well as the setting-up of the Amitié judéo-musulmane [Jewish-Islamic Friendship Association] in France in 2004.

significance. Henceforth, for the Church, the Jewish people is no longer held responsible for the death of Jesus; the Christian faith neither annuls nor replaces the Covenant contracted between God and the people of Israel; anti-Judaism, which has often paved the way for anti-semitism, and which may once have fed into the teaching of doctrine, is a sin; the Jewish people is no longer held to be in exile; and the State of Israel has now been recognized by the Vatican. This turning point is not only, for us Jews, a happy new awareness. It also testifies to an unusual ability to question oneself in the name of the most fundamental religious and ethical values. In this, it sanctifies the name of God, compels eternal respect, and constitutes an exemplary precedent for all the world's religions and spiritual beliefs. What is our duty, now that the representatives of the highest Christian institutions have expressed the wish to re-plant themselves, to re-graft themselves on to the trunk of the tree of Israel? It is to welcome Christianity, in synergy with Judaism, as the religion of our brothers and sisters. We, the signatories of this declaration, recognize, with the support of historical research, that Rabbinical Judaism and the Christianity of the Councils built themselves, in the past, by opposing each other, in scorn and hatred. The Jews have often paid a heavy price for this in being persecuted. These twenty centuries of negativity have made us forget what is essential: our paths, although they are irreducibly singular, are complementary and convergent. Do we not, indeed, have it as our supreme hope that the history of human beings should have a single horizon, that of the universal brotherhood of humanity gathered around a God who is One and Unique? We must work together towards this, now more than ever, hand in hand. [40]

Symmetrically, it is fitting to quote the "Document for Human Fraternity on World Peace and Living Together" signed by Pope Francis and the Grand Imam of al-Azhar on February 4, 2019, in Abu Dhabi:

In the name of justice and mercy, the foundations of prosperity and the cornerstone of faith;

In the name of all persons of good will present in every part of the world;

In the name of God and of everything stated thus far; Al-Azhar al-Sharif and the Muslims of the East and West, together with the

---

40   "Déclaration pour le jubilé de fraternité à venir," November 24, 2015, https://fr.zenit.org/.

Catholic Church and the Catholics of the East and West, declare the adoption of a culture of dialogue as the path; mutual cooperation as the code of conduct; reciprocal understanding as the method and standard. (...) The first and most important aim of religions is to believe in God, to honour Him and to invite all men and women to believe that this universe depends on a God who governs it. He is the Creator who has formed us with His divine wisdom and has granted us the gift of life to protect it. It is a gift that no one has the right to take away, threaten or manipulate to suit oneself. Indeed, everyone must safeguard this gift of life from its beginning up to its natural end. We therefore condemn all those practices that are a threat to life such as genocide, acts of terrorism, forced displacement, human organ trafficking, abortion and euthanasia. We likewise condemn the policies that promote these practices.

Moreover, we resolutely declare that religions must never incite war, hateful attitudes, hostility and extremism, nor must they incite violence or the shedding of blood. [41]

This transformation of the ecclesial landscape, understood in the broadest sense of the term "ecclesial," is the product of a radical change in Western consciousness. This new radical spiritual paradigm should now be introduced. After recalling some of the main changes in the ecclesial landscape over the last twenty years, along with their principal characteristics, we will show how this new paradigm could be capable of resolving some points of tension between the different religious constellations inherited from the twentieth century. Lastly, we will introduce some concepts and tools which are contributing or which could contribute to a major development of the world's ecclesial identities. These concepts and tools could move from a strictly denominational self-consciousness to a spiritual self-consciousness, at once faithful to ecclesial tradition and open to a more radical form of commitment in the name of faith.

THE NEW RADICAL CONTEXT AND CHRISTIAN CONSCIOUSNESS

At the turn of the millennium, several religious leaders understood that the ecumenical winter was in good part the result of the self-centered logic of the churches.

---

41   www.vatican.va.

AT THE WORLD COUNCIL OF CHURCHES

The World Council of Churches published in 1997 a document entitled "Towards a Common Understanding and Vision,"[42] in which it reminded readers that its mission was not a purely institutional one. The authors of the document returned to the sources of ecumenical consciousness to justify their desire for a decentering process. The will of God, according to them, indeed, is to "bring the whole universe together under Christ as its sole head, 'both which are in heaven, and which are on earth'" (Eph. 1:10). Christ himself explained to his disciples that his mission was universal: "And I, if I be lifted up from the earth, will draw all men to me" (John 12:32). A few years later, there was a wish to deduce the consequences of this realization. A seminar organized by the WCC was held in December 2004 at Chavannes de Bogis in Switzerland. The Churches were aware of their responsibility to relaunch the ecumenical movement after the crisis which had become evident in 1998 in Harare.[43] Their consultations continued until 2012.[44] In their initial recommendations, the participants in this consultation, tasked with imagining "Ecumenism in the Twenty-First Century," affirmed "the need for renewal, for 're-freshing' the ecumenical movement in a way that focuses less on institutional interests and more on fostering a spirit of collaboration."[45] They agreed to adopt more effective methods of work "in order to witness to the world — in areas such as justice, reconciliation, and inter-faith dialogue."[46] Aram the First (Kechichian) the *katholikos* of the Great House of Cilicia in Armenia and the president of the central committee of the WCC, suggested that the ecumenical movement should be oriented towards a more holistic vision and directed more towards people's needs. Following these discussions, the WCC took the historic decision to make its main decisions on the basis of differentiated consensus, rather than on the basis of the balance of opinion as in a classic parliamentary system. Similarly, it was decided in 2006 at the General Assembly of Porto Alegre that the member churches

---

42   https://www.oikoumene.org/.

43   Rudolf von Sinner, "Ecumenism in the twenty-first century: theses for discussion," https://www.oikoumene.org/.

44   Continuation Committee on Ecumenism in the Twenty-First Century, "Final Report," https://www.oikoumene.org/.

45   *Ecumenism in the XXIst century, Report of the Consultation convened by the WCC* (Geneva: WCC, 2005), 10. See also the reflections of Cardinal Walter Kasper, "The Ecumenical Movement in the Twenty-First Century," https://www.oikoumene.org/.

46   *Ecumenism in the XXIst century, Report of the Consultation convened by the WCC* (Geneva, WCC, 2005), 10.

of the WCC would henceforth adhere to the Niceno-Constanitopolitan Creed as a matter of statute.

After this assembly in Brazil, which was a success when compared with the one in Harare in 1998, the World Council of Churches organized its tenth assembly at Busan in South Korea, from October 30 to November 8, 2013, on the theme "God of life, lead us to justice and peace." Numerous informal events were organized within this assembly, as at Harare. In particular, there was a session of the Global Ecumenical Theological Institute organized by Dietrich Werner, its creator and international coordinator. Konrad Raiser, who had participated in all the meetings of the WCC since 1968, argued on the occasion of this session that the ecumenical movement showed more evidence from this point onwards of a more Trinitarian and theanthropic consciousness than it had in the past.[47] He also emphasized the theme of pilgrimage chosen by the assembly, so as to remember that in matters of ecumenism, the path was already the destination:

> It can liberate the ecumenical movement from its institutional captivity and recapture the original thrust of a renewal movement for and through the churches. It can help us to discover again that the central notions of unity, justice and peace which describe the goal of the ecumenical movement are in themselves relational and dynamic concepts that signify a way of living together and a praxis, rather than a state of affairs or an ideal to be realized. The three important statements that will be before this assembly on unity, on economy for life, and the ecumenical call to just peace all underline this dynamic, relational and transformative quality of the ecumenical vision.[48]

In summary, the churches did not merely promise to *remain together*, as they had in 1948 in Amsterdam; in Busan, in 2013, they committed themselves to *walk together*. The ecumenical pilgrimage displays the basic elements of the form of popular piety which pilgrimage is, such as repentance and physical effort. It also, however, possesses great originality, given its plural and therefore non-linear character. Thus the Anglican Bishop of Colombo in Sri Lanka, Duleep Kamil de Chickera, put forward a suggestion in Busan that ecumenical celebrations involving foot-washing should be organized, as Christ had done for his apostles, to mark certain stages of the ecumenical pilgrimage. The gesture suggests humility, but also proximity,

---

47   Konrad Raiser, "The Busan assembly in the history of WCC assemblies and as an occasion to unfold a new ecumenical vision," https://repository.globethics.net/.
48   Ibid.

which could form a provisional substitute for the shared Eucharistic celebrations that were still rejected by the Catholic and Orthodox Churches. It is significant, in this respect, that the apostle John chose to relate the episode of Christ's washing his disciples' feet (John 13) rather than to tell the story of the founding of the institution of the Eucharist as do Mark, Matthew, and Luke. Unity, in John's Gospel, is first of all a sacrament of humility, of service, and of hospitality.

> Verily, verily, I say unto you, The servant is not greater than his lord; neither is he that is sent greater than he that sent him. (John 13:16)

This idea of the pilgrimage of justice and peace was developed by the pastor Olav Fyske Tveit, the Secretary General of the WCC, in his report to the assembly to serve as a framework for the WCC's work until its next assembly in Karlsruhe in 2022. He compares pilgrimage to a mosaic, that is, to a work of art which is at once individual and collective:

> I have been inspired in the last months by a mosaic I found in the church of Plateau d'Assy, not far from Geneva, a church built in the dark 1930s in a village of sanatoriums for people with tuberculosis. The mosaic brings together all kinds of colours and forms into a warm, friendly image of St Francis, the young person that gave up what he had to become a pilgrim — of justice and peace — for the healing and reconciliation of the church, the peoples, the religions and our life with nature.
>
> We are together here in Busan to make our own mosaic, bringing together our different parts through prayer, sharing, conversations, discernments, and decisions. Together we shall develop an image for us to be guided by in our next years.
>
> So where shall we go? Where are those places still in darkness, still needing our contributions? They can be anywhere and everywhere, where people are struggling against conflicts and injustices. This is where we shall go.[49]

Several important documents were adopted on a global scale twenty years ago, which testifies to the renewal of ecumenical thought: the document of mutual recognition of the validity of each other's baptisms by eleven Christian churches present in Germany at Magdeburg Cathedral in 2007 (and, especially, the German Evangelical Church, the Methodist

---

49   Olav Fyske Tveit, "Report of the General Secretary to the Tenth Assembly of the World Council of Churches," https://www.oikoumene.org/.

Church in Germany, the Conference of German bishops of the Roman Catholic Church, the main Orthodox churches present in Germany, the Council of Anglican Episcopal Churches in Germany; the Coptic Church also signed the document);[50] "The Ecumenical Call for a Just Peace" adopted in Kingston, Jamaica in 2001; the document "Together towards life" of the Commission on World Mission and Evangelism adopted by the WCC in Crete in 2012 (to which we shall return); the document on unity, "God's Gift Call to Unity — And Our Commitment," prepared in Geneva for the General Assembly of Busan in March 2013. In this last document, the level of ecumenical consciousness changes. In previous decades, the ecumenical movement sought unity through a mutual recognition of sacraments on the part of each denomination; then, after the work on the reception of the document "Baptism, Eucharist, Ministry," unity was sought through a shared conception of what the Church is. After 2013, the Churches began to understand that in order to work towards unity, they themselves had to put themselves in the eschatological perspective of the Kingdom of God on earth. Here is what the executive council of the WCC writes:

> The vocation of the Church is to be: foretaste of new creation; prophetic sign to the whole world of the life God intends for all; and servant spreading the good news of God's Kingdom of justice, peace and love.

AT THE VATICAN

The election of Pope Francis on March 13, 2013, also changed the situation. The Italian-Argentinian Jesuit, immediately upon being elected, asked the Church to move itself away from the center, with the help of a metaphor: "Christ is the sun, and the Church is the moon; the light of the moon comes from the sun alone."[51] The Pope has clearly integrated

---

50   Annemarie C. Mayer, "The Common Gift of Baptism, A Field for Catholic Learning, Ecumenical Investigations Along Ecclesiological Lines," *Sluzba Bojia*, 57 (2017), 2: 196–211, 197.
51   "Dans la vie chrétienne, 'l'attitude la plus dangereuse c'est l'orgueil' affirme le pape François lors de l'audience générale," *La Croix*, April 10, 2019, www.la-croix.com. The image of the sun and the moon used by Pope Francis was put forward by the German Lutheran theologian Edmund Schlink, a celebrated ecumenist: "We must not treat the other Christian Churches as circling around our own Church, as if it were at the center; on the contrary, we must recognize that we as it were gravitate, as do the other communities, like planets around Christ, the sun from whom we receive the light." Edmund Schlink, *Ökumenische Dogmatik, Grundzüge* (Göttingen: Vandenhoek u. Ruprecht, 1983), 695. I thank Martin Hoegger for having pointed me to this original quotation.

into his own thinking the radical spirit of the era, and has himself on several occasions condemned "anaesthetized consciences" and the forms of "spiritual sclerosis."[52] The Argentinian Pope, once elected, invited Christians to come out of their comfort zones and to turn themselves towards the margins. For Francis, if Christians placed Christ at the center of their lives, then there would be no further need to try to maintain their equilibrium. He also strongly demands that the clergy should free themselves from all forms of hypocrisy and duplicitous language. For him, the self-referential Church retains Christ inside itself instead of permitting Him to come out beyond its visible borders. "Structural and organizational reforms," says Francis, "are secondary; that is to say, they come second. The first reform must be that of our way of being." Pope Francis defines the Church at once as the "true Bride of Christ" and as the "people of God." This vision overturns the institutional conception of ecclesial life. In an interview with *Civiltà Cattolica* given shortly after his election, Francis explains this idea:

> The risk of seeking and finding God in everything is the wish to explain too much, to say, with human certainty and arrogance, "God is here." In this way, we shall find only a god of our own stature. The correct attitude is St Augustine's: seek God so as to find him, and find him so as always to seek him. If the Christian is legalistic or seeks a restoration, if he wants everything to be clear and certain, then he will find nothing.[53]

With this Pope, who has chosen the name of St Francis, the Catholic Church is entering a new missionary age. His first trips in 2013 were to visit the very poorest in Italy, especially the refugees on the island of Lampedusa,[54] and the inhabitants of the *favela* of Varginha in Brazil.[55] He has also resolutely committed himself to the ecumenical movement. His philosophical convictions are clearly personalist. For him, no one can be saved alone, as an isolated individual; rather, God draws men and women to him while taking into consideration the complex framework of interpersonal relations which are realized in the human community. Over the course of the years, the world has also discovered that Pope Francis

---

52   "Le Pape François met en garde contre 'la conscience anesthésiée,'" *Ouest France*, November 13, 2016, www.ouest-france.fr/.

53   "La première réforme, le style chrétien: interview du Pape François," *Études: revue de culture contemporaine*, October, 2013, https://www.revue-etudes.com/.

54   Frédéric Mounier, "À Lampedusa, le pape François fustige 'l'indifférence,'" *La Croix*, August 7, 2013, https://www.la-croix.com.

55   "Le pape visite une favela de Rio," www.francetvinfo.fr/, July 25, 2013.

is attuned to the theme of the Wisdom of God. Wisdom, he says in his catecheses, is the grace to be able to see everything with the eyes of God. The Pope is also resolutely committed to the interreligious dialogue undertaken along these lines by the Community of Sant' Egidio. At the height of the COVID-19 crisis, its president, Marco Impagliazzo, announced in the name of an interreligious group that the time had come for a prayerful fast and for works of charity on the part of all religious leaders, so as to plead with God to help humanity to overcome the coronavirus pandemic:

> History — which we had set aside to make our little stories triumph — calls to a unity that hinges on what unites us and leaves aside what divides us. The common prayer of Thursday 14th May becomes for all a spiritual and universal sign: despite the differences, we cannot be saved by ourselves, rather by recognizing ourselves close in a common humanity, facing together the struggle for the life of all. With the hope that, for the end of the pandemic, all civil authorities of the world could really adopt the "common collaboration as conduct" to which Pope Francis invites.[56]

This understanding of the world as a polyhedron rather than as a sphere with a center makes it possible to understand the rebalancing currently taking place between synodality and primacy in the Church. According to Francis, "it is not advisable for the Pope to take the place of local bishops in the discernment of every issue which arises in their territory. In this sense, I am conscious of the need to promote a sound 'decentralization.'"[57] Consequently, the bishops' conferences are, as Dominique Greiner explains in the newspaper La Croix, called to become spaces of discussion and reflection where responses to local challenges can be worked out. In this way, pastors come closer to their congregations. They can understand the latter's problems with empathy, and help them to engage in processes of growth.[58] It is in this way, for example, that the apostolic exhortation Amoris Laetitia, published in April, 2016 after two synods on the family, sets the bishops' responsibilities before them: at the local level, they are invited to find modes of discernment and ways of traveling alongside people, whatever their matrimonial situation, with all that this implies for the training of pastors.

---

56   "Prayer and Action. Editorial by Marco Impagliazzo on the World Day of Pray For Humanity, on 14th May," https://www.santegidio.org/.

57   Pope Francis, Lumen Gentium, 16, www.vatican.va.

58   "Pape François, Reformer l'Église," La Croix, February 9, 2018, www.la-croix.com.

THE FIRST FRUITS OF THE NEW SPIRIT

New forms of radical ecumenical commitment came into being very shortly after this arrival at new awareness on the part of the churches. It became evident that there was a desire to rediscover the sources of ecclesial commitment, and a pressing will to bring about development in individual churches' ways of thinking.

Of course, as Philip Jenkins has shown in his book *The Next Christendom*, this development has not been evenly spread across the world. The history of Christian missions, above all, has been deeply transforming the ecclesial landscape for more than a century. Non-existent at the start of the nineteenth century, Pentecostalist churches today number more than 386 million believers. [59] These changes to the religious landscape led Jenkins, like the American Episcopalian theologian Marcus Borg (1942 – 2015), to take a new, more radical, look at Christianity. Far from being a religion of the American or European middle class, the sociology of Christianity reveals instead that at the beginning of the twenty-first century the typical Christian is a poor person living in a country of the global South, in Africa, Asia, or Latin America. [60] Whereas, at the beginning of the twentieth century, Christians in Africa numbered only a few million, there are more than 450 million of them today, and there are expected to be 633 million by 2025. By the same date, there will be more than 460 million Christians in Asia, and 640 million in Latin America. The time when Peter Berger could announce a general secularization of the planet is, therefore, long gone. In 1999, the American Lutheran sociologist himself admitted his mistake. The world, for Berger, is in full de-secularization mode. [61]

New forms of commitment to solidarity have been brought about thanks to the emergence of a Christian identity markedly at ease with itself. Thus for example the member churches of the World Council of Churches in 2009 launched, together with the Lutheran World Federation,

---

59   Noel Davies and Martin Conway suggest the following figures for 2008: 2.1 billion Christians (33% of the world's population); 1.3 billion Muslims (21%); 1.1 billion non-religious people of various kinds (20%); 900 million Hindus (14%); 376 million Buddhists (6%); 360 million belonging to traditional Chinese religions (6%); 23 million Sikhs (0.36%); 14 million Jews (0.22%); 7 million Ba'hais, 412,000 Jains. Among the Christians there are 1.1 billion Catholics, 386 million independents (Pentecostalists); 342 million Protestants (Baptists, Lutherans, Reformed); 240 million Orthodox; and 80 million Anglicans. Noel Davies and Martin Conway, *World Christianity in the Twentieth Century* (London: SCM Press, 2008), 13.

60   Philip Jenkins, *The Next Christendom* (Oxford: Oxford University Press, 2011); *God's Gift and Call to Unity — and Our Commitment* (Geneva: WCC, March 2013), no. 9.

61   Peter L. Berger, "Desecularization," *The American Interest*, May 13, 2015, https://www.the-american-interest.com/.

a powerful non-governmental organization entitled Action by Churches Together (ACT). ACT collected more than fourteen million dollars for the year 2018 alone, money which it distributes in more than 127 countries.[62] More than a hundred churches, thanks to their faith in God and in mankind, contribute to the United Nations' goals of sustainable development, and intervene wherever ecological or humanitarian crises take place.[63] These churches declare their commitment in a radical way:

> United in the common task of all Christians to manifest God's unconditional love for all people, the ACT Alliance works towards a world community where all God's creation lives with dignity, justice, peace and full respect for human rights and the environment.
>
> As churches and church-related organisations, we work together for positive and sustainable change in the lives of people affected by poverty and injustice through coordinated and effective humanitarian, development and advocacy work.
>
> ACT Alliance members are bound together by several core values that are grounded in our Christian faith and which guide our humanitarian, development and advocacy work.
>
> We believe that all persons are created in the image of God.[64]

More recently, with the COVID-19 pandemic of 2020, appeals for solidarity and strong gestures of support with medical supplies have been made by the churches acting together, at a local and at a global level.[65]

---

62   https://actalliance.org/wp-content/uploads/2019/08/00_FR_ACT_AR2018_web.pdf.

63   https://actalliance.org/how-we-help/development/.

64   ACT Alliance — Action by Churches Together, "Founding Document," www.actalliance.org. The text continues as follows: "Therefore, we act in ways that respect dignity, uniqueness, and the intrinsic worth and human rights of every woman, man, girl and boy we respond to human suffering irrespective of race, gender, belief, nationality, ethnicity or political persuasion we will promote an integrated approach to our work, which includes development, humanitarian assistance, disaster risk reduction, rehabilitation and advocacy we promote a participative, open, enabling style in working relationships where communities are central to identifying their own needs and assets and in determining priorities, approaches and mechanisms for response we support women's participation and right to make decisions in all aspects of their own lives and that of their family and community we will reflect in communication and fundraising materials the dignity and initiative of affected communities and people will not be portrayed as helpless victims we will guard against the abuse of power by those responsible for protection and assistance to vulnerable communities."

65   "Churches gear up to assist refugees during the COVID-19 pandemic"; "French church leaders call for solidarity in the face of coronavirus"; *Health and Hope: The Church in Mission and Unity.* www.oikoumene.org/.

Friendships have been cemented across the boundaries of churches and continents, thanks to thousands of meetings and gatherings such as the Ökumenischer Kirchentag [Day for Church Unity] in Berlin in 2003 and Munich in 2010,[66] thanks to the new transportation and communication tools of the global village. The Christian Conference of Asia showed itself to be especially dynamic. The work published in 2005 in memory of Ahn Jae Woong, one of the Protestant leaders of the ecumenical movement in South Korea, testifies to the strength of the bonds that linked him to the great figures of the ecumenical movement, whether Catholic, Protestant, or Orthodox, figures such as D. Preman Niles, Sam Kobia, K. M. George, and Heup Young Kim. The work presents the high levels of convergence, from Japan to South Korea, from the Philippines to China, between Christians belonging to different denominations, on topics of such burning interest as the place of women in the Church, the actions to be carried out thanks to the theology of *Minjung* (which promotes a social justice respectful of the environment), the possible ways of reconciling Christianity with the various Asian religions, such as Confucianism, Taoism, Islam, Buddhism, and so on.[67]

One might also mention the many ecumenical working groups that have undertaken convergent readings of the scriptures and the Fathers of the Church, thanks in particular to new translations (such as the *traduction œcuménique* [ecumenical translation] of the Bible, or the collection *Sources chrétiennes* published by Cerf). In Switzerland, in 2017, the Catholic Claude Ducarroz, the Protestant Shafique Keshavjee and the Orthodox Noël Ruffieux arrived at agreements on many subjects thanks to their shared vision of the Church. Their vision shows that the inter- and trans-denominational period of ecclesial consciousness has given way to an ecumenism that is at once radical and creative:

> Together, we welcome the Church as a gift of God offered by Christ, rich with many treasures. Guided by the Holy Spirit, the Church has kept a lively memory of the Gospel; she vibrates in her heart with the communion with God the Trinity; and in Christ, she continues to celebrate the sacraments of alliance, and gathers to her generous breast the vast variety of Christians. Moreover, she does not cease to send us out into the world so that

---

66   The most recent *Kirchentag*, bringing together hundreds of thousands of people, took place digitally from May 12 to May 16, 2021 at Frankfurt am Main, https://œkt-frankfurt.de/.

67   *Windows in Ecumenism: Essays in Honour of Ahn Jae Woong* (Hong Kong: WCC, 2005).

we should know and love the paschal Christ, while testifying to the energies and inspirations of the Holy Spirit in the renewal of society. When we contemplate the New Testament, we are deeply marked by what the Church represents in the eyes of the Apostles who describe her: the cradle of Christ, the flock of the Good Pastor, the vine of the Lord, the building of God, the Body of Christ, the Bride-to-be of the Lamb, and so on. We receive the Church as a mystery who helps us to live, she who is our mother. (. . .) Together we also believe that a certain reforming spirit of prophecy must be bravely exercised, since the Church — and, in particular, the churches — will always need to look at itself anew in the mirror of the Gospel, so as to correspond ever more closely to God's plan for it, and to the needs of a humanity on the move. Are not renewals in the Church the product of faithfulness to what is Christically essential, as well as of the reforms necessary to present and offer this essential element at the present time?[68]

Another European example of growing convergence, this time at the level of church institutions: Metropolitan Emmanuel Adamakis, the vice-president of the Conference of European Churches, and Cardinal Kurt Koch, the President of the Pontifical Council for Promoting Christian Unity, published a book together in 2014 entitled L'Esprit de Jérusalem [The Spirit of Jerusalem]. In the book, they recall the celebrated meeting of January 5, 1964, between Pope Paul VI and Patriarch Athenagoras at the Church of the Holy Sepulchre. The two men exchanged a kiss of peace and launched a dialogue on charity under the title Tomos agapis. Cardinal Koch and Metropolitan Emmanuel agree on the reconciliation necessary between the Orthodox and Catholic Churches in the twentieth century, and also come to agreement on all the topics which have occasioned vexation, including on the necessary synthesis between synodality and primacy in the Church.[69]

It must be said that on October 25, 2003, the North American Orthodox-Catholic Theological Consultation had published a historic convergence agreement on the filioque, solemnly affirming that this question, if well understood by each theological tradition, could no longer be understood as a source of division among the Churches. The solution found to the thousand-year-old controversy was based on the previous convergence documents, and especially on the pontifical Clarification of 1995, which

---

68   Ducarroz, Ruffieux, and Keshavjee, Pour que plus rien ne nous sépare, 85.
69   Metropolitan Emmanuel and Cardinal Kurt Koch, L'esprit de Jérusalem. L'orthodoxie et le catholicisme au XXIe siècle (Paris: Cerf, 2014).

acknowledged a poor translation of the Greek term *ekporeusai* — which bears on the relations among the persons of the Trinity — by the Latin term *processio*, which concerns the life of divine Wisdom. The document also drew on the work of professional historians to remind its readers that the emergence of the *filioque* had the aim of rehabilitating the divinity of Christ in the struggle against Arius's supporters in the fifth and sixth centuries. What was new about the 2003 agreement, beyond the fact that it was the product of a long-standing friendship among the participants, was that it went back to the root of the disagreement, that is, to mistrust and a want of love. The American Christians overcame the latter by affirming that the Spirit could not be a source of division, since the fruit of the Holy Spirit is love and peace.[70] Pope Francis pursued this dynamic by offering, on June 29, 2019, on the feast of Saints Peter and Paul, the most precious relic of the Catholic Church to Patriarch Bartholomew: the relics of St Peter.[71] All around the world, from Canada to Australia, from the United States to Germany, the Lutheran and Reformed Churches have continued to pursue reconciliation, as happened in France in 2013 with the creation of the United Protestant Church of France.

As is well known, requests for solemn pardon have been issued by the Churches, particularly at the moment of the jubilee in the year 2000, with the publication of the text "Memory and Reconciliation: the Church and the faults of the past."[72] The latter contributed to reconciliation between Orthodox and Greek Catholic Christians in Central and Eastern Europe. The Orthodox recovery of sources, or *ressourcement*, undertaken by Metropolitan Andrei Sheptytsky (d. 1944) and continued by his successors made it possible for the Ukrainian Greek Catholic Church to free itself from the Latinization it had undergone in the nineteenth century. Moreover, this Church, which was completely banned under Soviet rule between 1946 and 1989, with the complicity of the Orthodox Church of the Moscow Patriarchate, benefited from the support brought to bear by several Popes

---

70   United States Conference of Catholic Bishops, "The Filioque: A Church Dividing Issue?: An Agreed Statement": "Our discussions and our common statement will not, by themselves, put an end to centuries of disagreement among our Churches. We do hope, however, that they will contribute to the growth of mutual understanding and respect, and that in God's time our Churches will no longer find a cause for separation in the way we think and speak about the origin of that Spirit, whose fruit is love and peace (see Gal. 5:22)." www.usccb.org.

71   "Pope Francis explains gift of relics in letter to Ecumenical Patriarch," *Vatican News*, September 13, 2019, www.vaticannews.va.

72   International Theological Commission, "Memory and Reconciliation: The Church and the Faults of the Past, December 1999," http://www.vatican.va/.

in the twentieth century on behalf of this persecuted Church. Once emancipated, the Church was able to establish better relations with the minority Latin Catholic tradition (about eight hundred communities in Ukraine) because of the spiritual, political, and cultural rapprochement between Poland and Ukraine. Finally, the international dialogue at Balamand (1993), and the conclusions arrived at by the French Joint Orthodox-Catholic Commission (2004), led to a clear rejection of proselytizing on the part of all the signatory Churches, as well as to the acceptance of a Church of Byzantine tradition into the Catholic communion.

The French Joint Commission, in particular, acknowledged that the main outlines of the Balamand document were correct. That is, on one hand, that proselytism irrespective of other Churches is a reprehensible attitude, and, on the other, that the Greek Catholic Churches have the right to exist within the framework of the Catholic Church. But the French theological commission also observed that some Churches had nevertheless had difficulty in endorsing this Balamand document. This is why historians — understanding that these refusals were linked to failures of understanding connected to differences of situation — published studies of the phenomenon of Uniatism.[73] It emerges from these studies that the Uniat phenomenon is complex, and that the sincere desire of the Orthodox Church of Kyiv-Halich to achieve communion with Rome in 1596 cannot be considered as equivalent to the very real proselytism of certain Catholic orders in Greece towards the end of the nineteenth century. On this point there is a full consensus on the part of all serious historians, whether Orthodox or Greek Catholic, such as Father Cyrille Argenti and Mgr Borys Gudziak. Cyrille Argenti affirmed that "the initiative for union did not come from Rome. At Rome, the spirit of the Council of Trent, rather than that of the Council of Florence, prevailed."[74]

For this reason, the Catholic and Orthodox theologians suggested that an ethical attitude adapted to each particular context should be adopted. The French Joint Commission made three main recommendations: scientific honesty, which consists in shared submission to the truth; the shared re-reading of the past, which can lead to a labor of repentance and of mutual conversion; and respect for the codes of conduct concerning

---

73   Father Robert Taft, S. J., "Anamnesis, Not Amnesia: The 'Healing Memories' and the Problem of 'Uniatism,'" *American Catholic Press*, www.americancatholicpress.org.
74   Father Cyrille Argenti, "L'Union de Brest," in *Catholiques et Orthodoxes, Les enjeux de l'Uniatisme* (Paris: Cerf, 2004), 100–1; cf. also Borys Gudziak, *Crisis and Reform: The Kyivan Metropolitanate, The Patriarchate of Constantinople and the Genesis of the Union of Brest* (Cambridge, MA: Harvard University Press, 2001).

conversion from one denomination to another, which must be accompanied with bringing about in both Churches, starting now, everything that conduces to unity.

This labor of repentance and this shared work was begun at the Velehrad Conference in Moravia organized in July 2007 by the Institute of Ecumenical Studies in Lviv with the participation of forty Roman Catholic, Greek Catholic, and Orthodox bishops. The first Velehrad conference took place in 1907 at the instigation of Father Stojan, the future bishop of Olomouc, and Metropolitan Andrei Sheptytsky, the head of the Ukrainian Greek Catholic Church. From the beginning, Roman Catholic, Greek Catholic, and Orthodox theologians participated in these meetings. Before the Second World War, seven congresses had been held; then, after 1945, two further congresses, mainly featuring the participation of Czechs and Slovaks, took place. In the interwar period, the Velehrad Congresses became the largest ecumenical forum (in the modern sense of the word "ecumenical") in Central and Eastern Europe. In the spirit of Velehrad, similar congresses were later held in Pinsk and in Lviv. The aim of the Velehrad congresses was to find new ways of bringing together the Eastern and Western Churches, on the basis of the tradition they both shared with Saints Cyril and Methodius.

At the anniversary conference of 2007, the Roman Catholic, Greek Catholic, and Orthodox participants, of whom the majority came from Ukraine, adopted the following text, whose first five points are characteristic of this new spirit of practical reconciliation promoted by the French Joint Commission:

> In the spirit of the founders of the Velehrad movement, recognizing the essential unity of the Eastern and Western Churches as fundamentally inseparable parts of the Body of Christ, we call the Christians of Europe of different traditions: 1) to provide testimony of mutual respect and solidarity, and not allow utterances or publications that would be offensive for the Christians of other traditions but, contrarily, to defend other Christians from such offences; 2) to seek, nourish and spread cooperation, solidarity and friendship among themselves in different spheres of life: social, cultural, artistic, pastoral and academic, thereby awakening a longing for the unity of the Churches and Ecclesial Communities; 3) to foster and spread the spirit of the tradition of Cyril and Methodius which is common to Catholics and Orthodox; 4) to accept and realize the proposals of John Paul II

(2000) and the World Council of Churches (2004) to formulate and implement an "Ecumenical Metrology" and even an "Ecumenical Calendar of Saints" which will be a concrete expression of the recognition and the celebration of the martyrs and saints of different Christian Churches; 5) to organize together and actively participate in social and charitable projects which touch upon the problems of the least socially protected, immigrants, the sick, and others.... [75]

The declaration concluded with a show of support for the Ecumenical Patriarchate on the part of Catholic, Greek Catholic, and Orthodox Christians:

> Expressing our profound solidarity with His All Holiness Ecumenical Patriarch Bartholomew I of Constantinople and all Christians in Turkey in spreading the Word of God in not very favorable conditions, we wish to address to the government of Turkey a letter supporting the Patriarchate of Constantinople in its right to enjoy its civil liberties and in particular its right to renew its seminary in Halki. [76]

---

[75] Jubilee Velehrad Conference Towards Deeper Solidarity Among Christians in Europe, "Communiqué." *Occasional Papers on Religion in Eastern Europe* 27 (3): 7. The final six points are the following: 6) to pay proper attention to the need for pastoral care for the mixed marriages, and promote their full participation in church life; 7) to show deep respect for the dignity of the person and the value of human life at all stages of its development, from conception to natural death; 8) in view of the new evangelization of Europe, to pay attention to the organization of joint measures, especially involving the participation of youth, in activities like pilgrimages, seminars, spiritual retreats, prayerful meetings, and so on; 9) in order to avoid any kind of mutual proselytism, to adopt the experience of joint commissions which will examine the passage of faithful from one Church to another, guided by the principles of respect for freedom of conscience, transparency, respect and acknowledgment of the other tradition and which would deal with each case with pastoral consideration and prudence; 10) to organize working groups for the joint publication of books on the history of Christianity, in which the representatives of various Christian denominations and unprejudiced historians would take part and which would present controversial events in their multiform aspects; 11) to express ecumenical solidarity with the Christians of Belarus and support them spiritually in their efforts toward a common witness to the Gospel, remembering that Belarus theologians from the very beginning were interested in the Velehrad Congresses (their participation began in 1927 at the 5th Congress), that the ideas of the Velehrad Congresses found their theological and pastoral expression also at the Pinsk conferences in the 1930s, and that the living tradition of saints Cyril and Methodius continues to be present in the conferences organized every year in Minsk with the support of the Belarus Orthodox Church.

[76] Ibid.

THE CHARACTERISTICS OF RADICAL ECUMENICAL CONSCIOUSNESS

New philosophical and theological syntheses have been arrived at thanks to the convergent reflection of great intellectual and spiritual ecumenical figures such as Pope Francis and Patriarch Bartholomew, Olivier Clément and Andrea Riccardi, Olav Fyske Tveit and Ellen Johnson Sirleaf, Marie Balmary and Jim Wallis.[77] Christian philosophers such as the Orthodox Bertrand Vergely, the Methodist Stanley Hauerwas, and the Catholic Jean-Luc Marion, have written vigorously to show the impasses of modern rationalism. To agnostic philosophers such as Jürgen Habermas or Gianni Vattimo, who agree on the need for modern reason to try to achieve humility, these thinkers remind us that "the true reason is love and love is true reason."[78]

THE PHILOSOPHICAL AND THEOLOGICAL TURN

The return to the sources of the faith and of evangelical universalism is especially noteworthy in Radical Orthodoxy, a current of philosophical and theological thought. The latter has attempted to theorize the new radically ecumenical paradigm. Born towards the end of the twentieth century, Radical Orthodoxy calls itself "orthodox" in order to get beyond denominational border lines. Since its beginning in 1997,[79] it has been much discussed, both in the Anglican world where the movement began and in the various Catholic, Protestant, and Orthodox denominations.[80] The members of this movement — John Milbank, Catherine Pickstock, Graham Ward, but also Rowan Williams, the former Archbishop of Canterbury, William Cavanaugh, Adrian Pabst, Christoph Schneider, and many others,[81] have been influenced by the great figures of classical Christian

---

77   One can also add some recent syntheses in ecumenical theology: Paul Avis, *Reshaping Ecumenical Theology: The Church Made Whole?* (London, T & T Clark, 2010); Gesa Elsbeth Thiessen, ed., *Ecumenical Theology: Unity, Diversity, and Otherness in a Fragmented World*, Ecclesiological Investigations 5 (London: T & T Clark, 2009); John O'Grady and Peter Scherle, eds., *Ecumenics from the Rim: Explorations in Honour of John D'Arcy May* (Berlin: Lit, 2007).

78   *Christianisme, héritages et destins*, sous la direction de Cyrille Michon (Paris: Le livre de poche, 2002), 324.

79   John Milbank, Catherine Pickstock, Graham Ward, eds., *Radical Orthodoxy, A New Theology* (London: Routledge, 1999).

80   Denis Sureau, *Pour une nouvelle théologie politique, autour de Radical orthodoxy* (Paris: Parole et Silence, 2008).

81   James Smith, *Introducing Radical Orthodoxy* (Grand Rapids, MI: Baker Books, 2004); Adrian Pabst, Christoph Schneider, *Encounter Between Eastern Orthodoxy and Radical Orthodoxy. Transfiguring the World through the Word* (Farnham: Ashgate, 2008).

theology (St Augustine, Thomas Aquinas, and the Cappadocian fathers) but also by French *nouvelle théologie* (Henri de Lubac in particular) and contemporary Russian sophiology (Sergij Bulgakov). They are also most of them experts in post-modern philosophy (Derrida, Deleuze, Lacan).

The provocative radicality of this intellectual and spiritual movement consists in the first place, as can be seen from its twenty-four theses published in 1997, in its wish to break with a theology which has embraced in an uncritical fashion the secular tendencies of thought in the modern epoch. The movement also wishes to conduct a dialogue with post-modern nihilism, which it believes to be "nearer the truth than humanism, because it recognizes the unknown and indeterminate in every reality."[82] It signifies at once a return to the sources of faith, a wish to get beyond the rhetoric of rupture and of the simulacrum, but also a desire to rediscover a plenitude of ecumenical ecclesial witnessing. Modern nominalist thought had reduced the notion of universality to its conceptual extension in space and time. Universality was broken up into multiple sovereign or denominational identities. The notion of catholic or ecumenical universality cannot be made visible again for so long as the notion of truth remains unrehabilitated. Milbank and his companions chose to lay this bare once again from both sides, philosophical and theological:

> Radical Orthodoxy is influenced by Postmodern thought, but at the same time contests it. Postmodernity tends to conclude that since we cannot ground truth in an absolutely certain intuitive presence, nor in discursivity (which is either tautologous or else goes on for ever and never vanquishes uncertainty), that in consequence there is no such thing as truth at all. Often this lack of truth is seen as the only truth, and so as disclosing a nullity at the heart of things. Radical Orthodoxy accepts that there are no foundations and that there can be no finite certainty, but concludes that this situation can be read as the need to refer time to eternity. Only in the infinite Godhead can there be an entire intuition which is also an infinitely concluded exposition. Truth is possible for us because we participate by an act of faith in this infinite truth. At the Fall, humans tried to erect truth for themselves: this is why rationalism is evil. But God himself descended

---

82　"Radical Orthodoxy: 24 Theses," thesis 7. It is now difficult to locate a publicly available English text of this document. At the date of typing (January 30, 2022), a copy is posted at https://indecentbazaar.wordpress.com, but its authenticity cannot be guaranteed. See also "Radical Orthodoxy, 24 thèses," trans. Olivier-Thomas Venard, "De la charité intellectuelle," *Kephas*, n°25, January–March 2008. — *Translator.*

to us and became the truth for us in time. Echoes of this resound
through everything ever since, but are concentrated in the Church.

At the same time, then, as it began to seem as though the Christian
world had entered into a long ecumenical winter, a new generation of intellectuals has sought to integrate the elements of truth in post-modernism,
while suggesting ways of overcoming the spiritual and epistemic crisis
manifested by this philosophy. It is time to introduce some of the movement's theses. The Christian re-appropriation of the radicality of the Gospel,
however, does not belong among them. It will be seen in a later part of
our discussion that the self-understanding of the churches has developed
along the same lines, as can be seen in a number of documents that were
adopted on a global scale a decade ago.

Only a liturgical politics can now save us from the violence of liberalism, wrote John Milbank at the turn of the century. The revolution
in Cambridge, situated not all that far from the City of London, one
of the motors of ultra-liberal globalization, seized the *kairos* of the need
for a new definition of universality. The transformation of the Church
of Christ into a private religion in the modern era left the field free for
the infinite power of the state and for the growing claims made by the
desires expressed in all the world's markets. Rediscovering Christian faith
as a meta-knowledge beyond all denominational appropriations of it, a
meta-knowledge capable of exiting from the impasses of secular rationality,
and re-imagining the Church as a "community of eros," as an anticipation
of the Kingdom: in this lay the movement's radicality.

The movement born in the 1990s in Oxford takes up with certain
aspects of post-modernism, such as the priority given to narration over
foundation. The authors concerned again put in question (following
Heidegger) the constitution of onto-theology from Duns Scotus onwards,
which gives rise to an autonomous rationality having for its object a concept of being applicable to all beings, God included. This loss of the sense
of God's action in the world corresponds to a forgetting of the relational
and Trinitarian dimension of divine being, to an incomprehension of the
sapiential logic of divine creation. Humanist thinking constituted itself,
very logically, around a duality between reason and revelation. But as
Milbank insists, "Once, there was no 'secular.'"[83] For the Church fathers,
and for scholasticism, faith and reason were included within the framework of the human intellect's participation in God.

---

83   John Milbank, *Theology and Social Theory* (Oxford: Blackwell, 1990), 9.

In order to counter modern and post-modern agnosticism, Milbank suggests that the Kantian conception of evil as a willed negation of the good, taken up in uncritical fashion by the postmoderns, is a form of perverse Gnosticism. It makes God responsible for the creation of evil. The Gospel and the patristic conception of evil as a privation of the good and of being make it possible, on the other hand, to rediscover the authentic countenance of the living God. As St James writes, "God cannot be tempted with evil, neither tempteth he any man" (James 1:13). God, therefore, has not withdrawn from the world, as modern and post-modern thought assert. Modern man, on the other hand, is no longer in a position to perceive the "subtler languages" of the divine-human alliance.

As Adrian Pabst has shown, the rediscovery of participation by the fathers of the West and the East makes possible a sapiential ontology for which nature is already penetrated and augmented by divine grace, which prepares in this way for the deification of man.[84] Radical Orthodoxy developed a theology of participation which accepted and welcomed mediation as a principle of the incarnation itself. As Graham Ward has written, this new trans-disciplinary current integrated postmodern philosophy's rejection of any essential dualism. It proposed a radical hermeneutics centered on language and culture and the expressive expansion of human beings, understood as a symbolic species:

> Radical Orthodoxy developed a theology of participation that accepted and welcomed mediation, all the way down, as a principle of the Incarnation itself. It called for a radical hermeneutics that recognised language (and culture as the expressive expansion of human beings as a symbolic species) as key. Put simply: made in the image of God, we are image-makers; we are creatures endowed with the creative capacity to imagine, because we are hidden in God's own imagining. There are no foundations: the mystery and depths of the Godhead reflected in the mystery and depth of being human. In a memorable phrase of Milbank's: we participate in "the divine linguistic being."[85]

This rediscovery of a possible friendship between God and men (instead of a conception of a violent God which it would be the task of social life to channel) put ritual practices back — as in Catherine Pickstock's

---

84   Adrian Pabst and Olivier-Thomas Venard, *Radical orthodoxy, Pour une révolution théologique* (Geneva: Ad Solem, 2004), 72.

85   Graham Ward, "Radical Orthodoxy: its ecumenical vision," *Acta Theologica* 37.1 (2017), 29–42.

work — at the heart of the new vision of the post-denominational world, beauty rediscovering its whole significance in a panentheist conception of the cosmos. In her book *After Writing*, the Anglican theologian shows that liturgical thought makes it possible to go beyond the limits of immanentist rationality: "orality and writing, space and time, gift and given, subject and object, active and passive, life and death."[86] In a radically orthodox rationality, by contrast, time, the moving image of eternity, allows a mediation between finitude and transcendence. Similarly, for Pickstock, language is radically doxological. It has as its first function to praise God, even before it is a way of representing reality:

> It is not the aim of liturgy in the first place to improve the qual-
> ity of our collective life; instead, it is the crowning moment of
> that collective life. When, out of the surplus of our production,
> we collectively make a work of beauty visible to God, we are
> working, whether we wish to or not, towards building a society
> founded on justice.[87]

We are witnessing, therefore, a rehabilitation of faith as a higher form of knowledge. Only faith guarantees us that the visible speaks of the invisible, and that, as Olivier-Thomas Venard emphasizes, "sensuous desire is neither the sole foundation nor an illusion." Drawing on the accounts given by Maurice Merleau-Ponty and Jean-Luc Marion of the excess of the visible and the saturated phenomenon, according to which the visible is only a dimension of the invisible, the Radical Orthodoxy movement promotes a new perception of the epiphanic aspect of the real. This important development in contemporary philosophy and theology heralds a conception of the universal that can properly be called ecumenical, in that it makes it possible to hold together the various meanings which the term has accumulated through the ages — eschatological, political, denominational, and inter-denominational. The transition from a postmodern rationality to an ecumenical rationality, moreover, makes possible a new synthesis between faith and reason which respects different levels of reality and of consciousness, while being capable of grasping them together in a single coherent loop. Unity has become "both a dynamic happening and a complex relation. (. . .) It is, in fact, transcendental peace which 'overflows in a surplus of its

---

86 Catherine Pickstock, *After Writing: On the Liturgical Consummation of Philosophy*.
87 Adrian Pabst and Olivier-Thomas Venard, *Radical orthodoxy, pour une révolution théologique* (Geneva: Ad Solem, 2004), 32.

peaceful fecundity' and 'preserving [all things] in their distinctness yet linking them together.'"[88]

This conception of the unity, harmony, and beauty of the emanation of difference retains what is for Milbank one of the most distinctive features of postmodern consciousness. It can no longer be anticipated in advance. Between the nihilistic promotion of dissonance, which unites only by means of conflict, and the baroque risk of a harmony extended to infinity, there is, for Milbank, something undecidable. For the Trinitarian Christian God is neither in the indifferent relation nor in the naked force which are denounced by the postmoderns. The Christian God of love creates a harmonious order that is capable of integrating all differences, since it is itself relation and difference. Creation is not an appearance, with its mixture of true and false, nor an Aristotelian hierarchy of successive identities, but the gradual coming in time — in proportion to the way in which it is creatively, imaginatively, and virtuously received — of a differential reality. Ecclesial traditions must play a determining role in imagining and participating in the coming of the Kingdom. For Milbank, "the thought of God as infinite Being, as difference in harmony, is this speculative imagining."[89]

This imperative to live according to the laws of the kingdom of God (and not "as if" the latter were present, as Giorgio Agamben suggests), here and now, is taken up by Michael Martin, the author of *Transfiguration: Notes Toward a Radical Catholic Reimagination of Everything*. In this book, Martin explains that it is by being attentive to the kingdom of God that the latter manifests itself. For Martin, only a sophiological understanding of the economy makes it possible for humanity to exit from its mortifying vision of the real, and to participate in the Real, and thus in Christ and in the Kingdom.[90]

THE ECUMENICAL AND POLITICAL TURN

Radical Orthodoxy presented itself from the start as an ecumenical movement. Among the twelve contributors to the founding collection, seven were Anglican and five were Catholic. Laurence Paul Hemming, a Catholic professor of theology at Heythrop College in London, organized from 1997 onwards several debates between thinkers belonging to

---

88 Milbank, *Theology and Social Theory*, 428, quoting the *Divine Names* of Pseudo-Dionysius, 949c, 952b, 912d–913b.
89 Ibid., 430.
90 Michael Martin, *Transfiguration: Notes Toward a Radical Catholic Reimagination of Everything* (Brooklyn, NY: Angelico Press, 2018).

different Christian denominations.[91] By the very fact of these debates, Radical Orthodoxy indeed represents a turning-point in the history of the Christian Church's awareness of itself in the age of a new globalization. As Graham Ward summarizes the situation, and as Pope Francis often insists, the denominational consciousness of the Church, while having its own value, must today learn to decenter itself. The Church's mission is to move towards the Kingdom of God on earth, together with all the religious and cultural traditions of the planet. Graham Ward writes:

> Ecumenism is a mark of the character of Christian culture. It is not merely the work of administrators and leaders. It is an aspect of true discipleship.[92]

The level of ecumenical consciousness is not the final stage of ecclesial consciousness, since truth cannot be possessed, and remains transcendent to all attestations of it. This truth is to be searched for and accomplished without ceasing.

The ideas of the Radical Orthodoxy movement have spread, and have been fertile for several other original schools of thought and denominational tendencies. New ecumenical metanarratives have appeared. Centered on Christ, who is "before all things, and by him all things consist" (Col. 1:17), they offer an alternative to the new "World History," which often lacks any metaphysical vision. One might mention as an example of this the movement in support of a second Council of Jerusalem, which imagines a reconciliation between Jews and Christians.[93] Authors such as the Catholic theologian Richard Rohr, or the Buddhist philosopher Ken Wilber, integrate this radical distinction between pre-rational thought, rediscovered by certain postmodern and New Age currents, and the transrational thought promoted by the radical ecumenical paradigm. Here is what Richard Rohr, writes on the topic of the new transrational ability to imagine and participate in spiritual realities:

> Remember, the opposite of rational is not necessarily irrational, but it can also be transrational or bigger than the rational mind can process. Things like love, death, suffering, God, and infinity are transrational experiences. Both myth and mature religion understand this. The transrational has the capacity to

---

91   Laurence Paul Hemming, ed., *Radical Orthodoxy? A Catholic Inquiry* (London: Ashgate, 2000).

92   Ward, "Radical Orthodoxy," 40.

93   "Uniting Jewish and Gentile Followers of Jesus," *Towards Jerusalem Council II*, www.tjcii.org.

keep us inside an open system and a larger horizon so that the soul, the heart, and the mind do not close down inside of small and suffering times. The merely rational mind is dualistic and divides the field of the moment between what it can presently understand and what it deems "wrong" or untrue. Because the rational mind cannot process love or suffering, for example, it tends to either avoid them, deny them, or blame somebody for them, when in fact they are the greatest spiritual teachers of all, if we but allow them. Our loss of mythic consciousness has not served the last few centuries well and has overseen the growth of rigid fundamentalism in all the world religions. Now we get trapped in destructive and "invisible" myths because we do not have the eyes to see how the great healing myths like the Exodus, Cross and Resurrection, Krishna and Arjuna in the chariot, and Buddha under the Bodhi Tree function and transform.[94]

Neither left- nor right-wing, the Radical Orthodoxy movement seeks a third way that will allow ecclesial consciousness to re-invest in the public sphere and to be faithful in this way to its calling to foreshadow the Kingdom of God on earth. Many works have been written on this question of the political, economic, social, environmental, and cultural incarnation of the radical ecumenical paradigm. John Milbank and Adrian Pabst published in 2018 a book entitled *The Politics of Virtue*. The two authors explain that in order to exit from the crisis of the liberal paradigm, it is necessary to free oneself from mental habits according to which most of reality is neutral, neither good nor bad. This vision of the world is not only false, but also harmful. The realization that there are qualitative degrees in the spiritual life does not mean, however, that it is necessary to adopt a moralizing and punitive position.

The ethics of virtue is to be distinguished from liberal amoralism and from Kantian or traditional religious moralism. It appeals to the human being's spontaneous inclination to see the good in nature, "in the mode of the flourishing of all things insofar as they fulfil their given character and realise their innate ends to circulate, grow, and propagate."[95] This means that the essence of politics must become virtuous; it is the duty of politics to be oriented in a coordinated manner towards the common good. To the blind economic liberalism which, since Adam Smith, has been

---

94 "Myths," *Center for Action and Contemplation*, September 29, 2015, https://cac.org/.
95 John Milbank and Adrian Pabst, *The Politics of Virtue: Post-Liberalism and the Human Future* (London and New York: Rowman and Littlefield, 2016), 4.

founded on a secularized conception of divine Providence, the politics of virtue opposes a civil economy that re-connects the spiritual, the social, the environmental, and the economic.

Against the biopolitical tyranny that radically abolishes the difference between the sexes, or, as in gender studies, absolutely separates nature from culture, Radical Orthodoxy thinkers imagine a society that respects all sexual orientations and offers new social understandings of the sexes on the basis of equality, complementarity, and reciprocity. A new universalism, therefore, appears, demanding more coherence between the collective goals of societies and the establishment of national accountability measures and budgeting. As Jim Wallis has written, budgets are above all moral documents. This politics in search of virtue invites the churches to organize and to act in the real world, beyond the sanctuaries.

> Allied to the ecumenical exigency, in turn, should be a new recognition that, for all the inevitably enormous area of acceptable disagreement, uncertainty, and debatability, there is a much greater political consensus implied by orthodox Christian belief than has recently been taken to be the case. This is somewhat witnessed by the new tendency of Christians in the British Parliament to cohere in roughly post-liberal views across the party divides . . . .
> It is clear that there are many non-religious people who, nevertheless, fully recognise the existence, mystery and irreducibility of the human spirit and respect the wider mystery and value of nature and Being itself.[96]

THE CHURCHES' NEW RADICAL SELF-UNDERSTANDING

The new understanding of the radicality of faith does not belong to the intellectual and spiritual movement of Radical Orthodoxy alone. It is found in a whole series of social and humanitarian commitments, in publications, and in international ecumenical conferences. In its reflections at the end of the 1990s on the direction of the ecumenical movement, the WCC reminded us that the search for visible unity was not an end in itself but should stand as a credible witness so that the world might believe, and to serve in caring for the human community and all of God's creation.[97]

The realization that the meaning of history is that of acceding to divine-humanity is present in the declaration in support of a new conception of the churches' mission in the world, drawn up in Crete in 2012 by

---

96   Milbank and Pabst, *Politics of Virtue*, 383.
97   https://www.oikoumene.org/en/about-us/self-understanding-vision/cuv.

the WCC. In 1961, the WCC absorbed into itself the International Missionary Council and created a Commission of World Mission and Evangelism. Two texts, in particular, were adopted by this Commission in 1982 and 2000 condemning proselytism — that is, the aggressive practice aiming to persuade Christians already belonging to a church to change their denomination.[98] But the accelerated globalization of the world reshuffled the deck of cards. For the Lutheran pastor Rudolf von Sinner, a Swiss theologian teaching in Brazil, ecumenism can no longer, in the twenty-first century, concern only a group of a few "mainline" denominations. It must reflect "the household of God and the wealth of its range."[99] That is why, in 2010, the CWME joined forces in Scotland with several other world missionary organizations, especially with Evangelical and Pentecostalist organizations, to celebrate the hundredth anniversary of the Edinburgh Conference of 1910 from which the International Missionary Council developed. It was remembered on this occasion that since the beginning the Church had had the mission of witnessing to the Kingdom of God in the world.[100] The Church, indeed, exists by means of mission, "just as fire exists from the fact that it burns." Strengthened by the success of the contemporary Edinburgh conference and the many comings-together which were expressed on this occasion, the CWME initiated, in 2012, the Kolymbari conference in Crete. This managed to bring several hundred churches to agreement on the question of the new forms which their shared action in the world had to take. The text "Together Towards Life: Mission and Evangelism in Changing Landscapes," adopted in Crete, reflects, as we shall see, the new radical ecumenical spirit. That is why it is important to study this new form of "ecumenism in tension" in detail: an ecumenism in tension between witnessing and service, celebration and evangelization.

The Churches affirm at this conference, in the first place, a spirit of mutual collaboration and shared witness. They admit that they have, in the past, competed with each other. But today, they affirm with a single voice that they wish to witness together to the good news of the imminence of the Kingdom in words and deeds.[101] "The Spirit calls us all towards an understanding of evangelism which is grounded in the life of

98   Jacques Matthey, ed., *You Are the Light of the World: Statements on Mission by the WCC (1980–2005)* (Geneva: WCC, 2005).

99   Daryl Balia and Kirsteen Kim, eds., *Witnessing To Christ Today* (Oxford: Regnum, 2010), 141.

100 Ibid.

101 "Together Towards Life: Mission And Evangelism In Changing Landscapes," www.oikoumene.org.

the local church where worship (*leiturgia*) is inextricably linked to witness (*martyria*), service (*diakonia*), and fellowship (*koinonia*)."[102] They wish to do this in a new spirit, not merely one of mutual cooperation, but also one of respect for all the religious and non-religious identities of the planet. They refuse to impose uniformity on the expression of faith, and hold that it is indispensable to build "relationships with believers of other faiths or no faith to facilitate deeper mutual understanding, reconciliation and cooperation for the common good."[103]

In order to demonstrate the denominational and regional diversity of the churches which have committed themselves to this document adopted by the central committee of the WCC, it is worth naming some of the hundred and fifty members brought together by the Secretary General of the organization, the Reverend Olav Fyske Tveit (Secretary General of the WCC between 2009 and 2020, he became in 2020 the Preses of the Church of Norway): Bishop Ivan Manuel Abrahams, (Methodist Church of South Africa); Dr. Agnès Abuom (Anglican Church of Kenya, who was elected "moderator," that is, president, of the WCC in 2013); Rev. Walter Altman (Evangelical Lutheran Church of Brazil, former president of the WCC); Met. Anastassios of Tirana (Metropolitan of the Orthodox Church of Albania); Archbishop Vicken Aykazian (Armenian Apostolic Church); Bishop Samuel Robert Azariah (Anglican Church of Pakistan); Met. Bishoy de Damiette (Metropolitan of the Egyptian Coptic Church); Rev. Sofia Camnerin (Protestant Church of Sweden); Rev. Fernando Enns (German Mennonite Church); Rev Ying Gao (China Christian Council); Met. Gennadios of Sasima (Metropolitan of the Ecumenical Patriarchate of Constantinople); Rev. Kondothra George (Malankara Orthodox Syrian Church); Met. Hilarion of Volokalamsk (Orthodox Church, Moscow Patriarchate); Father Heikki Huttunen (Orthodox Church of Finland); Mgr Irenaeus of Australia and New Zealand (Serbian Orthodox Church); Rev. Micheline Kamba Kasongo (Church of Christ in the Congo, Presbyterian community in Kinshasa); Mme Carmencita Karagdad (Philippine Independent Church); Rev Carmen Lansdowne (United Church of Canada); Marie-Christine Michau (Evangelical Lutheran Church in France); Rev. Jane Mutoro (Kenyan Quakers); Met. Nifon Mihaita of Targoviste (Metropolitan of the Orthodox Church in Romania); Rev. Renta Nishihara (Anglican Church of Japan); Bishop Carlos Poma Apaza (Evangelical Methodist Church in Bolivia); Rev. Bernice Powell Jackson (United

---

102   "Together Towards Life," point 85.
103   Ibid., point 90 (f).

Church of Christ, USA); Bishop Taranath S. Sagar (Methodist Church in India); Bishop Martin Schindehütte (Evangelical Church in Germany); Rev. Gretchen Schoon-Tanis (Reformed Church in America); Rev. Glenna Spencer (Methodist Church in the Caribbean and the Americas); Dame Mary Tanner (Church of England); Rev. Sharon Watkins (Church of the Disciples of Christ, USA); Rev. Hnoija Jean Wetewea (Evangelical Church in New Caledonia and the Loyalty Isles); H. G. Abune Zacharias (Ethiopian Orthodox Tewahedo Church); and so on. Here, then is what the representatives of this mosaic of the world's churches wrote together:

> The church is a gift of God to the world for its transformation towards the kingdom of God. Its mission is to bring new life and announce the loving presence of God in our world. We must participate in God's mission in unity, overcoming the divisions and tensions that exist among us, so that the world may believe and all may be one (John 17:21). The church, as the communion of Christ's disciples, must become an inclusive community and exists to bring healing and reconciliation to the world.[104]

The representatives of the world's churches also declared that "God invites us into the life-giving mission of the Triune God and empowers us to bear witness to the vision of abundant life for all in the new heaven and earth."[105] This rediscovery of the calling of humanity to participate in the divine life in Christ in the Holy Spirit,[106] and thus to deify itself, also passes by way of a recollection of human responsibility for the whole creation:

> The gospel is the good news for every part of creation and every aspect of our life and society. It is therefore vital to recognize God's mission in a cosmic sense and to affirm all life, the whole oikoumene, as being interconnected in God's web of life.[107]

---

104   Ibid., point 10.
105   Ibid., point 1.
106   "In the Hebrew Bible, the Spirit led the people of God — inspiring wisdom (Prov. 8), empowering prophecy (Is. 61:1), stirring life from dry bones (Ezek. 37), prompting dreams (Joel 2), and bringing renewal as the glory of the Lord in the temple (2 Chron. 7:1).... After his resurrection, Jesus Christ appeared to his community and sent his disciples in mission: 'As the Father has sent me, so I send you' (John 20:21–22). By the gift of the Holy Spirit, 'the power from on high,' they were formed into a new community of witness to hope in Christ (Luke 24:49; Acts 1:8). In the Spirit of unity, the early church lived together and shared her goods among her members (Acts 2:44–45)."
107   Ibid., point 4.

The signatories to the document, whether from the so-called liberal or the so-called socialist world, castigate the consumerism and human cupidity that give rise to the warming of the planet and to climate change. This realization of the churches' responsibility for creation is linked to a rediscovery of sophiology. The latter affirms, indeed, against all of modern anthropocentrism, that there are forms of consciousness in nature that do not take the form of persons and that are nevertheless very real, as Scripture reveals:

> We tend to understand and practice mission as something done by humanity *to* others. Instead, humans can participate in communion *with* all of creation in celebrating the work of the Creator. In many ways creation is in mission to humanity; for instance, the natural world has a power that can heal the human heart and body. The wisdom literature in the Bible affirms creation's praise of its Creator (Ps. 9:1–4; 66:1; 96:11–13; 98:4; 100:1; 150:6). The Creator's joy and wonder in creation is one of the sources of our spirituality (Job 38–39).[108]

This awareness is radical, not only on an ecological level, but also on a social and economic level. The signatories of the text "Together Towards Life" defend a vision of the world that is resolutely personalist, since, as they write, all forms of Christian commitment in the world "safeguard the sacred worth of every human being and of the earth (see Is. 58)."[109] This implies struggling for freedom of religion everywhere.[110] This means that ecological justice cannot be separated from salvation:

> We are living in a world in which faith in mammon threatens the credibility of the gospel. Market ideology is spreading the propaganda that the global market will save the world through unlimited growth. This myth is a threat not only to economic life but also to the spiritual life of people, and not only to humanity but also to the whole creation. How can we proclaim the good news and values of God's kingdom in the global market or win over the spirit of the market? What kind of missional action can the church take in the midst of economic and ecological injustice and crisis on a global scale?[111]

---

108   Ibid., point 22.
109   Ibid., point 42.
110   Ibid., point 96.
111   Ibid., point 7.

This revolt against the injustices of contemporary liberal capitalist globalization is not limited to the denunciation of unlimited growth. It also proposes solutions that are brought about in the first place by a work of discernment of spirits. It is not usually remembered today that according to Scripture and the Christian tradition, invisible spirits are at work in the world, angels, and demons. The Kolymbari text recalls the words of the apostle James, who enjoins us to "resist the devil" (James 4:7). This appeal to spiritual discernment is the condition on which we can be filled with the power of the Spirit, the source, according to the apostle Paul, of love, joy, peace, patience, goodness, benevolence, faith, gentleness, and self-control (Gal. 5:23). This renewal makes it possible to bring to fulfillment that which God has already created, rather than creating another world. It invites us to follow Christ, who placed the poorest at the heart of his mission. This is why the new evangelization of the world no longer sets out from the center towards the peripheries, as it once did. Henceforth it spreads from all the margins of the modern awareness of the world, from the poorest countries of the South towards the industrialized North, but also from the most marginal layers of society towards the dominant categories of the individualized, secularized, and materialistic world. This demands listening to the experience of the Pentecostalist and charismatic churches. The western world must open itself to those who have taken the gift of healing, and therefore of regeneration, seriously,[112] the gift which Christ passed on to his disciples in the Spirit, as was the case in the very earliest age of the Church (Acts 3).

The churches exhort their congregations to commit themselves to a labor of active resistance to all injustice and discrimination. For them, Christian mission means "deconstructing patriarchal ideologies, upholding the right to self-determination for Indigenous peoples, and challenging the social embeddedness of racism and casteism."[113] They go so far as to wish to become counter-cultural communities whose first task is to refuse to shelter the forces of oppression in their ranks. Strengthened by a divine-human conception of Christian witness in the world,[114] as

---

112   Ibid., point 52: "Healing is more about the restoration of wholeness than about correcting something perceived as defective. To become whole, the parts that have become estranged need to be reclaimed. The fixation on cure is thus a perspective that must be overcome in order to promote the biblical focus. Mission should foster the full participation of people with disabilities and illness in the life of the church and society."

113   Ibid., point 43.

114   Ibid., point 18: "Christian witness . . . unceasingly proclaims the salvific power

well as by a new understanding of mission as "the overflowing of the infinite love of the Triune God," the churches cannot be content with a schizophrenic situation. Oriented towards the spiritual transformation of the political and economic structures of the planet, they are led to formulate radical proposals:

> Jesus promises that the last shall be first (Matt. 20:16). To the extent that the church practices radical hospitality to the estranged in society, it demonstrates commitment to embodying the values of the reign of God (Is. 58:6). To the extent that it denounces self- centeredness as a way of life, it makes space for the reign of God to permeate human existence. To the extent that it renounces violence in its physical, psychological, and spiritual manifestations both in personal interactions and in economic, political, and social systems, it testifies to the reign of God at work in the world.[115]

Lastly, the new radicality expressed by the churches at the Crete meeting is the product of a new relationship to history. Christ's sending of the Spirit into human history must be balanced by an awareness of the eternal procession of the Spirit from the Father. In summary, from the point of view of ecumenical anthropology and theology, the meaning of history is eschatological and not chronological, even if it is re-echoed in cosmic time. The end of history, that is, is for Christians the coming of the Kingdom of God on earth, the moment when God makes Himself "all in all" (1 Cor. 15:28). It is the dwelling of God with men (Rev. 21:3), and not the product of successive moments. It is participation, here and now, in the Kingdom of Him who was, is, and will come (Rev. 1:8). As a result of their personalist, sophiological, and Trinitarian conception, the churches discover that their mission is more qualitative than quantitative. They realize that if there truly exists a ladder between earth and heaven, in the Biblical age as in the age of postmodernity, then their role is not to busy themselves in all directions so as to try to capture souls at the ends of the earth. It is to make themselves into a ladder.

> Mission is not a project of expanding churches but of the church embodying God's salvation in this world. Out of this follows a dynamic understanding of the apostolicity of the church:

---

of God through Jesus Christ and constantly affirms God's dynamic involvement, through the Holy Spirit, in the whole created world."
115   Ibid., point 47.

apostolicity is not only safeguarding the faith of the church through the ages but also participating in the apostolate.[116]

The task of Christians does not, then, consist in imposing their own religious systems, but in witnessing to the God who is already there, as the apostle Paul did before the Athenians (cf. Acts, 17:23 – 28). The ideal portrait of the missionary Church is therefore to renounce oneself, to renounce any temptation to power or wealth, so as really to put oneself in the service of Christ's mission in the world, while respecting cultural and religious differences. This consists — and here the title of the text "Together Towards Life" is justified — in human beings' receiving life in abundance (John 10:10).

The Catholic Church participates in some of the structures of the World Council of Churches such as Faith and Order, as well as the Commission on World Mission and Evangelism. It is very active on this latter level. With Pope Francis, one can even think that a true turning-point has taken place. In the interview that Francis gave to *Civiltà Cattolica*, he summarized in three sentences the new and radical missionary vision of the churches:

> I see clearly that the thing which the Church needs most today is the capacity to treat the wounds of the faithful and to give them heart, closeness, conviviality. I see the Church as a field hospital after a battle. It is useless to demand of someone who has been seriously wounded whether he has a high cholesterol count or too much sugar intake! We must treat the wounds. After that we can talk about all the rest.[117]

FROM INTERDENOMINATIONAL ECCLESIOLOGY TO SPIRITUAL ECCLESIOLOGY

Unable dramatically to change into a consciousness at once wholly faithful and wholly open, denominational consciousness today is unable to hold together in a balanced way the four major poles of the Christian faith (law, justice, glory, and memory) or the four poles of philosophical rationality (coherence, consensus, correspondence, and efficacity) or even the four poles of social and environmental economic life (identity, alterity, the sense of transcendence and the sense of immanence). This is why it is eaten away at more and more by the arrival of new transdenominational constellations.

116   Ibid., point 58.
117   "Rome: Le pape François invite l'Eglise à se décentrer pour mieux comprendre le monde," www.cath.ch, January 4, 2014.

One might even say that it is threatened with being choked, when these constellations fold back on themselves and lose their sense of ecumenicity.

Now this short history of Christian consciousness shows that ecclesial consciousness will only be able to exit from the ecumenical winter if it discovers an ecumenical metaphysics. Thanks to the uneven discovery over the last twenty years of personalism and of sophiology, ecumenical thought has managed to undo a certain number of denominational consciousness's long-standing blockages. There remains, however, one more hurdle to be crossed before it can be said to have passed from a modern or postmodern ecclesiology to a fully ecumenical ecclesiology: to take possession once again of the at once historical and eschatological structure of metaphysics. The change of ecclesial paradigm invites us, indeed, to grasp that "things which are seen were not made of things which do appear" (Heb. 11:3). This simple and radical reminder of the complexity and depth of the visible world might be able to undo the crisis which has supervened in the matter of ecclesiological reflection within the ecumenical movement.

We shall take two examples of the possible development towards a greater radicality in contemporary ecclesiology: the dialogue between Catholics and Orthodox at the international level (which, as we have seen, had come down to an institutional analysis of the relationship between primacy and synodality, to the detriment of a broader vision of the life of the Church), and the dialogue within the World Council of Churches on the nature and mission of the Church (which, as we know, suffers from a fixation on the imperative of visibility, to the detriment of the non-homogeneous and non-possessive dynamic of faith, which is nevertheless a source of essential unity founded in love).

TOWARDS A NEW BALANCE BETWEEN PRIMACY AND CONCILIARITY

On the "Orthodox" side, the Patriarchate of Constantinople is today oriented towards a more emphatic assertion of its primacy within the Church, but also towards a more explicit recognition of the primacy of the Bishop of Rome within the Church.[118] The honor of primacy is not merely a matter of protocol within the Church. It corresponds to a responsibility for unity. The ninth-century Patriarch of Byzantium, Photius, in his *Homilies*, acknowledged that Peter was "the master of the apostolic choir established as the rock of the Church, proclaimed by Truth as the guardian of the keys of the Kingdom of heaven."

---

118   "The Ecumenical Patriarch meets with Pope Francis and the C9 Council to Reform the Catholic Church," www.archons.org.

On the "Catholic" side, Pope Francis is aware that the Roman Catholic Church needs to move more towards conciliarity. For Peter depends on the correct faith of the people of baptism, as that faith is defined by him. Through the apostolic constitution *Episcopalis Communio*, published on September 18, 2018, Pope Francis gave more weight to the Synod of bishops, while strengthening episcopal collegiality and making it listen more to the faithful.

We can add that the balance between primacy and conciliarity definitively rests on a balance between descending and ascending ecclesiology. It is found in the gospels, where the word *ekklesia* is found only twice, first in a mode of descending authority, in Matthew 16:18:

> Thou art Peter, and upon this rock I will build my church; and the gates of hell shall not prevail against it. And I will give unto thee the keys of the kingdom of heaven: and whatsoever thou shalt bind on earth shall be bound in heaven: and whatsoever thou shalt loose on earth shall be loosed in heaven.

The mode of ascending authority is present in Matthew 18:16–17 (the gospel of brotherly correction):

> if he ["thy brother"] will not hear thee, then take to thee one or two more . . . and if he shall neglect to hear them, tell it unto the church . . .

But it would be wrong to think that the ecclesiology of the Gospel is a purely vertical one. The dynamic of ecumenical ecclesial consciousness is also constituted by the two other poles of the law (and thus of resistance) and justice (and therefore mission). This is why it is worth remembering that the ecclesiology of the earliest Church is in a state of tension.[119]

Between the Transfiguration on Mount Tabor and the entry into Jerusalem, we find in the gospels a teaching on Christ's part which is specifically dedicated to three of the apostles, to Peter (the pole of memory), to James (the pole of the law), and to John (the pole of glory). They are the only apostles whose name was changed into one of a cosmic nature: Simon into Peter, and James and John into "sons of the thunder" (*boanerges*). Christ led them with him up to the mountain, and then, before his entry into Jerusalem, he taught them how to deal with the most serious cases of possession, how to wield power within and outside the Church, what their relationship to wealth should be, and taught them about the question of

---

119   Antoine Arjakovsky, "Primauté et Juste gouvernance dans l'Eglise," Istina 58 (2013), 345–60.

taxation within the state and community and so on . . . . At the moment of the night in Gethsemane, he called all three of them to pray with him . . . .

This authority was acknowledged by Paul in Gal. 2:9: "And when James, Cephas, and John, who seemed to be pillars, perceived the grace that was given unto me, they gave to me and Barnabas the right hands of fellowship; that we should go unto the heathen, and they unto the circumcision." Saul thus became Paul, as an apostle to the Gentiles, which makes him the symbol of mission and of the fourth pole, that of the knowledge of justice. If Peter received the pastoral charism, John was adopted by Christ on the cross as his brother, and received the gift of vision (which was made evident in the Book of Revelation), while James was the first martyr in the Church, and Paul the organizer of the first collections, so as to demonstrate the solidarity that must exist among Christians, whether they are from Corinth or Jerusalem or anywhere else.[120] . . . And it is John who is the subject of John 21:21–22: "Peter seeing him saith the Lord, and what shall this man do? Jesus saith unto him, If I will that he tarry until I come, what is that to thee? follow thou me." The Church, as the foundation of the Kingdom of God on earth, must offer a governance that is non-exclusive and that is capable of bringing together several different types of charisms.

Thus it may indeed definitively be the case that, in order to keep the principles of synodality and primacy in tension with each other within the institutional pole, it might be necessary to bring them face to face with the poles of mission, praise, and moral rectitude. This makes it necessary to think the new ecclesiology in a fully baptismal, Eucharistic, and pastoral fashion.[121] The current tensions between Constantinople and Moscow show the difficulty of reconciling a Eucharistic ecclesiology (which, interpreted in a narrowly legal fashion, places the primacy of canonical territory above cultural and linguistic differences) with a pastoral ecclesiology (which, on the contrary, privileges the unity between the bishop and his cultural and linguistic community, even if that unity has become a distant one for historical reasons, sometimes to the detriment of the unity of the local church). Now the ecclesiology of the earliest Church is ternary: it is at once baptismal, Eucharistic, and pastoral. It has been forgotten that the

---

120   "The couple 'circumcision [i.e., Jews]: nations [i.e., Gentiles]' is not merely, therefore, reversed into that of 'nations : circumcision'; it is the very relationship between the nations and those of the circumcision which changes — with an emphasis on the priority, in the future of the communion, for the mission to the pagans." www.vies-consacrees.be.

121   For the Pontifical Council for Promoting Christian Unity, "All ecumenism is baptismal." "The Bishop and Christian Unity: An Ecumenical Vademecum," 24, www. christianunity.va.

sacrament of baptism, which is indissociable from theophany, from the irruption of the divine into history and the cosmos, is what makes possible the sacraments of ordination and the Eucharist. The gift offered to each baptized person of participating in the death and resurrection of Christ is the foundation of ecclesial life. It is faith, joined with eschatological hope for the Kingdom of God on earth, which makes it possible to affirm the priority of love over every other consideration. Indeed, faith proposes a hierarchy of truths, according to which the heresy of life, that is, the failure to recognize the brotherhood of all human beings, is considered as more serious than the denominational heresy, which is marked in the first place by an inability to see the epiphanies of Spirit in history and in the creation.

THE ECCLESIOLOGY OF FAITH, VIATICUM OF THE NEW ECCLESIOLOGY

For more than forty years, the essential weight of the work of the theologians of the Faith and Order Commission of the World Council of Churches has been concentrated on defining the nature and mission of the Church. After the qualified, or non-existent, or self-critical reactions to the Lima document *Baptism, Eucharist, Ministry* (1982),[122] those in charge of the ecumenical movement understood, after 1987, that they would only manage to get beyond denominational divisions over the sacraments by arriving at a deeper convergence, that is, by situating themselves at the level of ecclesiology.[123] At the Busan assembly in South Korea in 2013 the churches brought together by the WCC adopted a convergence document entitled "The Church: Towards A Common Vision," which is today undergoing a new cycle of reception on the part of the churches at a local and at a global level.[124]

The Limits of the Faith and Order Method

The text begins by recalling once again that the ultimate goal of the WCC is for the churches "to call one another to visible unity in one faith and one eucharistic fellowship."[125]

---

122   Cf. Gennadios Limouris and Nomikos Michael Vaporis, *Orthodox Perspectives on Baptism, Eucharist, and Ministry* (Brookline, MA: Holy Cross Orthodox Press, 1985).
123   Commission on Faith and Order, "Minutes of the Meeting of the Standing Commission, 1987, Madrid, Spain [Faith and Order Paper, 141]," 96. The papers are available at www.archive.org.
124   Peter de Mey, "The Missing Link between the Nature and Mission of the Church (2005) and The Church: Towards a Common Vision (2013): An Assessment of the Impact of 'A Catholic Contribution toward Revising The Nature and Mission of the Church (2008),'" *Exchange* 44/3 (2015), 250–69.
125   Faith and Order Commission, *The Church: Towards A Common Vision* (Geneva:

Later, after having defined the Church in a Trinitarian fashion as "God's great design," "the community of witnesses to Jesus Christ," and "the Church in mission since Pentecost," and after also having recalled the responsibility of Christians to proclaim the coming of the Kingdom of God in a more and more secularized world, the text adds two further paragraphs of convergence:

> Visible unity requires that churches be able to recognize in one another the authentic presence of what the Creed of Nicaea-Constantinople (381) calls the "one, holy, catholic, apostolic Church." This recognition, in turn, may in some instances depend upon changes in doctrine, practice, and ministry within any given community. This represents a significant challenge for churches in their journey towards unity.
>
> Currently, some identify the Church of Christ exclusively with their own community, while others would acknowledge in communities other than their own a real but incomplete presence of the elements which make up the Church. Others have joined into various types of covenant relationships, which sometimes include the sharing of worship. Some believe that the Church of Christ is present in all communities that present a convincing claim to be Christian, while others maintain that Christ's Church is invisible and cannot be adequately identified during this earthly pilgrimage.[126]

The first chapter on "God's Mission and the Unity of the Church" finishes with a paragraph in italics which testifies to disagreements it was not found possible to overcome:

> *Fundamental issues on the way to unity*
> Ever since the Toronto Declaration of 1950, the WCC has challenged the churches to "recognize that the membership of the church of Christ is more inclusive than the membership of their own church body." Moreover, mutual regard between churches and their members has been profoundly encouraged and advanced by ecumenical encounter. Nevertheless, differences

---

WCC, 2013 [Faith and Order Paper, 214]), 1–2. From the introduction: "The present text has been elaborated by the Faith and Order Commission, whose aim, like that of the World Council of Churches as a whole, is to serve the churches as they 'call one another to visible unity in one faith and one eucharistic fellowship, expressed in worship and common life in Christ, through witness and service to the world, and to advance towards that unity in order that the world may believe'" (*The Church*, 1–2).
126   *Towards A Common Vision*, 8–9.

on some basic questions remain and need to be faced together: "How can we identify the Church which the creed calls one, holy, catholic and apostolic?" "What is God's will for the unity of this Church?" "What do we need to do to put God's will into practice?" This text has been written in order to assist the churches as they reflect upon such questions, seeking common answers.[127]

In my view, if it has not proved possible to find a common answer to questions as fundamental as this, despite decades of dialogue, and if one finds more divergences than convergences in the Busan text, it is because there is a major defect in the method adopted by those who drafted the document. This defect is, at a wider level, one from which the ecumenical movement as a whole itself has suffered for the last forty years. It consists in taking the goal of the World Council of Churches to be that of bringing about, by means of global, intellectual, homogenous, and inter-institutional agreements, a secure and visible inter-denominational unity. Now, there is nothing to say that the Kingdom of God must supervene in an intellectual, homogenous, and inter-institutional way. The visibility of Spirit, indeed, has a complex structure. Let me explain further, for this is a crucial point.

It is worth starting from the scriptures. The New Testament contains several passages that offer a phenomenology of the Kingdom of God. Luke's gospel, in particular, relates (17:20 – 21) the following exchange between Christ and the Pharisees on the subject of the advent of the Kingdom:

> And when he was demanded of the Pharisees, when the Kingdom of God should come, he answered them and said, The kingdom of God cometh not with observation: Neither shall they say, Lo here! or, lo there! for behold, the kingdom of God is within you.

Then Christ explains to the disciples (and not to the Pharisees, who could not agree to what he had said) this complex idea of "one of the days of the Son of Man." Its salient characteristic is that it is not a spectacular or exterior event, but an event that is personal, and therefore existential and of concern to the community, which demands a rapid decision at the moment of divine judgement. In Matthew 24, as in Luke 37, Jesus insists on the fact that this day will not appear at either the time or the place in which one might have expected it. As gathering vultures are a

---

127   Ibid., 9.

sign of a corpse, Christ asks his disciples not to trust to exterior facts acknowledged by everyone, but to sharpen their sight so as to discern the signs of its coming.

Similarly, after his resurrection, Christ teaches his disciples to recognize him, even though his physiognomy has obviously changed. The pilgrims to Emmaus, who are, however, people close to the first circle of Christ's apostles, do not recognize him even in the course of a long journey. They only recognize him at the "breaking of bread." Mary Magdalene takes Christ for a gardener. In the same way, Peter and John do not recognize Christ when he is standing on the shore of the sea of Tiberias where they are (without success) fishing. It is only when this mysterious personage asks them to cast their net on the right side of the ship that John says to Peter that it is the Lord (John 21:7).[128] John constructs his whole gospel according to Semitic rhetoric, mirroring the beginning and end of his gospel, where he relates in the one how Christ called John, then Andrew and Peter (John 1:35–43) and then, in the other, how he made them fishers of men (John 21). In this way he suggests that his readers should sharpen their sight for the coming of the Day of the Lord, by keeping the first call that they heard from their Savior ceaselessly in their memory. Despite the fact that their spiritual eyes recognized Christ, thanks in particular to the sign of the miraculous catch of fish, "none of the disciples durst ask him, Who art thou?" (John 21:12). This phrase testifies to the strangeness of Christ's exterior physiognomy. Jesus finally manifests himself fully when he takes the bread and gives it to them. Then the disciples understand that, in Christ, they are really participating in the Kingdom of God on earth. Christ, indeed, had often compared the Kingdom to the "net, that was cast into the sea" (Matt. 13:47).

Examples could be multiplied. The important thing is to understand that the churches' mission is not to make visible what is kept secret, but to prepare their faithful to recognize here and now the coming of the Day of Christ, which is a completely different sort of task. The Kingdom is a

---

128   Might this personage be a woman? Several indications make this possible. The person expresses themselves more like an elderly woman than like a man ("Children..." (John 21:5). It is also surprising that John in his way of narrating the episode avoids the difficulty of specifying the person's gender. He explains at the outset that this person whom the apostles do not recognize is Jesus. In the end, the apostles had already well understood that Christ might manifest himself with different faces. Nevertheless, after the miraculous catch of fish, they continue to be astonished by the strangeness of the person on the beach, of whom they nevertheless know in their hearts that this is Christ.

fragile reality that neither imposes itself upon people, nor is guaranteed, but is participated in. It is here that the episode of the meeting of the resurrected Christ with Thomas is decisive for the ecumenical movement. Christ explains to Thomas that it is necessary to believe in order to see, rather than the other way round. One could say that in this gospel Christ is berating the churches today, as he had done Thomas in saying to him "be not faithless, but believing" (John 21:27).

The Faith and Order Commission was set up in 1927 on the basis of a Christocentric theology strongly influenced by the thought of Karl Barth, but also, later, by that of Father Georgij Florovsky.[129] The expression "faith and order" itself also conveys this institutional priority given to inter-denominational theological discussion. Ecumenical rapprochement has made it possible subsequently for a Trinitarian theology to spring up, a theology that has made possible decisive advances in ecclesiological matters. In particular, mention must be made of the visionary approach of the bishop of the United Reformed Church, Lesslie Newbigin, who was able to balance in a Trinitarian way, in a single sentence, the necessary combination of visibility *and invisibility* which made it possible to present to the world "the secret of reconciliation," on earth as in heaven:

> I do not believe that we can be content with anything less than a form of unity which enables all who confess Christ as Lord to be recognizably one family in each place and in all places, united in the visible bonds of word, sacrament, ministry and congregational fellowship, and in the invisible bond which the Spirit himself creates through these means, one family offering to all men everywhere the secret of reconciliation with God the Father.[130]

But as Odair Pedroso Matteus has recognized, after the New Delhi assembly in 1961, the objective of ecumenical commitment was centered on the imperative of visibility.[131] As if the other hand of the Father at work in history, that of the Holy Spirit, could not be taken into account

---

129   Antoine Arjakovsky, "The Limits of the Ecclesiology of Faith and Order," in Ashley John Moyse, *Correlating sobornost: conversations between Karl Barth and the Russian Orthodox tradition* (Minneapolis: Fortress Press, 2016).

130   Lesslie Newbigin, *One Body, One Gospel, One World: The Christian Mission Today* (London: International Missionary Council, 1958), 55–56. Quoted by Odair Pedroso Matteus, "The Ecumenical Vision: An Overwiew of World Council of Churches' Statements on Unity," 12. https://www.academia.edu/36443273/The_Ecumenical_Vision_An_Overview_of_World_Council_of_Churches_Statements_on_Unity.

131   Matteus, "The Ecumenical Vision," 12.

when recognizing ecclesial unity in progress. In other words, the ecumenical movement condemned itself to exteriority alone by preventing itself from valuing the benefits of interiority.

Now, the Church is not a visible reality like the Republic of Venice, as Cardinal Bellarmine thought. Father Sergij Bulgakov had a different conception of the life of the Church, for he remembered that the first miracles in the Church, as the book of Acts recounts (3:1–10), took place when Peter, the symbol of external authority, and John, the symbol of interior authority, were together. Similarly, for the Orthodox priest André Borrély, "unity within reconciled diversity must be the living synthesis of mission and vocation."[132]

It is true that the Trinitarian basis of the WCC, which recognizes that the churches are united by sharing the same faith in a single God, Father, Son, and Holy Spirit, was not adopted until 1961, only a short time before the return of the "Hegelian years" in Europe and in the world.[133] The Trinitarian character of the life of the Church has only been integrated recently, and then only intellectually, by the ecumenical movement. This is why it has not yet really been put into practice. Until the Busan assembly in 2013, the ecumenical movement went forward with a vision that was fundamentally Christocentric, static, and institutional, only integrating the work of spirit insofar as the latter could serve that conception.[134] Now, as the churches recognized at Kolymbari in 2012, the Holy Spirit never lets itself either be "domesticated or 'tame.'" "Among the surprises of the Spirit are the ways in which God works from locations that appear to be on the margins, and through people who appear to be excluded."[135] Thus the ecumenical movement must henceforth integrate a more mystical and more dynamic theology, a theology that is at once personalist, sapiential, and Trinitarian.

---

132   André Borrély, *L'œcuménisme spirituel* (Geneva: Labor et fides, 1988), 47.
133   Michael Hardt, "La renaissance hégélienne américaine et l'intériorisation du conflit," https://www.multitudes.net/La-renaissance-hegelienne/. In 1989, when the communist regimes collapsed, it was discovered, with Fukuyama and Huntington, that the philosophy and political science departments of American universities had been just as much influenced as European universities by the thought of Hegel.
134   The constitutional basis which the WCC gave itself at New Delhi, conversely, is indeed Trinitarian: "The World Council of Churches is a fellowship of churches that confess the Lord Jesus Christ as God and Savior according to the scriptures and therefore seek to fulfill together their common calling to the glory of the one God, Father, Son and Holy Spirit."
135   *Together Towards Life*, point 35.

For Sophiology, it is Free Action in the Spirit which makes Visible

As a Faith and Order document adopted in 2019 justly recalls (without coming to the same conclusions as the present author, so much has the expression "the visible" church taken on a hypnotic force within the WCC),[136] Christ, when he is questioned about where he lives, replies "Come and see" (John 1:39). Now Jesus of Nazareth, when he invited his disciples to follow him, is not in any way proposing a fixed and identifiable place. John's gospel, in any case, does not specify where Christ, Andrew, and John first met. This is why, when Andrew invites his brother Peter to meet Christ, he does not tell him where he has gone. Instead, he brings him the event of his meeting with "the Messiah."

Nor, when Christ later says to Nathanael, "I saw thee under the fig tree," is he reporting an event of a physical kind, but an event of a sapiential kind. This meeting, in fact, is comparable to the nocturnal meeting of the Patriarch Jacob with the angel of Wisdom related by the book of Wisdom (10:10). On that night, Wisdom *showed* the royalty of God to the patriarch. This is why what Christ says brings about Nathanael's conversion (John 1:45 – 51). The promise he receives from Christ that he will now "see heaven open" confirms that the optic of the Kingdom must be understood sapientially. Similarly, to Nicodemus, Christ explains that "except a man be born again, he cannot *see* the Kingdom of God" (John 3:3). In order to see Wisdom, to enter the Kingdom, it is necessary to "do truth" (John 3:21). God reveals himself to man not in the visibility of power relations, but in the light of Wisdom. This is why it is said that YHWH opens the eyes of the blind. There is always something magnificent, fugitive, and promising in the sight of a rainbow. Christ is inviting us to a journey, to the adventure of discovery. Later he will tell the Samaritan that God is to be worshipped neither at Jerusalem nor on Mount Gerizim, but in spirit and truth.

The Faith and Order Commission has the merit of not separating the ecclesial order, and therefore its ministers, from the life of faith. Odair Pedroso Matteus reminds us that the reformer John Calvin bestowed a growing importance towards the end of his life on the "visible Church" as the Sunday gathering or the synod, after having long considered the Catholic Church to be authentic as invisible, given the decadence which he saw within the Roman Church.[137] This is also what the Westminster

---

136 "Come And See: A Theological Invitation to the Pilgrimage of Justice and Peace," Faith and Order Paper, 224. www.oikoumene.org.

137 O. Matteus, "De la catholicité vulnérable: Les Réformés, l'œcuménisme et l'unité humaine," *Vers une catholicité œcuménique*, 129.

Confession proclaims; for it, the visible Church is catholic only "under the gospel." But as the example of Abraham and Sarah illustrates, faith consists in leaving without knowing where one is going. Matteus admits too, with Saint-Exupéry's fox, that "what is essential is invisible to the eyes." The ecumenical movement could free itself from its exclusive fascination with a guaranteed institutional unity, if it understood that this unity is an attempt, dated today, and strongly linked to a particular period of the Protestant world, to free itself from the dialectic "invisible-authentic Church/visible-heretical Church." Very few indeed today confess the form of exacerbated spiritualism which would associate the Church with visible things and the Kingdom with the invisible world.

A Trinitarian approach to the Church is inseparable from a ternary conception of rationality, capable of thinking the open, the closed, and the intermediary, or the provisional, or the half-open. As Olav Fyske Tveit proposes today, the Faith and Order Commission would gain by adding a third element to its understanding of the unity of the Church — that is, mutual accountability.[138]

> Mutual accountability is a matter of how we in the ecumenical movement seek the truth together by sharing insights into the truth we carry. This progressive, collaborative discovery of truth entails as much repentance and self-criticism as it does fidelity to traditions. Churches must be learners as well as teachers! Often your insights shed light on my oversights! Ultimately, the truth we owe one another is an accounting for our hope not just to ourselves and our kind but to others as well. We are as churches and followers of the crucified and risen Christ called always to be ready to give account of the hope that we carry. This is the criterion of our Christian witness. This is in fact the criterion of being church: Are we giving hope to others, real hope? This is also the criterion of what it means to be human, created in the image of God: How do we give hope to the other?[139]

In summary, Olav Fyske Tveit explains that the visibility of the Kingdom is acquired more by a dynamic *attitude*, a style of life, than by a static *state*, the result of an official agreement. The introduction of a series of new criteria that make it possible to describe the levels of unity

---

138   Olav Fykse Tveit, *The Truth We Owe Each Other: Mutual Accountability in the Ecumenical Movement* (Geneva: WCC Publications, 2016).
139   Olav Fyske Tveit, "What Does Mutual Accountability Mean For Christians And The Christian Life?" www.oikoumene.org.

achieved by the churches allows Christology and pneumatology to be balanced with each other, but also permits the "Faith and Order" pole to be balanced with that of "Work and Life" within the WCC's activities. It vivifies the notion of unity, and balances the need for visible institutions with spiritual action, which is often invisible. The poor widow who gives all that she has to the Church in a way which is *invisible* to the eyes of the world is *valued* — that is, made visible — by the words of Christ praising her total generosity (Mark 12:44). Conversely, Christ invites men to close the door of their chamber, that is, to hide themselves from men's eyes, when they wish to pray and meet the Father "which is in secret" (Matthew 6:6).

The WCC could launch research on the parables of the Kingdom in the Gospel so as to support this new ternary criteriology, founded on the state of spirit (and not on the supposed break between noumena and phenomena). Christ expresses himself in parables, indeed, in order to educate his disciples in spiritual discernment. After having told everyone the parable of the sower, he grants them the privilege of an explanation. He makes them understand in this way that not everyone has "ears to hear." There are levels of consciousness. The consciousness of the Pharisees consists most often in reducing what Christ says to the level of the calculating, possessive, and voyeuristic intelligence. By means of this pedagogy, Christ invites his disciples to understand that the Kingdom is not a reality beyond their grasp, despite appearances.

The Kingdom is not only close to them, but it is also much more exceptional than anything the apostles can imagine of it. Christ appeals to hope, to imagination, to trust, to the joy of his disciples, with images of "treasure hid in a field" (Matt. 13:44), a "grain of mustard seed" (13:31), or a "leaven . . . hid in three measures of meal" (13:33). All these parables are not calls to vote on "constitutions," but are rather invitations to change the ecumenical movement's level of consciousness. If faith requires a minimum of ecclesial order, it demands still more freedom, trust, daring, and creativity. This should encourage the churches to abandon the "visibilist priority" (in the sense of a homogeneity that is perceptible by all) and to give more freedom locally to bishops and to the recognition of initiatives on the part of the baptized. Pastors would then more easily be able to bless all the new forms of ecclesial life which exceed a strictly denominational framework. As was recognized by the Catholic Church at Vatican II, the bishops of the local churches, surrounded by their colleges of presbyters, deacons, and lay people, must, in particular, possess the capacity to recognize cases of Eucharist hospitality that go beyond visible denominational borderlines. In 2003, in *Ecclesia de Eucharistia*, John Paul II recognized the possibility of the occasional participation of non-Catholics in communion.[140]

The Catholic Church, in its response to the document "The Church: Towards A Common Vision," also holds that the call to visible unity must be made more specific.[141] Taking up chapter 30 of the Busan document, which refers to chapter 15 of the Acts of the Apostles, the Catholic theologians wonder whether the ecumenical movement might not have to follow the example of the primitive Church, when it was resolving the conflict over whether non-Jews had an obligation to be circumcised or not. This process of resolution began, indeed, by listening to all parties, to Jerusalem and Antioch, Peter and Paul, applying in this way an *ecumenism of reception*. Then the Church gave to James, the brother of the Lord, the possibility of *referring to Scripture*. This stage had the objective of attaining to the level of *moral discernment*. Afterwards, the Church *appealed* through *prayer to the Holy Spirit*, so as to take its decision calmly. By means of these four stages the Church spontaneously set in motion a *spiritual ecclesiology*. Lastly, it came to a decision in a conciliar fashion in support of the great issue of Christian mission in the world:

> For it seemed good to the Holy Ghost, and to us, to lay on you no greater burden than these necessary things; that ye abstain from meats offered to idols, and from blood, and from things strangled, and from fornication . . . (Acts 15:28 – 29)

This decision "that we trouble not them, which from among the Gentiles are turned to God" (Acts 15:19), made it possible for the first Christian community to open itself to non-Jews. It had incalculable consequences, and favored the expansion of Christianity. Now, the Church did not hold the visible [*visible*] *sign* of circumcision to be the decisive criterion. For what it had *in mind* [*en vue*] was in any case more important and more profound. It was a question of nothing more or less than allowing the Kingdom of God to show itself. Pope Francis, for his part, on April 1, 2020 interpreted the sixth beatitude, "Blessed are the pure in heart: for they shall see God" (Matt. 5:8):

---

140 John Paul II, Encyclical letter "Ecclesia De Eucharistia," www.vatican.va. Vatican II had, with *Unitatis Redintegratio*, already envisaged this possibility. Pope John Paul II also referred to this topic in *Ut Unum Sint*.

141 Pontifical Council for Promoting Christian Unity, "'The Church: Towards A Common Vision': A Catholic Response," www.christianunity.va.

> In order to see God, it is of no use to change one's spectacles or one's vantage point, or to change theologians so as to have the way pointed out to us: it is necessary to free the heart from its wounds. This is the only path. [142]

Thus the future of ecclesiology is neither to identify the Church of Christ with one's own denomination, nor to hold that the Church of Christ is invisible as do the authors of the Busan text. The spiritual consciousness is more subtle in matters of ecclesiology. It invites each Church to sharpen its sight freely. It grants more flexibility to the faithful, departing from an ultra-modern logic. The latter consists in wanting a world that could definitively do without faith. Ecumenical consciousness must remember that the "one, holy, catholic, and apostolic" Church is an object of faith and not a guarantee against risk. Moreover, the testimony of the gospels and the history of the Church reveal that manifest and visible signs of the power of God were not enough by themselves to convert hearts. The apostle Judas, who even *saw* Christ accomplishing many miracles, was the one who delivered Christ to his assassins. Christ, by contrast, organized his Church on a transformation *invisible to the naked eye*: the transformation of work and human joys, of bread and wine, into his Body and Blood.

The Visibility of the Church is Qualitative Before it is Institutional

Let us understand this point well. The radical ecumenical paradigm is not opposed either to the visible manifestation of the Kingdom, or to a common work making visible the communion of the Churches. On the contrary. The true question is "To what sort of visibility must the Church bear witness?" For the Church is a historical reality that takes its existence only from its participation in the life of the Trinity. If the Church is founded by Christ, it is constituted by the action of the Holy Spirit. John Webster, a professor of systematic theology at the University of Aberdeen in Scotland, expresses this in his article entitled "On Evangelical Ecclesiology," published in 2004. For Webster, communion with God is the mystery of which the Gospel is the overt manifestation (Col. 1:26). This manifestation does not merely take the form of an announcement. As a manifestation of God's plan for his creatures, it is infinitely more powerful and creative. It generates an assembly, a social space, a political regime and a culture. In this space, the Gospel of reconciliation's power to convert becomes visible in human relations, and in creative acts of justice,

---

142   "Pour voir Dieu, 'il faut libérer le cœur de ses blessures,' affirme le pape François lors de l'audience générale," La Croix, April 1, 2020, www.la-croix.com.

kindness, beauty, and truth. This visible form is not a simple natural quantity. It possesses a sort of special visibility, created by Christ and the Holy Spirit. It is, therefore, perceptible only at their request. Hence the form of historical and meta-historical assembly proclaimed by Christ when he explains to his apostles that the Kingdom is found in power among them is the "communion of saints." Webster draws the following conclusion:

> Rather than focusing on the church as a visible community of practices, contemporary ecclesiology would do well to recover a proper sense of the church's invisibility — that is to say, of the "spiritual" character of its visible life. And, as a corollary, the active life of the church is best understood, not as a visible realization or representation of the divine presence but as an attestation of the perfect work of God in Christ, now irrepressibly present and effective in the Spirit's power. This combination of emphases, on the "spiritual visibility" of the church, and on the character of its acts as "attestations" of God, reflects an orderly account of the relation between God's perfection and creaturely being and activity, neither separating nor confusing the divine and the human. The church is the form of common human life and action which is generated by the gospel to bear witness to the perfect word and work of the triune God.[143]

The Scottish theologian adds that, in accord with Calvin, the Church is an object of knowledge in the same sense as is God, the knowledge of whom comes from his self-revelation of his presence, and whose receptive human antenna is faith.

> The church is known as God is known, in the knowledge which comes from God's self-communicative presence, of which the human coordinate is faith. Only in this spiritual knowledge is the church known and its phenomena seen as what they are. Faith does not, of course, perceive a different, "hidden" set of phenomena, behind the natural-historical realities of the church's visible acts. It sees those acts as what they are: attestations of God.[144]

In summary, wherever acts of justice and reconciliation, of kindness and of creation, are brought about, the Church manifests itself. Each time the work of God is faithfully proclaimed, and each time God's sacraments are rightly conferred, God can act, and the Kingdom of God manifests

---

143 John Webster, "On Evangelical Ecclesiology," *Ecclesiology* 1 (2004), 9–35, 24.
144 Ibid., 27.

itself. For Webster, spiritual ecclesiology definitively precedes institutional ecclesiology:

> Ecclesiology is secondary; the life of the fellowship of the saints comes first, because it is in that fellowship that we keep company with God. [145]

Olav Fyske Tveit is right to say that the opposite of visible unity is not necessarily invisible unity. Conversely, the lack of recognition of an existing unity is not necessarily synonymous with visible division. [146] On the contrary, the ability to adopt responsible attitudes, such as being true to one's word, transparent accounting, rejecting duplicitous language and all forms of attempts at capturing souls for one's own denomination, sorrow in the face of others' distress, enthusiasm for others' victories, liturgical and artistic generosity and creativity: these are the things that make the Kingdom visible. This is also what Pope Francis said when he called the WCC to equip itself with a "seeing heart" on the occasion of his historic visit to Geneva in 2018 to mark the organization's seventieth anniversary:

> Let us be challenged to compassion by the cry of those who suffer: "the programme of the Christian is *a heart that sees*" (Benedict XVI, *Deus Caritas Est*, 31). Let us see what we can do concretely, rather than grow discouraged about what we cannot. Let us also look to our many brothers and sisters in various parts of the world, particularly in the Middle East, who suffer because they are Christians. Let us draw close to them. May we never forget that our ecumenical journey is preceded and accompanied by an ecumenism already realized, the ecumenism of blood, which urges us to go forward. [147]

This approach does not deny the validity of denominational identities. It simply contextualizes them. Nor does it seek to close down discussion of the differences existing between the different currents of the Church. Rather, it redefines the horizon that is to be reached, the methods to be used, and the order of priorities, applying an understanding that is less institutional and more eschatological (in the strong, rather than in the

---

145   Ibid., 35.

146   Tveit: "We have as the WCC reminded the partners that the opposite of 'visible unity' is not 'invisible unity' but 'visible division.'" "The report by the WCC general secretary Rev. Dr Olav Fykse Tveit to the WCC executive committee," June 2017, www.oikoumene.org.

147   "Speech of Pope Francis during the Ecumenical Meeting at the WCC," June 21, 2018, www.oikoumene.org.

millenarian, sense of the term) of the life of the Church. This is what the Faith and Order Commission began to do in 2019, speaking through its director Odair Pedroso Matteus:

> The manifestation of the One Church and its witness in history
> to the ongoing recapitulation of all things in and by the head of
> the Body are also eschatological. They are in and for the world,
> "for us and for our salvation."[148]

Visibility is more an effect than an objective. The mission of the ecumenical movement is not to make an exact map of infinite and divergent hermeneutics on the topic of the Church. Nor is it, either, to hand out certificates of guaranteed unity. As Jean-Luc Marion writes, "the question of the saint's sanctity begins, paradoxically, to be posed as a result of its invisibility."[149] The ecumenical movement's mission, then, is rather to invite the churches clearly to identify their positions, without ambiguous language, in support of the coming of the Kingdom of God. It also consists in asking ecclesial institutions to repent for their lack of love. It must invite church leaders and their local communities to make possible the participation of all those whom they recognize as baptized according to the sacraments of the Church.

Thus there could really be constituted a *fellowship* of churches founded on a hierarchy of truths, those of love, responsibility, service, openness, and the common good. The traditional churches could also find in this way a space in which they could meet emerging Evangelical and Pentecostal communities who are proposing a new, more informal way of living the Church.

The radical and spiritual ecumenical paradigm invites us to live and to present the Church as a desirable object of faith, as a place of hope open to all, as the anticipation of the Kingdom of God on earth. This is the whole meaning of Father Paul Couturier's "invisible monastery." Miss Spens, who was a member of this invisible monastery, explains her spiritual father's vision:

> This monastery of the Order of Jesus at Prayer is called "invisible"
> not because it is nebulous or lacks any precise existence, but, on
> the contrary, because it knows no limits and exists concretely as
> God wills under many forms of organization which are unknown

---

148 "Faith and Order from Today into Tomorrow," Director's Address, China, 2019, www.oikoumene.org.

149 Jean-Luc Marion, *Le croire pour le voir* (Paris: Parole et Silence, 2010), 209.

in their totality to anyone except Him. Sometimes it will function in "denominational" or "inter-denominational" groups, whose members know each other; sometimes even in visible monasteries devoted to Him so as to foster "the Unity which He wants by the means that He wants"; sometimes in the form of two or three gathered inwardly in His Name, perhaps even in the same place; it can even be in isolated individuals: but always in the Whole, praying Christ, in heaven and on earth. The variety of paths and forms in which they lived, prayed, and acted mattered little; the abbot always recognized in a flash the individuals and collectives which belonged to this Order of Jesus At Prayer, which he met in the Spirit. And with his incomparable charity — creative, considerate, comprehensive — he encouraged everyone to remain faithful to this very rare vocation received from the Spirit, in this All which was one, inexhaustible, and inseparable.[150]

For faith, as St Paul writes, is "the substance of things hoped for, the evidence of things not seen" (Heb. 11:1). Now, as Nikolai Berdyaev wrote, the Kingdom of God on earth, the true horizon of ecumenical ecclesiology, lives by other rules than the kingdom of Caesar. One can only participate in it, as the Catholic priest André Bach well understood, by dint of tough battles with oneself.

> The Kingdom of Heaven can only be made by all the people among whom we live every day, as they are, with their miseries, their needs, people who are hungry and to whom there have to be given things for them to eat, and even more, people who are sinners and who are doing harm, which must be undone, who are injuring us, and who must be forgiven.[151]

The Kingdom shows itself only to a look which is loving, faithful and open, humble and generous.

150 Maurice Villain, *L'abbé Paul Couturier: apôtre de l'Unité chrétienne; souvenirs et documents* (Tournai: Casterman, 1957), 334.
151 Abbé André Bach, *Le Royaume de Dieu est parmi nous* (Paris: Bloud et Gay, 1941), 122.

PART SIX

General Conclusion:
From Fundamentalist Radicalism
to Ecumenical Spirituality

NOTHING IS FIXED. CERTAINLY, THE WORLD of Twitter and TikTok is no longer that of *cujus regio ejus religio*. The sovereignty of states and of churches has become deterritorialized, and their peoples' aspirations to happiness have become more complex. The American psychologist and humanist Abraham Maslow (1908 – 1970) showed in 1943 that human physiological needs and needs for safety, the needs for belonging, for esteem, and for love, tend in all human beings towards the need for self-fulfillment.[1] In his last book, *The Farther Reaches of Human Nature*, published in 1971, Maslow also recognized the existence of a meta-motivation in human consciousness, one that runs through all the human psyche's levels of consciousness, and depends upon representations of transcendence. After having listed the different understandings of transcendence, including those in Christianity, in Taoism, and in Buddhism, Maslow defines this power of human consciousness, at once tangible and discrete, in the following way:

> Transcendence refers to the very highest and most inclusive or holistic levels of human consciousness, behaving and relating, as ends rather than means, to oneself, to significant others, to human beings in general, to other species, to nature, and to the cosmos. (Holism in the sense of hierarchical integration is assumed; so also is cognitive and value isomorphism.)[2]

Our history of ecumenical consciousness has indeed shown that a new realization, both progressive and chaotic, has emerged over the course of the ages, spurred on by the horizon of the Kingdom of God on earth. Depending on the level of consciousness of divine-humanity, the desire

---

1   Abraham Maslow, "A Theory of Human Motivation," *Psychological Review* 50 (1943), 370 – 96.
2   Maslow, *The Farther Reaches of Human Nature* (New York: Viking, 1971).

for self-fulfillment cannot finally and presently be fulfilled except with and through other people, to the benefit of the common good. This vision does not reject, but integrates, the best of modern consciousness (its sense of human dignity) and of postmodern consciousness (its recognition of human finitude).

But taken in isolation, the modern and postmodern levels of consciousness are a source of instability and violence. That is why the world can still evolve according to the scenarios described in the two last chapters of this book. The modern scenario, which has a tendency to separate faith from reason, is that of the strengthening of the four types of consciousness within the four constellations of prayer and tradition, virtue and justice. The postmodern scenario, which suppresses faith and reason or fuses them together, is that of the rise to an extreme degree of a conceptual and neutral universalism, on the one hand, and of an irrational particularism hungry for meaning, on the other.

These developments, of course, do not only concern the churches or religion. The "ecumenical winter" is not a marginal phenomenon. It is the pendant to, and the contemporary of, the "globalization crisis." We have seen when studying the history of ecumenical consciousness that it is the whole of the political, social, and cultural life of the peoples of the planet which is affected by the degree of awareness that is given to the foundations of ecumenical metaphysics and to what is at stake in it. It will not be possible to reform the Security Council of the United Nations towards a new humanist law, to reduce the amount of plastic poured into the oceans, or to give out free vaccinations to every citizen of the planet, unless one has first thought about the spiritual, epistemological, and political arsenal that makes developments of this kind possible.

Nor can the destiny of ecumenical consciousness be reconfigured in a way that is abstract and detached from the urgent current needs of the contemporary world. There is a third scenario, brought to light in this volume, of the gradual, if chaotic, emergence over the course of three millennia of an ecumenical consciousness that makes possible the coming of a spiritual civilization. This ecumenical consciousness becomes real in proportion to the degree of faith which the various communities have in the reality of living God, and according to the degrees of subtlety of human rationality. These two resources, indeed, allow humanity, on one hand, to discern the eminent dignity of the human person and the created character of nature, and, on the other, to participate in the action of Wisdom in the history of humanity and the cosmos.

From the perspective of an ecumenical metaphysics that has been re-ordered towards nature as creation, and towards the human being as microcosm and macrocosm, the role of each person in bringing about this taste for Wisdom becomes decisive. For symbolic life cannot be decreed; it is, rather, discovered within one's most private self, and is tested through a look, or in the middle of a storm. The role of spiritual leaders is more important than ever in bringing to emergence, with wisdom and daring, by words and through deeds, a faith that is capable of rationality and a conceptuality that is open to what transcends it.

It is quite clear in view of the preceding pages that one could mention many eminent figures of the present day. In illustrating my argument, I shall limit myself here to introducing Pope Francis's dream of the possible paths to the reconciliation of the churches. I shall finish with an appeal to other narratives, presenting the coming of this integral ecumenical consciousness from starting points in other worlds of religion and belief, a consciousness that alone can foster the arrival of a more spiritual world.

THE DREAM OF POPE FRANCIS

On June 21, 2018, on the seventieth anniversary of the World Council of Churches, Pope Francis set out in Geneva his vision of the coming reunion of the churches, a vision founded on the model of reconciled communion:

> As an ancient Father in the faith rightly observed: "When love has entirely cast out fear, and fear has been transformed into love, then the unity brought us by our Savior will be fully realized" (Saint Gregory of Nyssa, Homily XV on the Song of Songs). We are heirs to the faith, charity and hope of all those who, by the nonviolent power of the Gospel, found the courage to change the course of history, a history that had led us to mutual distrust and estrangement, and thus contributed to the infernal spiral of continual fragmentation. Thanks to the Holy Spirit, who inspires and guides the journey of ecumenism, the direction has changed and a path both old and new has been irrevocably paved: the path of a reconciled communion aimed at the visible manifestation of the fraternity that even now unites believers.[3]

---

3 "Ecumenical Pilgrimage of His Holiness Francis to Geneva to mark the 70th Anniversary of the World Council of Churches: Address of His Holiness," June 21, 2018, www.vatican.va.

The following year, on the feast of Saints Peter and Paul, he explained that this vision of full communion in mutual recognition of legitimate differences applied to the relations to come between Catholic and Orthodox Christians:[4]

> I am increasingly convinced that the restoration of full unity between Catholics and Orthodox will come about through respect for specific identities and a harmonious coexistence in legitimate forms of diversity. The Holy Spirit, for that matter, is the one who creatively awakens a multiplicity of gifts, harmonizes them and brings them into authentic unity, which is not uniformity but a symphony of many voices in charity. As Bishop of Rome, I wish to reaffirm that, for us Catholics, the purpose of dialogue is full communion in legitimate forms of diversity, not a monotonous levelling, much less absorption. For this reason, I consider it valuable in our encounters to share our roots, to rediscover the goodness that the Lord has sown and made grow in each of us, and to share it, learning from one another and helping each other not to fear dialogue and concrete collaboration. The scandal of divisions not fully healed can only be removed by the grace of God as we journey together, accompanying in prayer each other's steps, proclaiming the Gospel in harmony, working to serve those in need and dialoguing in truth, without allowing ourselves to be conditioned by past prejudices. Thus, in that sincerity and transparency which the Lord loves, we will grow closer to one another and come to appreciate more fully our own identity. We will grow in knowledge and mutual affection. We will experience the fact that, for all our differences, there is indeed much more that unites us and inspires us to move forward together.[5]

In 2020 the Pope suggested, this time to Europeans, that they should rise to a radically spiritual level of consciousness. This vision is eminently political, and represents the basis of a renewal of the project of Christian democracy. We have seen that after the 1960s, the latter was unable to combat a secularist conception of politics. That is why the Italian-Argentine Pope asks Europeans to rediscover themselves at a deep level before launching themselves into a new stage of the construction of the European Union. In particular, he suggests that Europeans should remember their

---

4 "Dialogue avec Constantinople: pour 'la pleine communion dans les diversités légitimes,'" June 28, 2019, https://fr.zenit.org.
5 "Address of His Holiness Pope Francis to the Delegation of the Ecumenical Patriarchate of Constantinople," June 28, 2019, www.vatican.va.

own most ancient history, and that they should repent of what has been worst in this history, while also recognizing the good which there has been in it. He mentions in particular the great figures of the European saints like St Benedict, Saints Cyril and Methodius, St Catherine of Siena, St Bridget of Sweden, and St Teresa Benedicta of the Cross (Edith Stein). One finds here the major figures in the history of the Church, who were able to hold together in harmony the four major kinds of expression of the faith: ascetic and missionary, mystical and political.

The Pope links the notion of roots to a radical consciousness, so as to allow the contemporary European political consciousness to make itself fully ecumenical. Let us therefore consider, in conclusion, his call for the rediscovery of "deep roots." His call puts history and eternity, as well as truth and justice, in tension with each other:

> Europe, find yourself! Rediscover your most deeply-rooted ideals. Be yourself! Do not be afraid of the thousands of years of your history, which is a window open to the future more than the past. Do not be afraid of that thirst of yours for truth, which, from the days of ancient Greece, has spread throughout the world and brought to light the deepest questions of every human being. Do not be afraid of the thirst for justice that developed from Roman law and in time became respect for all human beings and their rights. Do not be afraid of your thirst for eternity, enriched by the encounter with the Judeo-Christian tradition reflected in your patrimony of faith, art and culture.[6]

This reflection on shared history and values leads Pope Francis to wish to gather Europeans together around the dream of a new Europe. The latter is structured around the four poles of religious consciousness that have been set out here: law and justice, memory and glory. The Pope shows a pedagogical side so as to promote a spiritual transition towards an ecumenical consciousness, a consciousness that is at once personalist, sapiential, and ternary.

The first pole of the Pope's European dream rests on the moral law. His thought is presented here as personalist.

> Being a friend to others entails defending their rights, but also reminding them of their duties. It means acknowledging that everyone is called to offer his or her own contribution to society, for none of us is a world apart, and we cannot demand respect

---

6 "Letter of His Holiness Pope Francis on Europe," October 22, 2020, www.vatican.va.

for ourselves without showing respect for others. We cannot receive unless we are also willing to give.[7]

The second pole of the new European consciousness imagined by the Pope rests on transmission through the different levels of consciousness constituted by being-in-relation, from the family to the Church. This pole, as Francis writes, has a particular importance for him because it fosters unity:

> A divided Europe, made up of insular and independent realities, will soon prove incapable of facing the challenges of the future. On the other hand, a Europe that is a united and fraternal *community* will be able to value diversity and acknowledge the part that each has to play in confronting the problems that lie ahead, beginning with the pandemic and including the ecological challenge of preserving our natural resources and the quality of the environment in which we live.[8]

The Pope, then, defends an inclusive model that values creation and creatures. This sapiential vision is in his thinking inseparable from a commitment to sustainable human development, as he has written in *Laudato Si'* and *Fratelli Tutti*. He asks Europeans to fight for greater social justice, for their nearest neighbors, and for the migrant, as well as for those who are furthest away, with help for development and for international cooperation.

> I dream of a Europe that is inclusive and generous. A welcoming and hospitable place in which charity, the highest Christian virtue, overcomes every form of indifference and selfishness. Solidarity, as an essential element of every authentic community, demands that we care for one another.[9]

Finally, the Pope turns to the pole of glory, and asks Europeans not to lose sight of the fact that a purely secular approach is a cul-de-sac:

> I dream of a Europe marked by a healthy secularism, where God and Caesar remain distinct but not opposed. A land open to transcendence, where believers are free to profess their faith in public and to put forward their own point of view in society. The era of confessional conflicts is over, but so too — let us hope — is the age of a certain laicism closed to others and especially to God, for it is evident that a culture or political system that lacks

---

7   Ibid.
8   Ibid.
9   Ibid.

openness to transcendence proves insufficiently respectful of the
human person.[10]

Christians are therefore called to "revive Europe's conscience," and
that of all the peoples of the planet, with the help of a vision of an integral world, the vision of ecumenical metaphysics. This vision of Pope
Francis's also testifies to a ternary consciousness. At the beginning of the
twenty-first century, Europeans realized the limits of a more and more
postmodern secularist consciousness of political life. Tomorrow they may
discover that the future of their types of political organization is to be
found in new forms of ecumenical commitment, forms that are at once
transreligious, transpartisan, transnational, and nevertheless in conformity
with the foundations of Christian faith.

THE VALIDITY OF THE THIRD GRAND NARRATIVE OF WESTERN CONSCIOUSNESS

Thus the third grand narrative of Western consciousness is that of a
form of personal wisdom in search of universality, a wisdom which is
deployed along several axes, according to levels of affinity, mythological representations, conceptual categories, and the different forms of
commitment which human beings have. This awareness of self, of God,
and of the world, is oriented towards an eschatological fulfillment of
human history, in the sense of the beautiful, the good, the true, and the
just. It is a tireless quest for unity and alterity, despite and through the
chaos of events, which represents one of the main gifts of the Christian
faith to humanity's ecumenical consciousness. This ecumenical history
completes the other two narratives of contemporary consciousness, that
of intellectual deviation in relation to a putative golden age of Christian
faith, and that of the permanent transformation of humanity's moral
ideals. The "macro-ecumenical narrative" is not limited to the modern
inter-denominational movement. It originates in the event of Pentecost,
but exceeds the framework of Christian consciousness alone to extend
to "all the sons of Adam" on "the whole of the inhabited earth."

This new metanarrative is able to grasp within a single history personalities as different as Silouan the Athonite and Martin Luther King,
Francis of Assisi and John Wesley. But this ecumenical history of Western
consciousness is also able to integrate other narratives, coming from different spiritual horizons, by dint of its own capacity to hold together the

---

10   Ibid.

four poles of faith-reason. Beyond Christian consciousness, it is therefore now worth writing the history of this wider consciousness by integrating personalities such as Ibn Arabi (1165 – 1240), the Andalusian Sufi theologian and mystic, and Martin Buber (1878 – 1965), the Austrian and Israeli Jewish philosopher, but also, today, the agnostic American philosopher Judith Butler (b. 1956), or Trinh Xuan Thuan (b. 1948), the Vietnamese-American Buddhist and Confucian.

This ecumenical history relates the process of the formation, in the history of civilizations, of several levels of consciousness, polarized by acceptance or rejection of faith-reason, and attracted by divine Wisdom. These levels of consciousness, tugged at by different forms of representation of the Kingdom (or of paradise, or of the free market, or of the classless society), try to achieve unity in a way which is now conflictual, now convergent. Tied to an ecumenical metaphysics, this narrative also recalls, against the dominant discourse of the present age, that at all levels of consciousness every human being is a microcosm and a macrocosm. It also recovers the intuition of the greatest mystics of the East and the West, that every living corporeality, beginning with the Church and the nation, has its own form of consciousness.[11]

If the illusion of the liberal paradigm, in its "smooth and flawless" aspect, can be represented by a sphere, and if the "liquid society" beloved of the postmoderns can be characterized as a snowball, the ecumenic age of consciousness can be symbolized by the ridged sphere of a polyhedron combined with a hologram. The polyhedron is the symbol of a new, more personalist and more qualitative form of globalization, one that is more respectful of otherness. This geometrical figure, according to Pope Francis, signifies the universal dimension of contemporary consciousness without, however, smoothing out its bumps and its discontinuities.[12] Jean Staune, the secretary-general of the Université Interdisciplinaire de Paris [Interdisciplinary University of Paris], is one of the representatives of this new ecumenical consciousness in France. In his preface to the book *Christ et karma* by the Orthodox Christian priest Jean Brune, he privileges the three-dimensional figure of the hologram:

> How is it possible to conceive that one can be at once part of a
> system and the totality of that system? That one can be truly

---

11   Marie-Anne Vannier, *Hildegarde de Bingen, une femme admirable* (Paris: Entrelacs, 2016); *En lisant François Jullien*, ed. Pascal David and Alain Riou (Paris: Bernardins, 2012).
12   "Le pape compare l'humanité à un 'polyèdre' qui respecte la pluralité," *La Croix*, November 22, 2013, www.la-croix.com.

a man and truly God? The problem of the incarnation and of the status of Christ is not only an enigma, even an absurdity for non-Christians, but has been a source of many divisions, schisms, and debates within Christianity. The metaphor of the hologram, even if it is only a metaphor, makes it possible to conceptualize this at last. When Christ says both "he that hath seen me hath seen the Father" (John 14:9) and "my Father is greater than I" (John 14:28), we have to understand him to be saying "I am the bearer of all the information in the system, at the same time as being only a part of that system."[13]

The development of the decisive action of ecumenical metaphysics has the advantage of offering a living link, a personal link one might say, with the history of the intellectual and spiritual journeys described by John Milbank, but also of grasping by means of new personal and collective practices those "subtler languages" of which Charles Taylor speaks. And above all, beyond the Western world that is the subject of Milbank's and Taylor's meta-narratives, this ecumenical paradigm invites each citizen of the world to become aware of all the potentialities of the real brought to light by great scientists, writers, and contemporary artists and poets such as Nils Bohr, Amedeo Modigliani, Philip K. Dick, and François Cheng.

The globalized and connected consciousness of today has been prepared for by preceding epochs. It is also built out of a thousand new ways of attaining to a level of reality at which the divine, the human, and the cosmic are articulated in an original way. The third great ecumenical narrative of contemporary global consciousness is indispensable in order to grasp its potentialities and its limits. John Milbank and Charles Taylor were both right in their explanations of the coming of a secular age in place of the age improperly called that of "Christianity." But their narratives do not by themselves explain why, from the Middle Ages to our time, Christian thought has had so much difficulty in thinking the new representations of the real which appeared in the fourteenth and fifteenth centuries. Despite all the depth of the Thomist synthesis, Christian metaphysics has not been able to oppose a separation between faith and reason, or a fragmentation into many denominations, each convinced that it has exclusive possession of the truth. The churches have had to cede their intellectual and moral magisterium to a new scientistic elite fascinated by objectivism, materialism, and power. Similarly, despite many very real

---

13 "Préface à la troisième réédition de Jean Brune, *Christ et karma*," cf. http://www.jeanstaune.fr/christ-et-karma.html.

epiphanies of Spirit, contemporary culture is more and more torn apart, as the Palme D'Or awarded at Cannes to the South Korean film *Parasite* symbolically showed, by a faith in an alternative reality, a cult of material power and a fascination with the goddesses of fatalism and irony.

Let us also recognize that our era is becoming more and more aware of the "twilight of the universal," to use Chantal Delsol's expression.[14] This universal still rested in 1948, at the time of the Universal Declaration of Human Rights, on a philosophy of natural Law, despite the inter-religious character of the committee that drafted it.[15]

This Declaration had the merit of declaring the "faith in fundamental human rights" and "in the dignity and worth of the human person" held by the peoples of the United Nations.[16] But it refused to say even the least word about the divine power as the source of all justice. Similarly, the biosphere is not even mentioned, and in this way humanity's mission of cultivating the earth is forgotten.

Today the modern consensus in support of "liberal individualism, cosmopolitanism, and the democracy of human rights" has been weakened, not only in Moscow or Islamabad, the strongholds of the contestation of Western universalism, but also at Palm Beach in Florida, where Donald Trump resides, and in the Cayman Islands, one of the main contemporary tax havens.[17] The time has thus probably come to rediscover an ecumenical metaphysics capable of fostering an authentic spiritual transition.

FROM THE NARRATIVE OF WESTERN CONSCIOUSNESS TO THE NARRATIVE OF GLOBAL CONSCIOUSNESS

It is thus a matter of the first importance to understand universality in an ecumenical way. Ecumenical metaphysics studies the link between the universal and the personal, but also between the knowledge of nature

---

14 Chantal Delsol, *Le crépuscule de l'universel* (Paris: Cerf, 2020).

15 Blandine Kriegel, "Les deux voies de la philosophie moderne": "the philosophy of the law-based State therefore finds its basis in a philosophy of nature. And let no one say here that these are simply my own wild imaginings, or claim, when the validity of this argument has been recognized, that it has always and everywhere been known. It is the political philosophy of the English revolution, or rather of the two English revolutions, which are at the origin of all modern political law, from Hobbes to Locke, who, themselves, speak to us still and always of natural law, and who inscribe natural law, that is, the norms proper to human beings, in a vaster law of nature which is that of the order of the forces of nature." www.blandinekriegel.com.

16 "Universal Declaration of Human Rights," www.ohchr.org.

17 François D'Alançon, "Donald Trump déménage sa résidence fiscale en Floride," *La Croix*, November 1, 2019, www.la-croix.com; https://panamapapers.org.

and the meaning of the moral law. It studies in a historical fashion a particular object, namely the consciousness of that which brings together and separates the human, the divine, and the cosmic. It is also fed by a spiritual effort, by a personal, non-homogeneous, non-conceptual, and non-verifiable capacity to discern and to listen to the voice of conscience, and to externalize it by means of an appropriate art of living.

Great figures in ecumenical thought such as Olivier Clément in the Christian world and Ken Wilber in the Buddhist world, have attained, each in their own way, to this post-eclectic level of consciousness, and to combine an attachment to living tradition with an open expectation of difference. Thus, in his book *You Are Peter* [*Rome autrement*], Olivier Clément imagines a science that would be capable of bringing together, in a respect for plurality, the Asiatic hemisphere, where the divine crops up everywhere, an impersonal divine that is manifested and absorbed back into the world, with the Semitic hemisphere, in which the transcendence of the personal God and the personal character of the human being is affirmed. The Orthodox theologian adds that from this perspective, the fundamental theme for the future is that of "divinized humanity, which is the space of the Spirit and of creative freedom."[18]

For his part, the Buddhist thinker Ken Wilber, taking up a whole tradition of thought from Plotinus to Schelling, proposes a non-dual definition of Spirit.

> Spirit knows itself objectively as *nature*; knows itself subjectively as *mind*; and knows itself absolutely as *Spirit* — the Source, the Summit, and the Eros of the entire sequence.[19]

As a result, he suggests that if Christianity thought God in opposition to man, and modernity man in opposition to God, the time has come to rediscover a religious thought capable of combining "ascending powers with descending powers." In Wilber's work, medieval and modern history is taken to have been a confrontation between the God of the ascending powers and the God of the descending powers. While the first God lived only in heaven, is Puritan and ascetic, and flees the multiple, finding its repose only in unity, the second is by contrast the God of pure immanence who blossoms only within the sensible and the various. This is why, for Wilber, ecumenical spirituality consists in thinking and living together the mysteries of the incarnation of the divine and the ascension of the

---

18   Clément, *Rome autrement*, 121–22; *You Are Peter*, 107.
19   Ken Wilber, *A Brief History of Everything* (Boulder, CO: Shambhala, 2017), 278.

human. In philosophical terms, this ecumenical quest for wisdom proceeds by means of wonder, but also by means of the closest possible attention to the interactions between *eros* and *agapē*. In Buddhist terms, meanwhile, for Ken Wilber, this ecumenical spirituality translates into an effort to bring together emptiness and form, nirvana and samsara, the energies of the world with those of Brahman.

> The more you contact the Higher Self, the *more* you worry about the world, as a component of your very Self, the Self of each and all. Emptiness is Form. Brahman is the World. To *finally* contact Brahman is to *ultimately* engage the world. If you really contact your Higher Self, one of the first things you will want to do is not ignore the elephant but feed the elephant. That is, work in all four quadrants to help manifest this realization, and treat each and every holon as a manifestation of the Divine.[20]

Although it requires supplementation by narratives from every cultural and religious tradition,[21] the third grand narrative of Western consciousness has a global dimension because of its metaphysical foundations. Indeed, it makes it possible to accede to a level of consciousness that is not limited by the conviction-based or denominational representations of the classical, modern, and post-modern epochs. It is, instead, a rehabilitation of each of these epochs that highlights the work of the Spirit in each of them. In contrast to German idealist thought, the ecumenical paradigm is *panentheist*, not pantheist, by virtue of its antinomial logic, which does not eliminate the old contradictory forms by overcoming them dialectically. It does not sacrifice personal experience in the name of the end of history. Nor does it separate processes of natural evolution from processes of spiritual involution. Instead, it aims, in an eschatological way, to inhabit each level of consciousness more intensely, and to grasp all the depths of, and the ways into, each of them.

Thus it is important to show next how ecumenical metaphysics can be a resource capable of illuminating the different disciplines of knowledge, and of inspiring the many different spheres of human activity, so that the citizens of the planet can put the necessary spiritual transition into practice.

---

20   Ibid., 290.
21   For example, the French scholar Hervé-Elie Bokobza has undertaken fundamental research on the perception of Christianity in Jewish consciousness.

INDEX OF NAMES

ABOUT THE AUTHOR

ANTOINE ARJAKOVSKY has a doctorate in History and is the Director of Research at the Collège des Bernardins in Paris, as well as the President of the Association des Philosophes Chrétiens. He is also the founder of the Institute for Ecumenical Studies in Lviv, Ukraine. Among his other commitments, he is a director of the Semaines Sociales de France, is a vice-president of the Artisans de Paix, and is a member of the executive board of the Platform of European Memory and Conscience.

Made in the USA
Monee, IL
07 August 2022